Anthropology Now And Next

ANTHROPOLOGY NOW AND NEXT

Essays in Honor of Ulf Hannerz

Edited by
Thomas Hylland Eriksen, Christina Garsten,
and Shalini Randeria

berghahn
NEW YORK • OXFORD
www.berghahnbooks.com

Published in 2015 by
Berghahn Books
www.berghahnbooks.com

© 2015 Thomas Hylland Eriksen, Christina Garsten, and Shalini Randeria

All rights reserved. Except for the quotation of short passages for the purposes of criticism and review, no part of this book may be reproduced in any form or by any means, electronic or mechanical, including photocopying, recording, or any information storage and retrieval system now known or to be invented, without written permission of the publisher.

Library of Congress Cataloging-in-Publication Data

Anthropology now and next: essays in honor of Ulf Hannerz / edited by Thomas Hylland Eriksen, Christina Garsten, and Shalini Randeria.
    pages cm
Includes bibliographical references.
 ISBN 978-1-78238-449-6 (hardback: alk. paper) -- ISBN 978-1-78238-450-2 (ebook)
 1. Anthropology--Philosophy. 2. Anthropology--Methodology. 3.Anthropological ethics. 4. Hannerz, Ulf--Influence. I. Eriksen, Thomas Hylland, editor of compilation. II. Garsten, Christina, editor of compilation. III. Randeria, Shalini, 1955- editor of compilation. IV. Hannerz, Ulf, honoree.
 GN33.A448 2014
 301.01--dc23
                    2014016265

British Library Cataloguing in Publication Data
A catalogue record for this book is available from the British Library

ISBN 978-1-78238-449-6 (hardback)
E-ISBN 978-1-78238-450-2 (ebook)

Ulf Hannerz

Photo by Kirin Narayan

Contents

Introduction	Ulf Hannerz and the Militant Middle Ground *Shalini Randeria, Thomas Hylland Eriksen, and Christina Garsten*	1
Chapter 1	Divided by a Shared Destiny: An Anthropologist's Notes from an Overheated World *Thomas Hylland Eriksen*	11
Chapter 2	Juxtapositions: Social and Material Connectedness in a Pottery Community *Brian Moeran*	29
Chapter 3	Connecting and Disconnecting: Intentionality, Anonymity, and Transnational Networks in Upper Yemen *Andre Gingrich*	48
Chapter 4	Global Swirl at Dupont Circle: Think Tanks, Connectivity, and the Making of "the Global" *Christina Garsten*	70
Chapter 5	Reflexivity Reloaded: From Anthropology of Intellectuals to Critique of Method to Studying Sideways *Dominic Boyer*	91
Chapter 6	On Anthropologists and Other Cultural Interpreters *Thomas Blom Hansen*	111
Chapter 7	Traveling between Knowledge Practices *Thomas Fillitz*	131
Chapter 8	Anthropologist in the Irish Literary World: Reflexivity through Studying Sideways *Helena Wulff*	147

Chapter 9	Reflections in and on the Hall of Mirrors *Gudrun Dahl*	162
Chapter 10	On the Shores of Power: The Cultural Diversity Turn, Cultural Policies, and the Location of Migrants *Ayse Caglar*	181
Chapter 11	Emergent Concept Chains and Scenarios of Depoliticization: The Case of Global Governance as a Future Past *Ronald Stade*	205
Chapter 12	Lusotopy as Ecumene *João de Pina-Cabral*	241
Chapter 13	An Anthropologist of the World: Interview with Ulf Hannerz, September 2012 *Dominic Boyer*	264
	Publications by Ulf Hannerz	277
	Notes on Contributors	291
	Index	295

Introduction

Ulf Hannerz and the Militant Middle Ground

Shalini Randeria, Thomas Hylland Eriksen, and Christina Garsten

Ulf Hannerz' published work spans more than four decades to date and has, since the beginning, contributed to shaping and reshaping the world of anthropology. The very titles of some of his major books—*Soulside* (1969), *Exploring the City* (1980), *Cultural Complexity* (1992), *Transnational Connections* (1996), *Foreign News* (2004), and *Anthropology's World* (2010)—reveal an anthropologist who has consistently been ahead of his time in exploring subjects that were not yet the academic fashion. Yet he has been both conversant with, and drawing energy from, his peers and the traditions of the discipline on both sides of the Atlantic, just as he has been contributing to extending the frontiers of the discipline. Through Hannerz' interest in networks, for instance, the influence of the pioneering analyses of the Manchester School (Gluckman, Clyde Mitchell, Epstein, and others) is acknowledged and evident. Yet Hannerz uses their approach not to study the dynamics of urbanization in southern Africa, but to explore transnational connections in a world on the move. In his dismissal of a clunky mid-twentieth century concept of culture, Hannerz acknowledges inspiration from anthropologists like Anthony Wallace, who wrote of culture in terms of "the organization of diversity." But his reflections on creolization add an original conceptualization, as does his emphasis on cultural complexity. His fine-grained ethnographies of urban life in Africa and the U.S.A. are in dialogue with a broad range of theoretical perspectives from both anthropology and sociology. His approach to urban life and cosmopolitanism, for instance, owes a debt to classical sociologists like Georg Simmel. For his writings on city life see it not merely as a recipe for alienation, but also as a potential means to liberation.

These and other continuities with twentieth-century social science need to be emphasized because so many of the topics and perspectives introduced in Hannerz' work appear to be novel. Indeed, many were novel for the discipline of anthropology. He was among the first to explore the relevance of modern mass media using ethnographic methods; he suggested to see culture in terms of flows rather than as bounded entities, as a result proposing new analytical terms such as "the global ecumene," "cultural creolization" and "network of networks." And though he was by no means the first urban anthropologist, Hannerz was among the first to see cities as cultural crossroads chiefly characterized by their urbanity, not by their constituent cultural or ethnic groups. His scholarship has thus consistently shown the limitations of confining our understanding of processes and phenomena to the localities in which we happen to study them. It has emphasized instead the need to keep in mind translocal flows and entanglements irrespective of where our research is carried out or on what theme.

It is thus mainly with the anthropology of globalization that Hannerz' name is associated inside and outside the discipline today. But as this collection shows, his œuvre covers a broad range of anthropological subject areas and has inspired colleagues whose work is very diverse. His work was also pioneering in that it called into question, and transcended in subtle but significant ways, the traditional disciplinary division of labor between anthropology and sociology. He carried out fieldwork in West Africa and in the U.S., an unusual undertaking for an anthropologist of his generation; he was equally at ease doing participant observation among poor African-American urban communities as he was, later, in interviewing cosmopolitan foreign correspondents all over the world. His rich ethnographic studies of these diverse contexts draw attention to the long-obsolete binary between the West and the rest as markers of disciplinary boundaries between sociology and anthropology, or between "us" and "them." Hannerz is a master at building bridges across rifts that may seem, to others, insurmountable, both in his anthropological analyses and in his theoretical inspirations. In his writings, strong impulses from American cultural anthropology merge seamlessly with the European microsociological traditions of network analysis and the Malinowskian-Barthian concern with individual agency. The division of labor between the study of culture and the study of society devised by Parsons and Kluckhohn in the 1950s (Kuper 1999) vanishes without a trace in Hannerz' work, which could perhaps be described as a form of intellectual Hinduism as opposed to the polemical monotheisms engaged in turf wars elsewhere in the global intellectual ecumene.

His ethnographic studies link the small to the large, moving effortlessly from fine-grained empirical analyses to theoretical issues, commenting in the process on some of the most salient transformations of the contemporary world. Small wonder then that his work has been widely read and well received both within and outside the confines of the discipline. Lucid in exposition, measured in tone, and with a refreshing lack of dogmatic tendencies or intellectual hobbyhorses, his essays are a delight to read not least for the wonderful, wry sense of humor with which they expound on a variety of issues in the contemporary world. They have thus done much to foster familiarity with, and respect for, an anthropological perspective on a wide range of subjects ranging from transnational processes, cultural complexity, networks, or urban transformations to fashion, music, or journalism. Catholic in his reading, sympathetic in his writings about others and a beacon of lucidity in developing his own thought, Hannerz appears to inhabit a monist world rather than a dualist or Manichean one; a world where complementarity and the "both–and" principle reign rather than conflict and "either–or." If there is one issue that runs through his entire scholarship, it is his consistent engagement with the kind of world we inhabit today and his striving to explore its changing contours.

An excellent writer in Swedish as well as in English, Ulf Hannerz' work in his native language tends to be more literary and informal than his academic publications, but his perspective on "the world in creolization" remains consistent. His fascination with the paradoxes of globalization and the deep humanism underlying his reflections come across beautifully in books such as *Café du Monde* (2011). As the reviewer in *Svenska Dagbladet* put it:

> It is a pleasure to read Hannerz' relaxed and stylish prose, full of exciting and important observations about anything from North American ghetto culture and postcolonialism to the particularities of the professional culture of foreign correspondents and the new forms of political power in a globalised world. Hannerz speaks with a fine formulation about the necessity of "the big conversation across cultural boundaries." (Persson 2011)

Viewed in the context of Hannerz' own writings about centers and peripheries, and not least his early collaborative work with Tomas Gerholm on non-metropolitan anthropologies (Hannerz and Gerholm 1982), it makes perfect sense that one of the most persuasive and influential contributions to the bridging of disparate anthropological flows and currents should come from a relatively peripheral country such as Sweden (see also Hannerz 2010). Here too his scholarship can be seen as a forerunner of what is today the debate around "world anthropologies," a project in the making, which has been subsequently institutionalized in the World Council of Anthropological Associations (WCAA). Ahead of his time, he addressed questions of anthropological knowledge production from a variety of locations and national traditions, but also pointed out that multiple transnational linkages shaped these differences too. Acutely aware of the importance of being attentive to the diversity of traditions within Europe and loci of knowledge outside Euro-American centers, Hannerz played an important role in the establishment of the European Association of Social Anthropologists (EASA), which he continues to support in a variety of ways. His unfailing presence and capacity for dialogue at EASA and American Anthropological Association (AAA) meetings has also contributed to the strengthening the ties between the two associations and communities of anthropologists. A quiet institution-builder, he is as attentive a listener and reader as he is prolific as a writer.

Ulf Hannerz belongs to that minority of anthropologists who have throughout their careers been bilingual in their writings. Not surprisingly, therefore, he has also argued for the importance of valuing publications in languages other than English, a point that he found necessary to make in the context of the audit culture driving evaluation of academic performance and excellence across Europe. Interestingly, his argument for the need to publish in various languages was driven neither by concerns about the hegemony of the English language nor primarily by a concern for publishing in languages accessible to those about whom we as anthropologists write and who are interlocutors in the "field." But with his insistence on valorizing non-English publications, he was equally concerned to foster the public engagement of anthropologists in their own societies as well as encouraging the kind of intellectual pluralism that results from the lived experience of sociocultural diversity. He very rightly reminds us that anthropologists write for a variety of publics: national and transnational, in academia and outside it. He thus makes a forceful argument for the need for us as anthropologists to engage with, and intervene in, public debates in our own countries of origin or residence by writing in the national language(s) in order to address a public outside academia and render our scholarship relevant to it. As a citizen-anthropologist and a public intellectual, Hannerz has not shied away from such intervention on matters academic and non-academic.

In the two decades that have passed since the publication of what was arguably Hannerz' most significant theoretical statement, *Cultural Complexity* (1992), the world has witnessed significant and accelerated change. Retrospectively, the book can be read as a prophetic statement about an incipient world and a program on how to study it. Its main line of argument has largely been made even more relevant by subsequent events, and the methodologies Hannerz developed to study unbounded cultural flows around 1990 now seem virtually tailor-made for research on phenomena such as deterritorialized warfare, Facebook events, migrant remittances, international terrorism, and mobile telephony. Indeed, Ulf Hannerz' more recent works testify to his keen eye not only for the present, but also for the crafting of scenarios for the future and the creation of future imaginaries (see e.g., Hannerz 2009).

Rarely overtly political, Hannerz' work nevertheless has clear political implications in its destabilization of concepts of bounded societies and cultures, and questioning of commonly held assumptions about the nature of social identity. Sensitive to cultural differences and aware of the frictions emerging from accelerated encounters, he shows the limitations of analyses positing "groups" or "cultures" as fundamental units, calling for more nuanced descriptions and more flexible analyses that make space for the paradoxical, the unexpected, and the new. As noted by Ronald Stade and Gudrun Dahl in an earlier appreciation of Hannerz' work: "Today, in a time of dystopias about clashing civilizations and coming anarchies, a cool-headed analysis of global processes that can provide tools for investigating cultural complexity may prove to be the best cure" (Stade and Dahl 2003: 203).

Perhaps the main question raised in Hannerz' wide-ranging but consistent work over more than forty years is simply, "Who are we?" or rather, "What does the word we mean?" He has helped us (*us*?) raise the question in new ways without reification or the dismantling of collectivities into atomistic individuals, which would have amounted to poor sociological thinking. In this move towards a more flexible understanding of the word *we*, Hannerz' work stands out not only as a contribution to social theory, but also—and in this we concur with Stade and Dahl—as a toolbox for dealing with the complexities of the new century both in terms of understanding and of practice. "Culture," as Hannerz rightly notes (1999), is often referred to today in contexts of conflict, and assumptions of cultural fundamentalism often become associated with xenophobia. On the other hand, a "cultural celebrationism" that tends to view cultural phenomena and processes in purely, or primarily, aesthetic and performative terms runs the risk of disregarding tensions around cultural difference. Hannerz proposes instead a processual view of culture as "work in progress" as one way out of this impasse and as an intellectual and practical resource for contemporary forms of belonging, such as citizenship.

Although Hannerz' contributions to anthropology have, in a substantial sense, largely concerned transnationalism, creolization, and globalization, they have implications for culture theory and theorizing of the social in general. Combining his decentering of the concept of culture with his interest in the complexities of interpersonal relations as a starting point, a next step, taken by several of the contributors to this volume, amounts to an exploration of the nature of the social, of cohesion and communication, in the ever shifting contemporary world.

Many languages distinguish between several words referring to different kinds of collectivities but which must perforce all be translated with the word we in most European languages; for example, "we, who are together in this room now," "we, that is you and I," "we, but one that excludes you," "we, that is my clan," or "we, the people of Z." The inclusion and exclusion denoted by the word we is, obviously, contingent on context and circumstance. When European politicians speak, possibly unthinkingly, about "our children and the immigrants' children" in debates about, for example, ethnic-minority numbers in schools, they reproduce notions of ethnic nationhood which are being contested by others. What is required to constitute a "we," be it big or small, depends on the context. While it may suffice in some contexts to take the bus together to feel ourselves to be part of a "we," in other contexts, it may be necessary to share language, religion, or place of origin.

Any complex society offers an almost infinite number of possible criteria for delineating subjective communities for whom the term "we" can be used meaningfully: Us, the members of the Swedish People's Party in Finland. Us commuters. Us lesbians. Us jazz musicians. Us Christians. Us copywriters. Us women. The question of commonality in collectivities remains, and is made acutely relevant in modern societies with regard to the underlying symbolic basis for a shared subjective identity that is overarching and totalizing, and which can make it meaningful still to speak of a country as a society that is something other than a mere administrative entity. Methodological nationalism, which limits the social to the boundaries of a nation-state, has come in for criticism as insufficient for identifying and understanding fundamental social processes taking place today, which are transnational as well as national and often blur the distinction between the two as well.

Nationalist ideology has likewise been criticized, often along normative lines, for standing in the way of a universalistic humanism. Yet, the nation still has, in many parts of the world, an indisputable and enduring ability to create strong abstract ties of community contrary to what many theorists of globalization predicted towards the end of the last century. The political struggles and debates dividing many European societies these days do not concern the nation as such, but how it should be delineated symbolically and demographically; who should be included, and on what conditions. The nation must now share the field of belonging with various other symbolic communities, many of them transnational, but it remains an important focus for identification.

Whether it succeeds or fails in relation to different persons and groups depends on what it has to offer, instrumentally and symbolically. The nation, seen as a metaphorical kin group or an abstract community, is nonetheless under pressure, thanks to a large number of transnational, supranational, and subnational processes that do not conform to its logic and indeed appear to threaten it. Yet a certain degree of national cohesion seems necessary for the functioning of economy, the public sphere, and civil society, since such institutions presuppose trust. A society arguably needs a "social glue," whether or not it is of the kind intimated by Godelier in his thoughtful analysis of changes wrought by colonialism and incipient modernity among the Baruya (Godelier 2009).

Nations were never homogeneous, even before the recent history of transmigration. As has been shown, it is possible to identify considerable cultural variation within any nation, and this variation does not necessarily follow ethnic lines. In terms of dialect, way of life, the role of religion, and kinship practices, intraethnic diversity is considerable even in small countries such as the Nordic ones. However, this kind of variation does not necessarily imply variation regarding the strength or degree of national identification. Jan Petter Blom demonstrated many years ago (Blom 1969) that there existed considerable cultural variation between mountain farmers and lowland farmers in central southern Norway, with no socially significant consequences for collective identification or exclusion/inclusion. There were no norms of endogamy or concerted politics of identity, in spite of clearly observable cultural differences.

This example shows that whereas culture is continuous, identities are discontinuous. Understood as symbolic universes of meaning, cultures flow and mix; one is influenced by one's experiences, surroundings, and impulses from near and afar, and many such impulses do in fact flow quite freely, unhampered by state boundaries, guardians of cultural borders, or capitalist profitability. Collective identity, on the other hand, is bounded: either one is a member of the group or one is not, necessitating criteria for group membership. The disjuncture between cultural flows and group identities is at the heart of contestations over the drawing of these boundaries. The central question in many societies today concerns the criteria for belonging. As far as the nation is concerned, Ernest Gellner famously wrote that nationalist ideology construes cultural boundaries as coterminous with political boundaries (Gellner 1983: 1), which is to say that a state should ideally only contain people of the same kind. Such a definition begs the question concerning the logic of national boundaries, however, since there is no consensus over ways of determining who is "of the same kind." When the map no longer fits with the territory, there is disagreement over whether the map (ideology of nationhood) ought to be changed, or whether one should rather change the territory (refuse citizenship to minorities, enforce their cultural assimilation, or stop migration etc.). The gap between the relatively free flows of cultural meaning and the fixed boundaries of identities is both a thorny political terrain and a fertile field for social research. There exists a grey zone, which expands and contracts situationally, but which as a whole grows, where the boundaries for inclusion and exclusion are under negotiation. The notion of "reflexivity" has long occupied a central place in Hannerz' writings, alerting us to the ways in which groups of people turn attention onto themselves, and thus onto the criteria for cohesion and for disintegration; for unity and for fragmentation. "The present world," he notes, "is also one of reflexivity" (Hannerz 2000: 15). In *Anthropology's World* (2010: 163), Hannerz looks towards the future of anthropology, refusing to provide predictions as to what lies ahead for anthropology, but nevertheless sticking to reflexivity as key to anthropology's mission:

> As a joint mission, anthropology should take care to stay world-building — to cultivate those cross-cutting ties, that mixture of research at home and away, that awareness of humanity as an interconnected but diverse whole toward which it has perhaps always been striving but which it may only rather recently have come close to achieving. ... What is involved here is not only satisfying the individual anthropologist's desire for travel, but having, in as many countries (or whatever are the units) as possible, access to a diversity of perspectives, both inside and outside, toward itself — and to insiders who know the outside.

An analytical approach to these issues must be dialectical in that it accepts that every phenomenon is defined through its opposite, implicitly or explicitly. Openness in one respect entails closedness in another. The French nation, based on Republican values at least in theory, has historically been open to newcomers, but the guardians of the French language, for example, have tried their utmost to close it off from unwanted impulses from the outside. If one says "similarity," one also says, implicitly, "difference": no two individuals are completely identical, and certain differences are tolerated, even in societies where the hegemonic ideology is founded on the principle of similarity. Integration also entails disintegration: when politicians and others talk of the need for immigrants to "be integrated," they conveniently forget that criteria for integration are by no means settled.

Since the Second World War, western European societies have changed dramatically due to processes of urbanization, migration, changes in the labor market, new family structures, new information technology, and so on, and it would be unwise to assume that these societies are today mere updates of their antecedents. For example, it is unclear which cohesive and fragmenting—centripetal and centrifugal—forces characterize contemporary European societies. It would be intellectually lazy to assume that a national sense of identity, for example, is a necessary condition for cohesion everywhere, or that it can easily be gauged and measured. No isomorphism can be assumed between society and culture, just as individuals are not bearers of national cultures, as Hannerz has always been at pains to point out. Different parts of a cultural universe change at different velocities, with resulting frictions and dissonances, and with little relationship between societal and cultural integration.

It is such innovative thought—reconstructing while deconstructing; rebuilding the ship at sea; using old concepts differently as well as trying out new ones—combined with a far-sighted vision of the discipline that transcends borders, boundaries, and fashions of the day, which characterizes Ulf Hannerz' scholarship. It is ecumenical in often bold and revolutionary ways, positioning itself firmly in the contested space of the militant middle ground.

References

Blom, Jan Petter. 1969. "Ethnic and Cultural Differentiation." In *Ethnic Groups and Boundaries: The Social Organization of Culture Difference*, ed. Fredrik Barth. Oslo: Universitetsforlaget, pp. 75–85.
Gellner, Ernest. 1983. *Nations and Nationalism*. Oxford: Blackwell.
Godelier, Maurice. 2009. *In and Out of the West: Reconstructing Anthropology*. London: Verso.
Hannerz, Ulf. 1969. *Soulside: Inquiries into Ghetto Culture and Community*. Stockholm: Almqvist and Wiksell.
———. 1980. *Exploring the City: Inquiries toward an Urban Anthropology*. New York: Columbia University Press.
———. 1992. *Cultural Complexity: Studies in the Social Organization of Meaning*. New York: Columbia University Press.
———. 1996. *Transnational Connections*. London: Routledge.
———. 1999. "Reflections on Varieties of Culturespeak." *European Journal of Cultural Studies* 2(3): 393–407.
———. 2000. *Flows, Boundaries and Hybrids: Keywords in Transnational Anthropology*. Stockholm: Research Program on Transnational Communities. Working Paper 2.
———. 2004. *Foreign News: Exploring the World of Foreign Correspondents*. Chicago: University of Chicago Press.

———. 2009. "Geocultural Scenarios." In *Frontiers of Sociology*, ed. Peter Hedström and Björn Wittrock. Annals of the International Institute of Sociology, 2. Leiden: Brill, pp. 267–288.

———. 2010. *Anthropology's World: Life in a Twenty-First Century Discipline*. London: Pluto Press.

———. 2011. *Café du monde: Platser, vägar och människor i världsvrimlet*. Stockholm: Carlsson.

Hannerz, Ulf and Tomas Gerholm, eds. 1982. "The Shaping of National Anthropologies." *Ethnos* 47(special issue): 1–2.

Kuper, Adam. 1999. *Culture: The Anthropologists' Account*. Cambridge, MA: Harvard University Press.

Persson, Magnus. 2011. "Njutningsfull kulturanalys." *Svenska Dagbladet*, 27 June 2011.

Stade, Ronald and Gudrun Dahl. 2003. "Introduction: Globalization, Creolization, and Cultural Complexity." *Global Networks* 3(3): 201–206.

Chapter 1

DIVIDED BY A SHARED DESTINY
An Anthropologist's Notes from an Overheated World

Thomas Hylland Eriksen

On his one hundredth birthday on November 28, 2008, Claude Lévi-Strauss was paid a visit by President Nicolas Sarkozy, France being a country where politicians can still build prestige by associating with intellectuals. In the press reports from the meeting, the centenarian, whose seminal book on kinship was published more than sixty years ago, said that he did not really count himself among the living any more. By saying this he referred, I believe, not just to his very advanced age and diminishing faculties, but also to the acknowledgement of the fact that the world he cherished was gone. Lévi-Strauss has devoted his life to the study of humanity under the most varying cultural circumstances imaginable, in order to develop his theory of human universals. Throughout his life—he was a cultural pessimist already in the 1930s—he has witnessed the accelerating disappearance of that world; that is, the world of radical cultural difference.

Elaborating briefly on his own comment to Sarkozy, Lévi-Strauss added that the world was now too full. *Le monde est trop plein.* Presumably he meant that it was overfilled by humans and the products of their activities. At the time of his birth in 1908, the planet was inhabited by a grand total of 1.7 billion persons; global population now stands at more than seven billion, and the percentage with their own Internet accounts and mobile telephones increases every year. No matter how you go about measuring degrees of connectedness in the contemporary world, the only possible conclusion is that far more people today are much more connected than ever before in history. There are more of us, and each of us has, on average, more links to the outside world than our predecessors, through business travel, information, communication, migration, vacations, political engagement, trade, development assistance, exchange programs, and so on. The number of transatlantic telephone lines has grown phenomenally in the last few decades; so has the number of websites and international NGOs. And one could easily go on and on.

It can indeed be argued that this is a new world, one which in significant ways differs from all epochs that preceded it. Most of us now live under the bright light of the powerful headlights of modernity, as genuine contemporaries, aware, however dimly, of one another. Lévi-Strauss bemoans the emergence of such a disenchanted world. By contrast, Ulf Hannerz welcomes it, armed with intellectual tools which he has to a great extent built himself (Hannerz 1992, 1996, 2010), which enable us to reenchant the world of global modernity by infusing it with the magic of anthropology. This is a new world, and as Hannerz has shown, it swarms with diversity and emergent cultural forms impatiently waiting for their ethnographer.

Among social theorists, a flurry of books, journals, articles, and conferences have, since around 1990, sought to redefine the human world—the post-Cold War world, the postcolonial world, the world of global modernity or the world of a deterritorialized information society—sometimes inventing new theoretical concepts, sometimes giving new tasks to old vocabulary (see Eriksen 2014 for an overview). A number of themes recur throughout this vivid and sometimes cacophonic discourse; let me just mention a few initially.

The concept of the network. Established as a staple in studies of globalization by at least two of the most prominent theorists in the field (Castells 1996 and Hannerz 1992, 1996), the concept of the network implies that stable hierarchies and structures are giving way to nodal, multicentered, and fluid systems, and that this change takes place in numerous fields of interaction. (This concept should not be confused with the Actor Network Theory (ANT) idea of the network developed by Bruno Latour, to which it is related: ANT networks include both human and non-human agents.) In Hardt and Negri's *Empire* (2000), a book which famously argues the fading away of territorial powers to the benefit of a jellyfish-like, omnipresent force that they call "empire," the influence from Deleuze and Guattari's contrasting of rhizomes and treelike structures (*rhizomes et racines*) in *Mille plateaux* (1980) is crucial, and Hardt and Negri's description of the world of global capitalism is also reminiscent of Castells' account of global networks based on the "space of flows" rather than the "space of places."

The glocal. Although the term itself is relatively uncommon in academic writings (it seems to have caught on in the business world, though), glocalization (Robertson 1992) is a standard theme in nearly all anthropological writing about globalization as well as most of the sociological and geographical literature. The argument is as follows. In real life, there exists no abstract, huge, global level of affairs on the one hand and local, lived realities on the other. The local level is in fact infused with influences from outside, be it culinary novelties or structural adjustment programs; but these "influences," on their part, have no autonomous existence outside their tangible manifestations. "Microsoft" thus exists as a company based in Seattle, and also as the computer software used to run most personal computers in the world, but it does not exist as a global entity except as an abstraction of debatable value. It has numerous concrete manifestations, all of them local, and it offers a shared language which makes transnational communication (and file exchange) possible, but as a global entity it exists only at the level of thought. Moreover, concepts describing impurity or mixing—hybridity, creolization, and so on—are specific instances of this general approach stressing the primacy of the local. The local–global dichotomy is, in other words, misleading.

Reflexivity and fluidity. Bauman's (2000) term "liquid modernity" sums up this theoretical focus, which emphasizes the uncertainty, risk, and negotiability associated with phenomena as distinct as personal identification, economies, and world climate in the "global era." That identities are not fixed and given once and for all is not exactly news any more, but it is widely held that the current "post-traditional" (Giddens 1991) era is characterized by an unprecedented breadth of individual repertoires, forcing people to choose between alternatives and to define themselves in ways which were not necessary in earlier, less unstable and more clearly delineated social formations. Ambivalence and fundamentalism in the politics of identity are seen to stem simultaneously from this fundamental uncertainty.

Rights issues. While it has become unfashionable to defend cultural relativism as an ethical stance, opinion remains divided as to the legitimacy of group rights and, more generally, the relationship between group and individual in the contemporary world. Since the mere existence of groups cannot be taken for granted, the individual is often foregrounded. The debates may concern intellectual property rights, cultural and linguistic rights, or multicultural dilemmas such as the conflict between individualist agency and arranged marriages among non-European immigrants in north Atlantic societies.

The globalization discourse tends to privilege processes over structures, rhizomes over roots, reflexivity over doxa, individual over group, flexibility over fixity, rights over duties, and freedom over security in its bid to highlight globalization as something qualitatively new. While this kind of exercise is often necessary, it tends to become one-sided. Many anthropologists talk disparagingly about the jargon of "global-babble" or "globalitarism" (Trouillot 2001), and tend to react against simplistic generalizations by reinserting (and reasserting) the uniqueness of the local, or glocal, as the case might be.

There is doubtless something qualitatively new about the compass, speed, and reach of current transnational networks. Now, some globalization theorists argue that the shrinking of the world will almost inevitably lead to a new value orientation, some indeed heralding the coming of a new, postmodern kind of person (e.g., Sennett 1998). These writers, who predict the emergence of a new set of uprooted, deterritorialized values and fragmented identities, are often accused of generalizing from their own European middle-class habitus, the "class consciousness of frequent travellers" (Calhoun 2002). The sociologist John Urry, lending himself easily to this criticism, argues in the final chapter of his *Global Complexity* (2003) that globalization has the potential of stimulating widespread cosmopolitanism (however, he does not say among whom). But, as he readily admits in an earlier chapter in the same book, the principles of closeness and distance still hold, for example in viewing patterns on television, where a global trend consists in viewers' preferences for locally produced programs.

The newness of the contemporary world was described concisely by Castells in 1998, in a lengthy footnote to the final volume of his trilogy *The Information Society*:

> Why is this a new world? ... Chips and computers are new; ubiquitous, mobile telecommunications are new, genetic engineering is new; electronically integrated, global financial markets working in real time are new; an inter-linked capitalist economy embracing the whole planet, and not only some of its segments, is new; a majority of the urban labor force in knowledge and information processing in advanced economies is new; a majority of urban population in the planet is new; the demise of the Soviet Empire, the fading away of communism, and the end of the Cold War are new; the rise of the Asian Pacific as an equal partner in the global economy is new; the widespread challenge to patriarchalism is new; the universal consciousness on ecological preservation is new; and the emergence of a network society, based on a space of flows, and on timeless time, is historically new. (Castells 1998: 336)

A few years later, he could have added the advent of deterritorialized warfare and political battles involving the question of humanly induced climate change to the list. He might also well have spoken of post-Fordist flexible accumulation (Harvey 1989) and mass migration (Castles and Davidson 2000). Be this as it may; Castells adds at the end of his long footnote that it does not really matter whether all this is new or not; his point is that this is our world, and therefore we should study it. I disagree. It does matter what is new and what is not, if we are going to make sense of the contemporary world.

This World Began in 1991...

There is simultaneously something very new and something very old about the contemporary world. The philosopher John Gray, towards the end of his essay on al-Qaeda and what it means to be modern (Gray 2003: 119), argues that "it is the interaction of expanding scientific knowledge with unchanging human needs that will determine the future of our species."

Put differently, shifting circumstances influence any narrative trying to make sense of the world. The growth of science and technology creates new frameworks for the enactment of human projects, which nevertheless remain rooted in the fundamental, and fundamentally contradictory, human experiences of community and alienation, security and individuality. Perhaps nowhere is this tension more evident than in the politics of culture and identity in the world of the early twenty-first century, which will be outlined below. The beginning of the twenty-first century, incidentally, could be dated either to September 11, 2001, or to January 1991. I am inclined to propose 1991, for the following reasons.

First of all, 1991 was the year when the Cold War was called off once and for all. The two-bloc system that had defined the postwar era was suddenly gone. The ideological conflict between socialism and capitalism seemed to have been replaced with the triumphant sound of one hand clapping. By 1991, it was also clear that apartheid was about to be relegated to the dustbin of history. Mandela had been released from prison the year before, and negotiations between the Nationalist Party and the African National Congress (ANC) had begun in earnest.

Secondly, Yugoslavia began to dismantle itself with surprising violence, fed by a kind of nationalistic sentiment many believed to have been overcome. Around the same time, the Hindu nationalists of the Bharatiya Janata Party (Indian People's Party, BJP) went from strength to strength in India. The identity politics of the state, or of statelike bodies, was thus not something of the past. In other words, openness and closure were still twin features of politics, but they were operating along new lines.

Thirdly, 1991 was the year in which the Internet began to be marketed to ordinary consumers, so that Mr. and Mrs. Smith could walk into the shop and buy their subscription to America Online. This was new, just as new as the pocket-sized mobile phones which all of a sudden began to spread across the world, from Mauritius to Iceland, around 1991. Deregulation of markets had taken place in the preceding decade, but many of the effects of a weaker state and a less manageable and predictable market were being felt only now, helped by new information and communication technology.

...and It Is an Overheated World...

This post-1991 world is, in addition to everything else, one of intensified tensions and frictions. One need only count the present number of transatlantic flights or the number of trans-Pacific telephone connections to realize that the webs of connectedness are hotter, faster, and denser than in any previous period, with repercussions virtually everywhere. The growth of urban slums throughout the Global South is an indirect result of economic globalization (Davis 2006), as is the growth of a transnational precariat (Standing 2011), a mobile labor force deprived of rights and predictability. The growth of militant Islamic identity politics across the Muslim world, the rise of a motley group of new social movements opposing global neoliberalism (Maeckelbergh 2009), the huge increase in social inequality in the U.S., and the double-bind between economic growth and environmental responsibility all indicate that globalization is anything but a tea party. Yet the networked capitalist world is a framework, or scaffolding, for almost any serious inquiry into cultural and social dynamics today, not least those movements that reject the hegemony of neoliberal capitalism; labeled "anti-globalizers" at the outset, they prefer the term "alterglobalizers" as it is not interconnectedness as such they oppose, but its neoliberal form.

This is an accelerated world, where everything from communication to warfare and industrial production takes place faster and more comprehensively than ever before. Speed, in physics, is just another way of talking about heat. In other words, when you say of someone that he or she is suffering from burnout, the metaphor is an apt one. The burnout is a direct consequence of too much speed.

This could be a main reason why the concept of global warming has caught on in such a powerful way in the north Atlantic middle classes. Climate change is a fact, but that is not the point: by focusing on literal heat as an unintentional consequence of modernity, the narratives about global warming fit perfectly with, enrich, and supplement, the other narratives about the contemporary age. It functions as a natural-science corollary of stories about terrorism and imperialism, roughly in the same way as chaos theory, in the 1980s, seemed the perfect natural-science companion for postmodernism in the humanities. All these narratives and their relations depict the contemporary world as one "out of control," fraught with alienation, powerlessness, global forces, and injustices brought about and reproduced by the rich and powerful—who are, without knowing it, digging their own grave. Above all, the notion of global warming feeds into a larger and more enduring story about acceleration, which, in a sense, is the story of modernity as such.

In a world of increased speed, intensified contact across boundaries and, as a result, the incessant questioning of these very boundaries, a sense—not only of vulnerability but also of instability and uncertainty—is very widespread. New zones of tension graft themselves onto the old and perhaps universal lines of conflict—power versus powerlessness, wealth versus poverty, autonomy versus dependence, recognition versus humiliation. Some of these emergent conflicts, which will probably define the present century, are:

- Globalization versus alterglobalization—the new social movements looking for viable, locally based alternatives to the "there is no alternative" (TINA) doctrine;
- Environmentalism versus development—saving the planet is posited as a threat to development, especially in less developed nations;
- Cosmopolitanism versus identity politics (including xenophobia and religious fundamentalism)—a main dimension of politics almost everywhere in the world now, frequently supplanting the Left/Right divide;
- Inclusion versus exclusion—walls, physical and metaphorical, preventing the free movement of people and their full inclusion in society;
- Uniformity versus diversity—shared templates of modernity articulating with the local and unique; and finally,
- Cultural autonomy versus the quest for recognition—finding the balance, as Lévi-Strauss once put it, between contact and isolation.

It is clear that the heightened speed with which encounters take place implies an unprecedented need for traffic rules. Movement has to be channeled. Laws regulating immigration and citizenship are obvious examples, but so are attempts—in some countries—to keep the language free of contamination from foreign (often English) influence and purification attempts taking place in some religious groups, such as the Deobandi movement in Pakistan that is seeking to purge Pakistani

Islam of Hindu elements. Purity is pitted against filth, order against chaos. A desperate need of tidiness in a messy world is making itself felt everywhere, albeit in different ways.

Amidst this flurry of contradicting claims, cultural change, and hotly disputed identities, boundary work is more often frantic than calm. Who is inside and outside the group, what are the criteria for being an insider, and what does it mean to be an individual with proper, socially recognized credentials and personal integrity? This exploration will begin with an examination of one of the most intriguing and shocking characters of the classic modern literature.

...Where Identities Are Uncertain...

Henrik Ibsen's plays from the latter half of the nineteenth century are widely admired for their psychological depth and their accurate depiction of profound contradictions in the bourgeois family of pre-First World War Europe. However, in some important ways, his earlier plays *Brand* and *Peer Gynt* (Ibsen 1972/1867–8) speak more directly to the sensibilities of the early twenty-first century than the dramas dealing with late-nineteenth-century bourgeois society. *Brand*, arguably Ibsen's first masterpiece, was a play about a Christian fundamentalist despairing at the moral decay and confusion he saw all around him, and his attempts to bracket off his own existence and that of his flock of faithfuls from the surrounding turmoil. His attempt to escape from modernity can be described as a project intended to create a controlled space where all questions could be answered, a community which was predictable and morally consistent.

Brand is a puritan in the literal sense of the term; he seeks purity and simplicity. By contrast, the protagonist of Ibsen's next play, *Peer Gynt*, is an entrepreneur and an adventurer who lies and cheats his way across the world, who makes a small fortune in the by then illicit slave trade, and who poses as a prophet in north Africa and as a cosmopolitan gentleman on a Mediterranean coast, before returning to his native mountain valley only to discover that his personality lacks a core. The struggles involving collective identification in the contemporary era, with which much of my research for nearly twenty years has incidentally been concerned, revolve around the questions raised by Ibsen in the 1860s. "Be who you are fully and wholly/not piecemeal and partially," proclaims Brand (Act 1: 25), a prophet not only of evangelical Christianity but also of the integrity of the person. Peer Gynt, for his part, boasts of having received impulses from all over the world, introducing himself in the fourth act as a "citizen of the world in spirit" (*Verdensborger af gemyt*, Act 4, Scene 1).

Whereas Brand can be said to inhabit a closed universe, Peer Gynt's universe lacks boundaries. The two characters cover, between them, the span between fundamentalism and collectivism on the one hand, and voluntarism and individualism on the other. Brand stands for destiny and security, while Peer stands for freedom and insecurity. The contrast between the two and attempts to stake out third ways are part and parcel of the experience of the children of immigrants in western Europe, to mention just one contemporary parallel.

In order to begin to understand social belonging and identity, we first have to consider personhood. I realized this, belatedly, when some years ago I was writing a book about identity politics (Eriksen 2004), discovering one day that I had not done the groundwork of studying the foundations of any kind of social identity—that is, the person (cf. also Cohen 1994). This led me, among other things, in the direction of developmental psychology and evolutionary theory, but that is another story. For now, we shall restrict ourselves to the person and his or her forms of attachment, seen as the basis for security.

The Latin term *persona* originally meant mask, which indicates that personal identity is shifting and can be treacherous (cf. Mauss 1960). Life is a stage (Shakespeare), and personality is like an onion—layer upon layer, but with no core (Ibsen). When all the layers of makeup and make-believe are peeled away, do we then encounter the real person—or do we instead meet a faceless monster? The answer from social science is: neither. Even "real people" have to play out their realness through an identity which is recognizable to others. He or she must, for example, possess a linguistic identity. The phantasmagoric point zero, where the "real person" coalesces with the faceless one, is tantamount to autism. There is no "other person" behind the social person.

Personal identity is shaped through social experiences. Some of them are easily forgotten, some can be interpreted to fit a present state one wants to belong to (it is never too late to obtain a tragic history or a happy childhood if one needs it), some may be more or less fictional, and yet others cannot be modified at all. In this sense, personal biographies are reminiscent of national historiography and religious myths of origin. Personal experiences are as malleable as national histories, neither more nor less. They can attach us to a great number of different communities based on gender, class, place, political persuasion, literary taste, sexual orientation, national identity, religion, and so on. Yet they cannot be bent indefinitely; certain facts about ourselves are unchangeable. One can deny them, but they keep returning—as the aging

Peer Gynt discovers in the final act. As Bob Marley put it in "Running Away," "Ya can't run away from yourself."

Peer tries to do just this, and he thus sacrifices security for the sake of freedom; Brand does the opposite. A parallel to the contrast between Peer Gynt and Brand is found in a metaphor used among some West African peoples. In describing what a person is they compare it with a tortoise. It may stick its head out, making itself visible and vulnerable, but it then retracts its head into the shell, rendering itself hidden and invincible. This metaphor seems to travel well into the world of mass media and reality television. Some of our contemporary tortoises prefer to stay inside their shells most of the time, while others live almost continuously with their heads stuck out for all to see.

What the tortoise metaphor does not claim is that there exists an insulated, pure self in the inner recesses of the individual, a self which is independent of its surroundings. Such a creature is, besides, difficult to envision. For example, we depend on thinking through linguistic categories, and if we should usually keep our thoughts to ourselves, at least we share them with a few confidantes. The metaphor of the tortoise, transposed to contemporary modern societies, is best understood as stating that human beings switch between being socially extroverted and directed towards the open, uncertain external world, and being socially introverted, limited to that which is secure and familiar. It deals not so much with the internal life of the individual as with two forms of sociality; the secure and the insecure, the closed and the open.

...and Nobody Knows the Precise Meaning of "We";

Secure sociality moves in a sphere of undisputed we-feeling. In this realm one may be backstage; one can speak one's dialect, laugh at in-jokes, savor the smells of one's childhood, and know that one has an intuitive, embodied cultural competence which one succeeds in performing without even trying. In a field of secure sociality, everyone is predictable to each other, and if they are not, there are ways of demarcating displeasure which are immediately understood by others. A relaxed intimacy engulfs secure sociality. It is related to the late-nineteenth century sociologist Ferdinand Tönnies' concept of *Wesenswille* ("natural, organic will") which in his view characterized life in the *Gemeinschaft*, that traditional community where everybody knew each other and had a limited horizon of opportunities. The *Wesenswille* recommends itself; it makes us behave along certain lines without asking critical questions.

Insecure sociality is to a much greater extent characterized by improvisation and negotiations over situational definitions. Those who meet in this kind of field are much less secure as to whom they are dealing with, and as a result, they are less certain as to whom they are looking at in the mirror. The opportunities are more varied and more open to a person in a state of insecure sociality than to someone who rests contented in a condition of predictable routines of secure sociality, but the risks are also much greater.

Insecure sociality appears, typically, in cosmopolitan cities, along trade routes and—especially after the industrial revolution—in societies undergoing rapid change. Suddenly, something new happens, and one finds oneself in a setting with no preordained script to be followed. One is faced with the task of rebuilding the ship at sea. A typical reaction to this kind of insecurity is withdrawal, but it is equally common to try to redefine the situation to make it resemble something familiar. When Columbus became the first European to set foot in the Caribbean, he was convinced that he had reached India. Later conquistadors were aware that they had arrived in a country which was not described in the Bible; that is, an entirely new land with unknown and undescribed inhabitants. Many of them still tried to interpret their experiences through Biblical interpretations. In *The Conquest of America*, Tzvetan Todorov (1989) shows that the Aztecs and the Spaniards interpreted each other into their respective preexistent worldviews. Neither group was ready to acknowledge that something entirely new had entered their world, which required new cognitive maps or even an intellectual revolution. In a word, they were not yet modern.

The work amounting to making insecure situations secure takes many shapes. Imperialist powers may try to reshape their new lands to make them less threateningly different, or erect physical boundaries against the aliens, as the architects of apartheid did in South Africa and Israel is doing presently. Dominated peoples either may try to imitate their rulers to mitigate the sense of insecurity on both sides, or by establishing their own boundaries—separatism, revolution, or independence.

Is insecurity a good or a bad thing? That depends. In social anthropological theory, different terms are being used, which provide different answers to the question. Mary Douglas (1966), who belongs to a tradition focusing on the study of social integration and assuming it to be a good thing, regards departures from the existing order as anomalies. They are cumbersome since they do not fit in. Many people who appear as anomalies, besides, become anomic—that is, normless; alienated, confused, and unhappy. In Douglas' great intellectual mentor Durkheim's view, anomie was an important cause of suicide.

An opposite approach is found in the early work of Fredrik Barth (1963), who, in the early 1960s, directed a research program about the entrepreneur in northern Norway. According to Barth's definition, the entrepreneur was someone who bridged formerly discrete spheres; who found new commodities to sell in new locations, new ways of running a business, new niches, and so on. He thrived on uncertainty and change, building his empire in the interstices. In his purest form, Barth's entrepreneur was a Peer Gynt; poorly integrated into the moral community, but hardly a candidate for suicide. It may perhaps be said that the entrepreneur fares like everybody else in the age of neoliberalism, which values freedom so highly but neglects security: whenever one has success, the range of options and the scope of personal freedom feel fantastic, but the moment one hits the wall, freedom is reinterpreted as insecurity and the choices as a kind of coercive compulsion. The entrepreneur becomes an anomaly the moment he fails to succeed.

It has been well documented that identification in our day and age can be an insecure kind of task with many difficulties and poor predictability. People who formerly had no mutual contact are brought together, new cultural forms arise, and the dominant ideology dictating that life should consist in free choices puts pressure on everyone. Good old recipes for the good life may not have been lost, but they are conventionally discarded as reactionary and inhibiting. The result may just as well be frustrated confusion as positive self-realization.

Even without the aid of this kind of freedom ideology, capitalism is capable of creating insecurity and new social dynamics. It has been a massive force, uprooting people from their conventional ways of doing things, moving them physically, giving them new tasks and bringing them into contact with new others. When mining began in the copper-rich areas of the eastern parts of present-day Zambia, just after the First World War, workers were recruited from all over the colony. They spoke many languages and had many different customs and kinship systems, but very soon, the workers began to sort each other, in a rough and ready way, on the basis of ideas about social distance. The people hailing from the western regions were seen as a category apart, likewise the Lozi speakers, the matrilineal peoples, and so on. Some of the groups had experienced regular contact before urbanization, and had conventionalized ways of dealing with each other. Some even enjoyed an institutionalized joking relationship with each other. (This wonderful African institution deserves being exported elsewhere. Perhaps

Jews and Palestinians, or Christians and Muslims, might want to give it a try?)

...Where Recognition Is a Scarce Resource...

Tzvetan Todorov, in his memoir from the twentieth century (Todorov 2000), describes three dangers facing the post-totalitarian world. One is instrumentalization of social relations—typically expressed as unfettered market liberalism, or rather, a loss of the social principles of solidarity and decency, which prevented markets from expanding outside the economy strictly speaking, and which also curtailed the power of state bureaucracies in liberal societies. In passing, it may be mentioned that these anxieties are neither uncommon nor new. Similar concerns with bureaucracies were expressed by the inventor of the theory of modern bureaucracy, Max Weber, and worries about the expansion of the market principle were voiced by Habermas in the 1960s, Lukács in the 1920s, and Marx in the 1850s. The second danger is moral correctness—sanctimonious and authoritarian conformism, in Europe typically expressed through the recently implemented bans on smoking in public places. The third danger identified by Todorov is the topic of the present discussion: fragmenting identity politics, where universal values are bracketed in the name of group self-determination, where commitment to shared societal projects is weakened, and where open conflict between identity-based groups may easily flare up—not so much because they are culturally different, but because they have few interests in common. This is a vision of a classic plural society without a colonial ruling class.

I share all his anxieties, although I might have wanted to add one or two of my own. Yet there can be no easy way out. The only credible responses to the challenges facing humanity have to be ambivalent, doubtful, cautious, and with instincts favoring pluralism and a multiplicity of voices, rather than universal recipes for happiness. It is, in other words, the open-mindedness of the Renaissance and the optimistic view of human nature of the Enlightenment we need to carry with us in this new, old world. It is an ironic fact—given that neither the U.S. of the Bush II era (2001–2008) nor its adversaries, real as well as imagined, are easily given to ambivalence—that the perhaps two most influential ideological thinkers of the U.S. Right are both partly correct, although they are wrong in crucial respects. Both are authors of widely distributed books about the "new world order," and both are keenly listened to in circles near the White House. However, they seem to be saying opposite things. Francis Fukuyama (1992) triumphantly argued that Western democracy is the only game in town worthy of the name, and that global politics nowadays simply consists in attempts, by the less fortunate nations, to achieve the same levels of consumption and liberal rights as those enjoyed by North Americans. In this context, he also argues that the quest for recognition is fundamental and accounts for various forms of identity politics. The late Samuel Huntington (1996), on the other hand, argued that current and future conflicts would take place not between ideologies, but between "civilizations"—that is, related clusters of cultures, such as the West, Islam, Hinduism, and Eastern Christianity. Both Fukuyama and Huntington have been severely criticized by academics and other intellectuals, and this is not the place to repeat all the criticisms. On the contrary, it may be conceded that they are both partly right. Fukuyama is right to assume that recognition by others is a notoriously scarce resource in the contemporary world, but he is wrong in believing that recognition can only be achieved through the successful adoption of Western values and ways of life. Huntington is correct in saying that cultural differences are important, but he is hopelessly off the mark when he tries to map out those differences—his concept of civilizations is theoretically inconsistent and empirically misleading—and there is also no reason to assume that such differences necessarily lead to conflict. In fact, it has been argued that none of the armed conflicts of the 1990s were in line with Huntington's predictions (Fox 2000).

It must nonetheless be conceded that these conservative American thinkers correctly claim that recognition and respect are important, and that cultural differences matter in politics. In an overheated, accelerated world, frictions between cultural worlds are accentuated, and other people's recognition becomes one of the scarcest resources in the world.

...and Boundaries Become Fuzzy Frontiers.

In the misty dawn of time, when the world was still young and fathomable for the common people—say, in the mid-twentieth century— not only was it seemingly possible to understand global politics, but one could also easily divide the world into discrete cultural regions: the world simply seemed to be a composite of cultures. Thus, in Denmark they spoke Danish, and the Danes were liberal Protestants with characteristic Danish features, a characteristic body language, and a love for red sausages and Pilsner beer; in Bangladesh the Bengali Muslims had their own customs and traditions; all the tribes in Kenya had their particular, unique cultures and languages, and so on. According to the prevailing worldview at that time there was not much contact between these cultures, although there was some exchange and mutual influence going on between them. Cultural contact, which developed through missionary work, aid, migration, and the diffusion of modern institutions such as the modern nation-state and the capitalist labor market, gave rise to a set of problems related to the encounter of separate cultures, each with its own special, internal logic. Often the results were misunderstandings and conflicts, and fairly often the stronger culture came to dominate the weaker. This was often referred to as cultural imperialism—a term which is today rarely used, though it was common in intellectual discourse a surprisingly short time ago.

This understanding of culture and cultural differences, which has been fundamental to European thinking ever since Romanticism and crucial both in nationalist ideologies as well as in cultural anthropological method, today, all of a sudden, appears old-fashioned and dated. This sudden change partly relates to a change in our way of thinking; however, far more important is the fact that the world has changed. Although cultures never have been completely isolated and without contact with other cultures, and despite the fact that cultural isolation often has been exaggerated both by scholars and others, the possibility of cultural isolation shrinks day by day. Both economy and politics have become globalized—that is, to an increasing extent processes affect people in different places at the same time as they cannot necessarily be traced back to one specific place. Because of advancements in communication technology, money, goods, people, ideas, and power travel across the world with little friction and at a high speed. There has been an enormous growth in air traffic during the past sixty years, and airline fares continue to drop. Satellite television, the Internet and related technologies have accelerated the development of a world without delays, where certain events can take place in all places at the same time and where distances are shrinking rapidly.

At the same time the huge contrasts in life opportunities across countries and regions create an unstable situation and make it advantageous for some people from poorer countries to move permanently or temporarily to rich countries. This is visible even in geographically peripheral regions such as Scandinavia, and questions concerning immigrants and integration are a recurrent issue in Scandinavian public debate.

Needless to say, changes of this magnitude will have consequences on a cultural level and consequently demand new ways of approaching culture and cultural differences. Some people believe that the processes of globalization will lead to the annihilation of cultural differences and that human beings throughout the world are becoming more and more alike. This view is shared by optimists and pessimists alike. A different perspective, which—for obvious reasons—is widespread among intellectuals in poor countries, focuses on the neocolonial aspects of globalization; how economic differences are sustained, and how the seemingly boundless openness that has characterized the era of globalization also has delimiting and marginalizing effects.

A third approach involves the new forms of cultural variation that are evolving in the context of global modernity, because modernity does not equal cultural homogeneity. As has been pointed out by Ulf Hannerz many times, the globalization of culture does not create global people. But globalization creates "cultural creoles," people who live at the intersection of different cultural traditions, constantly bombarded with impulses, expectations, demands, and opportunities from several different angles, and who continuously create themselves, not from ready-made prescriptions but by crafting their own unique, complex cultural fabric (Hannerz 1990; see also Stewart 2007).

Let us take the example of a country which enjoyed an undisputed, bounded, and rich national identity until very recently, and ask: Is Sweden still Swedish? To some extent, the answer naturally is yes. The country is a sovereign nation, with a number of common public institutions, a rich and diverse public life that includes everything from voluntary organizations to national newspapers, and certain customs and traditions that are perceived as typically Swedish. However, the notion of cultural "Swedishness" is under considerable pressure these days, and the content of the national cultural identity is as controversial, variable, ambiguous, and fuzzy in Sweden as it is in many other countries. The primary reason is that mobility and cultural creolization create a discrepancy between theory and practice; the map and the territory no longer fit together, as it were.

The old map reveals a world of cultural islands. On each island, people have their special way of living, with their own traditions and so forth, but there is relatively little contact between the islands. It is extremely difficult to navigate the world of today using such a map. That is a main reason that a significant part of the intellectual community has been at work revising that map for some time. (Naturally, it is also possible to change the territory so that it matches the old map—a solution which might take the form of ethnic cleansing.) This revision process is evident in the bifurcation of history into different narratives—stories or histories; new nuances and a new diversity are incorporated into the conception of Swedishness, and new groups of people attain a sense of subjective and objective belonging to Swedish society. The same work is being undertaken in other countries as well—the Swedish example was chosen more or less at random. Rebuilding the ship at sea has become a necessary task, and for more than forty years, Ulf Hannerz has offered tools, narratives, and analyses inspiring others to do their part.

In this kind of world, which is an irreducibly diverse, overheated world, we are all strangers in a strange land. At the same time, we are all in the same boat, divided by a shared destiny.

Acknowledgments

There is some overlap between the middle part of this article and the 2010 "Human Security and Social Anthropology" in *A World of Insecurity*, ed. Thomas Hylland Eriksen, E. Bal, and O. Salemink, London: Pluto, pp. 1–22.

References

Barth, Fredrik, ed. 1963. *The Role of the Entrepreneur in Social Change in Northern Norway*. Bergen: Universitetsforlaget.
Bauman, Zygmunt. 2000. *Liquid Modernity*. Cambridge: Polity.
Calhoun, Craig. 2002. "The Class Consciousness of Frequent Travellers: Towards a Critique of Actually Existing Cosmopolitanism." In *Conceiving Cosmopolitanism: Theory, Context and Practice*, ed. Steven Vertovec and Robin Cohen. Oxford: Oxford University Press, pp. 86–109.
Castells, Manuel. 1996. *The Rise of the Network Society*. Oxford: Blackwell.
———. 1998. *End of Millennium*. Oxford: Blackwell.
Castles, Stephen and Alasdair Davidson. 2000. *Citizenship and Migration: Globalization and the Politics of Belonging*. London: Palgrave Macmillan.
Cohen, A.P. 1994. *Self Consciousness*. London: Routledge.
Davis, Mike. 2006. *Planet of Slums*. London: Verso.
Deleuze, Gilles and Felix Guattari. 1980. *Mille Plateaux*. Paris: Minuit.
Douglas, Mary. 1966. *Purity and Danger: An Analysis of Concepts of Pollution and Taboo*. London: Routledge and Kegan Paul.
Eriksen, Thomas Hylland. 2004. *Røtter og føtter: Identitet i en omskiftelig tid* (Roots and Boots: Identity at a Crossroads). Oslo: Aschehoug.
———. 2014. *Globalization: The Key Concepts*, 2nd edition. London: Bloomsbury.
Fox, Jonathan. 2000. "Clash of Civilizations or Clash of Religions: Which Is a More Important Determinant of Ethnic Conflict?" *Ethnicities* 1(3): 295–366.
Fukuyama, Francis. 1992. *The End of History and the Last Man*. New York: Avon.
Giddens, Anthony. 1991. *Modernity and Self-identity*. Cambridge: Polity.
Gray, John. 2003. *Al-Qaeda and What it Means to be Modern*. London: Faber.

Hannerz, Ulf. 1990. "Cosmopolitans and Locals in World Culture." In *Global Culture: Nationalism, Globalization and Modernity*, ed. Mike Featherstone. London: Sage, pp. 237–252.

———. 1992. *Cultural Complexity*. New York: Columbia University Press.

———. 1996. *Transnational Connections*. London: Routledge.

———. 2010. *Anthropology's World: Life in a Twenty-first Century Discipline*. London: Pluto.

Hardt, Michael and Antonio Negri. 2000. *Empire*. Cambridge, MA: Harvard University Press.

Harvey, David. 1989. *The Condition of Postmodernity*. Oxford: Blackwell.

Huntington, Samuel. 1996. *The Clash of Civilizations and the Remaking of a World Order*. New York: Simon and Schuster.

Ibsen, Henrik. 1972/1867–8. *Oxford Ibsen: "Brand" and "Peer Gynt."* Oxford: Oxford University Press.

Maeckelbergh, Marianne. 2009. *The Will of the Many: How the Alterglobalization Movement is Changing the Face of Democracy*. London: Pluto.

Mauss, Marcel. 1960. *Sociologie et anthropologie*. Paris: PUF.

Robertson, Roland. 1992. *Globalization: Social Theory and Global Culture*. London: Sage.

Standing, Guy. 2011. *The Precariat: The New Dangerous Class*. London: Bloomsbury Academic.

Stewart, Charles, ed. 2007. *Creolization: History, Ethnography, Theory*. Walnut Creek, Calif.: Left Coast Press.

Todorov, Tzvetan. 1989. *The Conquest of America: The Question of the Other*. Oklahoma: Oklahoma University Press.

———. 2000. *Mémoire du mal, tentation du bien*. Paris: Robert Laffont.

Trouillot, Michel-Rolph. 2001. "Close Encounters of the Deceptive Kind." *Current Anthropology* 42: 125–138.

Urry, John. 2003. *Global Complexity*. Cambridge: Polity.

Chapter 2

Juxtapositions
Social and Material Connectedness in a Pottery Community

Brian Moeran

When the Third Stockholm Roundtable in Anthropology was convened in honor of Ulf Hannerz, back in 2007, several themes were picked out for discussion by the organizers. One of these was that of connections, which was due to be presented by Arjun Appadurai. Alas! At the last moment, Arjun was prevented from taking part in the Roundtable and it fell upon me to step into his place, with shoes that may be several sizes bigger than his, but with pertinent knowledge that is several sizes smaller. Scant comfort for both soul and sole!

Although I suspect that Arjun would have talked, among other things, about global cultural flows, scapes, disjunctures, and conjunctures (Appadurai 1990, 1998), I myself spoke about connections in three different ways. The first was sociological. I talked about networks, factions, and associations and the study of social forms rooted in connections that are primarily strategic exchanges between individuals. These evoke, on the one hand, anthropological discussions of different forms of reciprocity and, on the other, the question of how, in the world of business, the fragility of individual connections can be converted into corporate connections. In the context of media conglomerates, I noted that, in their attempt to control as many parts of the value chain as possible, corporate connections could create disconnections from competing firms, in addition to the uniformity of products, as part of their "organization of diversity" (Hannerz 1992: 46–52).

The second theme that I touched upon in the context of connections was technological. This, I suggested, is for ethnographers perhaps an issue of methodology more than anything else. Technology enables different forms of communication. One can send pictures from the field and write blogs, or "tweet," for computer users around the world when research is especially noteworthy (such as that associated with the recent earthquake, tsunami, and nuclear reactor disasters in Japan)—and, alas, even when it is not. So fieldwork accounts, in the form of monographs or journal articles, may no longer be the only, or even prime, means of communicating knowledge gained in the field, even though, in the context of tertiary education, formally they continue to be so. In this context, I expressed a concern that electronic media, with their emphasis on novelty and innovation, never allow us sufficient time for thought and reflexivity.

I then turned to methodology itself and to how connections have hitherto been the basic mode of engaging in anthropological fieldwork. As a number of anthropologists have pointed out, previously established relations with other people not only provide entry to a fieldwork site; new connections established after entry enable the continuous process of fieldwork over time, although some kinds of fieldwork—such as my own peregrination through the world of women's fashion magazines—rely more obviously on connections than do others. But, however much these connections come into play, a fieldworker inevitably comes up against an issue of ethics: of how to use, and return, favors often freely given. Once again, I concluded, issues of reciprocity and reflexivity come into play.

In a way, I suppose, I merely articulated in different words and in different contexts Appadurai's ideas about ethnoscapes, mediascapes, technoscapes, financescapes, and (in my case hinted at, but not developed) ideoscapes (Appadurai 1990). In the discussion that followed, one of the participants suggested that we needed to bring out such concepts in a clearer manner and consider how to relate connections to connectivity, and how to make use of clusters of potential connections (thereby emphasizing conjunctures over disjunctures, and thus indirectly taking up Hannerz' formulation regarding the organization of diversity). Others talked about temporality, about emergent connections, rather than those that are reproduced, although anthropologists themselves tended to reproduce the connections that they studied. But what was, and what was not, acknowledged as a "connection"? In this context, networks reared their head. How were we to distinguish between different kinds of networks? What kinds of diversity did we find in connectivity?

It seems to me now that one difficulty that emerged in this discussion was linguistic. The word *connection* has so many synonyms, which in turn produce their antonyms and metonyms, that it is hard to write about such "resonances" clearly. Different scholars have their different takes. For example, in the introduction to his book, *Transnational Connections* (1996), Hannerz talks about the kinds of connectedness that he makes therein (a Nigerian hotel, a demonstration in New York, and a small village in the south of Sweden). Among others, the following words form part of his theoretical discussion: *interactions, encounters, (social) relationships, networks, ecumene, culture, cultural continuum, boundaries, imagined communities, global village, globalization, transnational, multiculturalism, intercultural communication, (cultural) diversity, cosmopolitan,* and *creolization.*

This list reveals in itself the very broad nature of the subject of this chapter—a breadth that Hannerz himself sought to make manageable under the three headings of *culture, people,* and *places.* Since his concern was in large part with connectedness, it is different forms of connectedness that I will describe here in the context of my own fieldwork experiences among the potters of Sarayama Onta in Japan. By selecting certain "tales of the field" (Van Maanen 1988), and by then juxtaposing them in a particular way (part of it stylistic), I make connections where, like the Rosy Guest Inn in Kafanchan, central Nigeria, a Salman Rushdie demonstration in lower Broadway, New York, and the village of Utvälinge (from time to time inhabited by a fair-haired boy with an encyclopedic knowledge of tropical fish), none might otherwise exist.

Transactions/Exchanges

When, many years ago, I used to sit down at the kick wheel in the workshop of a pottery household in Sarayama, a remote community nestling deep in the hills outside the Japanese town of Hita, a lot of the work that enabled me to make my rather bad pots had already been done.[1]

The clay that I used to throw pots had been dug out of the hillside across the narrow valley by a bulldozer, which had disturbed the peace and quiet of the community for several noisy days some six months previously. This in itself had only been made possible through lengthy negotiations, accompanied by several bottles of *sake* rice wine, when nine potters in Sarayama had set about persuading the tenth that he should allow them access to land that they owned communally, but which lay a dozen yards back from the road. To dig the clay in this communal strip of land, the bulldozer had to pass through one potter's privately owned land—land which, until that point half a year earlier when a previously used source of clay adjacent to the road had been deemed inadequate for the potters' communal needs, had itself served no useful purpose.

Now, unexpectedly, a few cubic yards of scrub land, planted with a few small deciduous trees, became the focus of the entire community's attention. Its owner, Saburō, was not prepared to let a bulldozer dig its way through—or, in his words, "destroy"—his land in order to reach and excavate the clay that his fellow potters and, let us not forget, he himself needed.

This refusal led to many hours of negotiations and accompanying inebriation, which both helped and hindered the final outcome. Saburō was prevailed upon to grant his fellow potters access to the clay deposit through his land, for a one-off lump-sum payment in cash (so that the tax authorities would not know of his windfall) and the building of an open, shed-like garage, again at the other potters' expense, in which he could henceforth park his van. A few days later, the bulldozer arrived and began its "destruction." The potters got a supply of clay to last them many years, even a decade or two. Saburō, like many others who sold bits of forest or the occasional rice field, explained to me that he had "given" them his land.

But why all the fuss? Given that Saburō was a member of the potters' cooperative, and given that the cooperative owned the land in which the clay was to be dug, why did he take so much trouble to obstruct his fellow potters' aims? After all, the land in itself was worth nothing. It was not a big enough area on which to build a proper house or plant a substantial number of trees. To do either of these, Saburō would have had to purchase one or other of the larger plots of land on either side, or behind his own. And neither of his two neighbors, for reasons that I will soon come to, would have agreed to sell him their land. And, anyway, what was all this nonsense about "giving" away, rather than selling, his land? He had been handsomely paid for it. It did not make sense—at least, not to the resident anthropologist (nor, overtly, to the potters who went through the fiction that Saburō was acting irrationally). But it did make sense to Saburō himself.

For people living in the countryside, land is invariably important. It is something they use to satisfy their everyday needs, and something in which to invest for the future. Of course, the same is true of people living in cities where land is exploited as a means of increasing financial capital. In this sense, whether you grow rice, plant trees, or erect buildings on a piece of land makes little difference. But country people have an attachment to land that is often missing in an urban environment. After all, the fields that they plough, sow, and harvest, and the woodlands that they plant, prune, and cut are often not fields and woods that they themselves have purchased and now tend. Rather, they have inherited them from their fathers and forefathers. Land is ancestral.

Such was certainly Saburō's case. He had inherited the small plot of land beside the road that wound out of the village behind his house when, a couple of decades or so previously, his father had handed over the headship of the household when Saburō had reached the customary age of forty years. Originally that plot had been part of the land surrounding Saburō's father's house. But about a dozen years before my arrival to conduct my fieldwork, the local government in Hita had decided that a new road should be built between Sarayama and the Ōtsuru valley across the hills behind the pottery community. Along with two other households, Saburō's had been obliged then to sell some of the land behind his house to enable the road to be built. He had "given" it away for the better good.

In Japan, the household (*ie*) and local community (*buraku*) are the primary bricks with which rural social organization has been built. The two have formed an inseparable duality, obliging individual members to put the interests of now one, now the other, before the other (and the one). When his fellow potters asked for permission to cross his land to gain access to their clay deposits, Saburō found himself caught in a typical dilemma. On the one hand, he was himself a potter, one of ten in a community of fourteen households which specialized in a form of craft production and whose very structure, as we shall see, depended upon how clay was prepared for that production. On the other hand, he was head of one of those households, which he had inherited from his father, who had inherited it from his own father, and so on, back through more than eight generations to the time when the first member of his name group had brought the craft of pottery making to Sarayama from further north in Kyushu (and before that probably, although Saburō could not prove it, to Kyushu from Korea). Should he act as a member of the potters' community? Or should he represent his household?

In the event he opted to represent his household. After all, he owed everything to the hard work and self-sacrifice of those who had preceded him for more than 250 years. He could not just "give" away land that was not individually his; hence the negotiations and the need for some form of material compensation. In his own mind, Saburō had to justify "giving" away his household's ancestral land.

And "giving" away it was. Although handsomely paid for this small plot of land, which still remained in his household's possession, Saburō had engaged in an exchange which, he knew, would one day be reciprocated, maybe not with him, but with a future generation down the household line. Sarayama potters "owed" him for their clay.

Flows/Complementarities

Once the clay had been bulldozed out of the mountainside, it had to be distributed to Sarayama's ten pottery households. So early one morning, the potters gathered at Saburō's new parking lot and set about distributing the excavated clay equally amongst themselves. In the olden days, I was told, when they had dug the clay themselves and carted it down to Sarayama from the surrounding hills, they used to set up piles of clay in the road—one for each household—evenly distributed so that all had a fair share. Nowadays, things were easier. They shoveled their clay into three privately owned, identical light trucks (*kei jidōsha*) and carted it down to one pottery household after another until it was all used up.

If the excavation of the clay was a cooperative endeavor, its actual preparation for use at the wheel at which my fellow potters and I sat and worked every day was a household affair. As I have explained before (Moeran 1997: 89–98), the clay used by Sarayama's potters was extremely hard. It therefore had to be powdered, washed, sifted, and dried before being ready for the wheel. This work was carried out for the most part by the women in each household, although older men, who had more or less retired, occasionally helped out. Rock-hard lumps of clay were first hammered into smaller pieces, which were then taken down to clay crushers (known as *karausu*) powered by the community's two streams running down through the valley. Twice a day, once in the morning and once again in the evening, mothers- or daughters-in-law would go down to the clay crushers and turn over the deep piles of steadily powdered clay.

After a week or ten days, when the clay was completely powdered, the women would bring it back up their houses and start the laborious process of churning and sifting the clay in water tanks. Once all foreign matter had been removed, they let the water out of the tanks and ladled the clay onto straw mattresses to start drying. When it had become like soft ice cream in texture, they scooped it into large earthenware planters where it lay in the sun until it was hard enough to be used to make pots. It was only then, about one month after first being hammered into smaller pieces, that the clay was taken into the workshop and its transformation into pots took place, as it was kneaded, placed on the wheel, and thrown into different forms.

All this time, while the women prepared the clay, as well as glaze materials such as wood ash, rice straw ash, feldspar, and iron oxide, not to mention the need to dry wood for each kiln firing every six to eight weeks, fathers and sons sat at their kick wheels and threw, turned, decorated, and applied parts to their pots. There was a neat symmetry in this gender complementarity, one aspect of which was between insiders and outsiders: fathers and sons were (ideally at least) born into the household; their wives and mothers married in. Outsiders transformed each household's membership from one generation to the next, as they prepared the clay; insiders transformed the clay to pots, while preparing the next generation of potters.

Another aspect of this gender complementarity related to an almost universal distinction between form and content. Men were responsible for form: their names continued the household line; they made a variety of pots for functional use—teapots, dishes, lidded jars, and so on. Women contributed content: they provided the "wombs" that enabled heirs to each household to be born, to grow up, and to succeed to the headship held by their forebears; they also prepared all the ingredients that allowed the forms of pots to be decorated. A far-fetched analogy? Perhaps. After all, my informants did not necessarily see things this way. But, coincidentally, my survey of hundreds of visitors to Sarayama during fieldwork in 1977–79 revealed that men tended to buy pots on the basis of form, while women—who were the majority—based their preferences on the color of glazes and different kinds of decoration.

The "traditional" methods that were used in Sarayama to prepare clay—methods that attracted tourists from far and wide and that were the focus of attention for aficionados of the Japanese folk art (*mingei*) movement—had three social repercussions. Firstly, the *karausu* clay crushers provided sufficient clay for just two people to work full-time at the wheel; neither more, nor less. This meant that only one son could remain in the household and learn how to make pottery after he had grown up; other sons had to leave and make their living elsewhere. Secondly, precisely because there was a limited supply of clay, pottery remained within the household and outsiders, in the form of apprentices, were never taken in. And thirdly, the way in which the clay crushers pivoted, together with the lie of the land in which Sarayama is located, and the angle of incline of its two streams, meant that only ten households could prepare clay with which to make pots. Unless new technology was introduced, the potters' community was destined to remain fixed in a clay-crusher time warp that limited production while simultaneously attracting the attention of folk-art pottery aficionados.

This conjuncture of social norms and aesthetic ideals underpinned potters' talk about clay. When they explained its lack of plasticity[2] and how this affected the shapes of the pots that they formed at the wheel, shapes that could be praised or damned in aesthetic terms, potters were, on the surface at least, explaining why their pottery was different from pottery made in the nearby community of Koishiwara, as well as from other styles of pottery characteristic of *mingei* folk art. But because the clay was *their* clay, dug out of *their* land, and not purchased in bulk from far afield, potters' talk about clay inevitably reflected their awareness of Sarayama as a community. So, too, did their frequent rejection of the idea of taking in apprentices, or of allowing one of the non-potting households in the community to take up pottery again. Clay underpinned the whole structure of the community.

Adjacencies

Sarayama was founded, or so goes the mythical narrative, in 1705. In that year, three men with three different surnames decided to start pottery in this narrow valley located some seventeen miles from the nearest town of Hita and about the same distance, as the crow flies, from another Sarayama further north where Koishiwara pottery is still made. The potter was called Yanase; the financial investor, Kurogi; and the landowner, Sakamoto. Sakamoto came from the neighboring community of Onta, located a couple of miles across the mountain pass. It is the name of this community that eventually came to distinguish "my" pottery community of Sarayama from that of Koishiwara, as well as from other Sarayamas in Agano, Fukuoka, and Arita.

The relative importance of the three necessities of skill, money, and land was reflected in the location of the Sakamoto, Kurogi, and Yanase original households. Sakamoto took the highest position, where the narrow valley coming up from Hita opened up into rice fields; Kurogi built his house a little below; and Yanase further down, on the other side of the Sarayama stream. Over the years, each name group expanded so that nowadays there are seven Kurogi, five Sakamoto, and two Yanase households.[3] When establishing branch households, main houses have tended to locate them downstream from themselves. This is because branch houses that were to become pottery households needed to build a dam in one of the streams running through Sarayama in order to set up clay crushers, and it was recognized that raising the level of the water could adversely affect clay crushers upstream. In such cases, it was considered more sensible if the clay crushers affected were those of the main house establishing its branch. In this way, therefore, the flows of both wealth and skills have followed the flow of water.

Whose house is adjacent to whose has determined other forms of social interaction. Earlier on, I noted that all ten pottery households cooperated in digging and distributing clay. The same was also true of the slip clay that they dug from higher up the valley and carried down to

Sarayama. But other tasks—to do with both pottery and farming—were carried out in different household formations. When going further afield to dig iron oxide or feldspar, for example, main houses tended to go with one of their branch houses. They also tended to team up together when transplanting or harvesting rice, but such exchanges of labor could extend to neighboring houses that were not related by blood. Thus one of the Sakamoto households in the middle of the community would often help out the Yanase branch household across the road, as well as its own two branch households—one of which was located near the top of the community. Household adjacencies meant that those living in the middle of Sarayama had more frequent and more varied ties with one another than those, like the Kobukuro households, located at either end of the community.

In the centuries after Sarayama was founded, its potters always shared a single large, climbing kiln (*noborigama*). Initially containing four chambers, this cooperative kiln increased in size to contain eight chambers in the middle of the nineteenth century. Since the number of potting households was never completely stable, being on the increase slowly over the decades, and since none of the chambers was of the same size as the others, Sarayama's potting households developed a chamber-rotating system that ensured that each potter was able to fire more or less the same number of pots as his colleagues every year.

Two or three pre-war photographs show that kiln firing was very much a community affair. Everyone turned out to help load the chambers, fire the kiln, and unload the pots once they had cooled. There were plenty of stories about how the potters used to pass the time of day or night (it took at least forty-eight hours to fire the cooperative kiln), sharing numerous jars of sake rice wine, and about how one or two would feign drunkenness because they knew that one of their colleagues would help out and fire their chamber for them. If Onta pottery's clay revealed the social structure of Sarayama, the cooperative kiln pointed to the close-knit nature of its daily social interaction.

By the time I arrived in April 1977, however, the cooperative kiln was no longer the focus of community attention. The *mingei* boom had seen to that. In the early 1960s, one potter followed the example of his brother, who had been adopted into a house at the bottom of Sarayama, and built his own private climbing kiln on the grounds that it was "too far" to carry his pots from his workshop to the cooperative kiln. Coincidentally, these two households were the only houses at the time that had both fathers and sons working full-time at the wheel. They were thus able to produce more pots in less time than the others and used to drag their heels, they averred, as they waited for the others to complete enough pots for a firing. One of these other potters just could not keep up and, as a result, in turn built his own private kiln a few years later. In the space of a couple of decades, the cooperative kiln was being used by just five, instead of eight, households.[4]

How did they go about sharing kiln space? First of all, the five households were split notionally into groups of two and three. They then rotated evenly over the years between these two groups, which fired alternately as and when they had enough pots to fill the cooperative kiln. But they also had to distribute the kiln space among themselves within each group. This they did according to both chamber size and physical capability.[5] Thus participants in the three-household group drew lots, every year on New Year's Day, to find out who would fire the first, fourth, and eighth chambers; who the second, third, and sixth; and who the fifth and seventh, when they first fired the cooperative kiln that year. Thereafter, they rotated upwards, so that the household which started by firing the first chamber would next fire the second chamber, while the one that had first fired the second chamber would then fire the fifth chamber, and so on.

In this way, they resolved the issue that the first chamber was far smaller than any of the others, and that the upper chambers were in general larger than the lower ones, by evenly distributing available kiln space among themselves. This was extremely important because of its financial implications. By ensuring that all potters sharing the cooperative kiln actually fired more or less the same number of pots, the rotation system also ensured that, barring accidents, all potter households earned more or less the same income from the sale of their wares. In other words, the cooperative kiln was a mechanism designed to establish egalitarian relations among all potter households. Kiln chamber adjacencies led to financial adjacencies. In this respect, the upward flow of heat and fire through the kiln performed the same function as the downward flow of water into the clay crushers: a sense of "community." It was for this reason that those who built their own private kilns, for whatever reason, were seen as "betraying" the community.

Transformations

To become pottery that can be used by people in their everyday lives, clay has to go through two major transformations. The first I have already described. Raw clay is kneaded, placed on the wheel, and thrown into a variety of forms—cups, plates, dishes, and so on. After they have been partially dried, some of these forms can themselves be transformed:

a large sugar bowl becomes a side-handled kyuusu teapot through the addition of a spout and handle; a small dish is converted into a radish grater by using a wooden comb to indent its inner surface; a tea cup becomes a coffee cup by adding a handle.

The second main transformation takes place when the clay making up a pot is completely dry and is ready to be glazed and fired. It is here that decoration is added to raw forms. Onta pottery is known for its slipware. Slip is a more-or-less white clay mixed in water to a thick, liquid consistency, and then applied to a ready-made pot—either with a brush soon after being thrown, or ladled over its surfaces later on when it is semi-dry. A variety of decorative techniques—like *hakeme* brushing, *tobiganna* chattering, or combing—may then be used to bring out the contrast between the dark-colored clay used for forming the pot and the off-white slip used to decorate it.

Slip in itself, however, is insufficient to prevent a pot from being porous. This is where glazing and firing come in. By glazing his pots and then firing them to an appropriate temperature, a potter can ensure that they can be used for eating, drinking, and storing food and liquids. Glazes transform pots because they add colors to the clay while becoming hard and generally glossy when fired; firing itself transforms glazes into thin layers of melted glass to make the surfaces of a pot smooth and vitreous (and thus resistant to scratching).

In order to obtain different colors, potters use different combinations of materials when mixing their glazes. In Sarayama, potters have always used locally obtainable materials such as straw ash, wood ash, feldspar, and iron oxide. These they have prepared themselves, before blending to obtain the required color of a glaze: transparent, brown, greens, black, thick milky white, or yellow ochre. For green, they have added copper to their recipes. Because, as I have already noted, it is generally color (together with decoration) that sells a pot, each potter household has tended to guard its glaze recipes in secrecy, handing them down from one generation to the next, and allowing each potter to play around with the proportions of each ingredient in order to find the best solution of the particular materials being mixed. The fact that natural materials are used means that they tend not to be consistent from one year to the next, or from one source of supply to another. Cedar wood ash used nowadays, for example, is different in quality from the ash of deciduous trees cut down and burnt in previous generations; iron oxide varies considerably according to where potters are able to get permission to dig it.

However finely tuned a recipe may be, however, all will come to naught if a pot is not properly fired. By "properly" I mean three things.

Firstly, the kiln in which pots are fired must reach an appropriate temperature, allowing their glazes to melt and cover their surfaces so that they are no longer porous. Secondly, that temperature (for Onta pottery, somewhere about 1,280°C) has to be reached at the right pace—neither too fast, nor too slow—because overheating can deform or crack the clay surfaces of a pot. Thirdly, firing must also make use of an appropriate combination of air (oxidization) and smoke (reduction), since it is this combination that affects the final color of a glaze.

So far, so good. Onta potters, however, faced several further challenges that made the transformation of their pots into saleable products less than mechanical. In the first place, as we have already seen, they fired their wares in multichambered climbing kilns (*noborigama*). The difficulty here lay in the location and structure of each potter's kiln. Ideally, a climbing kiln should be located on a sunny, airy slope that prevents it from becoming too damp inside. Although the original cooperative kiln was so located, in the centre of the community, almost all the other individual household kilns suffered in one way or another from lack of sunshine and dampness (a situation which eventually led to the potters' building chimneys in the mid- to late-1970s to help draw the heat through the kiln during firing). Potters always had to be aware, and to take account, of such humidity when firing since it could seriously affect the rate at which a kiln chamber was heated and the finished glazes of the pots therein.

Secondly, although most individual household kilns consisted of four chambers (Kobukuro's was the exception), each chamber developed its own characteristics that differed from the other chambers in a kiln and affected how it should best be fired. These were due in part to the dimensions of the chamber, and in part to how humid it became at different times of the year. In order to ensure minimum damage during firing, potters had first to learn and then to adapt to these characteristics, which had two main consequences: one related to the placement of forms, the other to colors.

Because each chamber was fired with wood from the front, the front shelves of the kiln chamber tended to be hotter than those at the back. The lower shelves also received the full brunt of the heat from the wood as the chamber was fired. As a result, potters carefully separated out the different kinds of pots that they made, placing small teacups (without handles) at the front of the lower shelves, stacks of plates on the middle shelves, and larger wares such a pitchers, lidded pickle jars, and very large decorative plates at the very top of each chamber, where the temperature was subject to least variation. If the latter wares were placed lower down in the chamber, they would be unable to withstand the sudden rises in temperature caused by fueling the chamber and break. Pots with parts attached—teapots, coffee cups, and so on—were often, but not necessarily, placed towards the back of each chamber, together with a range of small dishes and cups.[6]

Adjacencies in colors, as well as in forms, were essential to the transformations wrought by potters from raw clay to glazed pots. The gradual increase in size of pots from the bottom to the top shelves of a chamber depended to some extent on how they were glazed. Since one glaze (translucent brown or *ame*) melted at a lower temperature than the others, pots so glazed were placed at the back of each chamber, the temperature of which was several degrees lower than elsewhere. At the same time, other glazes, such as copper green, had a rather high melting point, which meant that such pots as the famous Onta green teapot had to be placed at the front and in the middle of the kiln chamber, even though they were likely to come out bloated or damaged in some other way.

In other words, every potter in Sarayama had to get to know his kiln in such a way that he could calculate, while working at the wheel, how many trays of this form, and how many of that, to throw in order to be able to fill his kiln. At the same time, he also had to calculate how many pots of different forms had to be glazed in how many different colors, if he was to be able to fire his kiln successfully with minimum damage. Although this was something that each potter learned through the sheer repetition of firing his kiln six times a year, he always had to make minor adjustments according to orders that he received. Thus an order for one hundred large, brown-glazed kneading bowls, for example, would lead to his decreasing the number of plates and pitchers that he would normally make. This decrease, however, would not be on a simple one-to-one ratio, since plates of the same size as the kneading bowls could be stacked in piles of eight, while the latter could be stacked only in threes. Pitchers, however, took up slightly less space horizontally, but stood alone, so that the ratio here was more like four to nine. Transformations were thus frequently numerical.

Frames

The potters of Sarayama had not always devoted themselves full-time to making their wares. Indeed, when one of their black teapots was first "discovered" by Yanagi Sōetsu in the not-too-distant town of Kurume in 1927, they were both farmers and potters who made pots for use in local farmhouses. There simply was not enough demand for their work for them to be able to make a living full-time from making and selling pots. The working frame in which they functioned, therefore, was the fashioning of pots for use in rural households—large storage and pickle jars, kneading bowls, teapots, pitchers, cups, bowls, dishes, and other basic pots for eating from.

The *mingei* movement changed all that. The first real inkling potters had of what was to happen came in 1954 when Bernard Leach, not without considerable local government and media fanfare, visited Sarayama to "learn" the potters' craft. Leach was a well-known English potter who had befriended Yanagi Sōetsu, together with the potters Kawaii Kanjirō, Tomimoto Kenkichi, and Hamada Shōji, during his stay in Japan some forty years previously. Together with Tomimoto, he had also—seemingly without being conscious of it—introduced to Japan the ideas of William Morris and the British Arts and Crafts Movement on which Yanagi later drew so much when developing his ideology of *mingei* (literally, "popular art"). Over a month, Leach came and went between Sarayama and the neighboring town of Hita, throwing his own pots at the wheel, decorating other pots made for him by some of the potters, teaching them how to pull handles the English potters' way for their pitchers, and happily talking to them in his Meiji Period Japanese while enjoying their *sake* rice wine. All potters remembered Leach fondly for his humanity (and the fact that I first came to Sarayama armed with an introduction from the great potter himself certainly helped me ease my way into fieldwork). His visit was a watershed in their lives, as they readily conceded by talking about Sarayama "before Leach" and "after Leach."

But why did he go there in the first place? One of the things that appealed to Yanagi, Leach, Hamada, and other aficionados of *mingei* was that Onta potters lived "close to nature." They did not use modern machinery of any kind; no electric pug mills for preparing clay; no electric wheels for throwing pots on; no synthetic materials with which to glaze them; and no gas or electric kilns in which to fire them. It was the fact that potters kept their *karausu* to powder their clay, used only kick wheels to throw their pots, made glazes from natural raw materials, and used wood to fire them in their climbing kilns that appealed to the Folk Art Movement's leaders. The potters of Sarayama were almost unique in this approach to their craft. This was what made their work almost automatically "beautiful"—a far cry from the standardized goods of mechanized industrial production. Leach wanted to witness first-hand what had already been lost in his home country, where—in spite of the repeated calls for a revival of traditional, popular arts and crafts by the likes of Carlyle, Ruskin, and Morris—industrialization had destroyed the beauty of handmade crafts many decades previously.

There was something else, too, that appealed to Yanagi, Leach, Hamada, and the rest: the sense of "community" that they had heard about, but to little extent actually witnessed, in Sarayama. From digging clay and slip to firing the cooperative kiln, potters did everything "together." They even charged the same prices for their wares, so that, whichever of the ten households you visited to buy a teapot or pickle jar, you would be charged the same price—as fixed by the potters' cooperative at the beginning of every calendar year. The fact that the community consisted of just four name groups, intricately related through marriage and adoption practices, led to further close social interaction (in transplanting rice fields, for example, or seeking out glaze materials). In this respect, Sarayama was the epitome of their ideal of "community"—the imagined worlds (Appadurai 1998: 33) of Gothic cathedral craftsmen, medieval guilds, and rural hamlets before the industrial revolution. It was this sense of community that automatically seeped into each potter's work and made it, too, "beautiful."

Once the *mingei* aesthetic—or more strictly speaking, moral—ideal promulgated by Yanagi Sōetsu took off to become a consumer fashion fuelled by the media in the 1960s, the potters of Sarayama found themselves at the centre of attention. Suddenly, what had been a set of social ideals about how to live their everyday lives was transformed into a set of aesthetic ideals about how pots should be made. Subordinating individual interests to those first of one's household and then of one's community—standard ideal practice in the "good old days" of Japanese society—was now transformed into pottery ideals. By cooperating with their fellows, by continuing to use the clay crushers underpinning the social structure of their community, by making their glazes with natural materials, potters were able to make so-called "beautiful" pots.[7]

Because their pots were thus seen to be "beautiful," they sold—and sold in large quantities. And because—for a glorious two to three decades—they sold whatever they made, some potters decided to build their own private kilns, which helped them make and sell more, and so become richer. All the potters put in a mechanical device to help them throw smaller pots; five of them purchased ball mills with which to prepare their glaze materials; one made use of gas to fire the main mouth of his climbing kiln. To add insult to injury, one or two of the richer potters even charged higher prices for their work than others—although they tended not to get away with it for longer than the next drinking session, where vociferous arguments led to their toeing the line for a few weeks or months before going back to their errant ways.

And, of course, the more successful the potters were and the richer they became (even though what they earned was nothing like the amounts earned by real-estate speculators in Tokyo or even by fellow potters in Koishiwara), the more their work was criticized by the leaders of the Folk Art Movement. Onta pottery, they declared, was "destroyed"; it had "had it"; it was no longer as "beautiful" as it once had been. But they had to be careful with their criticisms. After all, Onta pottery represented "true" *mingei*. If it had "had it" and been "destroyed," that meant that "true" *mingei* had also had it. And, if that was so, then they themselves were out of a job!

So they tempered their critiques. Suddenly one potter would be extolled and his work selected for one of the prizes at the annual exhibition of Japanese folk arts at the Mingei Museum in Tokyo. Or a critic would write a reassessment of Onta pottery, saying that it had been really bad four or five years ago, but that now there was hope; some of the younger generation of potters had put commercial interests to one side and were focusing on making "good" work.

There were, then, two frames within which potters lived and worked. One was social and focused on the connectedness of households through shared occupation and work routines to make a "community"; the other was aesthetic and buttressed the social frame. The two were indissolubly linked: good social relations equaled "beautiful" pots; pots that were not "beautiful" suggested the breakdown of community, caused in large part by the evils of capitalism and an individual's desire for selfish profit. Although potters happily took advantage of Yanagi's *mingei* ideals, they by no means always agreed with them. Some were more vehement in their criticisms than others, but they had no means to give vent to their frustrations. The media were, of course, a potential outlet, but—like the Folk Art Movement's leaders themselves—potters had to be careful about what they said in public. There was little point in cutting off their noses to spite their collective face.

And then, one sunny afternoon in late April, an anthropologist arrived in their midst, carrying a notebook and writing things down as he participated and observed them over two whole years. And, as the saying goes, the snows of Mount Fuji that had sustained the purity of *mingei* aesthetic ideals slowly melted and flowed down to the sea, where prostitutes mixed it in their make-up. Nothing was ever quite the same again.

Coda

Transactions, exchanges, flows, complementarities, adjacencies, transformations, and frames are the stuff of connectedness. These are what I have here described in detail in the context of a Japanese pottery community, but we find them elsewhere and in more developed capitalist enterprises than family or household firms.

Take fashion magazines, for example. Well-known, multinational corporations in the fashion and beauty industries, in particular, enter into contracts with magazine publishers to publish a certain number of color advertisements in certain prime positions in a magazine (inside front cover, back cover, centre page, and so on). Other, slightly lesser known companies try to place their advertisements in the first half of the magazine, yet others within particular sections (travel, food, jewelry, and so on). There is a pecking order of advertisers in any issue of a fashion magazine.

In exchange for the income accruing from advertising revenues, editors write promotional material on behalf of their advertisers; dress and make up models in their fashion spreads in their advertisers' clothes and beauty products; photograph the glitterati (singers, actresses, models) wearing the latest fashions; and so on. In this way, women are transformed from the ordinary into the extraordinary, while beauty products take on magical, transformational qualities (Moeran 2010). Each complements the other.

Editors also strive to create a flow in textual matter that persuades readers to read from the first page to the last. Yet the advertisements are designed by advertisers to arrest that flow by "anchoring" readers (Barthes 1977), making them stop at a particular page. Magazine publishers may compromise by creating stylistic, visual, color, and linguistic adjacencies of textual and advertising matter on opposing pages to make readers move back and forth. Fashion magazines are commodities framed by the fashion and beauty industries, while simultaneously framing, as cultural products, the products of those industries (Moeran 2006).

This is by no means a feature of magazines alone and is to be found in other forms of cultural production. In his study of the making of the *Childhood* documentary series, for example, Barry Dornfeld discusses how producers and editors structured film footage into two distinct types of sequences. One of these he terms "extended," the other "juxtapositional." The former, which I see as equivalent to flow, refers to "edited segments featuring a single culture, following recognizable subjects through a series of events." The latter, a form of anchorage, refers to "sequences juxtaposing corresponding practices or events across cultures, constructed intercutting analogous material from more than one cultural setting. These structures represent two different documentary modalities between which *Childhood* moves" (Dornfeld 1998: 149). Extended and juxtapositional sequences, as Dornfeld notes, may not be entirely discrete categories since the former are "sometimes juxtaposed in longer comparative structures" (Dornfeld 1998: 150), but it is clear that flows and juxtapositions are two fundamental mechanisms for structuring cultural products and performances, whether we are talking of a piece of classical music, a theatre play, a catwalk show, or an art exhibition. In other words, the combined usage of flow and anchorage (by whatever name), first noted by Barthes of film, is found in all forms of cultural production, both within and between products. Of such juxtapositions—with their accompanying transactions, complementarities, adjacencies, transformations, and frames—is diversity organized and connectedness made. Herein may be found the complexities of culture.

Notes

1. Almost all of the detail that follows (unless referenced otherwise) may be found in my monograph, *Folk Art Potters of Japan* (Moeran 1997).
2. Plasticity is a complex quality that is difficult to define (and that consequently enabled me to get permission to make pots in Sarayama in the first place). It is influenced by the size and shape of clay particles, water, electrical attraction, carbonaceous matter, and aging.
3. Two of the original Kurogi households have undergone a name change to Kobukuro, while the original Sakamoto household has disappeared.
4. One Sakamoto household head decided to build his own kiln at the top of Sarayama when he took up pottery again during this period. Another (Kurogi) household had set up its own kiln back in 1927 and had been ostracized for its antisocial behavior for several years thereafter.
5. Each chamber takes approximately three hours to fire to 1,280°C. Ideally no potter should fire more than two chambers at any one time.
6. Variations in kiln chambers lead to variations in placements, so that this paragraph does not represent hard and fast rules.
7. For an extended discussion of these points, see Moeran (1997).

References

Appadurai, Arjun. 1990. "Disjuncture and Difference in the Global Cultural Economy." *Public Culture* 2(2): 1–24.

———. 1998. *Modernity at Large: Cultural Dimensions of Globalization*. Minneapolis and London: University of Minnesota Press.
Barthes, Roland. 1977. *Image Music Text*. London: Fontana.
Dornfeld, Barry. 1998. *Producing Public Television, Producing Public Culture*. Princeton: Princeton University Press.
Hannerz, Ulf. 1992. *Cultural Complexity*. New York: Columbia University Press.
———. 1996. *Transnational Connections: Culture, People, Places*. London & New York: Routledge.
Moeran, Brian. 1997. *Folk Art Potters of Japan*. London: Routledge-Curzon.
———. 2006. "More than just a Fashion Magazine." *Current Sociology* 54(5): 725–744.
———. 2010. "The Portrayal of Beauty in Women's Fashion Magazines." *Fashion Theory* 14(4): 491–510.
Van Maanen, John. 1988. *Tales of the Field: On Writing Ethnography*. Chicago: University of Chicago Press.

Chapter 3

CONNECTING AND DISCONNECTING
Intentionality, Anonymity, and Transnational Networks
in Upper Yemen

Andre Gingrich

Transnational connections or networks and global flows are two key concepts that have helped anthropology to move into the current era of postcolonial and global analyses. Both concepts have provided good service as buzzwords, orientating and setting the tone of recent debates and research and by consequence, leading to a rising awareness about global flows and transnational networks. That rising awareness, however, has been accompanied quite often by a diminishing amount of theoretical precision. This chapter sets out to differentiate the two concepts more closely in terms of how they relate to temporality, communication, and power. The chapter then proceeds to empirically examine the meanings and relevance of long-distance connections, and of transnational networks in the context of civil war developments in Upper Yemen. This is pursued by focusing upon specific tribal elites in the armed clashes before 2012 between government forces and a Shiite revolt, and on the tribal elites' connections to regional powers and to the anthropologist. The results of this investigation will suggest the necessity to consider anonymity and intentionality in transnational network analysis, and the power by those who are able to connect and to disconnect.

Transnational connections (or networks) and global flows therefore are more than mere buzzwords. In order to actually use them as analytical categories, it is crucial to continue relating them to the remainder of anthropology's tool kit along the lines suggested by authors such as Ulf Hannerz (1996) and Arjun Appadurai (1996). In view of this volume's overall rationale, the notion of "thinking with networks" (Hannerz 1992a) will be taken into account somewhat more closely than "assessing flows." It will be demonstrated how this notion can be particularly useful in exploring agency and intentionality in complex conflicts.

Introduction: Flows, Connections, Agency

Some authors tend to use *flows* and *connections* in an almost synonymous manner. These terms do address intersecting dimensions within the same kind of overall global developments. Still, some value can be identified in their non-exclusive, but differential focus. Evidently, the concept of transnational "flows" highlights powerful processes that take volatile and liquid forms. The concept of "flows" thus has greater potential for those historicizing perspectives that emphasize those sweeping dynamics characteristic of past and present (Bauman 2007) and their hegemonic drives towards an insecure future (Beck 2007).

Unfortunately, however, not everything in our world is as fluid or "liquid" as we perhaps would want it to be. For better or for worse, some phenomena and the relations they represent and effectuate are in fact more enduring than at first sight they appear to be. It is precisely with regard to these different modes, or rhythms, of temporality that I see a richer potential encoded in concepts like "connections" and "networks" for addressing slower movements of change, and somewhat less fluid forms of relations. In this sense, transnational connections and networks can be understood as the extension and elaboration for the present era of older concepts such as "social relations" and "structural relations"; i.e., as transformed versions of established anthropological concepts for a deterritorializing, globalized world.

The use of concepts like "connections" and "networks" is always informed by the choice of epistemological perspective. With their wide spectrum of differentiation, social sciences' network analyses may operate from various such perspectives, including actor- and agency-centered approaches. During the 1990s, these specific perspectives received more attention due to anthropology's new and useful emphasis on subjectivities and lived experience (Appadurai 1996; Das 2007). The combination of network approaches with a focus on subjectivity, in sum, has moved intentionality very much into the foreground of recent anthropological reasoning, together with intersubjectivity as one of its core dimensions (Duranti 2006). Bruno Latour (2005) is among those who have signaled their caveat that too exclusive a focus on subjectivity, intersubjectivity, and intentionality might result in unwarranted voluntarism. Subscribing to this caveat does not necessarily imply an adoption of a Latour-inspired version of actor–network theory. Yet it might be useful to distinguish between intentional and non-intentional connections in transnational and local spheres. In its theoretical dimension the subsequent analysis rather challenges most network analyses, by decentering ideas of both individual and system. These are some of the epistemological and terminological considerations that inform the present chapter. It sets out to further explore conceptualizations of connections through historical and present-day ethnography.

Reconnecting Transnationally

Through email and cellphone, I began to reconnect with my former host families in Yemen's northwestern mountain regions during the winter months of 2006/7. Friends who worked in Sanaa had established contact with them in the course of a very short, recent visit of their own to those remote northwestern mountains. I examined the pictures they sent me, and read their short email report. My desire to reestablish contact with my former hosts became irresistible. When these friends in Sanaa told me that they were planning another trip to the northwest, I emailed them from Vienna a letter for my previous hosts with my photograph attached, and asked them to put the printouts in an envelope with the family's name on it. Actually, chances were quite low that my friends in Sanaa would be able to reach the Munebbih area again, where I had carried out my main fieldwork in Yemen during the 1980s; but at least it was worth trying to contact my former hosts in this way.

Located in steep and rugged territories along Yemen's northwestern border with Saudi Arabia, the Munebbih Mountains were not often visited by strangers. For many years, special permits and official escorts had been required for most visitors. In the course of the "war against terror" since 2001, and in view of what had become known as the al-Houthi rebellion in parts of Upper Yemen since 2003, security precautions had become even tighter. In spite of all these difficulties, however, my friends played by the rules and managed to reach Munebbih territory, where they spent one night in the main weekly marketplace, Nayd al-Rakw. They asked after a member of my previous host family, and a member of the family actually came to see them. When they gave him my letter and the photograph printout in that envelope, he tore it open before them and immediately recognized my face.

Twenty years earlier, "Khaled"[1] had been a nine-year-old boy, and one of the brightest among the Munebbih paramount chief's grandsons. In fact, it had been Khaled from whom I had first learnt the Munebbih dialect. As a member of the chiefly lineages, he had enjoyed the rare privilege of several years of school education. For this reason, he was able to communicate with me in the standard Yemeni Arabic that I spoke when I began my fieldwork. Now, in late 2006, Khaled was one of the leading representatives of his tribe.

I was deeply moved when I read my friends' email report about their meeting with Khaled. Later I found out how surprised Khaled was to hear that I do not use cellphones. How so? Everyone among the leading families of Munebbih uses cellphones, he had exclaimed: they could not even do their jobs without these things. That part of the story made me smile, because of its contrast to the 1980s. Before my actual field sojourn began, Khaled's grandfather had often been asked why he was willing to accommodate a foreigner like me.[2] The paramount chief's answer to these questions had always been that his family and in fact the whole tribe needed to improve their relations with the outside world. Because of that answer, many tribal members had expected me to help in a very practical manner. In the provincial capital, Saada, they had seen telephone booths, from which everybody could connect to the outside world. Their own mountain region was then still far away from any tarmac roads or phone lines. When I arrived for my fieldwork, many of them in fact were quite disappointed, as they frankly told me in 1986, that I did not set up a telephone booth for them in their main marketplace. Now, in 2006, it was me who remained a cellphone skeptic, while the Munebbih chiefs all used them and could not imagine being without them!

During a short official visit to Sanaa very early in 2007, Khaled saw my friends again. He gave them his cellphone numbers, and they gave him my home and office phone numbers, which I had totally forgotten to indicate in that letter. We tried to call each other up, but the lines were busy. In view of this failure to reach me by phone, Khaled asked my friends if I could try to reach him a few days later during the evening hours, when he would be back in the high slopes of his home region. I later learnt that he had been in a hurry. The al-Houthi rebellion was on the rise again, and he was expected to play a support role in the government's efforts towards military containment. A few days later in Vienna, I canceled all appointments for the late afternoon and evening, and prepared everything for finally speaking to Khaled again in person. After three attempts, I got through. What an excitement and joy it was, hearing each other's voices again after two decades! We were able to speak for two or three minutes. Then, suddenly, the line was cut off. I tried to phone him again and again, but could not connect. Boundless disappointment and frustration set in.

Thirty or forty minutes had passed when the phone rang. Khaled was on the line again. He had driven up to the highest ridge of the Munebbih Mountains, where the reception was better, and he had switched onto his Saudi cellphone network connection. Now we were able to entertain half an hour of joyful and relaxed conversation. I extended an invitation to him and his family to visit me in Vienna in the near future. He accepted with pleasure, and we discussed the foreseeable details of such a trip. Its time schedule might be delayed, however, he warned me. If that conflict with al-Houthi's men were to continue, he might not be able to leave Yemen any time soon. Still, in that case we definitely should not give up the plan for his visit, but only postpone it. This is what actually happened. A new series of confrontations and fighting broke out in late winter and early spring 2007, between armed units of the al-Houthi movement and government forces and their allies.

Postcolonial Phase 1: A Cold War Scenario and its Background

The al-Houthi rebellion's name is derived from its leading family, and from that family's main ancestral residence in the plateaus of Upper Yemen. The al-Houthi family are Sada; i.e., descendants of the prophet Muhammad. The town of Houth is one among many enclaves that are the Sada's primary residence in the region. Such an enclave is called a *hijra* in the Yemeni highlands. Its safety is usually protected by those tribal groups in whose territory it is located. In turn, the Sada of such a hijra are expected to provide various services to the tribal groups in their neighborhood (Puin 1984). In Yemen's past, ideally, these were religious and legal services, but they always also included some more entrepreneurial and commercial interests. By their reputation, the Sada thus claimed to be representatives of scholarly theological erudition, while in practice this was always accompanied at least to some extent by business and politics. In short, the rebellion takes its name from its leading Sada family and its ancestral town, the hijra of Houth.

For many centuries, a majority of northern Yemen's highland and mountain population has followed the Zaydi version of Shiite Islam (Serjeant 1969). This is a legacy from almost one thousand years of rule by the Zaydi Imams, who always had one of their strongest bases of influence in the capital of Yemen's northernmost province, Saada, and in the tribal areas of that neighborhood. The Zaydi imams ruled northern Yemen until 1962, when an army revolt overthrew them and established the Yemen Arab Republic. A long and complicated civil war ensued, which also involved the Egyptian army on the republican side until 1967, while Britain and the Saudis assisted the royalists until they accepted that the tides had changed. The civil war ended shortly after 1970. Throughout the preceding centuries, the Zaydi imams had come exclusively from various, more or less prominent Sada families. The succession system was not hereditary in the strict sense; it also depended on meritocratic principles and on public recognition for whoever among the Sada claimed to be the new imam. Because Sada families therefore often competed among themselves for power and influence, the system had been relatively fragile. To a large extent, it also depended on sufficient support for Sada factions from tribal majorities and their powerful chiefs, which the chiefs had used to develop a fair amount of influence among themselves (Dresch 1989). In sum, the Sada of northern Yemen had been the Zaydi imamate's main power base. Together with the Sada, but to a more varying extent, large tribal groups of the northern plateaus and mountains had also continued to support the last imam during the civil war, until the republic prevailed. Contrary to this more general trend, many Sada also fought for the republic, while members of the same tribe often fought on different sides, and tribal leaders switched their allegiances repeatedly.

When I did my main fieldwork among the Munebbih in 1986, those civil war years were long gone. The Yemen Arab Republic gradually gained stability, while pursuing an intermediate course between the two main constellations of the Cold War era in the region: the U.S.A.'s powerful ally in the north was and is the "Wahhabi" Sunni Kingdom of Saudi Arabia; while in the south, the former British protectorate of Aden had become the pro-Soviet "People's Democratic Republic of Yemen." In the northwestern corner of the Yemen Arab Republic during the 1980s, Khaled's elderly grandfather still acted as the Munebbih paramount chief. He enjoyed a legendary status in northwest Yemen, and in government circles in Sanaa. Most other Yemeni tribes in the Munebbih's eastern and southern neighborhood had supported the last imam during the civil war (Weir 2006). On the other side of the border, the Saudis in the Munebbih's western and northern neighborhoods had also supported Yemen's royalists against the republic until 1970. By contrast, Khaled's grandfather at first declared the Munebbih should remain neutral in the civil war. Opting out in such an explicit manner was already a challenge to everybody else in the region. That challenge led to retaliation, in the form of some heavy air raids of Munebbih territory and settlements. In turn, the Munebbih paramount chief declared open support for the young republic throughout the final years of the civil war. While most of the Sada, and most of the other tribal groups and leaders in the northwest, continued to support the royalists until the end of the civil war, the Munebbih thereby emerged as the young republic's northernmost ally (Gingrich 1993).

There were several reasons for the Munebbih's stand in the civil war. One set of factors related to the tribe's history, in which their chiefs had never granted permanent hijra settlements to the Sada on their own tribal territory. This had allowed the Munebbih chiefs to play a more prominent role as commercial and legal mediators, primarily between groups from the hilly lowlands along the Red Sea coast in their western neighborhood, and the mountain and plateau regions around Saada to the east. In turn, this had resulted in a minimal degree of Sada and Zaydi religious, political, and fiscal influence among the Munebbih. During the civil war, the pragmatic evidence of the present therefore confirmed long-term historical experience. Out of their steep and inaccessible mountain fortresses, it was safer to oppose the Saudi and Zaydi royalists than let them in, and instead to support a weak, distant, and fairly secular republican government. A long, surprisingly stable alliance between the Munebbih's leadership and the republican authorities emerged from these civil war constellations. In return for guarding their own section of the border with Saudi Arabia and for keeping an eye on stability in the region, Munebbih were spared some of the republican tax burden, and they enjoyed more liberties from the state in most respects than many others in the north. Their paramount chief's family, the Banu Awfan, enjoyed a number of additional privileges.

Postcolonial Phase 2: A "Dethroned" Minority and its Opponents

During the 1970s and 1980s, the Yemen Arab Republic went through many changes, mostly of a social and economic nature. These were largely due to the gradual opening up of the country to the global market economy, to the Sada's integration into a new social environment in which they had fewer privileges, and to the gradual strengthening of the republican order. These developments were facilitated by the experience that from the outset, not all Sada had been royalist supporters. In fact, quite a few had been committed republicans. In terms of faith, the Zaydi Shiites still represented somewhat less than half of the overall population. Gradually, a majority among them more or less abandoned the idea of a return to the imamate, and they adjusted to the Yemen Arab Republic. Some among them developed certain sympathies for Khomeini's Islamic Republic after Iran's 1978 revolution. By contrast, the central government in Sanaa supported Iraq in Saddam Hussein's war with Iran in the 1980s. When Saddam's Iraq invaded Kuwait, the Sanaa government maintained its basically friendly attitude to Saddam. This led to serious tensions with Saudi Arabia, resulting in massive expulsions of Yemeni migrant workers from that country, and in cutbacks of what by then had become substantial budgetary assistance to the Sanaa government by Saudi Arabia, several other Gulf countries, and the U.S. A gradual demise into increasing poverty set in. Despite revenues from Yemen's recently activated but limited domestic oil resources, a process that made the country one of the poorest in the world could not be reversed until today. In the wider contexts of international developments, the Yemen Arab Republic by and large continued its neutralist position between its U.S.-backed Saudi neighbors in the north and the Soviet-sponsored regime in southern Yemen.

These contexts collapsed with the end of the Cold War, with the ensuing implosion of the communist regime in southern Yemen, and with Yemen's unification in 1990. In this unified, new "Republic of Yemen," the Sunnis now constitute at least two-thirds of the overall population (Dresch 2000). Internationally, the government in Sanaa was persuaded to abandon its former alliance with Saddam Hussein. After an al-Qaeda attack was launched in 2000 against the USS *Cole* in the port of Aden, the government in Sanaa agreed to intensify its cooperation with U.S. military, intelligence, and security forces. That cooperation was further reinforced after 9/11/2001, in view of convincing evidence indicating some local Yemeni Sunni support for al-Qaeda (Johnsen 2006). Gradually, Yemen has thus moved into a U.S.-dominated sphere of influence in which Saudi Arabia (together with most other Gulf countries) now is a somewhat uneasy and ambivalent ally.

If examined in the broader context of Middle Eastern upheavals and post–Cold War global developments, local events in northern Yemen are put into perspective. In turn, the shifting local relations between Shiites and Sunnis in southwestern Arabia thereby underline the fertility of a global and transnational approach that gives high priority to cultural diversity (Hannerz 1992b) and to ensuing changes in connections and relations. In the radically transformed, new domestic and international contexts outlined here, prospects have not in fact been improving for most of Yemen's Shiites. They are now definitely a minority with decreasing influence, in a country where they once were powerful. Perhaps the concept of a "dethroned" former majority in the political sense, which I developed out of the different historical contexts of imperial decay (Gingrich 2002), might also be applicable here. In that case, this would further highlight Shiite feelings of collective loss, and even humiliation for some, of being under some kind of pressure and siege, and of ensuing anger. At any rate, Shiite concerns have been aggravated by an uneasy and deteriorating economic situation, and by official legislation that they tend to see as increasingly favoring Sunni jurisprudence. In addition, some radical Sunni groups with growing influence, among them the Muslim Brotherhood and the Salafis, spread propaganda that treats the Shiite Zaydis as "infidels" and "heretics." Furthermore, the situation has not been improved by the well-funded, protracted efforts among "Wahhabi" Sunni circles to recruit and gain supporters within the Zaydi population itself, and to take over some of their institutions. Opportunities for strengthening and developing denominational pluralism and civil rights were available, but either they could not be sustained, or they were neglected and jeopardized. This is how the al-Houthi rebellion, against which Khaled was preparing himself while we had our first conversation in early 2007, flared up.

In 2003, Zaydi youth in Saada and elsewhere in the north protested against the U.S.-led invasion of Iraq. The protests were inspired by the "faithful youth," who were disciples of the religious scholar Badr al-Din al-Houthi and his son, Husayn al-Houthi, a teacher and former member of the parliament in Sanaa. Their branch of the Al Houthi family lives in Haydan, a major district centre in Saada province, close to where the first uprising broke out. These unarmed demonstrations were answered with arrests and detentions (Wedeen 2008). In 2004, when Husayn al-Houthi refused to hand himself over to the authorities, armed clashes broke out. Arms always were easily available in the north, and each tribal household has some at home. Moreover, it seems that arms also had been bought, stolen, or collected and put in store by some. Some reports suggest that Husayn al-Houthi toyed with, and sometimes instrumentalized the Zaydi conception of an "imam of war" (*imam al-harb*), whose legitimacy increases together with his determination to assume and to maintain the role of a war leader. Zaydi mass enthusiasm for al-Houthi, and the ensuing militant aggressiveness, came as a surprise to many, not least to the central government, which, in part, explains some of its own reactions. In September 2004, Husayn al-Houthi was killed, apparently by security forces. In the following year, one of Husayn al-Houthi's brothers, Yahya, emigrated to western Europe during a phase when confrontations had eased. Fighting reached a second peak, however, in early 2005. When the government announced an amnesty for many al-Houthi followers, the fights calmed down again towards the end of the year. Still, Zaydi religious institutions continued to be under increasing pressure from various Sunni sides. These were some of the main reasons why fighting erupted again in early 2007. At that point, Abd al-Malik al-Houthi had taken over the movement's leadership. The government in Sanaa sent thirty thousand additional troops into its northern province.

The al-Houthi revolt thus had widespread support among the Zaydi population when it began in 2003/4. Since then, several thousands have died. A number of attempts towards truce and reconciliation were made, partly assisted by several Gulf governments' diplomatic intervention, but these peace efforts did not last long, and were shattered by recurrent cycles of confrontation. Especially in Saada province, those cycles of armed fights resulted in extensive forms of destruction with few precedent cases in the region. Similar to the constant flow of shifting allegiances during the civil war, different members of the same tribal groups fought on both sides, and some tribal leaders shifted their allegiance several times (Brandt 2011). In such developments, it always takes more than just one side to allow things to go wrong (Gingrich 2011). Sunni propaganda in many mosques, and in several print media in Sanaa and Riyadh, has often portrayed the al-Houthi rebellion as instigated from outside. Primarily, Iran has been accused as the force in question. Except for several meetings between representatives of the al-Houthi family and the Tehran authorities, there seems to be little evidence to substantiate these allegations, but the propaganda nevertheless has had its effects in Yemen and internationally. Its opponents thereby tend to characterize the al-Houthi movement as part of a wider Shiite struggle for power and influence in the whole Middle East: Iran is seen as the centre of these aspirations (Johnsen 2007); Hizbollah in Lebanon and militant Shiites in Iraq are portrayed as the other components in a larger plan that also includes the Bashar al-Asad regime in Syria and the al-Houthi movement in Upper Yemen. Reports about actual demands by the movement's representatives themselves, however, indicate relatively pragmatic visions within a range of liberal realism, such as the liberation of political prisoners, mutual recognition as politically legitimate forces, or at one point, a Zaydi administration for Saada province.

To my mind, some local recognition of Zaydism in the province sounds fair. "But you know, the Sada are again fighting against our government," Khaled briefly remarked to me on the cellphone, thus at the same time indicating why his visit to Vienna might be delayed and where his own sympathies were in that conflict: not with al-Houthi, but as usual with the government in Sanaa. "He's alluding to his grandfather," I thought. The Banu Awfan were once again operating as the government's foremost ally in the tribal northwest. A few days later, international newspapers reported that a new series of armed conflicts had broken out between supporters and opponents of the al-Houthi rebellion in northern Yemen. Again and again, I tried to contact Khaled or somebody else from his family during the following weeks, but mostly in vain. Colleagues and friends in Yemen circulated reports via email that the government had decreed a relatively successful information blockade about the fighting in the northern plateau and mountain regions. Part of this policy was to make all telephone lines and all cellphone masts in these regions dysfunctional. It was obvious that this not only served the purpose of isolating the rebellion from contacts outside, but also, perhaps more importantly, of interrupting communication lines among its own forces.

In autumn 2006, international newspapers reported some heavy street fighting between government forces and rebels in Suq at-Talh, formerly a major black-market site to the north of the provincial capital, Saada. This news item might have passed war censorship precisely because it indicated that the government and its allies were believed to be gaining an upper hand, even in one of the core regions of al-Houthi support in the north. Through his Saudi cellphone connection, perhaps significant enough in itself, Khaled managed to contact me once or twice during these weeks, for very short conversations. He avoided any explicit comments about the conflict, of course. On one occasion he said: "We are doing what my grandfather did, remember?"

In various electronic and print media, the tribal name of Munebbih suddenly was being mentioned. Previously, the name had been virtually unknown among Yemen's general public. The Munebbih do not belong to the famous Hamdan federations of Hashid and Bakil on the plateau, but to the much lesser known Khawlan ash-Sham federation of the northwest (also known as Khawlan ash-Shimal, or Khawlan bin Amir). Even within their own federation, Munebbih's tribal name is rarely mentioned among the most important. The chiefs of the other main tribes of Khawlan ash-Sham on both sides of Yemen's border with Saudi Arabia admit that Munebbih are one of their own; though some of the Yemeni chiefs might see them as a maverick tribe: "very good fighters for their own independence, and sometimes very dangerous police units for the government in our region." In fact, already during the 1970s, and later, armed tribal Munebbih units had served as backup and as a fighting force for the government. That had been east of Saada, in one of the conflicts of the time. Their role as very effective support units had reinforced the proud Munebbih self-image and their more limited regional reputation of being the "best fighters of the north." In contrast to how the Munebbih see themselves, and how the chiefs from their tribal federation see them, the Sada usually try to avoid any mention of their name and that of their paramount chief's lineage. For many Sada, Munebbih and Banu Awfan were never part of Khawlan ash-Sham, because they never offered them a hijra residence in their own territory. While the Sada thus try to ignore them, and the general Yemeni public does not really know about them, the Yemeni government has not forgotten its old allies in the northwest. By contrast to preceding decades, the current government and its predecessor have had an influence on media that are actually consulted by the public.

In May 2007, the Sanaa daily *al-Ayyam* reported in a few lines that Shaykh Ali Hussayn al-Munabbihi was leading his tribal warriors towards Qatabir. Located not too far from the Munebbih Mountains, but at a distance from the provincial capital Saada, Qatabir is by far the largest and most important hijra in the northwest. It is situated in Jumaa territory, and Jumaa are the largest tribe among the Khawlan al-Sham federation. Qatabir is one of the main remaining strongholds of the al-Houthi rebellion. Khaled confirms to me that Shaykh Ali Hussayn al-Munabbihi now is "Shaykh al-harb": this re-activates an established Munebbih distinction between the paramount chief (i.e., the Ibn Awfan) as a leader in times of peace, and a tribal section leader who becomes the overall Munebbih "chief of war" in times of intertribal conflict. So, while most other information about events in the north cannot pass the current censorship, Munebbih support under their chief of war for the government did make it into the news.

Suddenly their name was known in the country, as a fighting force against one of the oldest hijras in the north. Later in the summer of 2007, Khaled confirmed this to my friends. About twenty Munebbih fighters were killed, while Munebbih tribal units themselves inflicted heavy losses against the al-Houthi movement near Qatabir. That movement had suffered a serious setback. A 2007 Doha truce settlement, mediated by Qatar, did not gain any lasting relevance despite several efforts to renew it in early 2008. In another effort to regain its authority in Saada province during spring 2008, the government mobilized new forces which also included Hashid tribal units and Salafi volunteer fighters. This is how the Salafi movement gained further momentum, with the most militant elements in it rising into leading roles. The United Nations Office for the Coordination of Humanitarian Efforts estimated in July 2008 (on the basis of figures by the Yemeni Red Crescent) that in Saada province at least 130,000 people lived as internally displaced persons as a consequence of recent fighting. In the early summer of 2009, the president of Yemen at the time proclaimed his government's determination to completely destroy the Shiite rebels in the north, even if it would take five or six more years. While confrontations between the Yemeni army and Shiite rebels continued in the north, unrest and tendencies towards a new kind of secessionism flared up in Yemen's south. Some international analysts began to categorize Yemen as a "failing state." International aid workers in Saada province were shot and kidnapped. Some among their desperate family members in Europe contacted me in early summer 2009, but I could do very little for them.

Then, during the last quarter of 2009, al-Houthi forces that included a group of local Munebbih supporters managed to establish themselves for a few weeks in and around Nayd al-Rakw. This is the most easily accessible village on the main ridge of the Munebbih Mountains, where a government building had been built in recent years. On YouTube the rebels showed images of their victims and of the government building's destruction with explosives by the insurgents. With apparent support from the Saudi side, a majority of pro-government tribal fighters drove the rebels out of Munebbih territory again in January 2010. Meanwhile, Saudi Arabia established a *cordon sanitaire* in the Red Sea and along the border with Yemen to cut possible international supply lines for the Shiite revolt. By then, prospects for the Shiite population in Saada province looked worse than ever.

In early 2010, an international conference in London called upon the responsible government in Sanaa to intensify its attention upon other and more pressing challenges (including Salafi support for al-Qaeda), instead of continuing its civil war against the Shiite rebels.

In January 2012, Yemen's president of thirty-three years, Ali Abdallah Salih, was forced to resign. The effects of the so-called "Arab spring," international pressure, and local revolts from various sides inside Yemen (including the al-Houthi rebellion) led to this result. Salih retained some of his former influence behind the scenes, but the new government in Sanaa called for a "national dialogue" and had to accept another provisional armistice. The civil war's effects were devastating in the north, yet by September 2013 the al-Houthi movement controlled most parts of the northernmost province, including some parts of Munebbih. A fragile peace set in, occasionally interrupted by local fighting in Munebbih and elsewhere. The al-Houthi leadership has begun to participate in the national dialogue, but reaching some basic consensus with all major parties involved still seems to be far away in early 2014. I feel a deep sadness and ambivalence about the outcome of a conflict that might have been solved by peaceful means during its earliest phases, and about the Munebbih's role in it. Khaled and I continue our attempts to reconnect, and to plan his visit to Europe.

Transnational Conclusions: Social Relations and Unintentional Connections

I have presented and discussed these encounters with Munebbih and their chiefly lineage's representatives from the time perspectives through which I have experienced them: long-term perspectives, featuring the medium- and short-term rhythms of interactions and connections, and of being disconnected. This form of written presentation now allows me to attempt a final analysis that again addresses the questions raised in the introduction to this chapter.

The agency-focused, actor-centered version of national and transnational networks in this chapter's case study is perhaps best exemplified through those connections which the Munebbih paramount chief's family maintains with its counterparts in Sanaa and Saudi Arabia, as regional U.S. allies, and through the connection the family has with me. These are all long-distance relations based on personal acquaintances and interactions that have grown over many years. They all have a contractual dimension, at least if seen through Munebbih customary law. The connection between the republican authorities in Sanaa and the Munebbih chiefly lineage dates back to the 1960s, passed on to the next generations by its original actors. Khaled continues to interact with a group of personal interlocutors among the Sanaa authorities, as his grandfather did. The current relationship with the Saudis merely dates back to the late 1990s, but it operates in a similar way. As officially entrusted guardians of the border along their section, Munebbih leaders are in fact entitled and obliged to communicate regularly with the Saudi authorities on the other side—which constantly is encouraged, in fact, by local Zaydi forces' unwillingness to recognize Munebbih as "belonging to them." Again, the Munebbih connection with the Saudis would not work without the crucial element of occasional personal encounters and some degree of trust. Both of these connections therefore include the stable participation of a few men from the Banu Awfan (Khaled today being one of them), and of a few men on the other side. These two connections are seen by Banu Awfan as extensions of their customary legal system of alliances with other, more powerful tribes and authorities. They may become less important at times, and they may be flatly ignored on specific occasions, but only to an extent that would then still allow for reconnection. Since the Saudis have become Yemen's new ally, this new constellation after the end of the Cold War has in fact opened up the opportunity for the Munebbih and their leadership to get the best for themselves from both sides (including cellphone connections). Strategically, however, this is only possible as long as they remain a force of their own—and as long as one of these two more powerful forces remains interested in connecting with them. In some important ways, the Munebbih leadership's present policies therefore represent a continuation of exploiting their border position, which is both peripheral and strategic. Yet at the same time, the conventional aspects of their "domestic" and "foreign" relations to the authorities in Sanaa and Riyadh also have transformed into new transnational relations through the massive presence of foreign powers inside the domestic arena during this conflict, and by the direct impact of technological, military, economic, and religious changes on a global level.

Banu Awfan's connections with me have developed in quite a different manner. Since Munebbih do not offer hijra status to anybody, they never categorized me as somebody with such a status. That has happened to ethnographers in other parts of Yemen, where they were hosted in ways that are comparable to the status of learned Sada, or of poor tanners (Caton 2005). By contrast, the Munebbih at first treated me as one minor factor in their overall effort of improving their relations to the outside world, similar to how they would deal with a guest of unknown social status. Subsequently, I was seen as part of the chief's escort, and finally, I was transformed into a regular tribal guest (Gingrich 1999). As a tribal guest, my status is still "weak" among them: I have to be protected and am not allowed to bear arms as they do. Still, when I am in my "own tribal territory in Vienna," as Khaled once laughingly phrased it, then I suppose I am a distant and minor tribal ally: such a person has to live up to a key element of tribal honor, and extend an invitation.

In all these three cases, then, long-distance relationships endure. They have lasted through several decades in two of these three cases and crossed hundreds and thousands of miles, with an element of local customary law from the Munebbih side as an ingredient that guarantees longevity, as they see it.

Still, despite their formal longevity, and in spite of the important emotional components of trust and friendship that may come with it, these more or less stable connections have changed somewhat in substance and quality. This is most obvious in the more recent and ambivalent case of the Banu Awfan's friendly relations with the Saudis, who were still seen as dangerous and unpredictable opponents during my fieldwork in the 1980s. Such changes can also be demonstrated in the Banu Awfan's more enduring relations with me, and with the Sanaa authorities.

As far as I am concerned, I had admired Khaled's grandfather for his stand in the civil war, and I was enthusiastic about the general political orientation and pragmatism that had inspired it. My relationship with Khaled as a boy was playful, but it was also based on my gratitude for the language lectures and the good company he provided. Today, we share an old friendship that will face a new test once I finally have a chance to host him as my guest. The friendly tensions of differences in age, language, and faith among two men represent an additional ingredient in this relationship. Still, I have serious doubts about the Munebbih's role, and about that of their leadership, which includes Khaled, in the al-Houthi rebellion, for the reasons outlined above. In this particular regard, I again find it useful to distinguish between empathy and sympathy (Gingrich and Banks 2006): I am still able to empathize, as I must for my ethnography, with the motives and decisions that led Banu Awfan into the Qatabir fighting. But this does not necessarily include my sympathy for a development in which violent confrontations gained priority over constructing civil society and religious pluralism.

This leads me to the Banu Awfan's contractual position as the Sanaa government's old ally in the northwest. Again, formal longevity does not exclude changes of quality and contexts but perhaps even facilitates them. In both the two historical contexts under consideration, the civil war of the 1960s and the al-Houthi rebellion of the early 2000s, Munebbih cooperated with the government in armed fights against movements that were led by the Zaydi Sada. Yet the international context and the local social contents of these two operations were entirely different. The Munebbih's role in the civil war resulted in military assistance towards overthrowing a royalist government and promoting tribal autonomy within a new republican order that was positioning itself in a neutralist constellation of the Cold War era. By contrast, the Munebbih's role in fighting the al-Houthi rebellion facilitated a globally hegemonic military solution in a conflict that initially might have had a chance at a peaceful settlement. Perhaps the Munebbih thus indeed have emerged for the time being as partial, bruised winners in the current phase of globalization, but the price for that was quite high.

Such an examination of long-term, personal connections therefore indicates, as a first result, that the intentional, face-to-face versions of transnational connections require an additional qualification: agency, interests, and practical usage are not included a priori in the concept of "connections" per se, but always remain an open question to be investigated. Any identification of interests and practical usage certainly does require a consideration of participants' self-presentation about their respective intentions. Yet this is never enough. Khaled's self-presentation of intentions, for instance, was: "We are doing what my grandfather did, remember?" Phrased in the terms, or in the "frame," of tribal leadership, that self-presentation of intentions sought legitimacy and support for Khaled's actual practices. The government's self-presentation of intentions claimed to fight an international threat emanating from Iran. Formulated in the frame of Yemeni national interests and of wider Sunni aspirations, that self-presentation sought legitimacy and the mobilization of support for the government's actual practices—by characterizing the rebels as local allies of, in fact, transnational Shiite interests that threaten the national cause.

Verbal intentionality therefore does not suffice to identify actual interests (Goffman 1974). An agency-centered approach to face-to-face connections (whether they are activated in their immediate or in their long-distance version) therefore has to consider more than verbally declared intentionality, and more than the explicit sides of lived experience and subjectivity. These self-presentations do not always include emotions, and they do not necessarily include all relevant practical effects. These are the main points to extract, in this context, from this ethnographic discussion of face-to-face relations in wider connections. This discussion, however, has also indicated some other dimensions in these transnational connections that, by definition, never rely on face-to-face encounters. The chapter will conclude with these more anonymous relations, inferred from what was said about the Qatabir fighting, about the blocking of phone communication, and about military censorship.

In general, the introduction of new electronic technologies in the Middle East seems to have contributed less to the strengthening of "civil society" elements than was the case in other parts of the global and postcolonial south (Korany and Dessouki 2008). Instead, the impact of new communication technologies appears primarily to have supported so far those military and secret police machineries that were firmly established from the outset, and gained additional relevance by absorbing these technological innovations much more rapidly than the rest of society, which not only is lagging behind in this regard, but sometimes also becomes fragmented, as in the Yemeni case. The hierarchical and dichotomizing potentials of these new types of communication lines are fully activated in conflicts such as the battles in Saada region between 2004 and 2012.

Connections in an operation like the Qatabir fighting of 2008 concern matters of life and death. They are at least of equal importance for the actors involved as those other connections that have been discussed already. Any military operation of such an order and size includes remote units, communicating to ground units the kind of information that comes with technological military superiority: the anticipation of larger enemy movements in the area, which are not yet visible for ground units; obstacles that still cannot be detected on the ground but can be identified much earlier by the remote unit; and so forth. In these forms of "new wars" (Nordstrom 2004; Robben 2011), of which the al-Houthi rebellion seems to be a fairly typical if only minor example, members of the tribal ground units have never personally met the staff of remote units in another region or country with whom they communicate, and they probably never will. All that matters is that they can identify each other at the right time, and that they are able to communicate to each other the military information that is required there and then. This works both ways, of course. For air raids in rugged mountain terrain, it may be crucial to have ground units who communicate clear directions about where to strike, and where to avoid friendly fire. These interactions depend on personal and identifiable communication between individuals who do not know each other in anything other than the present context of remote military communication. Communication among regular army units is different, in so far as all participants are part of the same organization. In contrast, "new wars" include by definition some of those shorter and more informal alliances between the smaller units of different organizations that may not reconnect any time soon.

As a second result of this analysis, it can be pointed out that this type of connection certainly is intentional and interactive, but, by definition, it has to remain remote to achieve its purpose. Its necessary long-distance quality introduces a certain amount of anonymity that is part of the operation's rules. Through their remote communication, the Munebbih tribal fighter and the Saudi or Yemeni army pilot identify each other by pre-arranged codes. They do not introduce themselves to each other in person. This type of remote connection is not confined, however, to military operations. It is part of any remote connection that requires anonymity and precision. In this sense, these remote connections largely resemble those other, anonymous relations that Monica Konrad aptly describes as "nameless relations" (2005) for British ova donors and recipients. Connectivity of this kind is currently expanding along transnational and global dimensions, through the market as much as through politics and legislation. It implies not only virtual connections of all kinds, but also anonymous and impersonal relations and networks. Konrad's cases and the example of Munebbih tribal fighters and army pilots therefore jointly demonstrate an additional feature of these versions of remote interactive connections: they entail encoded anonymity. That anonymity cannot be decoded intentionally by the participants themselves without breaking the rules. Usually, it would take a separate and specialized effort at a later point, by an investigative expert unit, for example, in order to decode who the actual participants previously were in that nameless remote connection.

This demonstrates another important point. Conceptualizing these intentional remote connections in larger networks with encoded anonymity sometimes unavoidably requires an introduction of some kind of systemic notion. The insight becomes even more evident if, in the end, "unintentional connections, and disconnections" is added to the inventory. Disconnecting all the telephone lines and cellphone masts of Upper Yemen in 2007 certainly was an intentional, strategic move by the government in the new war that was under way. For the population of Upper Yemen, the same event was against their intentions and took them by surprise. Interactive intentionality is always dependent upon the powers behind it, and if these are widely unequal, then intentionality becomes a one-sided process. The "lived experience" of one side then is of being powerless and angry, or fearful, faced with the powerful intentions of the other side. The powerful intentions of one side can be implemented because they are part of those wider forces that control systemic networks, in this case in the original modern sense of the term, i.e., communication systems. To this case of being disconnected against one's will and against one's intentions may be added the other case of being observed against one's will: long before the actual conflict began, the al-Houthi fighters in Qatabir in all likelihood were subjected to surveillance and to observation, by ground units as much as from air and space. This last point therefore identifies transnational connections that are unilateral and anonymous to the extent that those who are "being connected" (in the sense of being observed) or "disconnected" (e.g., from their access to cellphone networks) may or may not suspect what is going on, but they cannot be sure about it until it is too late. They do not have any "lived experience" of the operation while it is under way, except for the fear that it may be happening soon. They certainly have no intention that it happens, but they cannot do much about it. In most cases, such unilateral forms of being disconnected, or of being unwillingly connected through surveillance, require systemic control for their implementation.

It was said in the beginning that some connections and relations are more enduring than they at first sight appear to be. It can now be added that these more enduring connections and relations are often control systems of power. Their conceptualization cannot be ignored by anthropological approaches interested in transnational connections in a globalized world. Subjectivity is indeed a precondition of today's globalized world. Agency-centered approaches in anthropology, however, are facing the challenge that this globalized world continues to maintain, to enact and produce powerful systems and systemic power. Ignoring them conceptually is not too far removed from their belittlement. It is within these networks and "structures of the conjuncture" (Sahlins 1985), and sometimes against them, that history is made and enacted. For these reasons, acknowledging the different potentials of flows and networks remains both useful and realistic, if they are differentiated according to contemporary necessities, and as long as they are related to unequal relations of power.

Acknowledgments

A short version of this essay was first presented in September 2007 in honor of Ulf Hannerz on the occasion of his retirement from the University of Stockholm's anthropology chair. In line with that original occasion, this chapter is dedicated to Ulf Hannerz in recognition of the generous academic and intellectual inspiration he has been giving, and which he continues to provide for his colleagues and students. For suggestions and comments on earlier drafts of this chapter, I thank the anonymous reviewers provided by Mark Graham (Stockholm), by Marion Berghahn (Oxford), as well as several colleagues and friends in Yemen, in Europe and in the United States who prefer to remain unnamed. I gratefully acknowledge Julene Knox's (London) contributions in copy-editing this text.

Notes

1. Following normal standards of ethnographic descriptions, this name has been altered by the author. All Arabic terms and names in this text are rendered in conventional anglicized forms.
2. Many residents of the Munebbih area knew that I would soon be staying in the area for a longer period. I had traveled to the Munebbih Mountains in 1983 together with Johann Heiss for a shorter visit (Gingrich and Heiss 1986), which helped to prepare my 1986 main fieldwork sojourn.

References

Appadurai, Arjun. 1996. *Modernity at Large: Cultural Dimensions of Globalization*. Minneapolis: University of Minnesota Press.
Bauman, Zygmunt. 2007. *Liquid Times: Living in an Age of Uncertainty*. Cambridge: Polity Press.
Beck, Ulrich. 2007. *Weltrisikogesellschaft: Auf der Suche nach der verlorenen Sicherheit*. Frankfurt: Suhrkamp.
Brandt, Marieke. 2011. "Friedens-Shaykh und Kriegs-Shaykh: Der Übergang von Kriegsführerschaft bei den Banu Munebbih im Huthi-Konflikt in Nordwest-Jemen." *Anthropos* 1: 49–69.
Caton, Steven C. 2005. *Yemen Chronicle: An Anthropology of War and Mediation*. New York: Hill and Wang.

Das, Veena. 2007. *Life and Words: Violence and the Descent into the Ordinary.* Berkeley: University of California Press.

Dresch, Paul. 1989. *Tribes, Government, and History in Yemen.* Oxford: Clarendon Press.

———. 2000. *A History of Modern Yemen.* Cambridge: Cambridge University Press.

Duranti, Alessandro. 2006. "The Social Ontology of Intentions." *Discourse Studies* 8(1): 31–40.

Gingrich, Andre. 1993. "Tribes and Rulers in Northern Yemen." In *Studies in Oriental Culture and History: Festschrift for Walter Dostal*, ed. Andre Gingrich, Sylvia Haas, Gabriele Paleczek, and Thomas Fillitz. Frankfurt and Vienna: Peter Lang, pp. 253–280.

———. 1999. *Erkundungen: Themen der ethnologischen Forschung.* Vienna and Cologne: Böhlau.

———. 2002. "When Ethnic Majorities Are Dethroned: Towards a Methodology of Self-reflexive, Controlled Macro-comparison." In *Anthropology, by Comparison*, ed. Andre Gingrich and Richard G. Fox. London and New York: Routledge, pp. 225–248.

———. 2011. "Warriors of Honor, Warriors of Faith: Two Historical Male Role Models from South-western Arabia." In *Violence Expressed: An Anthropological Approach*, ed. Maria Six-Hohenbalken and Nerina Weiss. London: Ashgate, pp. 37–54.

Gingrich, Andre and Marcus Banks, eds. 2006. *Neo-nationalism in Europe and beyond: Perspectives from Social Anthropology.* Oxford and New York: Berghahn.

Gingrich, Andre and Johann Heiss. 1986. *Beiträge zur Ethnographie der Provinz Ṣa'da, Nordjemen. Aspekte der traditionellen materiellen Kultur in bäuerlichen Stammesgesellschaften.* Vienna: Verlag der Österreichischen Akademie der Wissenschaften, Sb. d. phil.-hist. Kl. Bd. 462.

Goffman, Erving. 1974. *Frame Analysis: An Essay on the Organization of Experience.* London: Harper and Row.

Hannerz, Ulf. 1992a. "The Global Ecumene as a Network of Networks." In *Conceptualizing Society*, ed. Adam Kuper. London: Routledge, pp. 34–56.

———. 1992b. *Cultural Complexity: Studies in the Social Organization of Meaning.* New York: Columbia University Press.

———. 1996. *Transnational Connections: Culture, People, Places.* London and New York: Routledge.

Johnsen, Gregory D. 2006. "Yemen's Passive Role in the War on Terrorism." *Terrorism Monitor* 4(4): 7–9.

———. 2007. "Yemen Accuses Iran of Meddling in its Internal Affairs." *Terrorism Focus* 4(2): 3–4.

Konrad, Monica. 2005. *Nameless Relations: Anonymity, Melanesia and Reproductive Gift Exchange between British Ova Donors and Recipients.* Oxford and New York: Berghahn.

Korany, Bahgat and Ali E. Hillal Dessouki, eds. 2008. *The Foreign Policies of Arab States: The Challenges of Globalization.* Revised edition. Cairo and New York: American University in Cairo Press.

Latour, Bruno. 2005. *Reassembling the Social: An Introduction to Actor-Network-Theory*. Oxford: Oxford University Press.
Nordstrom, Carolyn. 2004. *Shadows of War: Violence, Power, and International Profiteering in the Twenty-first Century*. Berkeley: University of California Press.
Puin, Gerd R. 1984. "The Yemeni Hijrah Concept of Tribal Protection." In *Land Tenure and Social Transformation in the Middle East*, ed. Tarif Khalidi. Beirut: American University of Beirut, pp. 483–494.
Robben, Antonius. 2011. "Neue Kriege." In *Handbuch der Globalisierung*, ed. Fernand Kreff, Eva-Maria Knoll, and Andre Gingrich. Bielefeld: Transcript, pp. 296–299.
Sahlins, Marshall. 1985. *Islands of History*. Chicago: University of Chicago Press.
Serjeant, Robert B. 1969. "The Zaydis." In *Religion in the Middle East: Three Religions in Concord and Conflict*, ed. Arthur J. Arberry. 7 vols. Cambridge: Cambridge University Press, vol. 2, pp. 285–301.
Wedeen, Lisa. 2008. *Peripheral Visions: Publics, Powers, and Performance in Yemen*. Chicago: University of Chicago Press.
Weir, Shelagh. 2006. *A Tribal Order: Politics and Law in the Mountains of Yemen*. Austin: University of Texas Press.

Chapter 4

GLOBAL SWIRL AT DUPONT CIRCLE
Think Tanks, Connectivity, and the Making of "the Global"

Christina Garsten

Dupont Circle in Washington D.C. is at once a large traffic circle, a park area, an intersection of diverse neighborhoods, and a historic center. The roundabout connects Massachusetts Avenue with Connecticut Avenue, New Hampshire Avenue, P Street, and 19th Street, all of which are major arteries of Washington D.C. A major point of connection for locals, commuters, and visitors, it is alive with city buzz. In the green park area in the inner section of the traffic circle, people break out from their offices for lunch, walk their dogs, preach to passersby of their religious or political conviction, or enjoy a moment of calm in the shade of the big trees.

Pretty much any type of subcultural inclination can be satisfied at Dupont Circle. Ethnic cafes and restaurants blend with gay clubs, fancy bars, trendy coffee houses, and upscale retail stores. Social clubs concentrate as well around the hub, which offers convenient locations for professionals to meet up with friends, acquaintances, and business associates after work. Intellectuals find their watering holes here as well, in places such as Kramerbooks & Afterwords, with its popular bar and bistro. Several Starbucks cafes cater to the needs of students and others, winding down during lunch breaks or after work, or spending their study hours there, latte in hand.

Dupont Circle is also a dynamic node for some of the nation's most prestigious organizations: think tanks and research institutes, including the Brookings Institution, the Carnegie Endowment for International Peace, The Eurasia Center, and the Peter G. Peterson Institute for International Economics. Less than two blocks away is the renowned Paul H. Nitze School of Advanced International Studies of The Johns Hopkins University. Not far away, the offices of the World Bank and the International Monetary Fund (IMF) are located.

Across the street from the Brookings Institution, the Carnegie Endowment for International Peace, and the private Sulgrave Club are located. This is also where the Center for Global Development (CGD) is to be found.[1] This is a think tank focused on providing research and knowledge that can influence policy for global development. The building in which CGD is housed strikes a clear contrast to the rounded and ornamented shape of the Sulgrave Club building on the opposite side of the street. This Beaux Arts-style house, the Wadsworth House, was built of light yellow Roman brick and cream-colored, molded terra cotta. The CGD building, on the other hand, is a light grayish, modernist cement complex, with large, shaded windows. In the entrance area, the guard asks visitors to enter their name in the register, and to name the person they are meeting with. Once every month, the neutral professionalism of the entrance area is enlivened by free popcorn or oversized muffins and a soft drink, offered to employees and visitors by the landlord company. The Center for Global Development was the central node in the vast network of think tanks that I was studying during my fieldwork in Washington D.C. It became the site from which I ventured out to grasp the social world of think-tank experts, with the aim to understand how think tanks work to influence decisions related to policy (Garsten 2013).

The "soul" of the D.C. area that I got to know was surely different from the one that Ulf Hannerz experienced and described in his landmark book *Soulside* (1969) forty-five years ago. The time I was there, spring 2011, was a highly turbulent time for Washington, for the U.S., for the world economy, and for world politics. There were the uprisings and an overthrow of power in Tunisia and Egypt, protest movements in Bahrain and Yemen, public mobilization in Syria, and the revolt in Libya that turned into a painful civil war. At this time, Japan was struck by a devastating earthquake, followed by a tsunami and the leakage of the Fukushima nuclear power plant. This was also the time when Osama Bin Laden was found and killed in Pakistan, and when debates about U.S. involvement in peacekeeping, war, and aid were intense. Domestically, turbulent spring weather caused hundreds of deaths and left people homeless in the south. And the budget deficit reached record highs. These events were the talk of the day in the streets, created media headlines, and were continuously debated in a variety of fora. Foreign news outlets were feeding into the buzz of Dupont Circle. And yet, despite the massive influx of news from across the world, public intellectuals talked about being in "the D.C. bubble." The D.C. bubble was a social world in itself, housing policy experts, public intellectuals, lobbyists, corporate leaders, and politicians, zealously engaged in mapping the outside world.

This chapter intends to provide some insight into how D.C.-based think tanks work to provide knowledge intended to influence policy making, and how they in the process also craft and disseminate knowledge that contributes to creating and mapping "the global." In targeting their messages to intended audiences by way of a range of publication outlets, media technologies, and data metrics, think-tank experts act as brokers between spheres of knowledge and expertise. As brokers, they play key roles in creolizing knowledge and in creating knowledge that can be counted on as credible and relevant. Think tanks are highly attractive organizations to study, not least since they bring ideas to bear on the much wider question of the relation between academic knowledge and public action. There is a double edge to the way think tanks have been, and are being, positioned in U.S. society; as citadels for public intellectuals and testimony to the rising significance of expert knowledge (Weidenbaum 2008: 2), on the one hand, and as heirs to the long and deep-seated anti-intellectual tradition that commentators since Alexis de Tocqueville have identified as part of the national culture, on the other (Medvetz 2012: 20). They are as well one of the most distinctive ways in which Americans have sought to link knowledge and power (Smith 1991: xv, see also Barley 2010; Gusterson 2009). With roots in the Progressive Era reform and the "scientific management movement," and nurtured by their capacity to "help government think," as it were, U.S. think tanks proliferated in the 1970s and 1980s, and have since experienced a steady and exceptional growth.[2] The term *think tank* itself "was created after World War II, when the government sought to marshal sophisticated technical expertise for both the Cold War national security enterprise and the short-lived domestic war against poverty" (Smith 1991: xv), and reflects the ambivalence that people feel about experts.

Tracking: Studying down, up, sideways, through, backward, and forward

Think tanks are bestowed with multifaceted organizational images. On the one hand, they embrace notions of openness, accessibility, and transparency. They aim to provide an alternative platform for dialogue, debate, and knowledge creation, more tied in with daily political events than universities, offering larger scope for thought than corporate research and development departments, and more long-term analysis than media agencies. To this end, they offer a stage onto which academics, politicians, corporate leaders, and NGO representatives can enter to flesh out their views and encourage debate. On the other hand, they also cultivate a sense of exclusion, inaccessibility, and opacity around themselves. Not anyone can enter and become a member of a think tank, and exactly how their priorities are set and their activities are funded remains unknown for the larger public. This double image provides think tanks with a set of public connotations, as slightly mysterious yet attractive places where ideas are being crafted, worked upon, and neatly packaged.

For me, the pressing question was, how do I approach think-tank people? The question of how to engage with the field of think tanks occupied my thoughts for quite some time before starting the actual fieldwork. Looking back at the organizations I have studied, I realize I have in some sense had an inclination to seek out fields that are not immediately accessible, but that require some kind of entry ticket (see, for example, Garsten 1994, 2008). I do not mean to suggest that other communities do not entail considerable challenge in terms of access, but studying formal organizations demands a badge, signing in, or being taken on board by some kind of inside host. Most probably, the challenge attracts me. Pondering about how to engage with think tanks was thus a puzzle I enjoyed. How was I to nestle into the network of public intellectuals and senior fellows? What entry points were most likely to work? What kinds of resources, skills, and tricks would I have to draw upon for doors to open?

Studying the world of think tanks comes with a set of methodological challenges (Garsten 2013). For a start, it is not evident what makes up the "field" as such. Indeed, it is a common concern of both research subjects and fieldworkers these days that the field, or "locality," must now be maintained and represented in relation to widening and fragmenting social frames and networks (Coleman and Collins 2006). The fact that think tanks are organizational entities, with recognized legal status, occupying office buildings into which only employees with badges are allowed, does not suffice to define the field. A closer look at how the professional and personal ties of think-tank employees stretch across organizations shows that as organizations, they are tangled into other organizations, other professional communities. The senior fellows are often academics affiliated with a university department; ex-government staff; and board members in other think tanks. Their professional networks extend vastly beyond the think tank in which they are housed, and should do so. Maintaining both strong and weak ties to relevant others, to manage one's network, is key (cf. Rothkopf 2008). Janine Wedel, in her study of U.S. policy professionals and their flexible roles and repertoires, granted them the label "flexians" (Wedel

2009). "Flexians" thrive on cultivating informal network ties to relevant others. It is through such ties and connections that information and knowledge may be passed on, *before* becoming official, *besides* the official, and as reflexive criticisms *after* the official. Working the network is essentially how "deep lobbying" (Wallace-Wells 2003) is done. Think-tank workers are also people in continuous motion, crisscrossing between meetings, conferences, and social clubs, within walking distance, or anywhere in the world. So, the field is a relational one, delineated by the reach and depth of network connections. The field of think tanks is to be found "here, there and everywhere" (see Hannerz 2003). Tracking networks means studying down, up, sideways, through, backward, and forward, as Hannerz has it (2010). Locating the field is thus more a question of tracking networks than about establishing boundaries (Marcus 1998).

In relation to my research into the area of corporate social responsibility (CSR), I have suggested that it may be studied "by the anthropologist positing herself at the crossroads, or interface, of such linkages and connections" (Garsten 2009: 76). Oftentimes, it is at the very interfaces of organizations that the field becomes mostly clearly articulated, where one can get a sense of the different stakes involved and negotiated, especially when dealing with the interactions of people representing different organizations and different interests, and with their own individual preferences, experiences, and perspectives. This methodological stance enables us to track processes of meaning-making that may be translocal, but it also invites some challenging questions regarding the "thickness" and density of ethnography in practice. Attending to actual practice, and to practices crisscrossing organizational boundaries, also allows us to understand the ways in which organization is done, how social as well as organizational fields are produced and reproduced, and how struggles over different forms of resources and values organize those fields (see Calhoun and Sennett 2007).

My first experiences of doing fieldwork in Washington D.C. involved moving along the interface, as it were. My academic credentials from Sweden counted for very little in this community, and to get connected to think-tank experts, yet alone to get "inside" a think tank as an outsider and a "nobody," took some effort, perseverance, and strategizing.[3] It also meant learning to make my way forward in a highly politicized landscape, where the "ease of privilege" (Rahman Kahn 2011) relied on signals that were, in part and at first, unintelligible to me, as an outsider to the "D.C. jungle."

After a few weeks, tracking the networks between people in the D.C. policy landscape, I got in touch with one of the directors at CGD.

Mike, as we may call him, was only three referrals away from the initial contact I had in D.C. He became my key interlocutor and my main connecting node both in CGD and from the organization outwards. His curiosity for an anthropologist's ability to contribute to the understanding of the organization opened several doors. In Westbrook's (2008) terms, the interlocutor (Mike) provided the navigator (me) not so much with a map of the culture, as with data that could be used to help me determine where it was and where I could go. Think-tank people are engaged in what Holmes and Marcus (2005) have called "para-ethnography," attempting to understand the environment in which they operate, to find ways to interpret and make sense of what is transpiring and to communicate their insights—activities that resemble those of the anthropologist. This shared concern provided a common ground for our discussions. This common ground did, however, also point to a key methodological concern. How was I to maintain awareness of the differences that may underlie the surface similarity in our reasoning? How could I engage with interlocutors around shared concerns and concepts, whilst articulating my own analytical position and keeping to my own place on the map? An "adjacency," in the terminology of Rabinow et al. (2008: 55–61), a certain amount of ethnographic untimeliness in a fast-moving field, seemed necessary.

I ventured to ask Mike if CGD would consider hosting me for the remainder of my fieldwork in D.C. I reasoned that my understanding of the operation of think tanks in the policy arena would be significantly enhanced by the opportunity to follow issues and practices on a day-to-day basis and over time. My question was favorably received, and I was invited to be their guest for some three months and was given my own office space. This meant that I could participate in all kinds of meetings and events in the organization and talk with and interview staff. The Communications and Outreach Team by which I was hosted comprised a dynamic group of young people in charge of making the research results of CGD more visible and available to the media, to people "on the Hill" (Capitol Hill—a metonym for the U.S. Congress), and to a wider audience. Considering my interest in the way knowledge is produced, packaged, and disseminated, this was an ideal vantage point.

A Think and Do Tank

The Center for Global Development had just celebrated its tenth birthday when I arrived in Washington D.C. The organization was founded in 2001 by Edward W. Scott Jr., C. Fred Bergsten, and Nancy Birdsall. Ed

Scott, a former technology entrepreneur, a philanthropist, and a former senior U.S. government official, took the initiative, based on the conviction that he wanted to make a contribution to improving the world. He provided the vision and a significant financial commitment that made the creation of CGD possible. Fred Bergsten, Director of the Peterson Institute for International Economics, an influential D.C.-based think tank, had the necessary standing in the area to put the visions into action. He lent to the cause his formidable reputation in policy circles and among academics. He also provided the new organization with an initial platform within the Peterson Institute, about one hundred meters from the CGD location. Nancy Birdsall, a former head of the World Bank research department and Executive Vice-President of the Inter-American Development Bank, with a solid academic background, was recruited to become the first president of CGD. Her intellectual leadership and personal charisma attracted a cadre of researchers and other professionals dedicated to CGD's mission, which is to influence policy for global development.

The dynamic duo—Chair of the Board Ed Scott and President Nancy Birdsall—represents and embodies the dual "thinking and doing" focus of CGD: to produce top-level research and to create an impact on policy making. The emphasis on "rigorous research" and "thinking" lies at the heart of CGD, and the academic profile is a central aspect of the organization. Based on research and policy analysis, the people at CGD want to "turn ideas into action." It is, in this sense, a "think and do tank" (http://www.cgdev.org/page/about-cgd, accessed April 15, 2014), combining research and analysis with an ambition to influence policy making in its areas of engagement. Formally, CGD is an independent, non-partisan, and non-profit think tank. Research is undertaken on a wide range of topics relating to the impact of policy on people in developing countries.

The entire CGD staff of eighty-seven people comprised executive, finance, operations, communications, and outreach people; research assistants; resident, visiting, and non-resident fellows; and program staff. Approximately sixty of the entire staff were resident. The spinal cord of the organization is made up of the experts, or fellows. At the time of my fieldwork, there were forty-eight experts associated to the CGD, about one-quarter of whom were visiting fellows. Most of them had academic backgrounds and Ph.D. degrees. Many of them had experience from working in the government administration, Republican or Democratic. The majority, however, had been recruited from one of the big multilaterals, like the World Bank. Most of the non-resident fellows had previously spent time at CGD as visiting fellows or as resident experts. There were also eleven research assistants, who worked with the senior experts on specific projects. Research assistants are typically younger college graduates, for whom a couple of years in an organization like CGD serves as valuable experience before they embark on a Ph.D. program or apply for a more senior position elsewhere. Also part of the organization was a distinguished advisory group, consisting of people well connected and experienced in the D.C. policy world, and an equally illustrious board of directors. Donors may join the CGD Society network and gain preferred access to the center's public conferences, events, and informal meetings. Financial contributors may also join the Partners Council, which is a non-governing membership body, with participants supporting CGD through financial contributions, by attracting other potential supporters and by serving as advocates for CGD's mission in their professional and social communities.

The Center for Global Development is a loosely integrated organization, with boundaries to the outside environment that are continuously in flux.[4] Forms of affiliation vary from permanent to short-term, and members' degree of engagement in the organization varies significantly. A vast and dense network of contacts connects CGD with other think tanks, corporations, and foundations; with Congress and the Administration; and with multilaterals, NGOs, and universities. From this viewpoint, CGD may be seen as an assemblage of people, resources, and ideas, extending over and beyond the physically located and formally bounded organization into a meshwork of transorganizational ties with other experts, business leaders, policy makers, and politicians. The trope of the "inside" (Marcus 1998), in the sense of aspiring to get "inside" a particular field entity, so cherished by anthropologists, thus proved to no avail in this context. Tracking ties and straddling the network was all the more important.

Improving the World: Ideas, Impact, Influence

Think tanks have emerged as key "sites for normativity" for the global order (Sassen 1998). In these sites, information is gathered, processed, and packaged, and knowledge is produced and distributed. Most think tanks aim to generate knowledge that is policy relevant, and that may influence decisions in Congress, in multilaterals, and in other decision-making arenas. Consequently, think tanks place great emphasis on dissemination and outreach. In practice, they operate as highly productive publishing houses, generating both traditional and multimedia publications. A substantial portion of their financial and human resources is devoted to assembling information and articulating and diffusing ideas and perspectives. In this process, important tools and outputs are monographs, reports, policy briefs and recommendations, workshops, and seminars, as well as briefings and informal discussions with government officials, policymakers, business leaders, and other key stakeholders.

Think tanks are motors in the diffusion of normatively charged ideas about how the current state of affairs should be understood, dealt with, and improved. These processes signal the emergence of a multisited, though partial, disruption of the existing formal, geopolitical architecture (Sassen 1998). This in turn raises questions about the future of crucial frameworks through which modern societies, economies, and polities (under the rule of law) have operated; about the social contract of liberal states, representative democracy as it has come to be understood, modern citizenship, and the formal mechanisms that render certain claims legitimate and others illegitimate in liberal democracies. Assemblages of institutional arrangements are emerging alongside and entangled in established national and international collaboration and decision-making, assemblages that are able to exert a degree of authority and to promote certain normative perspectives on selected issues. Such global organizational constellations to a large extent escape "the grid of national institutional frames" (Sassen 2008: 61). An essential feature of think tanks is their ability to exert influence beyond the formal organizational boundaries, by way of vast networks of connections to both individuals and organizations. Through their assemblage-type organization, think tanks can de-border, and even exit, what are today still ruling normative orders. Furthermore, they can establish particularized future "normative" orders specific to these assemblages.

Think-tank experts are part of a growing cadre of professionals engaged in producing global scenarios of cultural flows and borders that enter "the public geocultural imagination," in Hannerz' (2009) sense of the term. Such scenarios are aimed to capture the imaginations of politicians and policy makers, often by way of seductive sound bites, like "the clash of civilizations," "the end of history," or "the world is flat."[5] In Anna L. Tsing's (2005) terms, they are engaged in "scale-making" activities.

Think tanks compete for attention, visibility, and impact of their knowledge. Their knowledge products may be understood as "attention direction devices," in Power's words (Power 2003). They strive to get the attention of significant actors and to create visibility for themselves and their views. And it is a crowded scene on which they operate. Weidenbaum (2008) has referred to the world of think tanks in terms of a "competition for ideas," underlining the intense competition for visibility and attention of ideas and policy propositions that characterize this sector.

At CGD, research is undertaken on a wide range of topics relating to the impact of policy on people in developing countries. There are research programs on aid effectiveness and innovation, climate change, global governance, global health and education, migration, private investment and access to finance, and the links between trade and poverty reduction. Research topics can evolve in various ways. They may emerge from the interests and expertise of scholars, the priorities of the leaders, available funding opportunities, or interests of strategic partners. It is often a combination of available funding opportunities and the priorities of senior management paired with scholarly ambitions that eventually channels resources into a program.

How, then, do these educational activities translate into influence? CGD, like most U.S. think tanks, is organized under U.S. corporate law on the same terms as charities and educational organizations: as a 501(c)3 organization. As such, it is not permitted to use more than 5 percent of its total resources for lobbying and political advocacy. Hence, it must be inventive in finding ways of educating and informing public officials about critical issues. The center works actively to ensure that its research products and policy recommendations reach policy makers, advocates and public-opinion leaders, and continuously experiments with new, more effective ways to turn ideas into action. Experts produce an extensive range of print and online materials, such as books, peer-reviewed working papers, essays, policy briefs, congressional testimonies, and short policy memos addressed to specific policy makers. Policy recommendations and analytic findings are adapted in format and length to suit diverse audiences. The experts also write their own opinion editorials (op-eds) and may also have their own web pages. Online engagement is crucial. The center has a lively website and a presence in such social media networks as Facebook and Twitter. Its members produce policy blogs, in which senior experts provide their views on topical issues and advocate policy changes. Trying to get an overview, let alone to stay abreast of the production of documents, as "artifacts of knowledge practices," in Annelise Riles' (2009: 7) terms, was a daunting but crucial task. Moreover, CGD organizes a range of events that feature the work of its experts and other influential policy thinkers, with the aim of reaching a wider audience of policy makers, academics, diplomats, analysts, advocates, and journalists.

Among the varied audience groups that CGD targets, the U.S. Congress deserves special mention. The critical role that Congress plays in shaping, funding, and overseeing U.S. global development policies requires CGD's policy outreach team to work to ensure that the center's research and analysis is readily accessible to audiences on Capitol Hill. A great deal of effort goes into ensuring that the experts are given the opportunity to provide testimonies on development issues before the House and Senate Committees—testimonies that serve as critical milestones in the work of experts. The experts are also encouraged to submit written statements on relevant topics for the Congressional Record and to create opportunities for participating in discussions with members of Congress and their staff.

So, how are they faring? It is difficult to present evidence of the influence of think tanks on policy. As noted by Weidenbaum (2010: 134), "there is an inevitable amount of puffery in the claims of individual think tanks, especially when they are raising money or reporting to their supporters." It is clearly a temptation for think-tank experts to claim credit for the public policy statements of nationally known legislative figures. And because they cannot lobby in the strict sense of the term, their influence must come through the shaping of agendas and perceptions through education and the dissemination of information.

A distinction is made at CGD between influence and impact. Influence is the less tangible but nonetheless valuable change in the way key actors frame or approach a pressing problem. Impact refers to specific changes that can be largely or partially attributed to their work. Impacts are listed on the website and highlighted in seminars, web features, and blogs. The initiative with significant impact that was most frequently discussed during my fieldwork was "Shaping the Financial Access Agenda." On the website (http://www.cgdev.org/page/impacts-and-influence, accessed April 15, 2014), it is claimed that "CGD is shaping the international agenda on ways to increase access to financial services for poor people and for small and medium-sized businesses in the developing world"—which is seen as "a key to shared global prosperity." The task-force report that resulted from the initiative, "Policy Principles for Expanding Financial Access," released in 2009, proposed ten principles for financial-sector policy makers—including national authorities, donors, private-sector participants, international financial institutions, and others—on the facilitation, regulation, and direct provision of financial services. In June 2010, the G-20 summit in Toronto had adopted "Principles for Innovative Financial Inclusion" that closely mirrored those of the CGD task-force report. Senior Fellow Liliana Rojas-Suarez, who led the task force, was featured in *Business*

Week America, was quoted in the *Washington Post*, the *Latin America Advisor*, and *Diario Financiero*, appeared several times on CNN, and posted her own blogs on issues related to this topic. Her expertise in this topical area of global concern was a valuable asset for CGD and achieved great traction.

How to measure impact and influence in the public policy arena was a constant concern that fueled activities with a certain spark. The "so what?" can never be left unattended.

The Brokering of Knowledge

Think-tank experts are savvy in the creative acts of knowledge brokering. Positioned at the interface of spheres of activity and knowledge, think-tank experts function as intermediary actors, negotiating interpretations of events and data, and crafting representations of developments and future trajectories to be diffused to other organizations and cadres of experts. Bierschank et al. (2002) have suggested that interlinked and networked social realities are best captured through attention to the roles of brokers, who assume a growing importance in mediated cultures. The interlinked and connected worlds of think tanks, and the assembly-like type of organization they represent, alert us to the role of brokers and brokerage in claims for robust and neutral policy-relevant knowledge.

Brokerage is a long-standing theme in political anthropology, in which structural-functionalist models have been challenged by work—such as that of the Manchester school—highlighting the ways in which social actors operate as active agents, building social, political, and economic roles rather than simply following normative scripts (Bierschenk et al. 2002; James 2011). In this approach—exemplified by the work of Bailey (1969) in India and Boissevain (1978) in the Mediterranean—brokerage is viewed as an outcome of a weak state unable to impose its rationality on local areas and enlisting patron–client relationships to reduce the unpredictability of the state's efforts at intervention and control. In a similar fashion, think tanks operate at the margins of state power, outside state mandate, yet entangled in it, providing a link between political power of decision-making and corporate resources.

Brokerage is seen to occur at every instance in the outreach activities of think tanks. It is not enough, as the *bricoleur* would, to craft something new and interesting out of what knowledge there is at hand. To achieve traction, a think-tank fellow must also master the language, vocabulary, and tone of voice of the desired audience. She must be able to address the recipient with credibility, authority, and trust, and to "translate" or "creolize" findings and views into the vocabulary of the other. Strategic timing is important here, since the reports, blogs, op-eds, and other outlets need to be tuned in to relevant events in the surrounding world. Sniffing the news value and relevance that a certain message may have for readers and listeners whilst pushing the agenda of the organization one represents is a highly valuable skill, not least since think tanks in the U.S. are not allowed to engage in lobbying per se. "We want to influence, but we do it by seeding ideas, not by lobbying," as one of my informants expressed it. Planting knowledge at the right moment often makes up for arduous lobbying.

The notion of brokerage brings to the fore the active role of think tanks in producing and mediating knowledge and information, often between audiences and spheres. But the notion tends to focus on the role and position of the broker, and less on the process. It tends to favor attention on the individual actor and his or her agentic capacities, rather than examine closely the structures of distributed agency and the processes of structuration involved (cf. Meyer and Jepperson 2000). This perspective, then, needs to be complemented by looking at the actual processes at work. In doing so, we should not assume the *a priori* existence of social and institutional realms for knowledge and scenario creation. All human beings, and not just experts, are involved in producing interpretations, and powerful actors offer scripts and templates to which others can be recruited for a period. This is essentially what think-tank experts do. In this sense their interpretations are performative: "they prove themselves by transforming the world in conformity with their perspective on the world" (Latour 1996: 194–195). The concern becomes, then, not how actors operate and strategize within existing arrangements of knowledge, but how projects become real through the work of generating and translating interests, creating context by tying in significant people and so sustaining interpretations (Latour 1996; Mosse 2005). Latour's concept of 'translation" here refers to the mutual enrollment and the interlocking of interests that produce project realities. The notion of "creolization" (Hannerz 1987, 1992, 1997) may be deployed to make visible the interactive processes through which think-tank experts model and craft knowledge that they then package with a keen ear for the priorities of the intended audiences.

Where an interactionist approach emphasizes the brokering of an almost endless multiplicity of actor perspectives, strategies, and arenas, the metaphor of creolization may assist us in examining the production, packaging, and protection of unified fields of knowledge creation. Indeed, it is the appearance of congruence between problems and propositions, the coherence of policy logic, and the authority of expertise that are really surprising and require explanation (Moore 2000: 657; Mitchell 2002). The ethnographic task is thus to show how, despite fragmentation and polyphony, actors are continuously engaged in scale-making activities and a certain ordering and mapping of the world through creative acts of composition. A creolist view, Hannerz suggests (1997: 325), "is particularly applicable to processes of cultural confluence within a more or less open continuum of diversity, stretched out along a structure of center-periphery relationships which may well extend transnationally, and which is characterized also by inequality in power, prestige and material resource terms."

Windows to the World: Tools, Technologies, Imaginaries

There are many ways in which think tanks may work on projecting their knowledge and their arguments toward the outer world. As mentioned above, the publishing activities of think tanks are intensive and comprise an impressive range of activities and tools. These include a central technology of CGD, made up of aggregated data: the Commitment to Development Index (CDI).

On my very first day at CGD, I was introduced by Susan, one of the research assistants, to the CDI. This index is one of the most valuable information tools of the organization—a so-called "initiative." CGD initiatives are practical proposals aimed to improve the policies and practices of rich countries, international bodies, and others of means and influence to reduce global poverty and inequality. They draw upon the center's research and engagement with decision-makers to pursue these aims. Each year, since 2003, the CDI has scored wealthy governments on their record of helping poor countries. It ranks twenty-two of the world's richest countries based on their dedication to policies that benefit poor nations worldwide. The index is intended to educate and inspire the rich-world public and policy makers about how much they could do to help the global poor. It is intended to spark new debates about the effects of rich-country policies on developing countries and to encourage research about how best to measure them. It hopes to inspire a "race to the top" by motivating advocacy inside and outside government for more development-friendly policies.

Data for the annual CDI is compiled from a variety of sources, including the Organization for Economic Co-operation and Development and its Development Assistance Committee, the World Bank, the United Nations High Commissioner for Refugees, the United Nations

Framework Convention on Climate Change, the Centre d'Etudes Prospectives et d'Informations Internationales, the International Energy Agency, and other organizations, along with inputs from academic researchers. When large, standardized data sets are not available for certain indicators, CGD and its collaborators collect and compile information country by country. All index data and code is available for download in accordance with CGD's data transparency policy. The CDI has become a valuable tool for policy makers around the world. As stated on their website: "Finland and the Netherlands use the index as an official performance metric for their development policy, and the UK's Department for International Development lists the index as a measure of overall Whitehall policy coherence. Most recently, a senior USAID official confirms that the Obama White House, 'views the CDI as a key metric by which to assess over time the results of President Obama's anticipated global development policy'" (http://www.cgdev.org/page/impacts-and-influence, accessed April 15, 2014).

The index is a major tool in making the knowledge base of CGD legible, in Scott's (1998) words, to a wider audience, and to manifest accountability through transparency, as Marilyn Strathern (2000, 2005) has suggested. It reflects as well the general reliance on quantification and measurement, and the rise of a "culture of indicators" (Merry 2011), in which indicators and similar technologies are trusted to be able to organize complex information.

Another tool that works as a window to the world, providing close-up insights into complex global problems, is the so-called Wonkcast. I was acquainted with this on only my second day at CGD, at the weekly Communication Team Meeting. The meeting is convened in order to coordinate the planning of upcoming events, to help members decide which expert is to be featured on the website and what the lead story of the week will be, and to pick up on unforeseen events.

We were seated in the kitchen area that Tuesday morning—an open, light area with large windows overlooking the greenery of Dupont Circle, adjacent to the library area and to the open-office landscape. The team comprised close to twenty people, including research assistants, most of whom were present. Mike greeted everyone, and introduced me as their "in-house anthropologist," who was going to be their guest over the next couple of months. He said he expected everyone to greet me with their usual warm hospitality. Introductions around the table followed, with team members briefly presenting themselves, their backgrounds, and their areas of responsibility. Most of them were relatively young college graduates in their mid-to-late twenties, sparkling with talent and ambition. I had a difficult time recalling all their names, but over time, as things settled into some sort of daily rhythm, I received a relatively good overview of who did what and their educational and professional experiences and aspirations.

Mike then turned our attention onto the Wonkcast: "We need to think about possible Wonkcasts. Something post-Pakistan." "What on earth is a Wonkcast?" I asked myself. Jamie, who was in charge of publications, later explained to me that:

> The Wonkcast is the name we came up with for the podcast. So that's the weekly audio interview that Mike does, usually with one of our fellows, but sometimes with a visitor. So we tried to come up with a name that—something more interesting I guess than CGD's podcasts. So I think it was Mike's idea of the Wonkcast, and I can't remember who came up with it [at first], but he liked it.

I asked him whether *wonk* actually meant something, and was told:

> Well, wonk, it plays off—it might be someone who spends much time studying and has little or no social life, but policy wonks are people who are I guess kinda technocratic and into the details of policies and kind of—I don't what the word is—it's probably something like nerd.... Yeah. So there are a lot of wonks in D.C., and I guess we are—we house a few of them.

So, in the Global Prosperity Wonkcast, Mike interviews CGD experts and others on innovative, practical policy responses to poverty and inequality in a globalizing world. This interview is then placed on the website.

The CDI, the Wonkcast, and other tools though which the CGD collects, packages, and distributes information and knowledge are crucial to the mission of the think tank. These tools do not just report on the world as it is, but capture particular dimensions of it, and contribute to providing images and scenarios of the world. They provide a narrative of world events and nurture imaginaries of possible trajectories.

The D.C. Bubble: The World Writ Large?

Scale-making, Anna Tsing (2005: 88) notes, "is a foundational move in establishing the neutrality and universalism of Nature; only if observations are compatible and collapsible across scales can they be properly described by a universal logic. Yet to 'think globally' is no easy task." Although the focus of her study is a different one, undertaken in a different part of the world (the "zone of awkward engagement" between various organizational and community interests, in the rainforests of

Indonesia), the basic idea is valid for the practices of think-tank experts as well. The tools and technologies used by them, such as the indexes, the blogs, and the reports, are instances of scale-making that render the complexity of the world graspable and actionable. The knowledge that is produced by think-tank experts needs to be crafted and packaged in a manner that makes it possible to act upon it: to advance a point of view, provide a grand narrative, propose policy, and make decisions. Only by being actionable can knowledge gain traction and eventually influence and impact. The daily operations of think tanks are geared to this end and followed through in a sophisticated set of routinized practices. Practices form part of scale-making projects, with their sights set on different scales: the D.C. community of intellectuals and politicians, the domestic political scene, the regional, and the global. Linking U.S. domestic concerns to larger issues, such as development aid to Pakistan, or linking the U.S. budget crisis to global financial crisis and regulation gaps, knits the world together and projects images of the global.

The interface position of think tanks as both citadels for public intellectuals and event-driven advocates for policy change places them in an ideal position of brokerage between spheres of action, between the academic community and the political stage, and between scientific expertise and lobbyists. Think-tank experts are creolizers *par excellence*. This capacity also relies on a cultivated capacity for reflexivity, which involves not only a continuous deliberation and debate on how events are to be understood and interpreted, providing layers upon layers of interpretations and renderings, but also on a continuous questioning of the very ground on which they operate. Think-tank organizations may very well be instances of condensed power and expertise, manifestations of the workings of "soft power" (Nye 2004, 2011), but they are liquid fields, continuously undermined and reconstituted by way of strategic networking investments and savvy acts of brokerage. The global swirl around Dupont Circle is in constant motion.

The think tank, then, derives its position and influence mainly based on its ability to produce expertise and robust knowledge that may then enter and move in politically charged policy circuits. The relation between expert knowledge and public action is a complicated one. In the last instance, these circuit flows are purposeful. There are places to which think tanks do not go and issues with which they do not engage. The policy wonk's concern with and critique of global inequality is thus bounded by the interests of the funding base, the political inclinations of the organization's experts, and the political and media channels that are left ajar. Furthermore, knowledge and expertise are packaged, creolized, and targeted to intended audiences in acts of brokerage. In this sense, despite the ambitions of mapping the world at large, the map remains partly patchy, and there are still large territories to explore.

Notes

1. In late 2013, the Center for Global Development moved to a new nearby location on L Street.
2. For a fuller description of the history of think tanks in the U.S., see Abelson (2006), Dickson (1971), McGann (2007), Medvetz (2012), Rich (2004), Smith (1991), Stone (1996, 2001), and Weidenbaum (2008).
3. Melissa Fisher (2012) experienced similar challenges to access in her fieldwork among female Wall Street investors, where her way into the field was to a large extent dependent upon getting the right connections from the right person.
4. Think tanks therefore resemble what Ahrne and Brunsson (2011) have described as "partial organizations." As a partial organization, they make use of some, but not necessarily all, the organizational elements that characterize a complete, formal organization, and they exist in a partly organized environment.
5. The expression "the clash of civilizations" was proposed by political scientist Samuel P. Huntington. It suggests that people's cultural and religious identities will be the primary source of conflict in the post-Cold War world. This thesis was developed in a 1993 *Foreign Affairs* article entitled "The Clash of Civilizations?" in response to Francis Fukuyama's (1992) book, *The End of History and the Last Man*, and expanded in Huntington's (1996) *The Clash of Civilizations and the Remaking of World Order*. Fukuyama's view was that the advent of Western liberal democracy may signal the end point of humanity's sociocultural evolution and the final form of human government. The expression "the world is flat" emanates from the international bestselling book by Thomas Friedman (2005), *The World Is Flat: A Brief History of the Twenty-first Century*, which analyses globalization, primarily in the early twenty-first century. The title is a metaphor for viewing the world's commerce as a level playing field, where all competitors in the global market are seen to enjoy equal opportunities, and where historical and geographical divisions are becoming increasingly irrelevant.

References

Abelson, D.E. 2006. *A Capitol Idea: Think Tanks & US Foreign Policy*. Montreal and Kingston: McGill-Queen's University Press.

Ahrne, A. and N. Brunsson. 2011. "Organization outside Organizations: The Significance of Partial Organization." *Organization* 18(1): 83–104.

Bailey, F.G. 1969. *Stratagems and Spoils: A Social Anthropology of Politics*. New York, NY: Shocken Books.

Barley, S.R. 2010. "Building an Institutional Field to Corral a Government: A Case to Set an Agenda for Organization Studies." *Organization Studies* 31(6): 777–805.

Bierschenk, T., J.P. Chaveau, and J.P. Olivier de Sardan. 2002. *Local Development Brokers in Africa: The Rise of a New Social Category*. Working Paper No. 13, Department of Anthropology and African Studies. Mainz: Johannes Gutenberg University.

Boissevain, J. 1978. "Of Men and Marbles: Notes towards a Reconsideration of Factionalism." In *A House Divided: Anthropological Studies of Factionalism*, ed. M. Silverman and R.F. Salisbury. Halifax: Memorial University of Newfoundland, pp. 99–110.

Calhoun, C. and R. Sennett. 2007. "Introduction." In *Practicing Culture*, ed. C. Calhoun and R. Sennett. Oxon: Routledge.

Coleman, S. and P. Collins. 2006. *Locating the Field: Space, Place, and Context and Anthropology*. London: Berg.

Dickson, P. 1971. *Think Tanks*. New York, NY: Atheneum.

Fisher, M. 2012. *Wall Street Women*. Durham, NC: Duke University Press.

Friedman, T.L. 2005. *The World Is Flat: A Brief History of the Twenty-first Century*. New York, NY: Farrar, Straus & Giroux.

Fukuyama, F. 1992. *The End of History and the Last Man*. New York, NY: Free Press.

Garsten, C. 1994. *Apple World: Core and Periphery in a Transnational Organizational Culture*. Stockholm Studies in Social Anthropology, No. 32. Stockholm: Almqvist & Wiksell International.

———. 2008. *Workplace Vagabonds: Career and Community in Changing Worlds of Work*. Basingstoke: Palgrave Macmillan.

———. 2009. "Ethnography at the Interface: 'Corporate Social Responsibility' as an Anthropological Field of Enquiry." In *Ethnographic Practice in the Present*, ed. M. Melhuus, J. Mitchell and H. Wulff. Oxford: Berghahn, pp. 56–68.

———. 2013. "All about Ties: Think Tanks and the Economy of Connections." In *Organizational Anthropology: Doing Ethnography in and among Complex Organizations*, ed. C. Garsten and A. Nyqvist. London: Pluto Press, pp. 139–154.

Gusterson, H. 2009. "The Sixth Branch: Think Tanks as Auditors." New York, NY: Social Science Research Council. Working Paper, March.

Hannerz, Ulf. 1969/2004. *Soulside: Inquiries into Ghetto Culture and Community*. Chicago, IL: University of Chicago Press.

———.1987. "The World in Creolisation." *Africa* 57: 546–559.

———. 1992. *Cultural Complexity: Studies in the Social Organization of Meaning*. London: Routledge.

———. 1997. "Flows, Boundaries and Hybrids: Keywords in Transnational Anthropology." *Mana* 3: 7–39.

———. 2003. "Being There…and There…and There! Reflections on Multi-sited Ethnography." *Ethnography* 4(2): 201–216.

———. 2009. "Geocultural Scenarios." In *Frontiers of Sociology*, ed. P. Hedström and B. Witrock. Annals of the International Institute of Sociology, 2. Leiden: Brill, pp. 267–288.

———. 2010. *Anthropology's World: Life in a Twenty-first Century Discipline*. London: Pluto Press.

Holmes, D. and G.E. Marcus. 2005. "Cultures of Expertise and the Management of Globalization: Toward the Re-functioning of Ethnography." In *Global Assemblages: Technology, Politics and Ethics as Anthropological Problems*, ed. A. Ong and S.J. Collier. Malden, MA: Blackwell Publishing, pp. 235–252.

Huntington, S.P. 1993. "The Clash of Civilizations?" *Foreign Affairs* Summer 72(3): 22–49.

———. 1996. *The Clash of Civilizations and the Remaking of World Order*. New York, NY: Touchstone.

James, Deborah. 2011. "The Return of the Broker: Consensus, Hierarchy, and Choice in South African Land Reform." *Journal of the Royal Anthropological Institute* (N.S.) 17: 318–338.

Latour, B. 1996. *Aramis, or the Love of Technology*. Cambridge, MA: MIT Press.

Marcus, G.E. 1998. *Ethnography through Thick and Thin*. Princeton, NJ: Princeton University Press.

McGann, J.G. 2007. *Think Tanks and Policy Advice in the United States: Academics, Advisors and Advocates*. New York, NY: Routledge.

Medvetz, T. 2012. *Think Tanks in America*. Chicago, IL: University of Chicago Press.

Merry, S.E. 2011. "Measuring the World: Indicators, Human Rights, and Global Governance." *Current Anthropology* 52(3): 83–95.

Meyer, J.W. and R.L. Jepperson. 2000. "The 'Actors' of Modern Society: The Cultural Construction of Social Agency." *Sociological Theory* 18(1): 100–120.

Mitchell, T. 2002. *Rule of Experts: Egypt, Techno Politics, Modernity*. Berkeley, CA: University of California Press.

Moore, D.S. 2000. "The Crucible of Cultural Politics: Reworking 'Development' in Zimbabwe's Eastern Highlands." *American Ethnologist* 26(3): 654–689.

Mosse, D. 2005. *Cultivating Development: An Ethnography of Aid Policy and Practice*. London: Pluto Press.

Nye, J.S. Jr. 2004. *Soft Power: The Means to Succeed in World Politics*. New York, NY: Public Affairs.

———. 2011. *The Future of Power*. New York, NY: Public Affairs.

Power, M. 2003. "The Invention of Operational Risk." London School of Economics, Centre for Analysis of Risk and Regulation, Discussion paper no. 16.

Rabinow, P. and G.E. Marcus, with J.D. Faubion and T. Rees. 2008. *Designs for an Anthropology of the Contemporary*. Durham, NC: Duke University Press.

Rahman Kahn, S. 2011. *Privilege: The Making of an Adolescent Elite at St. Paul's School*. Princeton, NJ: Princeton University Press.

Rich, A. 2004. *Think Tanks, Public Policy, and the Politics of Expertise*. Cambridge: Cambridge University Press.

Riles, A. 2009/2006. "Introduction: In Response." In *Documents: Artifacts of Modern Knowledge*, ed. A. Riles. Ann Arbor, MI: The University of Michigan Press, pp. 1–38.

Rothkopf, D. 2008. *Superclass: The Global Power Elite and the World They Are Making*. New York, NY: Farrar, Straus & Giroux.
Sassen, S. 1998. *Globalization and Its Discontents*. New York, NY: The New Press.
———. 2008. "Neither Global nor National: Novel Assemblages of Territory, Authority and Rights." *Ethics & Global Politics* 1(1-2): 61–79.
Scott, J.C. 1998. *Seeing Like a State: How Certain Schemes to Improve the Human Condition Have Failed*. New Haven, CT: Yale University Press.
Smith, J.A. 1991. *The Idea Brokers: Think Tanks and the Rise of the New Policy Elite*. New York, NY: The Free Press.
Stone, D. 1996. *Capturing the Imagination: Think Tanks and the Policy Process*. Portland, OR: Frank Cass.
———. 2001. "The 'Policy Research' Knowledge Elite and Global Policy Processes." In *Non-state Actors in World Politics*, ed. D. Josselin and W. Wallace. London: Palgrave, pp. 113–132.
Strathern, M. 2000. "The Tyranny of Transparency." *British Educational Research Journal* 26(3): 309–321.
———. 2005. "Robust Knowledge and Fragile Futures." In *Global Assemblages: Technology, Politics and Ethics as Anthropological Problems*, ed. A. Ong and S.J. Collier. Malden, MA: Blackwell Publishing, pp. 464–481.
Tsing, A.L. 2005. *Friction: An Ethnography of Global Connection*. Princeton, NJ: Princeton University Press.
Wallace-Wells, B. 2003. "In the Tank: The Intellectual Decline of AEI." *Washington Monthly*, December. (Retrieved April 15, 2014, from http://www.washingtonmonthly.com/features/2003/0312.wallace-wells.html)
Wedel, J.R. 2009. *Shadow Elite: How the World's New Power Brokers Undermine Democracy, Government, and the Free Market*. New York, NY: Basic Books.
Weidenbaum, M. 2008. *The Competition of Ideas: The World of Washington Think Tanks*. New Brunswick, NJ: Transaction Press.
———. 2010. "Measuring the Influence of Think Tanks." *Society* 47: pp. 134–137.
Westbrook, D.A. 2008. *Navigators of the Contemporary: Why Ethnography Matters*. Chicago, IL: The University of Chicago Press.

Chapter 5

Reflexivity Reloaded
From Anthropology of Intellectuals to Critique of Method to Studying Sideways

Dominic Boyer

"Reflexivity" is a term that has currency in contemporary social-cultural anthropology but not always clear or positive connotations. I recall a telling conversation with a colleague from another university several years ago in which she rolled her eyes when I said that I thought her work was exemplary reflexive anthropology. I had meant this as a compliment but she began shaking her head immediately: "Oh, I'm not interested in *that* kind of a project. I'm not interested in solipsistic and self-satisfied anthropology." She had in mind, as it turned out, the anthropology she associated with the so-called "reflexive turn" of the 1980s, with works of James Clifford (1998) and George Marcus (Clifford and Marcus 1986; Marcus and Fischer 1986) and with their works' critical reception (e.g., Behar and Gordon 1996). My colleague identified herself as an activist anthropologist, as someone whose work was collaboratively oriented to the social challenges and political struggles facing the people with whom she worked. Reflexive anthropology had little to contribute to such work, she thought; it was too insular and narrowly academic a discourse that, for example, mulled abstract concerns with representation and knowledge, at best with the politics of representation and knowledge, rather than pursuing an "engaged anthropology," as she termed it—an anthropology that sought to address and, if possible, to remediate some human condition external to itself. I nodded along as she spoke because we all are familiar with this vision of reflexive social science (perhaps especially reflexive anthropology) as a self-cocooned and somewhat enigmatic enterprise; as a mode of criticism that has often focused in theory, textuality, and autobiography rather than extending itself into obvious political engagement or other ethical concerns. Historically speaking, reflexive social science's interventions in the domains of philosophy and theory have often been quite magnificent (Mannheim 1936, 1993) but even in their most politicized modes (e.g., Bourdieu and Wacquant 1991) they have often been restricted to matters of theory and knowledge (see Boyer 2005: 278–279), thus easily leaving themselves vulnerable to the assertion that the core of reflexivity is a virtuosic critical self-interest in social science's own analytic and representational methods that has little to offer anthropology other than a certain narcissistic pleasure of deeper self-concern. As one of my former teachers, Marshall Sahlins, used to joke, "As the native said to the postmodern anthropologist, 'that's enough about you, let's talk about me for a while.'"

Since I do not see narrow self-orientation as being an acceptable understanding (not to mention practice) of reflexivity, however, I would like to take the opportunity of this essay to revisit the past, present, and future of reflexivity in anthropology especially in light of recent research in the anthropology of knowledge and expertise. As more ethnographers have come to be interested in professionals, intellectuals, and other experts as interlocutors, and in knowledge practices, networks, and institutions as sites of ethnographic inquiry, and as they have probed the internal dynamics and political efficacy of "cultures of expertise," I believe that the horizon of reflexive anthropology has expanded laterally in a rather dramatic fashion. This expansion is recasting the ethical and political dimensions of anthropological reflexivity in ways that very effectively unsettle a distinction of "reflexive" from "engaged" anthropology (see, for example, Boyer 2008; Brenneis et al. 2005; Hannerz 2003; Holmes and Marcus 2004, 2008; Powell and Schwegler 2008; Rabinow 2009; Shore et al. 2009; Strathern 2000).

As will be discussed in this chapter, reflexivity has become increasingly central to anthropology (and to the social sciences more generally) as part of the transformation and pluralization of social knowledge formation in western intellectual cultures. Reflexivity, as I conceive it, is not, or not only, a voluntary condition of intellectual practice (e.g., a particular critical or analytical disposition one chooses) but also an ideological reflection of the growing phenomenological and epistemological salience of contingency in intellectual culture. By attending to the ideological dimension of reflexivity, this chapter traces the historical emergence of what can be viewed as increasingly engaged and ethically attentive modes of reflexive anthropology. In conclusion, it is argued that the burden of justification could well be shifted to those who wish to maintain an "engaged anthropology" purified of reflexivity to explain on what ethical and epistemic grounds it is possible and valid for them to do so. Engaged anthropology freed of reflexive attention to its social-historical contingencies of production would seem to me a blueprint for dogmatic epistemic conservatism (which I would suspect is the opposite intention of my colleague and many other critics of "reflexive anthropology").

Anthropological Reflexivity 1.0: Paul Radin's Anthropology of Intellectuals

Reflexive anthropology, it should be emphasized, was no invention of the 1980s. On the one hand, reflexive anthropology should be situated within the development of the social sciences since the eighteenth century and its gradual investment of epistemic attention in contextual contingency as a mediating factor shaping positive science and its forms of knowledge. Indeed, one could actually see reflexivity's emphasis on self-knowledge-in-context as a somewhat distilled figuration of the core legitimating condition of the social sciences more generally: that is, recognition of the importance of biographical, social, historical, and cultural conditions for the pluralization of human ways of knowing and forms of knowledge. The ideological truth conditions of reflexive awareness are discussed below, but it is just as important to identify the more specific prehistory of distinctly anthropological modes of reflexivity. In the 1920s and 1930s, some members of the Boasian school of American anthropology were already thinking critically about the place of intellectuals in society and about the ethnographic challenge of producing expert knowledge about other kinds of cultural experts (such as shamans, for example). The emblematic text from this tradition is Paul Radin's *Primitive Man as Philosopher*, a text that deserves to be read as the prolegomenon to any future reflexive anthropology. Published in 1927, Radin's book was the first sustained effort in professional anthropology to discuss the effects of the social specialization of knowledge upon practices of field research, analysis, and intercultural representation central to ethnographic methodology.

A major argument of Radin's text is that ethnologists of so-called "primitive" societies had hitherto misapprehended the ideational capacity of non-Western humanity because of the ethnologists' own socialization as cultured scholars. Instead of identifying a division of mental and material orientations in primitive societies parallel to those of more "civilized" societies—a division which Radin argued produced genuine, philosophically oriented "thinking men" among all primitive peoples—ethnologists had perpetrated the fallacy that all primitives simply had less differentiated logical and cognitive capabilities than moderns (here Radin had the works of E.B. Tylor (1970), Sir

James Frazer (1890), and especially Lucien Lévy-Bruhl (1996) in mind). In Lévy-Bruhl's case at least, Radin's reading offers some of its own fallacies. Although no less critical of Lévy-Bruhl, E.E. Evans-Pritchard later clarified that Lévy-Bruhl's category of the "Prelogical does not mean alogical or anti-logical. Prelogical, applied to primitive mentality, means simply that it does not go out of its way, as we do, to avoid contradiction[;] … he means by 'prelogical' little more than unscientific or uncritical, that primitive man is rational but unscientific or uncritical" (1965: 82).

More relevant to this discussion is why Radin felt that ethnologists such as Frazer and Lévy-Bruhl had underestimated the logical capabilities of so-called "primitive men." The key to the ethnological misapprehension lay, for Radin, in the greater sensual and pragmatic orientation of primitive man that first estranged the rationalist ethnologist-scholar and then encouraged him to focus on the sense-dependency of the primitive men rather than their cognitive capabilities. Radin wrote, "Paradoxical as it may seem, it is nevertheless a fact that few people are, on the whole, so unfitted by temperament to study the simpler aspects of the life of primitive people, and by implication their emotional and intellectual manifestations, as the average cultured scholar and university-trained ethnologist. It is really a marvel that they have done so well" (1927: 11).

Prone to overestimate and to overvalue the role of thought in culture because of their own cultured intellectualism, Radin continued, the ethnologists' efforts at achieving balance often "fall into the opposite error—that of reducing most of the spiritual values of primitive civilizations to those of mere delight in sensations" (ibid). Since sensualism is the antithesis of the Western intellectual's own life, it transitively becomes the locus of distinction for what is defined as "primitive." Thus, according to Radin, ethnologists are oriented, unintentionally perhaps, toward neglecting the subtlety of ideation among their fellow thinkers in primitive societies in favor of the more overtly sensual or mechanistic cultural expressions of non-intellectual social actors.

One of the more unsettling implications of Radin's argument is that the ethnologist and the primitive philosopher actually have more intellectually and sociologically in common with one another than either might share with the "men of action" in their own societies. This is, when one considers it, an idea that would have radical consequences for the legitimacy of anthropology to decipher the distinctive social and semiotic orders that unify and represent, in the tradition of Durkheim (1995), entire collectivities. On the one hand, Radin argues that the native "collectivity" of cultural order is fictitious insofar as its expectation of predictable collective order occludes a continuous dialogical politics of cultural knowledge and representation between intellectuals and non-intellectuals. On the other hand, where a sense of collectivity does emerge, it originates in the interpretation of native philosophical works by ethnologists since both groups of intellectuals share a common orientation toward objectifying cultural knowledge, an orientation toward ordering, indeed collectivizing, knowledge that loses its residue of intellectual artifice and is made instead "cosmological" in the process of anthropological analysis. As Bernhard Giesen has written, intellectuals are best understood as specialists in generalization (1998: 45). According to Radin, anthropological knowledge is thus a kind of interpretive objectification and generalization of native intellectual work, a knowledge that purports to represent collective cultural knowledge even though it is only, in fact, partially representing the cultural labors of a particular social class.

The moral of Radin's text, in my reading, is that all anthropology is in some ways already the anthropology of intellectuals. Any process of anthropological representation seeks to formalize the knowledges inhabiting another place and time and involves the cultivation of intellectual exchange systems to mediate the acquisition and evaluation of local knowledge. In these exchange systems, anthropologists typically rely heavily upon the intellectual labors of local knowledge specialists, who provide not just testimony but rather socio-cultural analyses that prefigure and orient the attention and analytics of the anthropologist. In U.S. anthropology such interlocutors have traditionally been called "key informants." They are people who, like Victor Turner's collaborator, Muchona the Hornet, help the anthropologist from their places within, or on the margins of, their own societies to objectify and to interpret epistemic, symbolic, and habitual orders in the practice of everyone else's everyday life (Turner 1967: 131–150). With such intellectual collaboration central to all anthropological research, Radin's anthropology of intellectuals might be seen as more than a marginal curiosity, or as an early anticipation of Laura Nader's famous call to "study up" (1969). Like later research in the anthropology of intellectuals (e.g., Bourdieu 1988; Boyer 2005; Feierman 1990; Herzfeld 1997; Lomnitz 2001; Taylor 1997; Verdery 1991; Warren 1998), it draws attention to the constitutive social tensions and relations within the process of making anthropological knowledge.

Radin's project thus already occupies the terrain of what much later came to be termed the "reflexive turn" in anthropology. Yet Radin also highlights what seems to me an enduring ethical dilemma for anthropological practice. If anthropological knowledge is indeed driven by a collaborative engagement between specialized knowledge-makers (or "intellectuals") then the real question is not how to do an anthropology of intellectuals but rather how *not* to do an anthropology of intellectuals; that is, how to prevent oneself from becoming so seduced by and invested in the aesthetically and ideationally familiar knowledge-work of one's sociological counterparts that one comes to ignore the understandings and lives of social actors with other epistemic dispositions. This could be just as much a dilemma for contemporary "engaged" anthropology as for "reflexive" anthropology, depending on the kinds of research methods and spectrum of interlocutors involved. Radin's work gestures very clearly toward the epistemic and ethical considerations that have come to orient contemporary reflexive anthropology of experts and cultures of expertise.

On the Eventual (Re)invention of Reflexive Anthropology

The timing of Radin's intervention suggests that "reflexive anthropology" has a certain redundancy to it. Rather than considering reflexivity as something that anthropology discovered (or that discovered anthropology) some time between the late 1960s and the mid 1980s, it seems more appropriate to consider reflexivity (meant here as attention to the contingencies of knowledge) as an integrating epistemic and methodological feature of anthropology from its disciplinary origins. Or, if one insists that "reflexive anthropology" be viewed as a subdisciplinary orientation in its own right, one would have to acknowledge that it has been invented more than once. One might add that the modern profession of anthropology established itself through a series of debates over the character of knowledge and rationality within which the character of scientific anthropological knowledge was contentiously discussed (Darnell 2001). The comparativist method of figures such as Edward Tylor and Sir James Frazer was eventually labeled amateurish and displaced to the margins of a new inventory of conceptual and methodological techniques associated with the modern, "professional" anthropology. Here, the chartering disciplinary works of self-identifying "anthropologists" such as Bronislaw Malinowski and Franz Boas (for example, participant-observational methods and non-unilinear, pluralist models of culture and cultural development) were already reflexive actions aimed at challenging the Victorian evolutionists' claim to rigorous empirical science. Disciplinary consolidation around the legitimating professional pillars of field research, participant observation, and pluralist-historicist methods of cultural analysis set the stage for a period of relative comfort with structural-functional field studies of bounded cultural and social assemblages in the years after the end of the Second World War. This was also, not incidentally, an era of significant disciplinary growth as abundant governmental and foundational funding for Cold War area studies research (notably the Foreign Area Fellowship Program) and for international development and democracy initiatives created the platform for a massive expansion in anthropology's professional ranks. According to data gathered by the American Anthropological Association, in 1950 there were only twenty-two anthropology Ph.D.'s awarded in the United States. By 1974, the annual Ph.D. production rate had risen twenty-fold to 409, reflecting the establishment of a raft of new anthropology departments and faculty lines, an equivalently massive expansion in the research output of the discipline, and a professional association that was measured in the thousands rather than the hundreds of members. The 1950s and 1960s were the boom years of professional anthropology, with the attentions of critical reflexivity perhaps somewhat dulled by the thrills and headaches of rapid disciplinary expansion.

It seems interesting, and again likely not incidental, that the return of anthropological reflexivity came precisely as the boom years ended. There was no "bust" exactly; a "plateau" would be more accurate. The average annual output of Ph.D.'s, for example, remained remarkably steady (from 360 to 460) between 1974 and 1995. But federal funding of graduate training dropped off dramatically (from 39 percent of doctoral students in 1972 to only 19 percent in 1990) and especially striking was the decline in governmental support for field research funding (from 51 percent of projects in 1972 to only 17 percent in 1988). Most importantly, the percentage of anthropology Ph.D.'s who were able to move from doctoral training into professorial positions in academic anthropology dropped very significantly from 74 percent in the early 1970s to under 40 percent by the late 1980s. Some of this drop was accounted for by the increasing success of anthropology Ph.D.'s at finding academic positions outside of anthropology, but not all of it. Even as the ranks of the professional community of anthropology swelled, it was hard to avoid a sense of abandonment by former benefactors and anxieties about a downward trajectory and growing irrelevance. Not only was a phase of rapid growth ending but normative social reproduction (in the form of Ph.D.'s finding positions in the field) was becoming compromised as well. Indeed, the difficulty of finding academic employment (either in anthropology or outside of it) has become an unavoidable presence and standard index of "professional crisis" ever since. But the sheer mass of knowledge and plurality of anthropological voices since the 1970s is surely part of this crisis story as well. As anthropology became a professional community measured in the tens of thousands rather than the hundreds, it appeared to lose its unifying conversations, concepts, and luminaries. But this is not an unambiguous sign of crisis; perhaps anthropology had simply become such an expansive and heterogeneous field of knowledge that it was difficult to define its core any more.

Moreover, trends such as the evident overproduction of Ph.D.'s and the increasing marketization of professional life can surely not be restricted to academic anthropology. Broader political-economic processes such as the postwar Keynesian expansion of public education across the world (which guaranteed both a boom in academic enrollments and positions and their subsequent plateaux) and the 1980s rise of neoliberal policy regimes with decreased governmental expenditures in research and higher education clearly generated similar trends within a great many academic disciplines and institutions. But this is somewhat beside the point: trends are almost inevitably enigmatic in their origins and scale. Sometimes, conspiratorial and/or transparential fantasies (West and Sanders 2003; Boyer 2006) are invoked to explain a sense of collective anxiety or downward mobility (as, for example, when German intellectuals in the late nineteenth century translated their own impressions of political blockage and social decline into a grand language of the assault of "mass culture" on the nation; see Boyer 2005). But blame can also be fantastically hyperlocalized. If anthropologists, for example, sense that their conditions of social reproduction have been made vulnerable then is it not reasonable for them to assume that this vulnerability has something to do with anthropology? Perhaps it is a problem with anthropology's theories or methods? Perhaps with its declining relevance or audience or ascending marketization or professionalism? As epistemically inclined actors, displacing one's own anxieties about "ontological security" (Jackson 1998) onto alleged crises of discipline and disciplinary knowledge makes perfect sense. For, it is precisely the insecure contingencies of professional life (the anxieties and opacities of competition and reproduction, for example) that invite explanation and redress, not its often more experientially secure core of professional practice (research, writing, teaching) and institutions. Disciplinary knowledge offers a perfect site of insecurity as a circulating "form" whose intrinsic polysemy guarantees uncertain value and efficacy. And disciplinary knowledge thus invites—demands, even—reflexive attention under the social conditions just outlined. One could even think of reflexivity as a kind of therapeutic impulse in response to the intensification of social vulnerability, a displacement of rising social vulnerability into a sense of rising epistemic vulnerability where vulnerability itself can be addressed and worked at under less immediate, and thus ontologically threatening, terms.

This is, to my mind, the ideological basis of reflexivity, where we should consider "ideology" not as "false consciousness" but rather as the transformation of practical intuitions into truth propositions (Boyer 2010: 89–90; Marx and Engels 1932). Reflexivity has long played this role; it really is just another name for the ideological recognition of epistemic contingency that has accompanied modern western social theory and philosophy since its origins in a seventeenth- and eighteenth-century metropolitan, European intellectual culture desperately struggling to organize an increasing volume of cultural data arriving at the hands of its legions of social mediators (missionaries, tradesmen, soldiers, explorers, naturalists, and administrators, among others). Most often, early European social theory did everything it could to dampen down the radical potential of this data to undo Christian and European exceptionalism under the signs of civilizational errors, inadequacies, and eventually pathologies (and, for this reason, the strongest civilizational challenger to the West, China, always found itself at the bottom of some scale of validity). But to see the various theologies of early social theory solely as acts of domination is to miss also their recognition of epistemic vulnerability in the context of accumulating signs that European societies were a few among a multitude and that the cultural and technical elements of their civilization were by no means incontrovertibly distinct, let alone superior. Reflexive attention to the conditions of epistemic contingency increasingly became a focus of social theoretical enterprise during the nineteenth century and beyond. Hegelian philosophy could be seen as the tipping point: one finds in Hegel's philosophy of history the first (paratheological) articulation of a theory of universal contingency in his centering of dialectical relationality as the motivating principle and method of being.

To return to anthropology, one can see a decisive shift between the late 1960s and the late 1980s to reincorporate reflexive attention as a central feature of anthropological knowledge. The structural-functionalist paradigms of the 1950s and early 1960s that emphasized not only the organicity of societies and the unity of cultures but also that these organic unities were more or less transparently accessible to and decodable by anthropological methods were slowly modulated into the symbolic, interpretive, and praxiological paradigms of the late 1960s and 1970s. Reflexivity was reinvented here, particularly by Marxian praxiologists, as part of a critical engagement of social power and inequality, not least of professional anthropology's longstanding conviviality with the extension and exercise of Western colonial, imperial, and postcolonial power (e.g., Hymes 1969; Asad 1973; Rosaldo and Lamphere 1974).

However, the critique of social power was only the leading edge of what could be termed "second generation" reflexive anthropology. With the growing intuitiveness of the cybernetic semiologies of French structuralism and poststructuralism, textualist paradigms of analysis became more salient in the 1970s and 1980s and anthropologists began to explore the critique of ethnographic representation and fieldwork method (e.g., Rabinow 1977; Dumont 1978). Likewise, landmark constructivist praxiological accounts (e.g., Anderson 1983; Hobsbawm and Ranger 1983) popularized the analytical language of "imagined communities," "invented traditions," and "cultural practices" in anthropology. This involved a qualitative shift in the validity claims of anthropological knowledge. Instead of committing oneself as an anthropologist to surfacing a social/cultural ontology construed as already present in the world and ready to be worked over interpretively, one committed oneself instead to situating the dynamic practices and processes through which such a social/cultural ontology might be conceived, constituted, and reproduced. In other words, the contingent (often historical) constitution of social and cultural knowledge emerged as a central object of anthropological research practice either in tandem with or to the exclusion of studies of collective cultural knowledge (in the Durkheimian sense of *sui generis* collective representations). Before Clifford and Marcus's *Writing Culture* had even been published, reflexive attention to epistemic contingency was thus well established in anthropological knowledge. *Writing Culture* was a lightning rod of the transition, certainly, but the project only generated the controversy that it did because it spoke an intuitive truth whose principles were widely understood even if its implications were still unaccepted: that is, anthropology had entered a phase of decisive social transformation. The 1980s debates over representation cemented the ideological displacement from social to epistemic vulnerability in the space of anthropological self-knowledge rather than generating it (in contrast to the impression at the time that the "reflexive turn" was itself stimulating the disruption of anthropological practice).

James Faubion has reflected that the true stakes of second-generation reflexive anthropology was a "professional self-critique" of "the disciplinary pretension ever to have produced anything that could count as genuine knowledge," given the "prevailing ethics of anthropological connectivity" (2009: 149). The stakes were thus something more foundational than a settling of accounts with the discipline's imperial and colonial legacies; second-generation reflexive anthropology reactivated and massively elaborated the reflexive critique of method (involving, of course, field methods, analytical methods, and representational methods) that had begun with the Boasians but largely lain fallow during the boom years. It did so for ideological reasons—to create disruptions in anthropological knowledge symmetrical to the "ontological" disruptions already being sensed in professional anthropological life—but, as Faubion rightly notes, also for ethical reasons: the opening of the question of what would make for better anthropological method and "connectivity." In retrospect, this was perhaps one of the most successful outcomes of the second generation of reflexive anthropology. Opening the problem of method to creative intervention resulted in the legitimation of a plurality of new modes of anthropological engagement, including perhaps most famously "multi-sited" methodology (Marcus 1995) and deepened anthropological engagement with science and other "cultures of expertise" (Holmes and Marcus 2004). The shift from critique of method to these new, positive programs of anthropological inquiry is, to my mind, the gradual (but also decisive) threshold between second- and third-generation reflexive anthropology.

Third-Generation Reflexive Anthropology: Studying Sideways, Epistemic Partnership, and Para-sitism

With the gradual centering of reflexivity in anthropological knowledge since the early 1970s, it would be difficult to identify anthropological research practice that incorporated no reflexive attentions whatsoever. Third-generation reflexive anthropology is thus in some respects indistinguishable from mainstream social-cultural anthropology more generally, which is in large part why I argue below that it would be better to talk about "anthropological reflexivity" (as an aspect of anthropological knowledge) rather than "reflexive anthropology" (as though reflexivity were a thematic subfield of inquiry like "political anthropology" or "medical anthropology"). At the same time, it is clear that some research and writing in anthropology is more reflexively concerned with and attuned to its own reflexivity than others. In particular, I would like to draw attention here to the growing body of research on and with other expert and professional formations (including most notably scientists), a research domain that has not only been extremely conceptually generative (e.g., Haraway 1991; Latour 1988; Rabinow 2003) but also helped advance second-generation reflexive concerns with anthropological methods and ethics into new experiments with collaborative epistemic partnership.

Ulf Hannerz' pathbreaking research on foreign correspondents is exemplary here. Hannerz deliberately modulated Nader's critical injunction to "study up" into a proposal to "study sideways;" that is, to look "at others who are, like anthropologists, in a transnational contact zone, and engaged there in managing meaning across distances, although perhaps with different interests, under other constraints" (1998: 109). What is both epistemologically and ethically important in Hannerz' proposal (and subsequent ethnographic practice: see Hannerz 2003) is his resistance to the kinds of interprofessional politics of jurisdiction that drench so many potential epistemic contacts in suspicion and caricature.

> We have again and again been made somewhat irritatedly aware of the presence of these other kinds of transnational practitioners in our habitat, and of the affinities between their lines of work and ours, even as we frequently dispose of that irritation with a shrug or a sneer. Mostly, it is clear, we have tended not to approach them as allies in the pursuit of knowledge and the enlightenment of publics, but rather we quietly keep our distance, holding our own efforts to be either intellectually or morally superior (or both). (Hannerz 1998: 109–110)

Hannerz' "studying sideways" suggests instead a method of reflexive connectivity that takes the intimacy of shared practices and concerns as a baseline for the development of dialogues that help to interilluminate (both critically and affirmatively) the techniques both kinds of practitioners have developed in the field of transnational representation and analysis (as well as their shared and divergent interests and conditions of knowledge-making).

Hannerz' sideways comparisons of models of intellectual practice among cultures of expertise have been extended by others into the exploration of more full-blown collaborative connectivities (see, e.g., Falzon 2009). Doug Holmes and George Marcus's work on "para-ethnography" (2004) and "epistemic partnership" (2008) is one of the most extensive examples of this move. "Para-ethnography" is a conceptual designation for the reflexive ethnographic awareness that exists more or less latently in other cultures of expertise and bureaucratic-institutional settings and whose recognition can set the stage for projects of epistemic partnership to solicit ethnographic and reflexive insight valuable to both ethnographer and expert practitioner (for a parallel discussion of the existence and significance of "para-theory" see Boyer 2010). Holmes and Marcus recognize the danger of ignoring the para-ethnographic, even para-anthropological, modes of knowledge circulating among our research interlocutors as well as the opportunities that such knowledge affords anthropological research within other cultures of expertise. As Hannerz also argues, there is more to be gained from treating our interlocutors not simply as data-delivering "informants" and more as collaborative "allies" or "partners" in processes of ethnographic exploration, analysis, and representation (also Westbrook 2008). After all, we should not underestimate the extent to which experts' (or others') reflexive awareness of their ways of knowing and forms of life could helpfully co-inform our own research process, just as the research intervention may offer our partners a much-needed excuse for self-reflection, feedback, and experimental reconfigurations of their own. In my own research experience, I have found that the para-ethnographic awareness of journalists both to their own professional contingencies and to the difficulties of social analysis and representation have been immensely instructive, representing a kind of ceaseless second education for me in ethnography and social theory. At the same time, my ethnographic work of research and social analysis has generally been welcomed by my journalistic partners as a kind of "para-journalism" that operates as a gathering and discussion point for their own reflexive attentions to their professional activity. This dual commitment to temporarily suspending the habitus of everyday professional knowledge in order to listen to Lévi-Straussian "other messages" seems to me a much better and indeed more ethical model of anthropological knowledge-making than the usual "epistemophagy" (Boyer 2008) in which one culture of expertise is allowed to absorb another's self-knowledge without the demand or expectation of reflexive transformation in the process.

A series of lateral institutional forms that have emerged from third-generation reflexive research appear to confirm this impression. Paul Rabinow's ARC (Anthropological Research on the Contemporary) "collaboratory" has been one very active instance and the platform for several successful collaborative projects (http://anthropos-lab.net/about). George Marcus's Center for Ethnography Initiative at the University of California-Irvine has been another and one that has helped to extend conversations on para-ethnography in very fruitful ways (http://www.socsci.uci.edu/~ethnog/). Rabinow and Marcus have published a lengthy discussion of contemporary concept work and research design in anthropology (Rabinow et al. 2008) with an eye toward extending the third-generation shift away from critique of method and toward positive, reflexive "refunctioning" of anthropological research, especially in the context of work among experts. One of the more impressive of these experiments in research design has been the Irvine Center's emphasis on creating the basis for a particular kind of modular research experiment and technique of graduate pedagogy that Marcus terms "para-sites."

The Center's online charter for the para-site reads:

> In the absence of formal norms of method covering these de facto and intellectually substantive relations of partnership and collaboration in many contemporary projects of fieldwork, we would like to encourage, where feasible, events in the Center that would blur the boundaries between the field site and the academic conference or seminar room. Might the seminar, conference, or workshop under the auspices of a Center event or program also be an integral, designed part of the fieldwork?—a hybrid between a research report, or reflection on research, and ethnographic research itself, in which events would be attended by a mix of participants from the academic community and from the community or network defined by fieldwork projects. We are terming this overlapping academic/fieldwork space in contemporary ethnographic projects a para-site. It creates the space outside conventional notions of the field in fieldwork to enact and further certain relations of research essential to the intellectual or conceptual work that goes on inside such projects. It might focus on developing those relationships, which in our experience have always informally existed in many fieldwork projects, whereby the ethnographers finds subjects with whom he or she can test and develop ideas (these subjects have not been the classic key informants as such, but the found and often uncredited mentors or muses who correct mistakes, give advice, and pass on interpretations as they emerge).

As Marcus has recently explained, one of the key motivations for the para-site was to "find ways of doing theory in continuous relation to the distinctly non-'meta' immersive quality of thinking during fieldwork" (Deeb and Marcus N.d.: 40; Deeb and Marcus 2011). The para-site is thus a kind of deliberate experimental interruption or "disruption" in the field research process with the intent of staging a reflexive (and potentially collaborative) encounter between research partners: "It embraces the opportunity to deal in unsettled working concepts, analytic strategies, and ethnographic ways of thinking that the fieldworker may appropriate critically for her own eventual individual purposes." Moreover, "para-sites thus can be seen as precociously enacting collaborative norms in the conduct of fieldwork that still tends to be conceived canonically in professional culture as individually conducted and reported" (Deeb and Marcus N.d.: 9). The para-site thus (ideally) creates a foundation in graduate pedagogy for the early enactment of collaborative norms and practices. This is what I find to be the most intriguing and important feature of the model from the point of view of the future of anthropological reflexivity. The move to focus on pedagogy as a site of reflexive intervention (Faubion and Marcus 2009) completes, in a certain sense, the work of "reflexive anthropology." What began as a critical concern with the methods and ethics of anthropological connectivity has now moved into an experimental, and undoubtedly positive, phase of play, care, and remediation. There is no blueprint here and no telos. But it seems clear to me that if experiments like the para-site are able to further develop, diversify, and circulate that reflexive anthropology will have finished its long journey from the ideological companion of vulnerable professional reproduction to the (far more interesting if no less ideological) project of transforming the methods of anthropological research and reproduction. Although I should be clear that I think this passage remains incomplete, there is no harm in looking further ahead.

Conclusion: From Reflexive Anthropology to Anthropological Reflexivity

To return to my opening anecdote, there is certainly nothing wrong with questioning the political relevance and ethical intentions of reflexive anthropology. But to define reflexive anthropology as a subfield as precisely that part of anthropology where political and ethical concerns are neglected in favor of the solipsistic pursuit of precious self-knowledge seems to me almost willfully ignorant. Reflexivity is a commonplace rather than an exceptional attention in anthropological knowledge today and it has helped shape and attune many of anthropology's most original and important contemporary engagements, including a great many projects that are explicitly political in their objects and objectives (e.g., Graeber 2009). So one might turn the question around and ask: on what basis could one legitimately divorce one's research and oneself from reflexivity in anthropology today? I think the colleague mentioned in my opening anecdote would have been aghast at the implications of this question for precisely the reason that the willful suspension of attention to epistemic contingency is more or less how we could define "political conservatism." At the very least, suspending reflexivity is a hallmark of a great many ideological projects ("ideological" here in the more classical Althusserian sense of dominant and dominating knowledge) that seek to establish some regime of epistemic certainty by disabling or damping down recognition of that regime's epistemic contingencies. On the contrary, I believe my colleague had a great appreciation for "anthropological reflexivity" (the centering of concerns of epistemic contingency), even though she rejected the banner of "reflexive anthropology." The banner is, needless to say, not what should concern us. Recognizing the centrality (and plurality) of anthropological reflexivity to (and within) contemporary anthropological knowledge is.

That is also to say that anthropologists need to work harder, or more obviously, at extending the political commitment and ethical intentions of their reflexivity. Third-generation reflexive anthropology is in the process of leaving an inspiring but also challenging legacy in this respect and future anthropological reflexivity needs to engage and to build upon it; but, in keeping with the experimental ethos of contemporary reflexivity, I do not see the need for any singular, programmatic model of extension. Rather, to stay within the framework of ethics, two general considerations seem important: the ethics of language use and the ethics of publicity. With regard to the former, anthropological reflexivity needs to find language(s) through which to articulate its reflexive impulses and attentions that communicate better and more widely than has often been the case in the past. In other words, we need to develop ways of thinking and talking about the core concern of reflexivity (epistemic contingency) that are not sealed by expert jargon into the pathways of professional discourse. Rather, we need languages that seek constantly to vernacularize themselves. I do not want to underestimate the difficulty of vernacularization since the contingent reflections of reflexivity often thrive productively in opposition to the commonsense languages of both professional and popular knowledge. In the former case, we need to continue to articulate reflexivity as a positive program in anthropological knowledge rather than a horizon of more or less self-referential criticism. In the latter, we need to develop means of communication that are persuasive and generous with non-experts—media that destabilize the caricaturing tendencies of dominant ideologies without utilizing "expertise" and expert registers of communication as weapons to bludgeon other interlocutors into pedagogical relationships. I agree with Matti Bunzl that constantly asserting the complexity or subtlety of our knowledge is not a very effective tactic for reaching a wider audience (2008: 58), especially in a distracted field of knowledge circulation in which simplicity is sometimes not just elegance but necessity. I also agree with Bunzl's critics that there is a necessary friction between "ethnography's interest in nuance and the glibness of some punditry" (Besteman and Gusterson 2008: 63) for which we need not apologize. Here again, I think the metaphor of "therapy" is apt—persuasion must be uniquely tailored to its communicative environment; it only works effectively when there is self-aware, generous, and caring intersubjective exchange. We should think about anthropological reflexivity as foremost a persuasive practice, as a communicative commitment to translate the concerns of epistemic contingency into knowledge-forms that are intelligible and relevant to experts and non-experts alike.

Regarding the ethics of publicity, it is true that anthropologists would do well to become much more aggressive and active in their dealings with intellectual culture at large (González 2004; Besteman and Gusterson 2005). Ultimately, the best defense against a phenomenology of seclusion and loss is to take our craft beyond the more limited networks of academic communication. Anthropological reflexivity can build upon the work of third-generation reflexive anthropology to develop productive relationships and partnerships with other professional and intellectual communities, other cultures of expertise, all of whom possess their own internal traditions of reflexive awareness and thinking. Indeed, building alliances of reflexive awareness both among and beyond a plurality of "cultures of expertise" seems to me an excellent goal for anthropological reflexivity. The para-site is one exemplary model but we can and should develop other parallel interventions as well. Another goal, which I have advocated previously (Boyer 2005: 279–280), would be to work to exceed the phenomenology and culture of expertise by making reflexivity into a method of life rather than a method of expert knowledge. I take inspiration here from colleagues—again, many of whom would not identify themselves as "reflexive anthropologists"—who have followed the threads of their academic work into other kinds of humanistic commitments (or vice versa), including social activism (David Graeber, Hugh Gusterson, Barbara Rose Johnston, Laura Nader, Terence Turner), prose and poetry (Ruth Behar, Paul Friedrich, Amitav Ghosh, Michael Jackson, Francis Nyamnjoh), film and media production (John Jackson, Meg McLagan, Maple Razsa, Lucien Taylor), health and medicine (Paul Farmer, Nancy Scheper-Hughes), and performance art and curation (Craig Campbell, Lina Dib, Tarek Elhaik), among many other possible domains.

Rather than valorize these or any other particular forms or agendas for future reflexivity, however, I would rather highlight the common sense of restlessness with professional anthropology that is expressed by all of these trajectories. What is vital, I think, is to develop a collective appreciation for, and valuation of, the importance of transprofessional experiments and forays in anthropological practice. If we take the ethics of anthropological reflexivity seriously, they should urge us to undermine, rather than imitate, specialized, exclusionary, and connoisseurial economies of elite cultural production. In practice, such reflexivity would have little patience with professional crisis narratives and redemption proposals. These would be rather besides the point of extending the horizon and circulation of our attentions to epistemic contingency. Anthropological reflexivity should therefore above all refocus its time and energies into the practice of persuasions and partnerships that look beyond a narrow disciplinary definition of the anthropological.

References

Anderson, Benedict. 1983. *Imagined Communities*. New York: Verso.
Asad, Talal, ed. 1973. *Anthropology and the Colonial Encounter*. New York: Humanities Press.
Behar, Ruth and Deborah A. Gordon, eds. 1996. *Women Writing Culture*. Berkeley: University of California Press.
Besteman, Catherine and Hugh Gusterson, eds. 2005. *Why America's Top Pundits Are Wrong*. Berkeley: University of California Press.
———. 2008. "A Response to Matti Bunzl: Public Anthropology, Pragmatism and Pundits." *American Anthropologist* 110(1): 61–63.
Bourdieu, Pierre. 1988. *Homo Academicus*. [Translated by Peter Collier.] Stanford: Stanford University Press.
Bourdieu, Pierre and Loïc J.D. Wacquant. 1992. *An Invitation to Reflexive Sociology*. Chicago: University of Chicago Press.
Boyer, Dominic. 2005. *Spirit and System*. Chicago: University of Chicago Press.
———. 2006. "Conspiracy, History, and Therapy at a Berlin *Stammtisch*." *American Ethnologist* 33(3): 327–339.
———. 2008. "Thinking through the Anthropology of Experts." *Anthropology in Action* 15(2): 38–46.
———. 2010. "On the Ethics and Practice of Contemporary Social Theory: From Crisis Talk to Multiattentional Method." *Dialectical Anthropology* 34(3): 305–324.
Brenneis, Don, Cris Shore, and Susan Wright. 2005. "Getting the Measure of Academia: Universities and the Politics of Accountability." *Anthropology in Action* 12(1): 1–10.
Bunzl, Matti. 2008. "The Quest for Anthropological Relevance: Borgesian Maps and Epistemological Pitfalls." *American Anthropologist* 110(1): 53–60.
Clifford, James. 1988. *The Predicament of Culture*. Cambridge, MA: Harvard University Press.
Clifford, James and George E. Marcus, eds. 1986. *Writing Culture*. Berkeley: University of California Press.
Darnell, Regna. 2001. *Invisible Geneaologies*. Lincoln: University of Nebraska Press.
Deeb, Hadi and George E. Marcus. N.d. *The WTO as Para-Site: Seeking Illumination in the Green Room*. Unpublished Ms.
———. 2011. "In the Green Room: An Experiment in Ethnographic Method at the WTO." *PoLAR* 34(1): 51–76.
Dumont, Jean-Paul. 1978. *The Headman and I*. Austin: University of Texas Press.

Durkheim, Emile. 1995. *The Elementary Forms of Religious Life*. [Translated by Karen Fields.] New York: Free Press.
Evans-Pritchard, Edward Evan. 1965. *Theories of Primitive Religion*. Oxford: Clarendon Press.
Falzon, Mark-Anthony, ed. 2009. *Multi-sited Ethnography: Theory, Praxis and Locality in Contemporary Research*. Burlington: Ashgate.
Faubion, James D. 2009. "The Ethics of Fieldwork as an Ethics of Connectivity, or The Good Anthropologist (Isn't What She Used to Be)." In *Fieldwork Is Not What It Used to Be*, ed. James D. Faubion and George E. Marcus. Ithaca: Cornell University Press, pp. 145–164.
Faubion, James D. and George E. Marcus, eds. 2009. *Fieldwork Is Not What It Used to Be*. Ithaca: Cornell University Press.
Feierman, Steven. 1990. *Peasant Intellectuals*. Madison: University of Wisconsin Press.
Frazer, James G. 1890. *The Golden Bough*. New York: MacMillan.
Giesen, Bernhard. 1998. *Intellectuals and the Nation*. [Translated by Nicholas Levis and Amos Weisz.] Cambridge: Cambridge University Press.
González, Roberto J. 2004. *Anthropologists in the Public Sphere*. Austin: University of Texas Press.
Graeber, David. 2009. *Direct Action: An Ethnography*. Oakland: AK Press.
Hannerz, Ulf. 1998. "Other Transnationals: Perspectives Gained from Studying Sideways." *Paideuma* 44: 109–123.
———. 2003. *Foreign News: Exploring the World of Foreign Correspondents*. Chicago: University of Chicago Press.
Haraway, Donna. 1991. *Simian, Cyborgs and Women*. New York: Routledge.
Herzfeld, Michael. 1997. *Portrait of a Greek Imagination*. Chicago: University of Chicago Press.
Hobsbawm, Eric and Terence Ranger, eds. 1983. *The Invention of Tradition*. Cambridge: Cambridge University Press.
Holmes, Douglas and George E. Marcus. 2004. "Cultures of Expertise and the Management of Globalization: Toward the Re-functioning of Ethnography." In *Global Assemblages*, ed. Aihwa Ong and Stephen J. Collier. New York: Blackwell, pp. 235–252.
———. 2008. "Collaboration Today and the Re-imagination of the Classic Scene of Fieldwork Encounter." *Collaborative Anthropologies* 1: 81–101.
Hymes, Dell, ed. 1969. *Reinventing Anthropology*. New York: Vintage Books.
Jackson, Michael. 1998. *Minima Ethnographica*. Chicago: University of Chicago Press.
Latour, Bruno. 1988. *Science in Action*. Cambridge: Harvard University Press.
Lévy-Bruhl, Lucien. 1996. *How Natives Think*. [Translated by Lillian A. Clare.] New York: Washington Square Press.
Lomnitz, Claudio. 2001. *Deep Mexico, Silent Mexico*. Minneapolis: University of Minnesota Press.
Mannheim, Karl. 1936. *Ideology and Utopia*. [Translated by Louis Wirth and Edward Shils.] New York: Harcourt, Brace and Company.
———. 1993. "The Problem of a Sociology of Knowledge." In *From Karl Mannheim*, ed. Kurt H. Wolff. New Brunswick: Transaction Publishers, pp.187–243.

Marcus, George E. 1995. "Ethnography in/of the World System: The Emergence of Multi-sited Ethnography." *Annual Review of Anthropology* 24: 95–117.

Marcus, George E. and Michael Fischer. 1986. *Anthropology as Cultural Critique: An Experimental Moment in the Human Sciences*. Chicago: University of Chicago Press.

Marx, Karl and Friedrich Engels. 1932. "Die deutsche Ideologie." In *Marx/Engels Gesamtausgabe*, I(5), ed. Vladimir Adoratskij. Berlin: Marx-Engels Verlag.

Nader, Laura. 1969. "Up the Anthropologist—Perspectives Gained from Studying Up." In *Reinventing Anthropology*, ed. Dell Hymes. New York: Pantheon, pp. 284–311.

Powell, Michael G. and Tara Schwegler. 2008. "Unruly Experts: Methods and Forms of Collaboration in the Anthropology of Policy." *Anthropology in Action* 15(2): 1–9.

Rabinow, Paul. 1977. *Reflections on Fieldwork in Morocco*. Berkeley: University of California Press.

———. 2003. *Anthropos Today*. Princeton: Princeton University Press.

———. 2009. "Prosperity, Amelioration, Flourishing: From a Logic of Practical Judgment to Reconstruction." *Law & Literature* 21(3): 301–320.

Rabinow, Paul and George E. Marcus (with James Faubion and Tobias Rees). 2008. *Designs for an Anthropology of the Contemporary*. Durham: Duke University Press.

Radin, Paul. 1927. *Primitive Man as Philosopher*. New York: D. Appleton and Company.

Rosaldo, Michelle and Louise Lamphere, eds. 1974. *Woman, Culture and Society*. Stanford: Stanford University Press.

Shore, Cris, Susan Wright, and Davide Pero, eds. 2009. *Policy Worlds: Anthropology and the Anatomy of Contemporary Power*. London: Berghahn.

Strathern, Marilyn, ed. 2000. *Audit Cultures*. London: Routledge.

Taylor, Lucien. 1997. "Mediating Martinique: The 'Paradoxical Trajectory' of Raphael Confiant." In *Cultural Producers in Perilous States*, ed. George E. Marcus. Chicago: University of Chicago Press, pp. 259–330.

Turner, Victor. 1967. *The Forest of Symbols: Aspects of Ndembu Ritual*. Ithaca: Cornell University Press.

Tylor, Edward B. 1970. *Religion in Primitive Culture*. New York: Harper & Row.

Verdery, Katherine. 1991. *National Ideology under Socialism*. Berkeley: University of California Press.

Warren, Kay. 1998. *Indigenous Movements and their Critics: Pan-Maya Activism in Guatemala*. Princeton: Princeton University Press.

West, Harry G. and Todd Sanders, eds. 2003. *Transparency and Conspiracy*. Durham: Duke University Press.

Westbrook, David A. 2008. *Navigators of the Contemporary*. Chicago: University of Chicago Press.

Chapter 6

ON ANTHROPOLOGISTS AND OTHER CULTURAL INTERPRETERS

Thomas Blom Hansen

A decade ago, a colleague of mine in the U.K. told me: "I think anthropology is dying. Everything is so full of consciousness and reflexivity. The days when we could describe alien worlds that just *were there*—incomprehensible, contained, and in themselves—they are over for good. Even ethnography has been hijacked by other disciplines."

For all its nostalgic gloominess, this sentiment captures something important about the profound transformations of the conditions under which cultural interpretation, including anthropology, can be performed and presented today. Let me outline three contradictions that mark the work of anthropology today. Firstly, there is little doubt that anthropology today experiences something of a global triumph as a perspective and as a set of methods. The social sciences have undergone a narrative and interpretative turn as a whole—although one finds strong and assertive countercurrents such as the dominance of rational-choice models and formal and mathematical modeling in much of political science, economics, and sociology. However, the prestige of anthropology—its theories, the value of long-term fieldwork, the importance of understanding the world of one's informants by learning native languages and idioms, and the overall value of ethnographic methods—has never been higher. As anthropology left its islands and isolated mountain ranges and entered the cities and their diverse modernities, it did in many ways become the royal road to understanding different and surprising social worlds. This has been recognized by major organizations and governments and today there are thousands of anthropologists working in aid agencies, government services, financial institutions, global corporations, NATO, and the U.S. Army. Ethnography is no longer the preserve of anthropology. Many sociology programs take ethnography more seriously as a method than many anthropology departments. The fundamental idea of studying a "field" and the "natives" that inhabit this field—even if it exists down the road from one's own dwelling—has taken firm root in the social sciences. Yet, anthropologists experience a recurrent sense of marginality in the universities and in the public. Anthropologists feel perpetually undervalued and neglected in public debates that invariably feed on simplified assumptions about identity, religion, and the territorial boundedness of cultures. At the moment of its real breakthrough in a world which increasingly understands itself in terms of cultural clashes and frontlines, many anthropologists feel that no one is interested in their actual insights and fine-grained analyses of agency, meaning, alterity, and experience.

This sense of loss, it will be argued here, is linked to the second contradiction at work: the conceptual vocabulary of anthropology—culture, memory, identity, religious attachment, ritual, senses of *communitas*, ideas of proper kinship and sexual morality, and much more have now become central elements in vigorous, well-articulated, vernacular public debates across the world. Many of these themes were first explored by colonial ethnographers, and subsequently taken up by nationalists in their search for authentic ethnic and national cultures.[1] Later, across the postcolonial world, notions of cultural attachment, collective religious sentiment, and cultural heritage became central to national curricula in schools, social reforms, and struggles between governments and popular movements, religious institutions, and so on. Arguments that base themselves on cultural practices and discrete cultural identities have more purchase today, in most of the world, than just a few decades ago. We live in an age of cultural objectification and cultural heritage where the right to have and own cultural meaning, authentic belonging, inviolable religious sentiment, and a native identity is stronger and more legitimate than ever. Objects of craft and art are no longer just artifacts in museums signifying territorialized cultures (e.g., "Statuette, Eastern Malawi, ca. 1700 AD"). They are now conceptualized as works of art and expression that can be precisely dated and given authorship; or be commodified as tourist art and ethnic chic emblematic of a specific culture.[2] Cultural artifacts, music, medicinal herbs, etc. are rapidly becoming legal entities, copyrighted brands that can be owned and claimed as property of a whole class of people, albeit often controlled by a tiny entrepreneurial elite (Comaroff and Comaroff 2009). Not only modernity is at large, as Appadurai formulated it almost two decades ago (Appadurai 1996), but also cultural authenticity as a right, an entitlement, and a naturalized element of human life is at large across the world. In such an environment of extensive "culture talk" in our public cultures, it is very difficult to claim expertise on cultural knowledge as such, or even expertise on how to interpret cultural expressions and identities. In our increasingly textualized and articulate public cultures across the world, every assertion or analysis of a cultural expression, ritual, or practice by an anthropologist will be contested by local intellectuals, by those with particular political agendas, by ethnic entrepreneurs, and so on—invariably insiders whose knowledge of the vernacular tongue, local history, and the subtleties of their societies is often more than a match for the anthropologist's knowledge. This is not a new phenomenon and well known to any social scientist who has worked in areas of the world with old and established literary and intellectual traditions. Among anthropologists, the longstanding suspicion among Native Americans vis-à-vis anthropology as a profession is perhaps one of the best known examples of the brittle standing of the "anthropologist-as-expert."

This leads on to the third contradiction we live with: the general depletion of the authority of expert knowledge of academics and experts in the social sciences and humanities. Populations are becoming ever-better educated and societies are suffused with easily accessible information on virtually every conceivable subject via resources accessible through the Internet, from Google to Wikipedia. Neither knowledge, nor interpretation, nor cultural competences in languages and ritual practices can be said to be a scarce resource commanded and controlled by academics and specialists. In the richer parts of the world, both educated, financially secure people and recent labor migrants living in polyglot and multicultural environments are often more widely traveled than the average anthropologist. Even in her secure institutional environment at the university, the anthropologist encounter many students with broader, more multicultural and multilingual backgrounds than her own. How can one even begin to claim expertise and authority on cultural interpretation in such an information-rich environment where every piece of information, textualized statement, blog commentary, or authentic YouTube clip has already been interpreted, framed, and debated many times over?

When Culture Writes Itself

It has been customary for more then twenty five years now to introduce students of anthropology to the reflexive turn in our discipline that is widely attributed to the publication of Clifford and Marcus's volume *Writing Culture* (Clifford and Marcus 1986). This volume began to sensitize anthropologists to their responsibility vis-à-vis the wider world of cultural and textual representation—to the powers and perils of textual objectification and authorization of certain representations through books and texts published by recognized university presses and journals. It was indeed a critique of the self-proclaimed "expert knowledge" of anthropologists. It was an important and seminal intervention but today this text reads as dated. Its diagnosis of the authority of textual representation seems somewhat overblown, considering the real depletion of the authority of texts as a whole and the current transformations of the conditions of cultural interpretation summarized above. It even seems as if the volume, and the many texts that followed in its wake, take a much too limited and almost purified view of the relationship between a powerless, non-textualized set of cultural practices of various natives and the powerful and authoritative voice of the (Western) academy. For someone who has spent all his career working in contexts and countries marked by highly articulated, vernacular intellectual cultures and extremely politicized everyday practices (in India and South Africa), the tenor of *Writing Culture* has always seemed to exaggerate the real authority of the academy. Like much of the older anthropology it critiqued, it downplayed the plurality of native voices, the many local people who eloquently claim the authority to represent and interpret their own cultural practices.

In today's world, the anthropologist is merely one voice among others producing cultural interpretation. The authority of scholarly work is guaranteed neither by institutional position and a standing among peers, nor by a detached or "objective" point of view, although many of our informants still willingly accord us such a privilege. Anthropologists swim in a sea of narratives and stories, including accounts by local vernacular historians and works by journalists and fiction writers, whose stories often are more compellingly written and more dramatic than those of the average anthropologist. The standard criticism from anthropology of such competing accounts is that they are shallow, or based on relatively uncritical recirculation of already existing standard narratives and prejudices one finds well established in one's field site. This criticism implies, of course, that anthropology, through close engagements of people over time and by employing reflexivity and sophisticated theoretical tools, can produce a more comprehensive, authentic, and also more ethically defensible picture of people, situations, and communities.[3] If this is so, the most complex challenge that anthropologists are facing at this particular juncture is to make themselves relevant, readable, and compelling in a cacophony of voices in a larger market of texts and representations where academic authority counts for less than ever before.

This has been brought home to me in the last decade by the surging public interest in my most intense and absorbing field site ever, the megacity of Mumbai in India. When I began my work in the city in 1990, the scholarship was almost entirely dominated by labor history and sociological enquiries into the rich working-class history that had developed during the twentieth century around the city's massive textile mill districts. My own work on the mass support for the city's most important ethnoreligious political movement, the nativist and rightwing Shiv Sena movement, was not unprecedented. However, broader anthropological studies of the city and its many overlapping, antagonistic, and adjacent sociocultural worlds were sparse at this point. When my book on the city was published in 2001, a host of very able scholars, such as Sujata Patel, Arjun Appadurai, and the historian Raj Chandavarkar, were doing research on the city as such (Chandavarkar 1994, 1998, 2009; Appadurai 2000a, 2000b; Patel and Thorner 1997; Patel and Masselos 2005); but the real change only came a few years later when a range of popular books, films, and novels on the city, and especially its mythical underworld, achieved phenomenal success in a wider public.

The bloody conflicts and pogroms in the city in the early 1990s had been the theme of several documentaries and Mani Ratnam's controversial Bollywood film *Bombay* from 1995. Yet, it was only in the beginning of the new century that the underworld and the seamy sides of the city really caught the imagination of a wider public and, as always in India, it involved Bollywood. With popular films like *Satya* (1998), *Company*, (2002) and *D* (2005) (referring to Dawood Ibrahim, the city's most notorious don), the director Ram Gopal Varma set an influential trend. Many others followed, among them the more art-house inspired *Maqbool* (Vishal Bhardwaj, 2003) (*Macbeth* adapted to a contemporary gangster drama), and the scene was set for a much more colorful and romantic take on the city and its underworld. In the world of English-language literature, Salman Rushdie had put the city firmly on the map, albeit more as a backdrop to parts of *Midnight's Children* (1980) and *The Moor's Last Sigh* (1995) than as an object in its own right. The Canada-based author Rohinton Mistry had for some time portrayed life in Mumbai in gritty detail but it was only with the highly successful book *Maximum City* (2004) by Suketu Mehta that the city as such became part of the consciousness of a mass reading public both globally and within India itself. Mehta tells his own story of a Bombay-born boy who after many years in the U.S.A. returns to explore and understand the enormous and diverse world that is Mumbai. He goes in search of the secrets and hidden sides of the city, and, as in local lore, he finds its true heart of darkness in some of the old Muslim neighborhoods that also have given birth to its biggest and most famous criminal organizations. Mehta explores this world and its semipsychotic "shooters" and errand boys. He also ventures into the seedy and mysterious world of the beer bars—the places where girls dancing to Bollywood tunes entice the city's small businessmen, daredevils, gangsters, policemen, and many others. The men shower their favorite girls with cash and favors and indulge in intense fantasies of romance and true love. The bars allow for a relatively instant and plebeian version of the grand romances between landlords and their favorite courtesans that remain a crucial trope in the cultural repertoire of romantic love on the Indian subcontinent.

In Mehta's work, and even more in Vikram Chandra's thriller Sacred Games (2007) and in the earlier account of the deadly serial blasts in Mumbai in 1993, *Black Friday* (2005) by the journalist Hussain Zaidi, the policeman assumes a central position as interpreter and raconteur of the city. Chandra's massive novel tells the intertwined story of the life of a gangster and a policeman, both of them superior connoisseurs of the city, its people, and its dirty secrets. The last decade has also seen a virtual explosion of the mediascape across India with a proliferation of television channels. Among them multiple 24-hour news channels and the highly popular crime channels that follow police officers on duty as they bust criminal rackets, arrest corrupt officials, and line up suspects, mostly lower caste and poor Muslims, in front of the cameras. In all these cases, the police have become the central pivot around which both knowledge and certainty in the city revolves.

For the Mumbai police force, which a thorough public investigation in the late 1990s indicted for its shameful, corrupt, and brutal pro-majority conduct during the riots in 1992–1993 (Hansen 2001), the new publicity and their newfound roles as protectors of the city have been much welcomed. Here lies a serious problem in many of the highly entertaining accounts of the city. When I did my fieldwork in Mumbai in the 1990s, it soon became clear to me that the very notion of "the underworld" itself is highly unstable and heavily mythologized. The main providers of information about the underworld to journalists, writers, scriptwriters, and anthropologists are, in fact, police officers, who have a clear and vested interest in reproducing a narrative of a fearsome and all-powerful world of gangsters. This portrait is often rendered in the tradition of Mario Puzo's classic *Godfather* trilogy and justifies almost unlimited discretion in eliminating, torturing, and incarcerating suspects. The clear majority of the convicts in the city's prisons are Muslims, although they as a group make up less that 17 percent of the population. A series of bomb blasts culminating in a bloody attack on landmarks in the city in 2008 afforded the police another opportunity to portray Muslims as terrorists, "anti-nationals," and traitors.

Another thing I learned in Mumbai in the 1990s was that the police force is almost entirely dependent on local informers who sell information to the police in exchange for protection and business opportunities. The system of transfers of police officers from district to district at short intervals was originally designed to limit corruption but rarely allows higher-ranking officers to build up an independent knowledge of localities. They remain dependent on lower-ranking officers and constables and their longstanding relationships with local semi-legal businesses, real estate developers, and local busybodies. The result is that the stories and powerful fictive accounts of the city of Mumbai that now circulate worldwide are incredibly indebted to a certain structure of knowledge reproduced by the police department and devoured by the dominant, Hindu middle classes and elites in the city. In this new and emerging story, the normal and secure life of a city is constantly threatened by criminals, terrorists, and a corrupting underworld. With global aspirations, the city's elite has imported an essentially American (North and South) idea of urban life as necessarily pervaded by security considerations. Like other Indian cities, Mumbai has a stunningly low rate of common and violent random crime, except the internal and often domestic violence that is endemic to many low-income neighborhoods. Instead, a burgeoning privatized security industry has become a technology devoted to keeping the city's poor majority out of its many new privatized public spaces—shopping malls, promenades, and parks. In Mumbai, security is not really protection from crime: it is mainly a form of "social security."

This is the context in which the anthropologist must find his or her niche: as a producer of disavowed perspectives, non-standard narratives, minority accounts, and alternative mappings and understandings of the city, rapidly being recast by a powerful new bourgeoisie. Classical anthropology saw its role as providing counterpoints to a homogenizing and universalizing narrative of Western modernity as the unquestionable standard against which everything else could be measured. The pockets of unadulterated wildness and primitiveness on islands and in remote highlands were supposed to teach "us" about our own past, and that the category of the human was wider and more diverse than could be ascertained in Europe and North America alone. This older project challenged neither colonialism nor bourgeois culture and mainly affirmed the boundaries between the primitive, the traditional, and the modern. Modern anthropology has a different role to play in telling the disavowed and unacknowledged stories of the undersides of contemporary capitalist modernity—the margins, the slums of Mumbai, the ethnic underclass in Europe, the new, criminalized "Muslim villains" of India's self-confident modernity, and much else. However, unlike classical anthropology, we must attempt to represent these worlds in a way that is not patronizing. We must have due respect for the multiple ways in which people, however marginal and impoverished, desire to represent themselves and to speak for themselves.

In practice, this is a complicated challenge, as the next example will show.

Writing Your Culture—No Thanks!

I have recently published a book based on a ten-year-long engagement with social life in a formerly Indian township in Durban. (Hansen 2012) The township was created as a flagship for apartheid's great project of socioracial engineering in the 1950s, the Group Areas Act, according to which race was to be converted into a spatial category, as each racial group would inhabit its own townships and areas in the country. The official apartheid ideology was a form of colonial multiculturalism aiming at reducing tension and conflict in a diverse society. The reality was of course a systematic protection and furthering of the interests, livelihoods, and good life of approximately five million whites who have since the 1960s enjoyed one of the highest standards of living anywhere in the world. The varied groups of people who had come to South Africa as indentured laborers and traders from different parts of the Indian subcontinent from 1860 onwards were gradually compressed into a single racial category: Indians. Indians were also regarded as a "permanent minority"—as people who were intrinsically alien to the African soil and thus never to be expected to fit into what the colonial authorities and later apartheid state saw as an intrinsically Christian society built on Western values.

The people who lived in the present-day township were diverse in caste, in linguistic background, and in religion (Hindus, Muslims, and Christians) and had been forced into the area from a variety of locations in and around the city. After almost forty years of forced coexistence, the notion of a specific and shared South African Indian identity had nonetheless become quite well articulated. However, as apartheid collapsed in the early 1990s, Indians were, like other communities in the country, forced to redefine themselves vis-à-vis the new democratic state and vis-à-vis their neighboring communities. Like everybody else, they were trying to make sense of what living in freedom actually entailed. More than a decade after the moment of freedom, many of my informants were disappointed and appalled by the changes that have taken place in the country. Many have experienced the loss of secure jobs in the erstwhile protected labor market that today gives preference to the Africa majority; thousands of Africans have moved into the erstwhile purely Indian neighborhoods and schools; crime rates have shot up throughout the country; and much more. Their experience is not unique but their intense anxieties about (re)defining and representing their identities in a new South Africa were very pronounced.

The view of Indians as an "alien" minority has not really changed since 1994. Well-entrenched anti-Indian feelings among the Zulu-speaking African majority in the city and the province resurfaced at regular intervals. The old colonial stereotype about Indians as uniquely steeped in family life, tradition, and religion had been firmly rejected by many young, well-educated, and politically radical Indians during the apartheid era. However, in the 1990s this notion of a deep Indian culture has in a paradoxical way returned. The township I worked in was suffused by religious fervor and cultural activism of every conceivable variety, often appended to global formations: neo-Hindu sects, Pentecostal churches, radical Muslims, Hindu nationalist and traditionalists, modern gurus. All of these found in the township a receptive audience that frantically searched for new foundations, new certainties, and affirmation in a diverse and often perplexing global cultural economy.

Enter the anthropologist with a good deal of experience from South Asia who walked around the township, lived there, and became known as the "white *ou* (man) who writes a book about us." Several things happened that no textbook on fieldwork could have prepared me for: first, I became a very minor local celebrity who regularly appeared in the local media, and in photographs of social and cultural events of an Indian hue around the city. I was often the only white person present, routinely touted as "a specialist on India and on our culture," or as a "professor of Hindu studies," etc. These were descriptions that added much-wanted cultural capital to a community that feels permanently under-recognized. Second, these imputed qualities soon made me something of an involuntary adjudicator of the authenticity, quality, and even "correctness" of Indian rituals and practices in South Africa. How did they compare with India? Were they better, shorter, less beautiful, or more old-fashioned? My opinion was sought on many matters where I had none, and only some politeness and a good deal of prodding by my hosts made me produce impromptu, probably misguided, verdicts on the length of wedding rituals, the propriety of dancing, the comparative quality of *bhangra* performers in different parts of the world, and much else. I had in other words become an almost native informer of that other and supposedly more authentic world of India that my friends did not know except from the Bollywood films.

Third, and most intriguingly, I also became known as someone who would "write about us as we really are," as my friends would put it. This position produced a variety of responses that seemed very far from the anguish about power differentials and objectification expressed in *Writing Culture*. I was constantly navigating a hotly contested terrain of friends, informants, and people with various political and cultural agendas who all wanted me to write about them, to include them in my book. Many wanted me to describe what is locally known as "the community" (of Indians in South Africa) in a particular way and with particular emphasis on their subgroups, or their understanding of recent history. However, I was also someone who knew the locality well, including the more intimate and unofficial sides of life in the township. Many of my friends had ambivalent feelings about how, and if, I should incorporate some of these elements into my book. What became clear to me as I began writing up was that my book was no longer seen as just "my book" but as a screen, a showcase, an account that qua my status as an outsider and academic could become seen as a comprehensive and intimate account of life in the township. It was important to influence me. For me, the main question quickly became one of trust and betrayal. How could I portray and write about this very literate but also anxious group of people, who live in fear of being further ostracized by local nativist Zulu forces who would rather see them leave the country?[4] How could I write critically, and truthfully, about ordinary life in the township without confirming some of the stereotypes of racism, introversion, and cultural cocooning among Indians: the often shallow fascination with India in some quarters; the determined disavowal of South Asian roots in favor of becoming "Arabic" among richer Muslims; the alienation from political life as a whole among the poorer Indians; their general hostility to the African National Congress (ANC); and much more?

All the analytical terms I employ in my work are potentially loaded with political significance and import. I sympathize, at least in principle, with the notion that anthropologists to some extent must turn themselves into local chroniclers, local storytellers who write the histories of communities and places with due respect given to their internal differentiation and their historical specificities. I also realize that it is an impossible task. No stories of "cultural practices" or even "everyday life" can be told without being profoundly selective, and without being shot through with political implications.

The inevitable conclusion is of course that we as anthropologists never can hope to stand above the political and cultural struggles we portray—merely by claiming a quasi-neutral scholarly ground. We will always be held accountable for what we write, and whom we write about, by our informants or those belonging to the same world. This is the inevitable situation of the anthropological undertaking in the twenty-first century: we are commentators who compete on a playing field with local academics, writers, bloggers, and amateur historians. This field may not be even in terms of institutional power, prestige, or imputed "expertise," but it has many and diverse audiences, many of whom are not automatically swayed or impressed by the institutional address of the visiting anthropologists. This has been the case for other disciplines, such as history, for some time and anthropologists might as well get used to it. The problem today is not one of textual objectification, which my informants in fact so desired from my writing, and so happily engaged in themselves on innumerable websites and blogs. It is not even undue "othering," which in benign renditions can be read as statements of distinction and authenticity. Rather, it boils down to something as ephemeral as "quality"—that is, reflexivity as well as loyalty to one's material, and an imaginative understanding of the local scene one is depicting. Such a position entails a new form of responsibility, sensitivity, and ethics more attuned to the sentiments and agendas in one's field than previous generations were used to. I keep a file of letters, often deeply unpleasant letters, from people in India who have read my work and disagree with me and are offended by it. I am sure I will receive an equally mixed reaction when I launch the South Africa edition of my new book in Durban in 2014. This is the condition anthropologists have to work under and I find it sobering and important. This does not mean that theoretical debates and agendas are unimportant but merely that one no longer, as an ethnographer, can assume that one "has" data of one's own—they are always coproduced with reflexive individuals one has met in the field and the data "belongs" to the field, not to the anthropologist.

Natives, Stop Talking!—I Am Busy Observing You

At this point where the privileged voice of the anthropologist is under systematic erasure and where the discipline finds itself questioning the real value of much of its older canon, it is little wonder that many anthropologists are disoriented. For those of us who attend the mega-meetings of the American Anthropological Association on a regular basis it is clear that the discipline no longer has a center but instead sees an enormous proliferation of subjects and specializations that range from the hardcore scientific, over the quasi-philosophical, to work that is closer to cultural studies and art history than to the classics of the discipline. This is a sign of spectacular success and popularity but also of fundamental confusion in a discipline overwhelmed by the fact that its informants and material now talk back, write back, organize, publish, and upload videos on the Web, interpreting themselves faster and more competently than most anthropologists. The productivity of the so-called linguistic turn and poststructuralist attention to language is gradually waning, overwhelmed by, among many other things, the sheer magnitude and complexity of texts and speech now available. Maybe language and the voices of "the native" count for less today because they have lost a deep sense of authenticity. I found it very interesting to ponder how young people in a township collect wisecracks and lyrics from American rap and sprinkle their own vernacular with it, along with many Standard English expressions, and other phrases sampled from other circulating languages. To many anthropologists steeped in a more classical mode of enquiry, the many half-globalized mongrel tongues we meet in our fields may appear as already de-purified; parts of a global linguistic-sampling culture saturated by news, circulating standard frames, global religious discourses, and global pop culture rather than anything local, historical, or truly authentic. Instead, authenticity and the "real" are sought in the manners of being, bodily movement, spirit possession, and other forms of somatic religious experience.

The current turn away from language and discourse in anthropology is both remarkable and counterintuitive. This "non-linguistic turn" is informed by many sources—from Bruno Latour's turn to things and objects as standing in an active and agentive relationship with the world (Latour and Weibel 2006), to the increasing interest in neuropsychology and cognitive science, and not least, the turn to the senses and to the notion of affect as another way to study the relationship between culture and human agency. The senses have for a long time been a focus of anthropological work (see Goody 2002 for a summary), by ethnomusicology pioneers such as Steven Feld (1990), ethnographers such as Paul Stoller (1987, 1989a, 1989b), and cultural historians such as Constance Classen (1993, 2012). However, in the last decade or so, the anthropology of the senses has increasingly been portrayed as a new approach in the discipline (see Meyer 2010; Pink 2009, 2012; Van de Port 2011), ostensibly an alternative to the customary reliance on discourse and text. Philosophical works on affect, mainly inspired by Gilles Deleuze (e.g., Bennett 2001; Connolly 2002; Massumi 2004), have in the last few years been hailed as the latest "big thing" and have emerged alongside a broader interest in the senses. The fundamental assumption guiding both these fields of studies is that the human relationship with the world, and other beings, cannot be captured by language and consciousness alone. Human beings are conditioned, swayed, seduced, scared, enraged, and affected by natural phenomena, smells, sounds, vibrations, and interhuman bodily energies long before, or alongside with, converting their perceptions into conscious thought, and maybe linguistic expression. One of the most compelling studies in this tradition is Hirschkind's recent book on the art of self-making among Muslims in Cairo, as they listen to and apprehend the popular taped sermons by Muslim scholars (Hirschkind 2006).

While there indeed is much to be said for this line of research and exploration, it often tends to produce a form of reverse Cartesianism—that is, a reversal of René Descartes's famous distinction between a realm of thinking and consciousness (*res cogitans*) and an inanimate realm of nature (*res extensa*). To Descartes, this distinction enabled reasoning men to systematically study the natural and physical world created by an omnipotent God who had then withdrawn from it (Descartes 1641/1998). With a reversal of this privileging of human consciousness comes an assertion of the relative independence of matter, and of the body and its associated powers of perception and affective energies. This celebration of a holistic and non-mediated relationship between humans and their world is prefigured in much nineteenth-century Romanticist philosophy and in Henri Bergson's idea of an *élan vital* that pervades both the human and the natural world. (Bergson 1911/1998). This philosophical vitalism informed the *Négritude* movement of the 1930s and 1940s, where Léopold Sédar Senghor and Aimé Césaire famously argued that blackness was an embodied sensation, lodged in and spontaneously experienced by black bodies. In this tradition, consciousness and speech emerged as de-purifying and inauthentic faculties, distortions of the more primary and embodied sensations. It is no coincidence that Senghor's preferred medium was poetry (Jones 2010).

This grounding of experience in the body and experience is not new in anthropology but the distinct hostility to language and meaning among those promoting a "new materialism" (Coole and Frost 2010) is remarkable. Within a few years, Latour's playful notion of the "Parliament of Things" (Latour 2004), for example, has acquired a semi-canonical status despite its glaring vagueness on what non-human actors (or "actants") actually are, other than loose assemblages of things, devices, and people in networks almost invariably designed and operated with distinct commercial, bureaucratic and scientific purposes. How can the popularity of the "agency of things" be accounted for, when even a careful thinker like Jane Bennett, in her attempt to define a "vital materialism" (Bennett 2010), is unable to define material agency much beyond what appears as "second order human agency"—unintended consequences and complex effects emanating from machines, networks, and practical arrangements erected and designed by people in the first place? What is it that makes this withdrawal from "meaning" and discourse so attractive that it makes even a deeply thoughtful ethnographer like Hirschkind virtually ignore that the effects, and affects, generated in his informants' minds and bodies by the cassette tapes have as much (if not more) to do with the rich meanings and connotations of the words recited and uttered by the Islamic preacher, as with the sounds and vibrations of the preacher's voice?

I suggest that there is a very intimate connection between this intellectual movement (which also encompasses "science and technology studies") and the ever more uncertain role of the anthropologist in the global cultural economy as discussed above. What Latour-inspired anthropology, cognitive science, and the anthropology of affect and the senses all have in common is the primacy of observation: conducting experiments (especially in cognitive science), recording highly structured procedures and manuals in laboratories, and sharing key moments of embodied sensations and persuasion with informants. In all of these cases, native speech and interpretation is irrelevant, or at best peripheral. What counts is the immediacy between bodies and affect, between sensations and event, and thus between observation and event. In that move, the anthropologist is suddenly catapulted to a new position of centrality—as the research instrument par excellence by virtue of "being there" as a sensing organism that can share the moment; and by virtue of devising a new theoretical language of interpretation that is largely inaccessible to the informants because it belongs to a completely different order of discourse.

In this move, a recognizable order seems to be restored in the anthropological universe. This order seems uncannily close to the methodologies and ethos that for decades have governed the very Cartesian assumptions and methodologies of mainstream biological anthropology, for instance. Here, the populations studied (small, "primitive" communities, or social and cultural minorities, for instance) are entirely objectified as clusters of inter-bodily effects and outcomes, devoid of reflexivity and language: pure *res extensa*. The natives speak but we do not listen (that much) unless they speak in a language of true alterity.

What matters is what they do, how they do it, and how they sense and act in the world as a holistic unit, all observable through the now fully reconstituted and legitimate ethnographic gaze. We, the anthropologists, have won back a form of a metalanguage of scientific interpretation that cannot be easily be contaminated by the social world and the de-purified vernacular of our natives and the legions of local intellectuals and vernacular interpreters of culture: elegant and simple, and yet deeply problematic, and surely not far beyond Descartes. This may be a bit of a caricature, but not that much.

The resurrection of ethnographic authority is also at stake in the recent emergence of "ontology" as an alternative to the way social constructivism in the past decades has been focused on representation and epistemology. While the followers of Latour employ the term *ontology* to designate objects or states that are socially produced and naturalized as facts (see Woolgar and Lezaun 2013 for a clear discussion), the followers of Marilyn Strathern and Viveiros de Castro deploy *ontology* to designate the inner logics of unyielding and stubborn worlds of absolute alterity. Using the example of ostensibly absurd claims such as "The Nuer believe that twins are birds," Holbraad argues that "[t]he anthropological task, then, is not to account for why ethnographic data are as they are, but rather to understand what they are ... [. W]e use the ethnography to rethink our analytical concepts" (Holbraad 2010: 185). While some of this labor of reconceptualization of Western truisms was begun by Strathern with respect to kinship (see especially Strathern 2005) and Clastres with respect to political authority (Clastres 1989), it is as yet unclear what the more generalizable theoretical contribution of the ontological turn is aiming at. The advocates of "ontology" as a perspective insist that it is not tantamount to an older, objectivist notion of "culture" and cosmology but instead "a set of assumptions postulated by the anthropologist for analytical purposes" (ibid.) The latter formulation is, however, strikingly close to what most philosophers would call epistemology. It certainly reveals that the epistemological pivot of this school of thought is the ethnographer's authoritative gaze and perception turned into the "new" (but actually old) frontier of analytical innovation. The "natives" are back in their familiar role as pure fonts of authentic alterity and most of the key natives in these ethnographies are indeed shamans, spirit media, and other ritually initiated people (see for instance Holbraad 2012; Pedersen 2011). Of late, "ontology" has been hailed as "critical anthropology," as opposed to "modernist anthropology" (i.e. most of the discipline), which, according to Ghassan Hage, amounts to nothing but a form of sociology.[5] The ironic and often reflexive narrators and raconteurs of identity and culture one increasingly finds in many ethnographic accounts today seem to be of little interest to the "ontologists." In this new/old tradition, natives speak little, mostly in oblique keys, and predominantly through the pen of the ventriloquist ethnographer-interpreter, the undisputed hero of the "ontological turn." Ontology is not really about how the world of the native is lived or understood by people themselves but, as Pedersen puts it, "a new analytical method from which classic ethnographic questions may be posed afresh ...[:] a technology of description, which allows anthropologists to make sense of their ethnographic material in new and experimental ways" (Pedersen 2012). This begs the question, whose ontology is this? Is it that of Cambridge-trained anthropologists, or of people who appear in ethnographies? Later in the same piece, Pedersen comes clean and admits that the "ontological turn" is but a "certain moment in the recent history of the discipline" (ibid.). What purports to explode categories in a major way in a dynamic global moment turns out to be a form of analytical introversion of little consequence outside certain strands in the British social anthropological tradition.

Quo Vadis?

The key question remains whether the celebrated "reverse Cartesianism" or the rediscovered love of alterity effectively address or take into account the momentous changes in the very conditions of cultural interpretation that were sketched above. Is anything gained by trying to analytically isolate the non-linguistic moments of human behavior, or by isolating kernels of incommensurable alterity gleaned from the statements of shamans and healers that precisely are expected to be obscure in order to be effective? Is not the task of anthropology to study the complexity of the human in its totality? Does this not mean, for instance, to understand how human experience is suspended between the subjective perception of one's bodily being and the "exteriority of the flesh," the social conventions and material strictures that interpret and frame this body and its speech (Merleau-Ponty 1945/2004, 202–223)? Does it not mean understanding how speech and structures of meaning are renewed, deflated, and also enabled by globally circulating concepts and sound bites; how materiality is integral to the most intimate and banal of activities (Miller 2005, 2007); and how things are often anthropomorphized and made agentive (Gell 1998)? Does it not mean to understand how the spirit medium's always brittle claim to authority depends on an ability to deploy frames and "ontologies" that are at odds with the flow and categories of everyday life? In short, is it not the task of anthropology to study how our informants, like us, swim in a sea of speech, narratives, and interpretations whose validity and veracity always are open to debate and questioning?

At stake is whether anthropology's old category of "the human" remains meaningful. On the one hand, one sees a broad church of "reflexive storytelling," which focuses on the human as a unique form of consciousness and capacity for desire and imagination. This branch of anthropology is forced to constantly engage with a proliferating range of competing accounts in the vernacular in its broadest linguistic and non-linguistic sense. On the other hand, there are the contemporary posthumanists who question the category of the human as a self-evident entity and whose interests drift towards non-linguistic behavior, objects, materiality, animals, and neurological approaches to the brain and the human mind. Some of these approaches, such as that of the ontologists, claim to expand and deepen the range of what is conceivably considered human.

The older anthropology, whose demise was bemoaned by my colleague, belonged to the colonial world and its enduring (perhaps Cartesian) epistemological distinction between those who study and reason and those who can be studied and reasoned about. That distinction is still with us, albeit in a new form. Today, the privileged locus of anthropological reason is defined less by geographical and institutional parameters and more by analytical language and by the (multiple) definitions of what *anthropos* may mean. We live in an era where the epistemological status of the human is more uncertain among scholars than ever before, while "the human" as a universal legal, political, and religious category has never been stronger or more varied in our public cultures across the world. This is an extremely interesting paradox that calls for more reflection and study. In this light, the calls by many anthropologists for abandoning the category of the human, however complex, contradictory, and annoyingly reflexive it may seem, at a point where it at long last emerges as a truly global vernacular, appear both untimely and strangely myopic.

Notes

1. The classical example is of course that of Jomo Kenyatta, the father of modern Kenya whose book *Facing Mount Kenya* was heavily influenced his teacher at the London School of Economics in the 1930s, Bronislaw Malinowski (see Berman 1996).
2. There is a burgeoning literature on heritage and history in many fields and "Heritage and Museum Studies" is now a well-established academic

career path. For a very interesting, philosophically inflected argument on heritage as living practice, see Herwitz 2011.
3. On the difference in style and ethics between anthropology and journalism, see Emma Tarlo's recent discussion of Katherine Boo's bestseller *Behind the Beautiful Forevers* and Aman Sethi's *A Free Man* (Tarlo 2013).
4. A recent survey in Johannesburg of attitudes among South Africans relating to the very controversial issue of immigration and the status of migrants have confirmed the well-known groundswell of hostility to continued immigration into South Africa from other African nations. It also showed that among Black South Africans not even 10 percent think that whites should leave the country whilst more than 30 percent feel that the country was better off without Indians. (L. Landau, Centre for Forced Migration, University of the Witwatersrand, 2008.)
5. In a recent article, Ghassan Hage argues that for anthropology to be truly "critical" it must retain the insights of an older, "primitivist" anthropology that enables the ethnographer to recognize that "alterity exists everywhere" in the form of other possible life worlds, other forms of sociality, that a conventional focus on "modernist categories"—such as race, ethnicity, or government—will not be able to discern (Hage 2012).

References

Appadurai, Arjun. 1996. *Modernity at Large: Cultural Dimensions of Globalization*. Minneapolis: University of Minnesota Press.

———. 2000a. "Spectral Housing and Urban Cleansing: Notes on Millennial Mumbai." *Public Culture* 12(3): 627–651.

———. 2000b. "Grassroots Globalization and the Research Imagination." *Public Culture* 12(1): 1–19.

Bennett, Jane. 2001. *The Enchantment of Modern Life*. Durham, NC: Duke University Press.

———. 2010. *Vibrant Matter: A Political Ecology of Things*. Durham, NC: Duke University Press.

Bergson, Henri. 1911/1998. *Creative Evolution*. London: Dover Publications.

Berman, Bruce. 1996. "Ethnography as Politics, Politics as Ethnography: Kenyatta, Malinowski, and the Making of Facing Mount Kenya." *Canadian Journal of African Studies / Revue Canadienne des Études Africaines* 30(3): 313–344.

Chandavarkar, Raj. 1994. *The Origins of Industrial Capitalism in India*. Cambridge: Cambridge University Press.

———. 1998. *Imperial Power and Popular Politics: Class, Resistance and the State in India, c. 1850–1950*. Cambridge: Cambridge University Press.

———. 2009. *History, Culture and the Indian City*. Cambridge: Cambridge University Press.

Chandra, Vikram. 2007. *Sacred Games*. New York: Harper Perennial.

Classen, Constance. 1993. *World of Sense: Exploring the Senses in History across the World*. London: Routledge.

———. 2012. *The Deepest Sense: A Cultural History of Touch*. Chicago: University of Illinois Press.
Clastres, Pierre. 1989. *Society against the State: Essays in Political Anthropology*. New York: Zone Books.
Clifford, James and George Marcus. 1986. *Writing Culture: The Poetics and Politics of Ethnography*. Berkeley: University of California Press.
Comaroff, J. and J. Comaroff. 2009. *Ethnicity Inc.* Chicago, IL: University of Chicago Press.
Connolly, William. 2002. *Neuropolitics: Thinking, Culture, Speed*. Minneapolis: University Of Minnesota Press.
Coole, Diana and Samantha Frost, eds. 2010. *New Materialisms: Ontology, Agency, and Politics*. Durham, NC: Duke University Press.
Descartes, René. 1641/1998. *Discourse on Method and Meditations on First Philosophy*. Indianapolis: Hackett Publishing Co.
Feld, Steven. 1990. *Sound and Sentiment: Birds, Weeping and Song in Kaluli Expression*. Philadelphia: University of Pennsylvania Press.
Gell, Alfred. 1998. *Art and Agency: An Anthropological Theory*. Oxford: Clarendon.
Goody, Jack. 2002. "The Anthropology of the Senses and Sensations." *La Ricerca Folklorica* 45(April).
Hage, Ghassan. 2012. "Critical Anthropological Thought and the Radical Political Imaginary Today." *Critique of Anthropology* 32(3): 285–308.
Hansen, Thomas B. 2001. *Wages of Violence. Naming and Identity in Postcolonial Bombay*. Princeton: Princeton University Press.
———. 2012. *Melancholia of Freedom. Social Life in an Indian Township in South Africa*. Princeton: Princeton University Press.
Herwitz, Daniel. 2011. *Live Action Heritage*. New York: Columbia University Press.
Hirschkind, Charles. 2006. *The Ethical Soundscape: Cassette Sermons and Islamic Counterpublics*. New York: Columbia University Press.
Holbraad, Martin. 2010. "Response" in "Ontology Is Just Another Word for Culture Symposium." *Critique of Anthropology* 30(2).
———. 2012. *Truth in Motion: The Recursive Anthropology of Cuban Divination*. Chicago: University of Chicago Press.
Jones, Donna. 2010. *The Racial Discourses of Life Philosophy: Négritude, Vitalism, and Modernity*. New York: Columbia University Press.
Latour, Bruno. 2004. *Politics of Nature: How to Bring the Sciences into Democracy*. Cambridge, Mass.: Harvard University Press.
Latour, Bruno and Peter Weibel eds. 2006. *Making Things Public: Atmospheres of Democracy*. Boston: MIT Press.
Massumi, Brian. 2004. *Parables for the Virtual: Movement, Affect, Sensation*. Durham, NC: Duke University Press.
Mehta, Suketu. 2004. *Maximum City: Bombay Lost and Found*. New York: Vintage.
Merleau-Ponty, Maurice. 1945/2004. *The Phenomenology of Perception*. London: Routledge.
Meyer, Birgit. 2010. "Mediation and Immediacy: Sensations, Semiotic Ideologies and the Question of the Medium." *Social Anthropology* 19(1): 23–39.
Miller, Daniel, ed. 2005. *Materiality*. Durham, NC: Duke University Press.

Miller, Daniel. 2007. *The Comfort of Things*. Cambridge: Polity Press.
Patel, Sujata and Alice Thorner. 1997. *Bombay: Mosaic of Modern Culture*. Delhi: Oxford University Press.
Patel, Sujata and Jim Masselos. 2005. *Bombay and Mumbai: The City in Transition*. Delhi: Oxford University Press.
Pedersen, Morten A. 2011. *Not Quite Shaman: Spirit Worlds and Political Lives in Northern Mongolia*. Ithaca: Cornell University Press.
———. 2012. "Common Nonsense: A Review of Certain Recent Reviews of the 'Ontological Turn.'" *Anthropology of this Century*, Issue 5. Available at: http://aotcpress.com/articles/common_nonsense/ (accessed April 1, 2014).
Pink, Sarah. 2009. *Doing Sensory Ethnography*. London: SAGE Publications.
———. 2012. *Situating Everyday Life*. London: SAGE Publications.
Stoller, Paul. 1987. *In Sorcery's Shadow: A Memoir of Apprenticeship*. Chicago: University of Chicago Press.
———. 1989a. *The Taste of Ethnographic Things*. Philadelphia: University of Pennsylvania Press.
———. 1989b. *Embodying Colonial Memories: Spirit Possession, Power and the Hauka of West Africa*. New York: Routledge.
Strathern, Marilyn. 2005. *Kinship, Law and the Unexpected: Relatives Are always a Surprise*. Cambridge: Cambridge University Press.
Tarlo, Emma. 2013. "Two Journalists Get Up Close and Personal with Urban Poverty in India." *Anthropology of this Century* 8 (2013). Available at: http://aotcpress.com/articles/journalists-close-personal-urban-poverty-india/ (accessed April 1, 2014).
Van de Port, Matthijs. 2011. *Ecstatic Encounters: Bahian Candomble and the Quest for the Really Real*. Amsterdam: Amsterdam University Press.
Woolgar, S. and J. Lezaun. 2013. "The Wrong Bin Bag: A Turn to Ontology in Science and Technology Studies." *Social Studies of Science* 34(3): 417–443.
Zaidi, Hussein. 2003. *Black Friday: The True Story of the Bombay Blasts*. Delhi: Penguin.

Chapter 7

TRAVELING BETWEEN KNOWLEDGE PRACTICES
Thomas Fillitz

In his note for the "Third Stockholm Anthropology Roundtable" (September 2007) Ulf Hannerz positioned *reflexivity* as one of four keywords characterizing the anthropological enterprise. Among the various uses of this notion, Hannerz suggested as a frame of discussion "the broader sense of human modes of individually or collectively representing oneself, portraying oneself, measuring oneself" (personal communication, June 2007). This perspective on reflexivity may also refer to our common sense use of reflexivity, an idea going back to Descartes's *cogito*, an inner contemplation or "introspective representation" (Sandywell 1999: 39). In such processes, the "I" is reflecting inner representations of external events. Representing oneself (either as individual or as collectivity), then, refers to reflexivity as producing substantial, cultural uniqueness. In this more general sense reflexivity is a process occurring in everyday life, and is a also a general tool of scientific endeavor. People reflect on their consumption activities, and scholars reflect on their research and analyses. This is, broadly speaking, considered as a general reflexivity (or essential reflexivity): an integral part of our lives.

Beyond such a general reflexivity, Hannerz points to processes of reflexivity within societies or collectivities that create consciousness, a feedback, and may result in readaptations or reconfigurations of sociocultural institutions, ideas, etc. Over the past decade several issues of the journals *Social Anthropology/Anthropologie Sociale* and *Ethnos* have dealt with these subjects. A special issue of the former focused on "Religious Reflexivity," and one of the latter on "Reflexivity in Other's Context."[1] In his introduction to the former, Højbjerg highlights that the articles in the issue deal with three different types of religious reflexivity: (a) "the organisational form of ritual action"; (b) "the experience of events and the presence of alternative 'worldviews'"; and (c) "the objectification of religious representation stemming from the conflict over doctrine" (Højbjerg 2002: 6). In the special issue of *Ethnos* Gershon invites the reader to look at the reflexivity practiced by interlocutors in debating with anthropologists, and most importantly the reflexivity that "highlights the multiple social orders that may exist in a single context" (Gershon 2006: 451).

On the one hand, apart from its general form, reflexivity appears as a cultural technique for reflecting upon oneself, which in particular forms was and is present and enacted in all societies. Myerhoff and Ruby mention among others the activities of dreaming, collective memories, celebrations, rituals, and public performances (Myerhoff and Ruby 1982: 3). Demian analyses loss as involving such a technique among a group of mainland Massim (Demian 2006). On the other hand, Beck emphasizes reflexivity as a characteristic of what he considers "second modernity" and speaks of a "reflexive modernization" as characteristic of modern Western societies today (Beck 1994).

> [The model of reflexive modernization tries to take into account the whole breadth of the modernization process. The structural break is explained not as a result of exogenous factors but as a consequence of modernization itself. Once modernization has been radicalized, it affects *all* spheres of society. (Beck et al. 2003: 13; italics in original)

"Reflexive modernization," however, encompasses variable understandings of reflexivity. For Beck the idea of "reflexivity" is understood in the context of his notion of unintended consequences, incomplete knowledge, and the possibility of multiple modernities. Giddens (1994) posits post-traditional societies as being reflexive in novel ways, while Lash (1994) emphasizes the non-linearity of the notion—its dimension of *bricolage*, of creating connections.

This chapter will focus on notions of reflexivity "in the world," as differentiated from notions of reflexivity related to the production of scholarly knowledge (Hervik 1994: 96). It begins by asking: When does reflexivity matter? Even if reflexivity is adopted, it does not automatically lead towards new insights, readaptation, restructuration, or "a liberating perspective" (Gershon 2006: 447). On the contrary, as a tool for more objectivity, some authors question if it could actually contribute in any way to better knowledge production, and stress possible negative uses and abuses of such objectification (see for example Lynch 2000; Pels 2000; Salzmann 2002).

Looking at when reflexivity entails consequences, George Marcus' notion of "derived (ideological) reflexivity" will be adopted here. Marcus emphasizes how reflexivity is handled for particular purposes—in his case, of course, by arguing about the postmodern reflexive turn in anthropology (Marcus 1998: 190). The notion of "ideological reflexivity" will be used here to refer to those circumstances where the tool of reflexivity leads to a fundamental transformation of specific sociocultural phenomena. It is used to understand developments in modern art in Ivory Coast in the period between the 1970s and early 1980s. An art teacher, Serge Hénelon, encouraged his students to rely less on European art concepts in which they had been trained so far, and to go into their villages and study what forms of artistic expressions and materials were being used by local artists. The tensions and appropriation of this new knowledge culminated in the creation of the *vohou-vohou* movement.[2] It will be argued here that the advent of this artistic movement not only was the result of a general introspection, a mirror game, but also consisted in a reconfiguration, by producing new perspectives and connections in this cultural field.

The second question addressed here highlights the spatial dimension: Where does such a form of reflexivity occur, either in geographical terms, or in terms of particular sectors of a society? The notion of "reflexive modernization," for instance, is primarily a Eurocentric concept, elaborated for European and North American "second modern societies" (see Alexander 1996; Therborn 2000: 51; Adams 2003; Beck et al. 2003: 7). This concept is based on the expansion of intensive webs of information and communication. On the basis of inclusion in or exclusion from such webs, this system produces winners and losers (Lash 2003). One could point in this context to the elaboration of working programs of the European Union. Its periodical, different research-programs and their cyclical reformulations (such as FP-5, FP-6, FP-7) clearly delineate the spaces where the reflexive endeavor should be particularly intensified.

This second question will be dealt with here with regard to the global art world. Within this complex global culture one has to understand *where* the idea of global art is materialized. From among the multiple domains—to name but a few: the production of a global art (see e.g., Appadurai 1999), the creation of global art collections (e.g., the Contemporary African Art Collection), problems of a global art history (e.g., Summers 2003; Belting 2007; Elkins 2007), and the art market (galleries or auction houses)—this chapter will merely focus on the phenomenon of art biennials, in contrast to the model of European and North American museums of contemporary art (see e.g., Bydler 2004; Weibel and Buddensieg 2007; Belting and Buddensieg 2009). This example highlights another dimension of reflexivity, beyond personal introspection. Here, reflexivity is characteristic of the various connections produced in specific art biennials in order to relate to each other artworks that have been created in various regions of the world by artists, who position themselves in different ways within this global culture.

Following a discussion of these two questions related to the when and where of the reflexivity in question, the third section will develop some arguments about possible trajectories of the discipline of anthropology. These thoughts are strongly influenced by the scholarship of Ulf Hannerz on cultural flows, cultural complexity, world culture, cosmopolitans, and geocultural scenarios.

In the examples analyzed in this chapter, reflexivity will appear not so much as the Cartesian inner reflection of the outer world, but rather as a process founded on relational experiences. The chapter will, therefore, argue in favor of focusing on such spaces or arenas of encounter, where different worldviews are connected, and discuss how such arenas are constitutive of the cultural. This approach may be considered as a further development of Marcus' and Myers' concept of a "critical anthropology of art" (1995). Reflexivity, as one of the characteristics of anthropology, then appears in the context of interconnections and regional variations.

When: Times of Reflexivity

The development of modern art in Africa in the European-North American sense goes back to the early twentieth century, and is generally linked to the Nigerian artist Aina Onabolu, who started in 1900 to paint in a European style, with European techniques and materials (canvas, oil, etc.). These works of art created in the first decades of the twentieth century were very much influenced by the well-known conventional European academic styles of figurative representation. Around the time of many successful national independence movements in Africa (1950s and 1960s), a major reflexive turn occurred in art production. As a contribution to the struggle against colonial powers, and with a vision of a new, emerging, national culture, artists adopted new politics of representation. In Ghana, some refused to create pictures containing any motifs of colonial modernity; in Nigeria a group of young artists known as the Zaria Rebels developed an entire program to depict the colonial exploitation and collaboration with colonial authorities, to bring their art to the local population, and to refrain from contacts with European collectors. In Senegal, the newly appointed President Léopold Sédar Senghor implemented, during the first decade of his presidency, the cultural concept of *Négritude*, which he and some of his friends had coined in the burgeoning cultural field of Paris in the 1930s. *Négritude* in the visual arts was associated with spontaneous expression, color, and rhythm, an artistic style that was free from European academic influences. What is widely labeled as the *École de Dakar*, however, never coincided with any all-encompassing, unitary, *Négritude* style in art production (see e.g., Harney 2004).

While the connection between the political transformations and the reflective turn in most of the new states is obvious, not much happened in Ivory Coast. Although the first and long-time president, Félix Houphouët-Boigny, was a collector of historical Occidental artworks, the new (post-independence) government was not particularly interested in supporting pictorial art creation. Its major activity in this field was the foundation of the national art school in 1966, the Institut National des Arts in Abidjan. Sculptor Christian Lattier, winner of the sculpture prize at the First Festival of Negro Art in Dakar (1966), nevertheless heavily complained about this disinterest.

The creation of *vohou-vohou*[3] goes back to the year 1972, but as an art movement in Ivory Coast, it was disseminated under that name only from the mid-1980s onwards. Artists of the *vohou-vohou* movement were fiercely opposed to artistic (Occidental) academism, which was then still dominant at the art school and among most of the Ivorian artists. *Vohou-vohou* implies fundamentally the use of local materials and a freedom of expression, combining regional art styles from African societies with those learned from Occidental art history. The most prominent, first-generation personalities are Théodore Koudougnon, Youssouf Bath, Yacouba Touré, and N'Guessan Kra.

Why can the creation of this art movement be considered as major moment of reflexivity? First, it should be mentioned that there was a general economic crisis in the region, due to a devaluation of the currency, the CFA franc. Until that date, art students had been provided with their materials—canvasses, paper, oil colors, brushes, etc.—by the art school. This could not be continued due to the economic situation, and local purchase was far beyond the means of the students. Their teacher, therefore, suggested they look for other means of realizing artworks.

Second, there was the outstanding personality of the art professor, Serge Hénelon, a French citizen originating from Martinique. He inspired the students not only to look for other materials but also to question the canvas as support for the picture. As early as 1969, he sent his students out into the villages to interact with local communities, in order to find other means of expression. They began experimenting with the use of bark-cloth, jute, feathers, bones, animal blood, pieces of metal, sand (kaolin), colors made from plants, etc.

> In those days we traveled to villages to collect old baskets, used wrap-around dresses of our kin, or bark-cloths. We reflected on whether the

canvas had to be the main support of a picture, an idea we had learned during our European academic training ... The *vohou* attitude was fundamental for us to develop a new consciousness regarding painting or sculpture and African art in general. (Théodore Koudougnon, July 30, 1997, Abidjan)

Hénelon's main impact consisted in reorienting his students to the local cultures instead of solely focusing on European-defined modern art. Théodore Koudougnon speaks of a "cultural initiation" they underwent under the guidance of Hénelon (Fillitz 2002: 57). They realized that artistic creation in these sub-Saharan regions was not confined to carving masks or figurines, an art concept largely propagated by European specialists of the time. They learned about weaving techniques and the historical memory within these, about the art of scarification, and about bodies as a support for pictures: they learned a different notion of art and the artist. The various social experiences of the young art students also prompted specific forms of artistic representation. Théodore Koudougnon's artistic themes were connected for a long time to the ritual body, as he comes from a region where old artistic expressions were connected to rituals. Yacouba Touré was strongly influenced by textiles and ropes as containers of cultural memory. "We need to talk of the village, as there are various elements I use which are rooted there. I originated in a society of weavers, and for them, the fabric is the bearer of meaning!" (Yacouba Touré, August 25, 1997, Abidjan). Youssouf Bath turned to bark-cloth as a support. *Vohou-vohou* was not a uniform stylistic school. It produced a novel cultural consciousness by connecting in multiple ways local, traditional cultural phenomena of the time to European modernity, and to a reflection of the impact of colonialism. The new visual forms of representations were related to a change of the gaze, a new awareness of local modernity, and a new consciousness of the process of visual representation beyond the dominant discourse of Occidental art in the Abidjan art world (figurative academism, easel painting, canvas, oil, and brush).

Third, while the "cultural initiation" and new techniques of representation were introduced around 1972, the *vohou-vohou* movement was launched in the early 1980s. One reason for this is the time these artists needed to obtain their diplomas in French art schools. This was the usual trajectory for art students given that France and Ivory Coast had contracted that those receiving their diploma in Abidjan would then be further trained for several years in French art institutions. This accord was canceled in the early 1990s. *Vohou-vohou* was not a school but a movement, which radicalized the approaches introduced under Serge Hénelon. As against the time spent at the Institut National des

Arts, it was conceived as a tool with which these artists could assert their vision of art within the arena of the Abidjan art world. There were, even in the late 1980s and early 1990s, confrontations with those who opposed these artists and who maintained and defended the old academism. The *vohou-vohou* artworks were not valued and the skills of the artists were not acknowledged: they were attacked, their insights ridiculed. The arena of these confrontations, however, was public. It comprised artists from different directions, journalists, collectors, and, as the main institution, the Institut National des Arts.

Applying the notion of ideological reflexivity helps us to understand the interrelated processes that finally led to a new art movement, which would be acknowledged by the mid-1990s as the most influential one in Ivory Coast. By then *vohou* artists were being considered as "masters of Abidjan" in the local art world. The field within which this process of reflexivity was launched is complex. The cultural contexts were the postcolonial urban society of Abidjan, and local Occidental-art academism. There was, further, a constellation of the economic crisis and the Martiniquean teacher, Serge Hénelon, that introduced another vision to cultural processes in the region. Both factors initiated a series of shifts in perspectives. They induced reflections on the meaning of art in the context of ethnic groups, which went beyond European understandings (mainly of carving) and practices of art. It became liberated from a "modern art" that was subaltern in European and North American visual discourses. The constitution of the loosely bounded *vohou-vohou* movement enabled its proponents to adequately position and confront the outcomes of this reflexive process against the defenders of old academism in the arena of the Abidjan art world. Ideological reflexivity, in this example, refers to the changes in viewing the world, a rejection of several academic, European art concepts, and a shift in visual representation. By the early 1990s, these transformations and new considerations had implications for the cultural politics in Ivory Coast. This turns our attention to when and how this reflexive process became most virulent.

Where: Spaces of Reflexivity

George Marcus' notion of the derived or ideological reflexivity refers not only to a time component, as discussed in the previous part, but also to the uneven distribution of processes of reflexivity. Scott Lash specifically highlights this dimension in his discussion of "reflexive modernization" (Lash 1994). Lash asks why, in second modern societies (Beck et al. 2003), reflexivity is found in some places and not in others, or in some economic sectors and not in others; for example, more in the software sector, and less among the so-called "junk-jobs" (e.g., working for McDonald's). He considers structural conditions of reflexivity as characteristic of second modern societies: "Reflexive production ... is possible only in the presence of optimal levels of information flow and knowledge (or information-processing) acquisition" (Lash 1994: 121).

This aspect of reflexivity, however, does not correlate with introspective reflection, based on the Cartesian *cogito*. To be reflexive for Lash means to rely on *bricolages*: "we put together networks, construct alliances, make deals" (Lash 2003: 51). Beck in the context of second modernity speaks of the choices we have today, based upon his notion of indeterminate knowledge. And here, too, can be found the full dimension of Anthony Giddens' concept of post-traditional society. For Giddens, (local) tradition loses its salience in second modernity, though it continues to exist (Giddens 1994: 95ff). Post-traditional society is reflexive in the context of intensifying globalization, and in as much as it disposes of all traditional contexts for agency.

Arjun Appadurai makes a similar argument in dealing with developments of art in the age of globalization. He combines the idea of unrestricted cultural flows with that of liberation from local cultural traditions. In Asia and Africa, he argues, modern art production is mostly restricted by references to local cultural traditions, a dilemma for representing the contemporary within the global contemporary.[4] An art that is truly embedded within globalization, and committed to coevality, has to be liberated from local cultural restrictions within a global framework; that is, by freely relying on whichever art traditions from wherever, as tools for visual representation at any place (Appadurai 1999: 56).

In the following, the question of particular spaces of reflexivity will be looked at in the context of the global art world, which is considered as a global culture. Such a global culture "is marked by an organization of diversity rather than by a replication of uniformity" (Hannerz 1990: 236). Some years ago, the project Global Art and the Museum (GAM) was launched at the Centre for Art and Media (ZKM) in Karlsruhe by Andrea Buddensieg, Hans Belting, and Peter Weibel.[5] It questions what global art is today, and whether museums of modern art, now renamed in many places as museums of contemporary art, are able to represent this global art (Buddensieg 2009: 10f.). The notion of "global art" is defined in opposition to that of "world art." "World art" is an older notion, encompasses all art of this globe in historical and geographical dimensions, and is inscribed within discourses of Occidental art history. "Global art" instead is connected solely to the age of globalization, and refers to the creation of different forms of contemporary art in the various regions of the globe. This latter notion acknowledges within the global context the existence of particular, local expressions of art, and is not subsumed under the hegemonic discourses of the European-North American art world (Belting 2007, 2009). The project coordinators and invited scholars further question, among other things, how and where such global art can be visualized, what contradictions are inherent in museums of contemporary art, and how a global art history can be conceptualized.

The problem may be clearly seen in the creation of the "Contemporary African Art Collection" (CAAC). Following the *Magiciens de la Terre* exhibition in Paris in 1989, curator André Magnin and collector Jean Pigozzi started this project. Both agreed to collect contemporary art from artists living in African countries, who had not been trained according to the canon of Occidental art history—i.e., they had not passed through any European- or North American-influenced academic training. Since then, André Magnin has been traveling widely throughout African countries to meet artists, and to buy works of art for the CAAC. Today, the CAAC encompasses more than six thousand works of art by artists from seventeen countries, and is still growing.

All these works of art have been created in the present day, and articulate in particular ways contemporary life in modern African states. It would, however, be quite problematic to subsume any of the artworks of the CAAC into the category of "contemporary" as a canonical criterion of Occidental art history (see Soulillou 1996). In hegemonic European and North American art-world discourses the notion of "contemporary" refers to works of art that are connected with present art discourses within that world—i.e., by artists who are acquainted with ongoing artistic reflections, and whose works may well be positioned within today's European-North American concept of contemporary art. In this respect, the works of art of the CAAC do not subscribe to these criteria. Non-academic European-North American training is not required; neither are interconnections with or references to Occidental art styles or the Eurocentric concept of (second) modernity. Neither would criteria developed by Occidental art history, therefore, be applied to subsume these works of art under discourse, nor would an inner matrix be developed that would connect all these works of art into an ideal global community of artworks.

Magnin and Soulillou have aimed at mapping the cultural connections created by the artists using the categories of Territory, Frontier, and World. Artworks placed in the category of Territory relate to traditional cultural expressions, such as the grave pillars (*aloalo*) by Efiaimbelo in Madagascar. Works of art are categorized as Frontier when they are between local traditional and European-North American contemporary art forms, such as the works by Calixte Dakpogan from Benin. His sculptures are related, on the one hand, to his earlier profession as a blacksmith, when he made sculptures (*asen*) for the local voodoo altars, and, on the other, to European *art brut*. The category of "World "characterizes those works of art that have strong interconnections with the global, as for instance the works of the Ivorian *vohou-vohou* artists mentioned above (Magnin and Soulillou 1996; Magnin 1998).

In the context of global art the CAAC is a radical example of a notion of "contemporary art" that is fundamentally different from that used by the European-North American art world, but that nevertheless is prominently present within it, in exhibitions such as in the Guggenheim Bilbao (2006–2007). The CAAC may, therefore, be considered as a particular place of reflexivity within the process of creating global art. It connects artworks from specific trajectories of modernities in various African countries, some of which are more vernacular, others more strongly influenced by European modernity. At the same time, it is placed within the European-North American art world. Rather than considering contemporary art from Africa as a by-product of European-North American contemporary art, in this perspective, there are multiple interlinked spaces of contemporary art. Centers and peripheries thus are viewed as entangled and as coeval.[6] The CAAC, moreover, reflects in a radical way various non-European and non-North American trajectories of what the contemporary may be in different social contexts in African countries. The GAM project, too, highlights the fact that museums of contemporary art in Europe and North America are not primarily places where interconnections, new alliances, and divergent visions for a global art are forged. Rather these museums are embedded within local social contexts, a majority of their audiences are local, and their collections have specific local histories. These aspects create a very specific constellation that does not allow a fundamental restructuring of these museums into institutions of "global art," i.e. exhibiting contemporary art from anywhere.

Rather, one has to turn towards art biennials, which have emerged since the late 1980s as arenas for new interconnections and various visions of global art. There are currently more than one hundred art biennials, and about half of them are located in countries of the global South. The most important principle of these venues is interconnectivity—i.e., connecting the art products of regions of the world that formerly seemed disconnected. Each art biennial is an arena within which global connections are specifically created. With its second edition in 1986, the biennial of la Havana, for instance, could position itself as the art biennial par excellence of the so-called Third World. The biennial of Dakar, Dak'Art, started in 1992 as an international art event, with artworks by artists from the Americas, Asia, Africa, and Europe. Such an approach, however, failed to convince as it brought neither a local, national nor a transregional West African perspective, and it did not succeed in positioning (West) African art within the context of the global art-biennial culture either. Thus in order to make its mark by gaining for itself a unique position, Dak'Art was reconceptualized by 1996 as a window on the contemporary art of Africa. Its 2004 exhibition included contemporary art by artists from the African diaspora too. Since then, each Dak'Art event reflects contemporary art of Africa, in relation to developments occurring within the global biennale culture at large. The Venice Biennale, one of the most important venues of the European-North American art world, is still largely built on a combination of both national pavilions and a movement away from this national dimension. In its fifty-third edition (2009), the artist duo Elmgreen & Dragset (Michael Elmgreen and Ingar Dragset) thematized, among other things, this dual "national and beyond the national" aspect. They curated a project, "The Collectors," which combined the Danish and the Nordic pavilions, and was the only one, where no national flag was hoisted at the entrance of the exhibition space.

This brief analysis should suffice to show that art biennials are arenas where different variations of the global are constructed by combining art products from different regions of the world. In doing so, each of them enhances a locally specific reflexivity of global art. The global system of art biennials, however, a global culture in Hannerz' terms (Hannerz 1990), shows a diversity of forms of reflexivity on the overall theme of global art.

Relational Reflexivity

Reflexivity appears as a technique in all disciplines, and as an everyday practice out there in society—what Marcus termed "essential reflexivity" (Marcus 1998: 190). In this concluding section of the chapter, I would like to raise the question of why reflexivity is particularly characteristic of anthropology, as Ulf Hannerz suggested by placing it among the four key notions he formulated for the discussions at the Stockholm Anthropology Roundtable.

In the context of fieldwork, Peter Hervik emphasizes the dialogical aspect of reflexivity, as part of the intersubjective process, within which the ethnographer and the interlocutor share their experiences, thus contributing to transforming social practice and the understanding of culture (Hervik 1994: 79). Okely argues in a similar vein, while stressing the participatory experience. "In its fullest sense, reflexivity forces us to think through the consequences of our relations with others, whether it be conditions of reciprocity, asymmetry or potential exploitation" (Okely 1992: 24). Interconnections, interactions, new alliances, networks, and *bricolages* are central themes in the work of Ulf Hannerz, particularly his thoughts on cultural flows, and more specifically the concepts of cultural complexity and the creole character of culture, global culture, or cosmopolitans. Even his interest in geocultural scenarios may be viewed in this framework, as extreme, hegemonic forms of picturing the interconnected world of today. The dialogical, intersubjective reflexivity that Hervik and Okely assert as characteristic for ethnographer and interlocutor, however, appear "out there" in the world, in processes inscribed in power relations. As against a self-reflective Cartesian concept of reflexivity, one may argue that such forms of reflexivity promote an "other-awareness" (Gershon 2006: 450).

In the examples dealt with above I have argued for reflexivity that is built on such other-awareness, on diversified relational gazes. The *vohou-vohou* movement in Ivory Coast consists of a transition from art production fully embedded within European modern art to visions of complex, non-linear trajectories propagated by artists in Ivory Coast. The CAAC, for instance, contributes to widening the ambit of contemporary art within a global framework. Art biennials, finally, may be conceived as arenas for picturing and debating ideas of global art in specific ways in particular places.

Reflexivity as "other-awareness" may be considered as a further critical function that anthropology may fulfill in our own societies. Two points are of interest in this context. The main thesis of Marcus' and Fischer's "anthropology as cultural critique" (1986: 111) was that the analysis of other cultures was the hidden agenda for a critique of one's own culture. Marcus and Myers proposed in 1995 a "critical anthropology of art," which transports the critical dimension further: such an anthropology of art would no longer translate non-European art to the European-North American art world. Marcus and Myers instead emphasize the appropriation and incorporation of the former within the Euro-American art world, while other works of art are excluded from it. "In this regard, the very specific anthropological critique would concern the art world's manner of assimilating, incorporating, or making its own cross-cultural difference" (Marcus and Myers 1995: 33). A critical anthropology of art, then, would unravel the circumstances and power relations of these processes, and further would show how images of other cultures are created by these processes of inclusion, circulation, and exclusion in European-North American contexts.

Reflexivity, as a key characteristic of anthropology, emphasizes the relational dimension of traffic between centers and peripheries. The anthropological gaze would focus on various regional trajectories thus producing entangled modernities (Randeria 1999: 379; see also Beck et al. 2003: 7f). Speaking of (reflexive) trajectories turns our attention to interconnections, to processes, which may as well include possible disjuncture. It also turns our attention to how people engage with modernization: how they express their complex global position and connections locally in a contemporary framework.

Concluding Remarks

This chapter focuses on reflexivity not as a methodological tool in anthropology, but as a cultural technique (see Myerhoff and Ruby 1982). On the one hand, reflexivity refers to a Cartesian introspection, the famous *cogito*. On the other, the concept of "reflexive modernization" (Beck 1994) corresponds less to an introspective process, than to a reflexive stance embedded in interconnections, networks, and alliances (Lash 1994). In using examples from the anthropology of art, the idea of reflexivity as constituted by entanglements (Randeria 1999) has been scrutinized here, examining the time and place of reflexivity. The chapter has examined, first, *when* reflexivity leads to a qualitative change in local art production, and second, *where*, in which specific arenas of world culture such processes of reflexivity might be located. It has argued that art biennials, for example, are spaces for the production of global entanglements of a different degree and kind than are museums of contemporary art. I have proposed to consider reflexivity in its relational dimension as one of the key characteristics of anthropology. The anthropological gaze might focus on documenting specific trajectories and arenas where power relations are enacted—in my particular case, that of the production of global art. A consideration of relational reflexivity would include notions of regional variations, of entangled trajectories, and of the production of particular interconnections by transcending former binary constructions of the self and other.

Notes

1. These were edited by Christian Kordt Højbjerg (*Social Anthropology/Anthropologie Sociale* 10(1), 2002) and Ilana Gershon (*Ethnos* 71(4), 2006) respectively.
2. For an in-depth discussion of this, see Fillitz (2002).
3. *Vohou* is a word in Gouro that was used by Jean Boni, a student of architecture in 1972, when he first saw the artworks of his colleagues at the Institut National des Arts. According to the artist Youssouf Bath, a prominent representative of the movement, it means "whatever," i.e. the application of any material to a support, just as a healer applies different medicines to the body of his patient.
4. Appadurai's argument about what he calls "anxieties of tradition" may be subject to criticism when considering the multiple contemporary art creations in these two continents (1999).
5. See Weibel and Buddensieg (2007) and Belting and Buddensieg (2009). I thank Hans Belting for giving me the opportunity of participating in one of the project's conferences, held in Vienna, entitled "The Interplay of Art and Globalization: The Cultural Practice of Global Art" (January 2007, International Research Center for Cultural Studies (IFK); see Fillitz 2009).
6. Randeria's notion of "entangled modernities" refers to the power structures which inform the interconnection of multiple modernities (Randeria 1999: 378).

References

Adams, Matthew. 2003. "The Reflexive Self and Culture: A Critique." *British Journal of Sociology* 54(2): 221–238.
Alexander, Jeffrey C. 1996. "Critical Reflections on 'Reflexive Modernisation.'" *Theory, Culture & Society* 13(4): 133–158.
Appadurai, Arjun. 1999. "Traditionsängste im globalen Kunstkontext—Anxieties of Tradition in the Artscapes of Globalization." *Springerin* 5(1): 54–57.
Beck, Ulrich. 1994. "The Reinvention of Politics: Towards a Theory of Reflexive Modernization." In *Reflexive Modernization: Politics, Traditions and Aesthetics in the Modern Social Order*, ed. Ulrich Beck, Anthony Giddens, and Scott Lash. Cambridge: Polity Press, pp. 1–55.
Beck, Ulrich, Wolfgang Bonss, and Christoph Lau. 2003. "The Theory of Reflexive Modernization: Problematic, Hypotheses and Research Programme." *Theory, Culture & Society* 20(2): 1–33.
Belting, Hans. 2007. "Contemporary Art and the Museum in the Global Age." In *Contemporary Art and the Museum: A Global Perspective*, ed. Peter Weibel and Andrea Buddensieg. Ostfildern: Hatje Cantz, pp. 16–41.
———. 2009. "Contemporary Art as Global Art: A Critical Estimate." In *The Global Art World: Audiences, Markets, and Museums*, ed. Hans Belting and Andrea Buddensieg. Ostfildern: Hatje Cantz, pp. 38–73.
Belting, Hans and Andrea Buddensieg, eds. 2009. *The Global Art World: Audiences, Markets, and Museums*. Ostfildern: Hatje Cantz.

Buddensieg, Andrea. 2009. "Editorial." In *The Global Art World: Audiences, Markets, and Museums*, ed. Hans Belting and Andrea Buddensieg. Ostfildern: Hatje Cantz, pp. 10–37.
Bydler, Charlotte. 2004. *The Global Art World Inc.: On the Globalization of Contemporary Art*. Acta Universitatis Upsaliensis, Figura Nova Series 32. Uppsala: University of Uppsala.
Demian, Melissa. 2006. "Reflecting on Loss in Papua New Guinea." *Ethnos* 71(4): 507–531.
Elkins, John, ed. 2007. *Is Art History Global?* London and New York: Routledge.
Fillitz, Thomas. 2002. *Zeitgenösssische Kunst aus Afrika: Vierzehn Künstler aus Côte d'Ivoire und Bénin*. Vienna: Böhlau.
———. 2009. "Contemporary Art in Africa: Coevalness in the Global World." In *The Global Art World: Audiences, Markets, and Museums*, ed. Hans Belting and Andrea Buddensieg. Ostfildern: Hatje Cantz, pp. 116–134.
Gershon, Ilana. 2006. "Reflexivity in Other's Context: An Introduction." *Ethnos* 71(4): 445–452.
Giddens, Anthony. 1994. "Living in a Post-Traditional Society." In *Reflexive Modernization: Politics, Traditions and Aesthetics in the Modern Social Order*, ed. Ulrich Beck, Anthony Giddens, and Scott Lash. Cambridge: Polity Press, pp. 56–109.
Hannerz, Ulf. 1990. "Cosmopolitans and Locals in World Culture." In *Global Culture: Nationalism, Globalization and Modernity*, ed. Mike Featherstone. London: Sage Publications, pp. 237–252.
Harney, Elisabeth. 2004. *In Senghor's Shadow: Art, Politics, and the Avant-Garde in Senegal: 1960–1995*. Durham, NC and London: Duke University Press.
Hervik, Peter. 1994. "Shared Reasoning in the Field: Reflexivity beyond the Authors." In *Social Experience and Anthropological Knowledge*, ed. Kirsten Hastrup and Peter Hervik. London and New York: Routledge, pp. 78–100.
Højbjerg, Christian Kordt. 2002. "Religious Reflexivity: Essays on Attitudes to Religious Ideas and Practice." *Social Anthropology/Anthropologie Sociale* 10(1): 1–10.
Lash, Scott. 1994. "Reflexivity and its Doubles: Structure, Aesthetics, Community." In *Reflexive Modernization: Politics, Traditions and Aesthetics in the Modern Social Order*, ed. Ulrich Beck, Anthony Giddens, and Scott Lash. Cambridge: Polity Press, pp. 110–173.
———. 2003. "Reflexivity as Non-linearity." *Theory, Culture & Society* 20(2): 49–57.
Lynch, Michael. 2000. "Against Reflexivity as an Academic Virtue and Source of Privileged Knowledge." *Theory, Culture & Society* 17(3): 26–54.
Magnin, André. 1998. "Welten, Welt." In *Triennale der Kleinplastik. Zeitgenössische Skulptur Europa Afrika*, ed. Trägerverein der Triennale der Kleinplastik e.V., W. Meyer, Künstlerischer Leiter. Catalogue. Osterfildern: Ruit, pp. 51–58.
Magnin, André and Jacques Soulillou. 1996. "Introduction." In *Contemporary Art of Africa*, ed. André Magnin and Jacques Soulillou. New York: Abrams, pp. 8–17.
Marcus, George E. 1998. *Ethnography through Thick and Thin*. Princeton, NJ: Princeton University Press.

Marcus, George E. and Michael M. Fischer. 1986. *Anthropology as Cultural Critique: An Experimental Moment in the Human Sciences*. Chicago and London: The University of Chicago Press.

Marcus, George E. and Fred R. Myers. 1995. "The Traffic in Art and Culture: An Introduction." In *The Traffic in Culture: Refiguring Art and Anthropology*, ed. George E. Marcus and Fred R. Myers. Berkeley: University of California Press, pp. 1–51.

Myerhoff, Barbara and Jay Ruby. 1982. "Introduction." In *A Crack in the Mirror: Reflexive Perspectives in Anthropology*, ed. Jay Ruby. Philadelphia: University of Pennsylvania Press, pp. 1–35.

Okely, Judith. 1992. "Anthropology and Autobiography: Participatory Experience and Embodied Knowledge." In *Anthropology and Autobiography*, ed. Judith Okely and Helen Callaway. ASA Monographs 29. London and New York: Routledge, pp. 1–26.

Pels, Dick. 2000. "Reflexivity: One Step Up." *Theory, Culture & Society* 17(3): 1–25.

Randeria, Shalini. 1999. "Jenseits von Soziologie und soziokultureller Anthropologie: Zur Ortsbestimmung der nichtwestlichen Welt in einer zukünftigen Sozialtheorie." *Soziale Welt* 50: 373–382.

Salzmann, Philip .C. 2002. "On Reflexivity." *American Anthropologist* 104(3): 805–813.

Sandywell, Barry. 1999. "Specular Grammar: The Visual Rhetoric of Modernity." In *Interpreting Visual Culture: Explorations in the Hermeneutics of the Visual*, ed. Ian Heywood and Barry Sandywell. London and New York: Routledge, pp. 30–56.

Soulillou, Jacques. 1996. "Für eine Phänomenologie der afrikanischen Kunst." In *Neue Kunst aus Afrika*, ed. Alfons Hug. Catalogue. Berlin: Haus der Kulturen der Welt, pp. 72–80.

Summers, David. 2003. *Real Spaces: World Art History and the Rise of Western Modernism*. London: Phaidon.

Therborn, Göran. 2000. "The Birth of Second Century Sociology: Times of Reflexivity, Spaces of Identity, and Nodes of Knowledge." *British Journal of Sociology* 51(1): 37–57.

Weibel, Peter and Andrea Buddensieg, eds. 2007. *Contemporary Art and the Museum: A Global Perspective*. Ostfildern: Hatje Cantz.

Chapter 8

ANTHROPOLOGIST IN THE IRISH LITERARY WORLD
Reflexivity through Studying Sideways
Helena Wulff

In his recent book *Anthropology's World*, Ulf Hannerz (2010: 1) starts out by pointing to the two meanings of this notion: "anthropology as a social world in itself—the community of a discipline, with its internal social relationships, its ideas and practices," and anthropology's world as "the wider outside world to which the discipline must relate in various ways." In what follows, drawing on an anthropological study of contemporary Irish writers as cultural translators and public intellectuals, the literary world in Ireland will be considered in a parallel way.[1] One defining idea of the social world of Irish writers, which relates to the outside world, is the distinction between on one hand a national reputation and on the other an international reputation. For this, choice of literary tropes—that is, common themes in storytelling—is vital. This chapter also follows Ulf Hannerz' (1998, 2004) strategy, in his research on the foreign correspondents of news media, of "studying sideways," which turns out to be a method with theoretical implications. Both writers and foreign correspondents can be seen as the anthropologist's fellow intellectuals. This adds another dimension to reflexivity.

The anthropology of literature and writing, which has expanded recently, goes a long way back and covers the role of literature and literary texts in anthropology as well as writing as process and form. This is evident in volumes such as *Literature and Anthropology* (Dennis and Aycock 1989) and *Novel Approaches to Anthropology* (Cohen 2013). In the 1970s, Victor Turner (1976: 77–78) saw how African ritual and Western literature were "mutually elucidating." Clifford Geertz (1988) wrote about the anthropologist as author and at the end of the twentieth century, there was the influential debate on writing culture (Clifford and Marcus 1986). Eduardo Archetti (1994: 13) formulated an anthropology of the written, which suggests that "a literary product is not only a substantive part of the real world but also a key element in the configuration of the world itself."

In the Irish Literary World

Irish writing also has its own long history. Looking back, Ireland's strong literary tradition was established by writers from James Joyce to Edna O'Brien and Seamus Heaney. Literature was a prominent part of the nationalist cultural revival in Ireland, at the end of the nineteenth century. Under the leadership of W. B. Yeats, a poet but also a senator, the literary movement had an impact on the passage of Ireland into political independence (Kiberd 1996; Ó Giolláin 2000). Literary theorist Declan Kiberd (1996) has even pointed out that it was with this literary movement that Ireland became a modern nation. A number of twentieth-century Irish authors have made the journey to Stockholm to receive the Nobel Prize in literature.

Today the literary tradition is developed further by an acclaimed generation of contemporary writers such as Chris Binchy, Roddy Doyle, Deirdre Madden, Éilís Ní Dhuibhne (pronounced in English "Ailish Nee Gwivna"), Colm Tóibín, and the winner of the prestigious Man Booker Prize in 2007, Anne Enright. Born in the 1950s or later, these writers of novels, short stories, plays, and journalistic essays tend to consider the new Ireland with its recent rapid social change. As with any artistic depiction, their literary representations are not direct reflections of what the writers observe around them, but intricate commentary. Many stories take the form of social satire, they can be both political and romantic, and are usually witty, but framed by a dark tone, even though the stories tend to end in a sudden sense of hope, looking forward with a certain optimism after all.

It is among this generation of writers I have been doing my fieldwork. Although the anthropology of literature is an established subfield with a history, my study has thus come to involve a number of current issues such as how to conduct ethnographic research on celebrity and fellow intellectuals. There is the changing role of the anthropologist in relation to the people we study. Some Irish writers have achieved a global celebrity-elite status, so that research with them entails "studying up" (Nader 1999). Yet writing about his study of the work of foreign correspondents, Hannerz (2004: 3, 226) points out that he prefers to think of this as "studying sideways": it is "not so much as a matter of power or rank" but a question of "trying to understand the workings of a neighboring group engaged in a somewhat parallel pursuit." Interestingly,

Sherry Ortner (2010: 213) has also recently pointed out that "much of what is called studying up is really 'studying sideways,' that is, studying people—like scientists, journalists, and Hollywood filmmakers—who in many ways are really not much different from anthropologists and our fellow academics more generally." Ortner (2010: 223) continues by indicating that not only do "the people being studied have the same kinds of educational background as the anthropologist," but also they are, she emphasizes, "working in the same general cultural zone as ourselves—the world of knowledge, information, representation, interpretation and criticism. This I think plays a large role in the fact that some of the most active areas in the 'studying up' game today are the anthropology of (the work of) the knowledge classes." This is an increasing trend in anthropology, which is reshaping fieldwork, knowledge production, and the writing process. Reflexive informants have, of course, always been there. Educated or not, but with an intellectual inclination, they are our best friends in the field. Not only can they be counted on to provide reliable replies to questions time and again, but admittedly they keep surprising us with analytical insights that sometimes can go directly into text. Yet in contrast to classic anthropology, it is now becoming common to study people that are the anthropologist's colleagues and counterparts (Holmes and Marcus 2005). A systematic, while internally diverse, studying sideways can bring new complexity to our reflexivity.

The argument about similarities between anthropologist and informant applies, again, to an anthropological inquiry into the work of writers in Ireland. Just like writers, anthropologists spend a lot of time reading and writing. A writer's job is not only writing, however, but also delivering public talks. Apart from reading their own work at festivals and other events, they give papers at academic conferences and teach university courses in creative writing and comparative literature (Wulff 2011b). They engage in what Ortner (2010), discussing her Hollywood study, terms "interface events." This is, again, quite similar to what academics do, which makes me feel close to the writers. With many of the writers I also share the task to comment on the new Ireland. This sense of affinity is accentuated by the fact that some of the writers write literary essays and reviews for magazines such as *The New Yorker* and the *London Review of Books* and daily papers such as *The Irish Times*, as well as academic volumes on literature. I too know something about what it is like to switch between genres, if not between fiction and culture journalism, at least between academic anthropology and culture journalism. I occasionally write journalistic essays and features on my research for the Arts and Leisure pages of a Swedish daily, and international dance magazines (Wulff 2011a; see also Boyer and Hannerz 2006 and Gottlieb and Graham 1994).

My field research involves interviewing, in the form of extended conversations, and as much informal interaction with writers and their social circles as possible—here is the literary world as a social world in itself. The interface events may be seen to occur at its margins, but they are also central in my ethnography. In large part, as they occur regularly but not so frequently, the study takes place on a number of visits back and forth from Stockholm to Ireland. Like many other contemporary field studies, that is, this study demanded recurrent visits over more than the traditional uninterrupted year in the field. It unfolded during week-long stints mainly about every third month over a three-year period, and subsequent follow up visits—what I have called yo-yo fieldwork (Wulff 2002, 2007a).

Tropes of Irish Storytelling

What, then, for the Irish literary world, is that world outside the community to which its members respond? Here the task is to scrutinize what the writers choose to write about. In his extensive review of *Irish Writing in the Twentieth Century*, David Pierce (2000: 1267–1281) identifies the central topics and issues of Irish writing: "history, politics and religion," "the city and the country," "culture and identity," "colonialism and post-colonialism," and "the Irish diaspora." Among the subtopics he mentions are "violence," "North of Ireland," "folklore and folk tales," "gender," "gay sexuality," "childhood," and "return" to Ireland. These topics are obvious in Irish society, and some of the stories by the writers in this study will be related to them here. This chapter will make use of literary tropes that correspond with topics that have come up frequently during my fieldwork with the writers: topics I have observed or that writers have brought up spontaneously during informal conversations. Some of the tropes discussed coincide with Pierce's topics; others do not. History, for instance, was emphasized early in my fieldwork by writers in many conversations as a strong structure in Irish society of which I should be aware. They have not mentioned family as a topic to include in my research, but often refer to family in other contexts. This centrality of family life strikes an outside observer as unusual. I have also had many opportunities to observe family life in Ireland.

Pierce's reader begins in 1892 and ends in 1999, while this study is taking place in the twenty-first century. This chapter will consider, in particular, novels published between 1999 and 2009, and discuss how

Irish tropes might be about to undergo transformation. To what extent does the new Ireland have new tropes? One new trope is the so-called Celtic Tiger, the economic boom in the late twentieth century and recently the economic downturn. The Troubles (and post-Troubles) in Northern Ireland is a somewhat older theme, going back not only to the late 1960s when the contemporary conflict broke out, but at least to the treatment of the moral ambiguities in the aftermath of the War of Independence. This period is portrayed in Sebastian Barry's (2008) novel *The Secret Scripture* through the tragic fate of a Protestant woman who marries a Catholic man in Sligo in the 1930s.[2] The big family with closeness and constraint is a classic trope in Irish literature and life. One or two of these tropes can be said to define each of the following novels, supported by subtropes. As will be shown, there are also overlaps. A major trope in one novel might appear as a subtrope in another one, and the same subtrope does recur in many novels. There are clusters of tropes and subtropes that belong together, such as the Celtic Tiger, politics, and morality. The Troubles are associated with violence and religion, and family is also associated with religion, as well as with childhood and gender.

Éilís Ní Dhuibhne's (2007a) novel entitled *Fox, Swallow, Scarecrow* was endorsed as a Celtic Tiger novel by Kate Holmquist on the first page as "searingly perceptive and wickedly funny in its stylish dissection of the rotten heart of contemporary Ireland's chattering intelligentsia." It is the literary world in Dublin, especially "the aspiring middle-class popular-fiction writers of south Dublin" (O'Donoghue 2007), which is Ní Dhuibhne's target. Talking about writing *Fox, Swallow, Scarecrow*, before it was published, she told me: "I've written it very quickly. It just flowed out," and that: "the story is going to be about relationships. It always has to be. The petty catting all the time." A much-quoted section in the novel describes one aspect of relationships in the new Celtic Tiger Ireland:

> Divorce was available in Ireland these days, but it had arrived, strangely enough, at the same time as the big increase in house prices.[3] When people could afford to divorce, it wasn't available, and then when it became available, it became unaffordable. Almost overnight. The free-market economy was doing what the Church had done for centuries. (Ní Dhuibhne 2007a: 45)

Incidentally, the novel *Open-handed* by Chris Binchy (2008) was also advertised as a Celtic Tiger novel, and this was how it was received. But here a new trope, that of immigrants from eastern Europe, is introduced. This makes it different from Ní Dhuibhne's Celtic Tiger novel. Ireland, which used to be an emigration country, is now also an immigration country. *Open-handed* features five characters. The three immigrants, Marcin, Victor, and Agnieszka, work the night shifts in hotels and bars. The two Irish characters are a businessman in the foreign property market and his driver. In their pursuits of success, from their different vantage points in Irish society, these characters get together in unexpected ways. One point made in the novel is that not only the immigrants are lost when it comes to "class codes and moral mores" (Hand 2008) in their new country; so are the Irish in modern Ireland. In a country with a history of fractured identities, the new immigration has brought out questions about who exactly is Irish. In the satirical yet serious short story "57 % Irish" by Roddy Doyle (2007), the protagonist considers how to measure Irishness. He invents a test based on people's reactions to video clips of the Irish dance show *Riverdance*, the traditional song "Danny Boy," and a goal scored by an Irish football player, Robbie Keane, against Germany in the 2002 World Cup.

When I asked Deirdre Madden, in an interview in Dublin in 2008, if she relates to the Celtic Tiger in her fiction, she replied that: "I want to think of bigger things than just what is happening now—not just reflecting or reporting on the Celtic Tiger. It takes time to consider what it was about, to really be thoughtful about it." Madden's (2008) novel *Molly Fox's Birthday* deals with the impact of the past on the present. Even though the novel unfolds during the course of one single June day in Dublin (as did the classic *Ulysses* by James Joyce (1922)), it is built around reminiscences from the past, especially an event from the Troubles. The narrator, who is now a playwright, went to Trinity College as a student, where she met Andrew, a Protestant from the North. Andrew's brother Billy was a Loyalist paramilitary. One morning:

> I slept in for my nine-o'clock lecture on Monday and was bumbling around the kitchen, still in my dressing gown, when the phone rang. As soon as Andrew spoke I knew by the sound of his voice that something was seriously wrong. He asked me if I had heard the news headlines that morning and I said that I had. "That man," he said, "the man who was shot, the body they found on the mountain—that was Billy." (Madden 2008: 41)

As Cressida Connolly (2008) remarked in her review in *The Telegraph*, "the reader is never introduced to Billy, the person who has had the most profound effect on anyone in this book. Instead, his death creates an empty space that his surviving brother must face and, ultimately, overcome." The narrator also has an older brother, Tom, who is a Catholic priest. Despite their differences in outlook and experiences, she loves him dearly. It was Tom who first took the narrator to the theatre, in Belfast, when she was a child.

A subtrope in this novel is clearly "family." The narrator has a big, congenial, Catholic family in the rural part of Northern Ireland, yet she is only really close to her brother Tom. Not only are the brothers of the narrator and Andrew important for the story, so is Molly Fox's brother Fergus, who sometimes has to go into hospital because of depression and drinking. Molly takes care of him, and he is said to be the reason that she, with her international fame as an actor, remains in Dublin. The fact that their mother left the family when they were both young probably matters also. Towards the end of the novel, which increases in surprise and suspense, it is revealed that Molly does not celebrate her birthday (she is away in New York on this day), and that the reason is not an actress's fear of old age, but the painful memory of her mother leaving her and her family—on Molly's birthday.

Family is the focus of Anne Enright's (2007) famous novel *The Gathering*, where a big Irish family gets together for the wake of Liam, one of the brothers, who has committed suicide. The past is prevalent here, too, just like in *Molly Fox's Birthday*, catching up with the characters. The novel opens with a hint of a haunting childhood memory. It is Veronica Hegarty who spins this story, which started when she was eight or nine years old: "I think you might call it a crime of the flesh" (Enright 2007: 1). Pedophilia has, of course, been a huge public issue in Ireland, leading to the collapse of the government in 1994 and numerous court cases. As *The Gathering* shows, the hurt and humiliation of such acts are monumental. *The Gathering* displays a lot of grief. In its connection with love, between siblings, parents, and children, as well as spouses, grief becomes a subtrope in this novel.

Family, premature death, and grief also feature in the novel *The Blackwater Lightship* by Colm Tóibín (1999). Published in 1999, the story takes place in 1993, which was the year when homosexuality was finally decriminalized in Ireland (Walshe 2008). *The Blackwater Lightship* is not as much a story about homosexuality, as it is a story about AIDS. The novel has been made into a film, and as Walshe (2008: 121) says, "this widely read novel, which was shortlisted for the Booker Prize, successfully brought an Irish AIDS narrative right into the mainstream of Irish culture." In the story, Declan is dying of AIDS in his grandmother's house by the sea. His family—sister, mother, and grandmother—have to come to terms with this, and with each other afterwards. The twist of the story is that these three generations of women, who have been incompatible for years, are brought together by this devastating event. There is also a gay couple, friends of Declan, who arrive one after the other. Larry comes first, which prompts a conversation between Declan's sister, Helen, and their grandmother.

> When Larry went and sat in front of the house, Helen's grandmother guardedly closed the kitchen door and made sure no one was coming.
> "Helen," she asked, "is this man Larry, is he going to stay here as well?"
> "I don't know, Granny."
> "Helen, are we going to put them into the same room?" [Declan's room]
> "I don't know."
> "I suppose we're all modern now," her grandmother said, going again to the window, "and I'm as modern as anyone, but I would just like to know. That's all." (Tóibín 1999: 130)

It turns out that Declan's grandmother has taken for granted that he and Larry were partners, which is something she has no problems with. Helen explains, however, that Declan does not have a partner: he has his family and friends. Their grandmother is deeply saddened by the fact that "he has nobody of his own" (Tóibín 1999: 130) and makes clear that "we have to do everything we can for him."

The Significance of Irish Soil

In a way, however, and to a degree, life as portrayed by the current generation of Irish writers can also be seen to involve two major kinds of stories. I want to explore literary accounts of the new Ireland in terms of Walter Benjamin's (1969: 84–86) idea of the two archaic types of storytellers: "the resident tiller of the soil" who "knows the local tales and traditions" and the traveler "who has come from afar," bringing "the lore of faraway places." The reason for the focus on the soil, or the link to the land (see Wulff 2007a), here is that the soil continues to have a special meaning in Ireland and thus is often referred to in literary renderings. One example of a writer who travels and "brings the lore from faraway places" is Colm Tóibín, whose novel *The Master* (2004) is a biographical fiction about the American writer Henry James. Tóibín devotes a long section in the novel to a Dublin visit by James—just one of the Irish connections in this story from afar.

It was when I was doing my previous study in Ireland (see mainly Wulff 2007a, but also Wulff, 2003 and 2005, among others), on dance and social memory, that I was impressed with the significance of the Irish soil. In an interview, a manager of The Project Arts Centre, an alternative theatre and exhibition space in Dublin, told me:

> We were a colonized country, an occupied country. What happens is that land becomes important for survival. The English took land and left the poorer land to the Irish. If you had no land, you had no status in the community, that has carried through: people have a very deep desire to own property. (Wulff 2007a: 51)

It is thus the legacy of colonialism in the Republic of Ireland that is the basis of the contemporary link to the land. Experiences of emigration and exile are prominent in Irish society and culture, both in Ireland and among the Irish diaspora communities, and keep contributing to the magnitude of this link to the Irish land. It seems to be more momentous than in many places. Remnants of colonial conflict, but also internal disagreement and controversy over land rights, have maintained the complexity of this link. Historically, it originates in the early colonization of Ireland when the English settled on plantations and estates in the sixteenth and seventeenth centuries. Penal laws that were introduced in the seventeenth century stated long-term restrictions on Catholics' practicing their religion or owning land. After the Great Famine in the mid-nineteenth century, landlords and tenants agreed to a system where tenants were allowed to leave rented farms to their own heirs. Just a few years later, landlords were faced with an agricultural decline and thus financial difficulties. This led to a wave of evictions of poor tenants (Fitzpatrick 1989; Power and Whelan 1990; Ó Giolláin 2000).

The physical form and location of a land are crucial for how it is perceived. It matters that Ireland is an island, that it is flat and surrounded by cliffs and long beaches. John Gillis (2001: 40) points to the quality of remoteness of islands, and goes on to say that remoteness does not always entail physical distance, as it might well occur through "travel through time." According to Gillis, remote places such as islands are often associated with "pastness," which may not be accurate. When it comes to Ireland, different forms of perceived "pastness" attract both expatriates and tourists to go there (Wulff 2007b).[4] In the novel *The Dancers Dancing*, Éilís Ní Dhuibhne (2007b) contemplates the map of Ireland when arriving by air:

> Imagine you are in an airplane, flying at twenty thousand feet. The landscape spreads beneath like a chequered tablecloth thrown across a languid body. From this vantage point, no curve is apparent. It is flat earth—pan flat, plan flat, platter flat to the edges, its green and gold patches stained at intervals by lumps of mountain, brownish purple clots of varicose vein in the smooth skin of land. Patterns of field, rough squares and rectangles, are hatched in with grey stone. The white spots, sometimes slipping disconcertingly out of focus, are sheep. (Ní Dhuibhne 2007b: 1)

The Irish landscape looks neat from above, but not everything on the ground is visible from there. "What you can't see is what it is better not to see: the sap and the clay and the weeds and the mess," Ní Dhuibhne (2007b: 2–3) goes on in her stream-of-consciousness style, and she brings out colorful details from "heart and kitchen and sewer" to "weep and laugh." By then we have landed on the Irish soil "in between, that is the truth and that is the story."

Stories from Afar

Born in Ireland, Colm Tóibín's upbringing was steeped in Irish history. His grandfather fought in the 1916 Uprising against the British and was interned in Wales. After having completed a degree in literature and history at University College Dublin, Tóibín left Ireland and lived for many years in Spain. He came back and worked as a journalist, writing essays that would develop into literary stories. In addition to his fiction, Tóibín writes literary essays and reviews for magazines such as *The New Yorker* and *The New York Review of Books*.

Living in London, "Henry James" in Tóibín's The Master (2004), is preoccupied with Oscar Wilde's trial and public disgrace, fearing that this might happen to him. "James, like Wilde, was of Irish Protestant descent, but kept his Irish ancestry 'hidden'" (Walshe 2008: 128). In a conversation about what spurred him to write *The Master*, Tóibín has said that he was drawn to James' abandonment. "I was interested in that. I was also interested in James versus Oscar Wilde, his Irishness being hidden, his homosexuality being hidden" (O'Toole 2008: 197). The fact that James was single out of choice has been confirmed by Tóibín (2007) in an essay entitled "Single Minded" in *The Guardian*. Solitude was the only way for James to be able to write. In this chapter, which is tracing Irish tropes, it is worth noting that it was after having experienced a major fiasco with the play *Guy Domville* in a London theatre that James, in Tóibín's biographical fiction, decided to go to Ireland for comfort. "He went to Ireland since it was easy to travel there and because he did not believe it would strain his nerves" (Tóibín 2004: 22). In the novel, James stays with friends who have not seen his play, enjoys the polite courting of a male servant at a distance, and observes intrigue at a ball—all against a backdrop of political unrest in Ireland. *The Master* had rave reviews, but in one of them the reviewer, who is otherwise clearly impressed by Tóibín's accomplishment, inserts a comment about the visit to Ireland, saying in a parenthesis that this is "(an excuse for a lightning sketch of late 19th-century British colonialism, a subject closer to Tóibín's heart than James's)" (Lee 2004). Nevertheless, it is a case in point here.

Tóibín's *The Blackwater Lightship* (1999) was shortlisted for the Man Booker Prize, but did not win. In an interview with Fintan O'Toole (2008), Tóibín explains how "the very bruising Booker Prize experience," when "you would have to go over to London and wash yourself and put on formal clothes, and have a TV camera in your face for about two hours" (O'Toole 2008: 199), had been essential when he wrote about Henry James' failure with the play. Eventually, *The Master* (2004) was shortlisted for the Man Booker Prize. The fact that it did not win the prize either is an event which other writers in the literary world in Ireland regard as a major mistake.

Based in Dublin, Colm Tóibín now spends a number of months in Spain and the United States every year, which is noticeable in his choice of topics. Many Irish writers have lived abroad, including Deirdre Madden, and many still do. Colum McCann was born in Dublin, but moved to the United States as a young adult and made an international name for himself there. He mostly writes about non-Irish topics, such as in the biographical fiction *Dancer: A Novel* (2004), inspired by the Russian dancer Rudolf Nureyev's dramatic life, moving from a provincial town during Stalinism to world fame in the West and gay jet-set life in New York during the 1980s. *Dancer* was published by Picador in New York. Picador has a London office, by which *The Blackwater Lightship* and *The Master* were published. In a sense, Irish writers who publish with U.S. and U.K. publishers bring Irish stories from afar, to American and British readers.

Conclusions: Reflexivity and Studying Sideways Reconsidered

The traditional Irish tropes, emigration and exile, are illustrated by Colm Tóibín in another novel, *Brooklyn* (2009), which opens in a small town in the 1950s Ireland. This is a story which is both from the soil and from far away as it combines the two perspectives. It traces the trajectory of a young woman, Eilis, who has to emigrate. She goes to Brooklyn in search of a job, which she finds, working in a department store. She falls in love with an Italian man, but is unexpectedly called home to Ireland when her sister dies. In the end, Eilis decides to go back to Brooklyn and make her life there. The painful pivot of the novel is the legacy of leave-taking in Ireland.

Comparing the resident storyteller and the one from far away, Benjamin (1969) argues that they are in fact quite alike in their work: the traveler might well have been resident before setting out on travel, and vice versa. Relating this to Irish writers such as James Joyce, Fintan O'Toole (1997: 83) finds both types of stories in the same literary pieces, but notes that a competition between the two is more common.

This is obvious in the contemporary literary world in Ireland, where it importantly has consequences for careers. In the social organization of the world of writers in Ireland, a distinction is made between those who combine their literary writing with cultural journalism and teaching creative writing at universities in Ireland, Britain, and the United States as a way to support themselves, on one hand, and those who work in museums or broadcasting media in Ireland, on the other. One senses here, both in kinds of Irish stories and in kinds of Irish writers' careers, parallels with contrasting concepts which are now familiar to anthropologists: anthropology at home and anthropology away, and cosmopolitans and locals.

There seems to be an expectation internationally that books coming out of Ireland deal with Irish tropes. I have discussed the Celtic Tiger, the Troubles, family, exile, emigration, and immigration, as well as a number of subtropes that surround them such as violence, religion, grief, childhood, and gay sexuality. Colonialism also belongs here. Another classic trope of Ireland is the Great Famine.

However, it is not only the choice of an Irish trope, or non-Irish trope, which defines a novel as a story of the soil or from far away, respectively. It also matters how Irish local knowledge is presented, to what extent explanations are provided about Irish circumstances. It can be something as simple as to specify that the DART (Dublin Area Rapid Transit) is a suburban train in the Dublin area. *The Master* (2004), *The Gathering* (2007), and *Brooklyn* (2009) were written with international readerships in mind. *Molly Fox's Birthday* (2008) was published with a London publisher, but is an example of a book that works both in Ireland and abroad. Novels by writers in Ireland that are published with U.S. or U.K. publishers in a global market can be classified as new world literature, referring to circulation rather than evaluation (Casanova 2004). In the competition between writers who stay with stories of the soil and those who venture into stories from afar, it is obviously prestigious to be able to make a living on literary writing in combination with cultural journalism, which also offers more time to write than having to work full-time on something else. This tends to involve those authors in twenty-first century Ireland who write of faraway places as well as the Irish soil.

Studying sideways in the Irish literary world, I now and then feel that I catch a glimpse of a mirror for anthropology. In the craft of writing, the making of a writer's career with relationships to colleagues, critics, readership, and the publishing market, and the fact that we to some extent share the task of cultural journalism, an anthropologist can look at fiction writers with a certain recognition of seemingly familiar experiences. But that would be too simple a notion of the possibilities of studying sideways. Importantly, the inhabitants of that world cultivate reflexivity in their own ways. In *Anthropology's World*, Ulf Hannerz (2010: 59ff.) also notes that anthropology's expansion over the last century has involved "studying down, up, sideways, through, backward, forward, early or later, away and at home." And while he points to a certain fondness among anthropologists for visual imagery (2010: 87ff.), he goes beyond the simple mirror as a metaphor. The range of optical tools for varied anthropological practices, he suggests, has included halls of mirrors, rear-view mirrors, microscopes, binoculars, telescopes, and dark glasses...

As studying sideways involves other people's reflexivities, not altogether similar to ours, we may well be stimulated, or provoked, to think again about what we study, how, and where; and about how we write, and for whom. As anthropology moves further into the twenty-first century, perhaps that can help us decide what to do next.

Notes

1. The study "Writing in Ireland: An Ethnographic Study of Schooling and the World of Writers" was funded by the Swedish Research Council in 2007–2009.
2. For classic literary accounts of this historical period, see for instance Frank O'Connor's short story "Guests of the Nation," first published in 1931, which depicts the execution of two Englishmen held hostage by the Irish Republican Army during the War of Independence. Liam O'Flaherty's novel *The Informer* (1925) is about an informer who betrays a friend in the aftermath of this war.
3. Since then house prices in Dublin have both decreased and increased again.
4. See the chapter "The Link to the Land" in Wulff (2007a). For an argument about the Irish land in relation to tourism, see Wulff (2007b).

References

Archetti, Eduardo, ed. 1994. *Exploring the Written: Anthropology and the Multiplicity of Writing*. Oslo: Scandinavian University Press.
Barry, Sebastian. 2008. *The Secret Scripture*. London: Faber and Faber.
Benjamin, Walter. 1969. "The Storyteller: Reflections on the Works of Nikolai Leskov." In *Illuminations*. New York: Schocken Books, pp. 83–109.
Binchy, Chris. 2008. *Open-handed*. Dublin: Penguin Ireland.
Boyer, Dominic and Ulf Hannerz. 2006. "Introduction: Worlds of Journalism." *Ethnography* 7(1): 5–17.

Casanova, Pascale. 2004. *The World Republic of Letters*. Cambridge, MA: Harvard University Press.
Clifford, James, and George E. Marcus, eds. 1986. *Writing Culture: The Poetics and Politics of Ethnography*. Berkeley: University of California Press.
Cohen, Marilyn, ed. 2013. *Novel Approaches to Anthropology: Contributions to Literary Anthropology*. New York: Lexington Books.
Connolly, Cressida. 2008. "Review. Molly Fox's Birthday by Deirdre Madden." *The Telegraph*, 15 August.
Dennis, Philip A. and Wendell Aycock, eds. 1989. *Literature and Anthropology*. Lubbock: Texas Tech University Press.
Doyle, Roddy. 2007. "57 % Irish." In *The Deportees and Other Stories*. London: Jonathan Cape, pp. 100–129.
Enright, Anne. 2007. *The Gathering*. London: Jonathan Cape.
Fitzpatrick, David. 1989. "Ireland Since 1870." In *The Oxford History of Ireland*, ed. Roy F. Foster. Oxford: Oxford University Press, pp. 174–229.
Geertz, Clifford. 1988. *Works and Lives: The Anthropologist as Author*. Stanford: Stanford University Press.
Gillis, John R. 2001. "Places Remoter and Islanded." *Michigan Quarterly Review* 40(1): 39–58.
Gottlieb, Alma and Philip Graham. 1994. *Parallel Worlds: An Anthropologist and a Writer Encounter Africa*. Chicago: University of Chicago Press.
Hand, Derek. 2008. "Stories of the Here and Now." *The Irish Times*, 13 September.
Hannerz, Ulf. 1998. "Other Transnationals: Perspectives Gained from Studying Sideways." *Paideuma* 44: 109–123.

———. 2004. *Foreign News: Exploring the World of Foreign Correspondents*. Chicago: University of Chicago Press.

———. 2010. *Anthropology's World: Life in a Twenty-first Century Discipline*. London: Pluto Press.

Holmes, Douglas R. and George E. Marcus. 2005. "Cultures of Expertise and the Management of Globalization: Toward the Re-functioning of Ethnography." In *Global Assemblages: Technology, Politics, and Ethics as Anthropological Problems*, ed. Aihwa Ong and Stephen J. Collier. Oxford: Blackwell Publishing, pp. 235–252.
Joyce, James. 1922/2008. *Ulysses*. Oxford: Oxford University Press.
Kiberd, Declan. 1996. *Inventing Ireland: The Literature of the Modern Nation*. London: Vintage.
Lee, Harmonie. 2004. "The Great Pretender." *The Guardian*, 20 March.
Madden, Deirdre. 2008. *Molly Fox's Birthday*. London: Faber and Faber.
McCann, Colum. 2004. *Dancer: A Novel*. New York: Picador.
Nader, Laura. 1999. "Up the Anthropologist—Perspectives Gained from Studying Up." In *Reinventing Anthropology*, ed. Dell Hymes. Ann Arbor: Ann Arbor Paperbacks.
Ní Dhuibhne, Éilís. 2007a. *Fox, Swallow, Scarecrow*. Belfast: Blackstaff Press.

———. 1999/2007b. *The Dancers Dancing*. Belfast: The Blackstaff Press.

O'Connor, Frank. 1931/1982. "Guests of the Nation." In *Collected Stories*. New York: Vintage Books, pp. 3–12.

O'Donoghue, Bernhard. 2007. "Tolstoy and the New Ireland." *The Irish Times*, 10 November.

O'Flaherty, Liam. 1925/2001. *The Informer*. Dublin: Wolfhound Press.

Ó Giolláin, Diarmuid. 2000. *Locating Irish Folklore: Tradition, Modernity, Identity*. Cork: Cork University Press.

Ortner, Sherry B. 2010. "Access: Reflections on Studying up in Hollywood." *Ethnography* 11(2): 211–233.

O'Toole, Fintan. 1997. "Perpetual Motion." In *Arguing at the Crossroads: Essays on a Changing Ireland*, ed. Paul Brennan and Catherine de Saint Phalle. Dublin: New Island Books, pp. 77–97.

———. 2008. "An Interview with Colm Tóibín." In *Reading Colm Tóibín*, ed. Paul Delany. Dublin: The Liffey Press, pp. 183–208.

Pierce, David. 2000. *Irish Writing in the Twentieth Century: A Reader*. Cork: Cork University Press.

Power, Thomas and Kevin Whelan, eds. 1990. *Endurance and Emergence: Catholics in Ireland in the Eighteenth Century*. Dublin: Irish Academic Press.

Tóibín, Colm. 1999. *The Blackwater Lightship*. London: Picador.

———. 2004. *The Master*. London: Picador.

———. 2007. "Single Minded." *The Guardian*, 28 April.

———. 2009. *Brooklyn: A Novel*. New York: Scribner Book Company.

Turner, Victor. 1976. "African Ritual and Western Literature: Is a Comparative Symbology Possible?" In *The Literature of Fact*, ed. Angus Fletcher. New York: Columbia University Press, pp. 45–81.

Walshe, Eibhear. 2008. "'This Particular Genie': The Elusive Gay Male Body in Tóibín's Novels." In *Reading Colm Tóibín*, ed. Paul Delany. Dublin: The Liffey Press, pp. 115–130.

Wulff, Helena. 2002. "Yo-yo Fieldwork: Mobility and Time in a Multi-local Study of Dance in Ireland." *Anthropological Journal of European Cultures* 11: 117–136.

———. 2003. 'The Irish Body in Motion: Moral Politics, National Identity and Dance." In *Sport, Dance and Embodied Identities*, ed. Noel Dyck and Eduardo P. Archetti. Oxford: Berg, pp. 179–196.

———. 2005. "Memories in Motion: The Irish Dancing Body." *Body & Society* 11(4): 45–62.

———. 2007a. *Dancing at the Crossroads: Memory and Mobility in Ireland*. Oxford: Berghahn Books.

———. 2007b. "Longing for the Land: Emotions, Memory and Nature in Irish Travel Advertisements." *Identities* 14(4): 527–544.

———. 2011a. "Cultural Journalism and Anthropology: A Tale of Two Translations." *Archivio Antropologico Mediterraneo online*, a. XII/XIII, 13(1): 27–33.

———. 2011b. "Creative Writing: An Anthropology of Literary Arts in Ireland." In *Blackwell Companion to the Anthropology of Europe*, ed. Ullrich Kockel, Máiréad Nic Craith, and Jonas Frykman. Oxford: Blackwell-Wiley, pp. 537–550.

Chapter 9

REFLECTIONS IN AND ON THE HALL OF MIRRORS
Gudrun Dahl

Reflexivity is an essential aspect of anthropology both in the sense that a reflexive approach to one's position in fieldwork is an established part of the traditions of the discipline, and in the sense that theoretical development in anthropology has often emanated from turning the analytical instruments used in studying other societies and cultures to the discipline's own concepts and practices. Even early theoretical reflections in anthropology consisted of the realization that the analytical concepts that the anthropologist brought into the field were ethnocentric, so that fieldwork elsewhere simultaneously could become an indirect fieldwork at home.

Doing fieldwork outside her own social setting, the anthropologist became aware of the cultural and historical contingency of her own concepts. In the last decade, notions that are well known to anthropology, such as social construction and reflexivity, have gained a wider currency in social science more generally. This chapter will first look at some uses of the term "reflexivity" in a broader social science context. It will then ask whether something has been lost (to anthropology) in the process of this diffusion, and in the increasing preoccupation of anthropology with Western culture. Have some aspects of anthropological self-reflection become lost and "reflexivity" become more of a formulaic demonstration of moral standing? What are the difficulties of reflexivity in the new settings of emergent phenomena, where the researcher is positioned in a constant flow not only of novel scientific fashions, but also of different standards of "timeliness" and "moral writing"? What are the consequences for reflexivity of a more Hannerzian view of culture as distributed, in flux and flow?

The concept of "reflexivity" as such has three important dimensions. First, it has connotations of the well-established metaphor of throwing light as a way of increasing understanding. Second, it points to a movement of feedback, and third, to a degree of conscious deliberation. However, beyond these core traits, the way that the term is used in social science varies a lot: it might even be that *reflexivity* is more of a shared word than one single, shared concept. A number of different conceptualizations of reflexivity are relevant to us as anthropologists, relating both to reflexivity as a methodological stance and to various forms of reflectivity in society as objects of analysis. These are: (a) the abstract notion of society reflecting on itself; (b) institutional practices of reflexivity as organizational self-improvement and self-presentation and the social and cultural context of such practices, taken as social facts to be studied; (c) individual practices of reflexivity as methods of self-improvement and self-presentation and their social and cultural context; and (d) scientific reflexivity as practice and virtue.

At the individual level, *reflexivity* as an everyday concept lies close to *reflectivity*: the concept evokes connotations of a subject thoughtfully scrutinizing his or her own activity. There are also connotations of a thoughtful look in the mirror, or just of a thoughtful mood. Different traditions in social science differ in the degree to which they regard reflexivity as a normal component of mundane human life. One end of the spectrum is represented by the ethnomethodological emphasis on reflexive accounting, whereby the actor normally constructs an explanation that will make her actions palatable to the social environment. The other end can be represented by Bourdieu's insistence that the most efficient strategies are those not rationally deliberated at all, but just representing embodied dispositions to act (see Mouzelis 2007).

When the concepts "reflectivity" and "reflexivity" are applied to the societal sphere, it is sometimes done in an aggregating manner—i.e., societal reflecting is seen as the aggregate of individual reflection and reflexivity. In other cases, various processes at the societal level are likened to the conscious reflecting and self-monitoring carried out by the individual human being, an example of how concepts that apply to the individual are commonly metaphorically transposed to the societal level, suggesting that society can be seen as a system akin to an organism. One example of the latter is Luhmann's model of how autopoetic social systems reproduce themselves (Luhmann 1995: 444). It has such a self-monitoring built into it: a first-order observation distinguishing the system from its environment and a second-order observation monitoring this very process of observation and separation, yet at a level explicitly distinguished from that of the conscious, reflecting, individual mind (Gershon 2005: 105). The concept is used in a purely metaphorical way, since Luhmann denies the existence of a collective consciousness. The reflective "observation" is hence situated in self-producing systems of meaningful acts of communication. "Social systems, of course, are not self conscious units like human individuals. Societies have no collective spirit which has access to itself by introspection. ... Self observing communication refers to the system which is produced and reproduced by the communication itself" (Luhmann 1982: 136). Luhmann's metaphorical concept of communicative self-reflexivity plays a critical part in his system-theoretical analytical model of society. Many scholars talk in the other, more aggregating manner, about society becoming more reflexive, where the reflexive and reflective agency lie with institutions or individuals, rather than with "society" as such.

When talking in a general way about society as becoming more reflexive, however, we need to clarify whether we are talking about reflexivity in the sense of unreflected feedback processes, about the sum of individual or institutional actions of conscious reflexivity, or about a more reflexivity-centered discourse. The notion of "reflexive modernization," as used by Beck et al. (1994), for example, suggests a number of processes that make society more reflexive in all these ways. The basis for this understanding is the realization that social institutions are "social constructions" or cultural conventions. For institutions relying to a large degree on their socially constructed images, reflexivity becomes an important aspect of institutional development: thinking about what you are doing and presenting it as part of your impression management is actually creating the organization as a fiction with real consequences.

Various researchers observe and comment upon different processes in modern society which encourage "reflexivity." First, reflexivity is seen as a response to competition (Garsten and Turtinen 2000, following Rose 1996), propelling self-improvement, self-presentation, and self-fashioning through profiling, styling, and branding. The rule of an unpredictable market encourages the individual to self-monitor and self-improve by making active choices, in order to be flexible (Rose 1996: 37). Information technology and expanding market economies are further seen to broaden the range of options for individual choice, making individual identity more and more the result of conscious and reflected self-fashioning. Such processes of competition-driven comparison are also identified at the level of organizations, such as universities, local communities, or nations, where intensified and facilitated communication provides for easier access to benchmarks for self-comparison.

Second, reflexivity is seen to be mobilized as a mode of decentralized or budget-cut governance and rule through self-control, for example on the organizational level when closely guarded reflexivity in the form of self-audit is used as a method for imposing values, subordinating a lesser unit under an expanding supersystem (Strathern 2004, quoted in Gershon 2005: 108). "Reflexivity as control" is also a mode of understanding industrial relations when rule-governed worker control is replaced by self-monitoring (Lash 1994: 111; Garsten and Turtinen 2000: 163).

Another arena for *reflexivity* as a buzzword has been that of aspiring occupational groups, who seemingly suffer from a low level of theoretical articulation of their foundational knowledge. "Reflexivity" has become a main tool for an organization to gain recognition as representing a fully fledged profession by raising the members' own awareness about habitual or prereflected activities. This is, for example, vividly demonstrated in the Scandinavian training of teachers, where all Nordic governments put an emphasis on developing the capacity for self-reflection, personal systematization, and reflection over experiences of teaching (Bronäs 2003; Lindhart and Lund 2006: 162).

Finally, human society at the global level is said to have become more self-reflexive with the realization that significant threats are generated by processes internal to society itself (risks) rather than by entirely external forces (dangers). Reflexivity, then, is thought to be linked to the growth of an imagined global community, a collective identity, in the name of which more and more actors ponder upon human activity as a shared problem. The proclamation in 2012 of the geological era of the "anthropocene" is a case in point. The idea of "reflexive modernity" among other things also implies a stage where "society," represented by new social movements, turns to a critical, decentralized self-reflection of its own fundaments (Anderson 2000).

There can be little doubt that there is an increased cultural and discursive emphasis on reflexivity, but it is more difficult to say whether the general trend is really toward more reflexivity in practice, and what the limits of reflexivity as an undertaking are. All the processes that researchers have summarized by using the term *reflexivity* do not necessarily stand out as such to the people undertaking the same reflexivity: reflexivity is mainly an "etic," not an "emic" term. Nevertheless, it might be that the term refers to a phenomenon or a trend coherent enough in today's world to warrant systematic ethnographic observation and comparison. Reflexivity as an intentional stance requires a frame of reference: a primary object for the ethnography of reflexivity must then be to map what the standards are, according to which people are monitoring themselves, and what are the sources and channels of such standards. Are the reflexive agents looking at their own original resources, the constraints they operate under, the results they are able to achieve, or the "performance" they are able to demonstrate? To what extent are the standards themselves objects of reflexive scrutiny?

Benchmarking as a managerial fashion provides for homogenization and centralization, constraining reflexivity to unidimensional criteria, such as universal measures of economic efficiency, productivity, and merit. Standardization, however, removes the criteria as such from scrutiny, and undermines the possibility to reflect and act upon the standards themselves, which are taken for granted. On the whole, we do not know if processes such as audit and branding increase or decrease our capacity to look through what is taken for granted.

In the self-awareness of social science, the images that are presented by the disciplines themselves have a particular bearing on the social constructions that are the basis of social life. Hence there is a need for reflection on the recursive process where articulated observations themselves influence that which is observed. "Radical reflexivity" refers to the practice of subjecting science itself to scrutiny—sometimes applying the very methods of study used to the research process itself, sometimes looking at the recursive process of research affecting reality. In the words of Lynch (2000: 44) paraphrasing Pollner (1991), it is "an unrelenting, unsettling, self critical examination of how any empirical investigation constructs the world it studies."

In anthropology, reflexivity came to the fore in the early 1990s and is nowadays one of the foundational pillars of anthropological methodology (see e.g., Aull Davies 2007). An early plea for reflexivity was made in an article by Jay Ruby in 1980. There were parallel movements in other disciplines. The breakthrough of methodological reflexivity in anthropology was similarly to that of other professions concerned with raising self-awareness, by articulating non-verbalized practices and experiences, in this case those involved in doing fieldwork and in writing. Scientific reflexivity, too, is closely related to the practice of elucidating uncodified or inexplicit knowledge, in order not only to scrutinize it, but also to make such knowledge amenable to formalizing as a professional toolkit. In anthropology, the epistemic consequences of fieldwork practices and literary conventions were central to this reflexivity. An interest in reflexivity as an empirical object of study, on the other hand, seems to have been spurred later, primarily by the process whereby British departments of anthropology and, later, other institutions, themselves became subject to neoliberal forms of control and governance by audit, self-monitoring, and a new emphasis on market competition.

Depending upon discipline, reflexivity may have different bases. Lynch (2000: 35), summarizing types of sociological reflexivities, states that they all involve a recursive turning back, "but what does the turning, how it turns, and with what implications differs from category to category and even from one case to another within a given category." Neither does the call for reflexivity preset whether the reflexive elaboration should mainly address issues of the agency of the researcher or the situation under which she is operating: the classic distinction from attribution theory of whether somebody thinks in terms of "who am I, acting?" or in terms of "how is a structure constraining me?" Apart from general considerations of research ethics and political and humanitarian matters, different disciplines can have their own take on what paradigms should guide the reflexivity that is applied to their own and other sciences. They may for example ask questions of how psychology, political contexts, economic interests or rhetorical strategies shape science or suggest that the results of research be evaluated from the point of view of either publication, economic efficiency, or moral contributions. The notion of scientific reflexivity in itself does not prescribe which. In anthropology, where fieldwork stands as a metonym for the discipline, an early, central issue for reflexivity was the interpersonal relations between researcher and researched. The question of how researchers and informants categorize each other in the fieldwork encounter lies close to the heart of anthropology. A recent volume on repeated fieldwork edited by Howell and Talle, for example, follows up this issue by looking at how returns to the field make it possible for the researcher to test different age statuses and follow the informants through their life cycle by parallel aging (Howell and Talle 2011). More traditional anthropological issues, however, do not exhaust the possible reflexivities applied to the encounter and how they influence the quality of data and description. Such a focus also actualizes psychological issues: your baggage of personal idiosyncrasy, suspicion or trust, and your emotions. Who were you allowed to be in the field? To use one of Ulf Hannerz' (1992) metaphors: were you allowed to share their "frameworks" and "perspectives"?

The second set of reflexive concerns in anthropology, that of text production, associated with Clifford and Marcus (1986), deals with similar worries. How do we depict the Other in our writing? And how do we in our writing establish truth claims? A third concern relates to Haraway's notion of situated knowledges (1988), requiring that the researcher spells out his or her own social positioning, since different social positions are seen to imply different perspectives on society. Particularly, the researcher is encouraged to try to switch positions, and to especially listen to the "subalterns" since their views are assumedly less ideologically skewed. However, many of Haraway's followers conventionally perform the role of critical anthropologists by showing their cards of identity in terms of a preset list of categories: gender, race, class, ethnicity (see, e.g., Amory 1997: 111), and sometimes sexuality. Bourdieu (2003; see also Bourdieu and Wacquant 1999), who does not afford much space to reflexivity in his general theory of action, does not care much for this type of reflexivity. Pleading for an awareness of the scholastic point of view and its limited relevance to an understanding of the logic of practical life, he nevertheless advocates a critical look at the different roles our academic structure offers us and at how the latter constrain such reflexivity on the part of the researcher.

To me, the basic reflexive perspective that we need to apply to anthropological practice relates less to preconceived ideas about how a limited set of personal identity dimensions are likely to predetermine our interests and analytical gaze. Rather, we need to be aware and observant of the shifting, time-specific, and contingent webs of meaning that we are stuck in as individuals and researchers. The purpose should be to wed the individual reflexivity of the researcher to the issue of reflexivity in its other sense: that of the interaction between social constructions afloat in our own social contexts, the organizational and institutional forms they refer to, and our own analytical contributions. The question that appears to have become closest at hand is how the analysis itself contributes to changing social constructions. Perhaps we should ask more often, and more clearly, how the history-contingent repertoires of mundane meaning that we as individual researchers bring to the job shape our understanding and analyses. Compared to the importance given to reflection on fieldwork interaction, relatively little attention has been given to the ways in which the anthropologist's concepts and models reflect more particular social, cultural, and political contexts. In the 2011 book edited by Howell and Talle, for example, the age of the fieldworker is actualized as a topic, but none of the contributors raise the issue of the life experiences of different cohorts of researchers. Researchers at different times of their life, or belonging to different generations, may bring very different ideas to the field, considering the rate of social and cultural change not only in the fieldwork society but also in the background society of the researcher (if these differ). Age does influence not only who you are allowed to be in the field, but also what ideological fads have shaped your biography. A particular local configuration or cultural repertoire is always culturally and historically contingent. The ideally reflexive researcher should foreground not only "the ways in which we anthropologists are historically and socially (not just biographically) linked with the areas we study," as Gupta and Ferguson (1997: 36) demand, but also how political, economical, and ideological fads structure the questions asked, the concepts and models used, and the interpretations made. These need to be seen as expressions of contingent cultural flows, set in history.

The reader might oppose the proposition that there has been too little focus on the anthropologist's background, by reference to the wide acceptance—especially in feminist anthropology—of the idea of situated knowledge, mentioned above. However, I would like to argue that the notion of situational knowledge, as it emerges in the literature, depends on an analysis of knowledge which does not recognize culture as transmittable. Instead, knowledge is mainly treated as on one hand, generated by direct experiences which are constrained by how the individual is categorized, and on the other, strongly shaped by interest. "Situation" and "position" are defined as "situation in the structure of power" or "function in a system" rather than "situation in the flow of interpretative frameworks." As a standard recipe for reflexivity, the mobilization of very general categories such as race, gender, class, and sexuality allows for an analysis at a distance which does not have to struggle with "emic" meaning, meaning becoming mainly a question of interest and function. Different perspectives are traced back to different situational experiences but without taking into consideration that the distribution of culturally specific stances, dispositions for action, and conceptualizations are also shaped by communication and flows of culture.

The dimensions along which reflexivity is expected are in this way themselves at risk of being essentialized. Rather than reflecting insights into how frames of interpretation are molded by cultural flows and historically and socially specific situations—that is, recognizing cultural diversity—the categorization mobilized for the reflective exercise tends to be based on generalizing and functionalist assumptions of how interests shape ideas. Meaning thus becomes read mainly as corresponding to function. The notion of social construction, simultaneously, has become more concerned with making a stand in opposition to naturalizing or biologizing explanations of gender and race, than with contextual variation and placing patterns of cultural interpretation in their temporally and spatially structured social, political, and economic settings.

In the analysis of situated knowledge, the categories of analysis used to denote positions often do not do justice to the realization that gender, race, class, etc. are all social constructions, and hence by necessity themselves culturally and socially contingent. As Thomas notes (1999: 271), they are problematized only insofar as they are shown to intersect. After a nominal bow to their constructedness, they are treated as context-independent and reified categories, transmittable from one national context to the other and used for legitimating self-presentation or for undermining rivals. Rather than tools for an open-minded look at what the anthropologist's cultural baggage implies, they become, as Gupta and Ferguson call them (1997: 38), "well-intentioned placemarking devices"; gestures "of expiation for more historical and structural understanding of location." Collier (1997: 127) relates this type of listing of variables to the establishing of "positions, from which ... to make claims to knowledge" and to meet demands for "minority scholars" (ibid.: 128). The labels become part of the self-fashioning performativity of the morally informed, politically conscious researcher.

Such typecasting, at the same time the target and the basis for identity politics, contradicts the notions behind social constructivism but has to be seen against a wish from the researcher to claim shared identity in order to legitimize representation. When this is used as a basis of critique of other researchers, such practices become problematical. While the identity of the studied group is seen as socially constructed, often in terms of an unjust categorization, and hence not fixed in a deterministic way, the perspective of the observer is read as an expression of an essential power interest from which he or she cannot break.

The formulaic list of different types of inequality (race, class, gender, sexuality) also acts as a kind of shortcut societal model. Although social constructivism logically implies cultural variation, the universality of the model is taken for granted. When all these categories are thrown into the same pot, however, there is often a general lack of discussion of the differences between the processes of social construction and categorization that govern these dimensions, each in its own particular way. For example, the connotations of gender and race may be equally culturally constructed, yet there is a big gap between race, a social category that is entirely based on arbitrary classification on the basis of superficial phenotypical traits, and gender, which is modeled on radical differences in relation to reproduction.

The idea of "intersectionality," although it suggests variability, does not solve the dilemmas associated with the preset list, since the word suggests sections between previously fixed dimensions rather than flows over fuzzy boundaries and hints that these dimensions are equal and of universal significance. The need to unite universally for political mobilization and solidarity leads to a failure to recognize other important structures of inequality or difference than the ones listed. Notably, in this classification of what structures knowledge positioning, there is often nothing between the wide generalization of "Western culture" and "ethnicity." National citizenship, for example, is mostly forgotten (though cf. Weston 1997: 171). For example, one rarely sees questions explicitly raised about the effects of a researcher being American, French, Ghanaian, or Swedish on fieldwork relations (however, see Yamba 1985). Despite the intellectual dominance of U.S. scholars, and the U.S.A.'s political and economic dominance, the problematization of how U.S. mainstream culture forms empirical descriptions or theoretical work about other parts of the world is still relatively rare. Among the exceptions, one can mention Bourdieu and Wacquant (1999), who lucidly described how U.S. understandings of race and resistance to racism were transposed to writings on race in Brazil, and Bartholdson (2007) has shown how this has impacted back on race relations in the latter country. Sarnecki (2001: 137) has noted how scholarly ideas of ethnic gangs in the U.S. have been spread partly by the international entertainment industry, partly by international sociology, yet are not particularly relevant in the Swedish situation. In her thesis (2011), Sarajeva argues for the irrelevance for the Moscow HBT (hetero-, bi- and transsexual) scene of American models of interpreting the local meaning of transsexuality and homosexuality in relation to mainstream gender structures. Critical science, gaining momentum from identity politics, here provides a risky bridge for ethnographic assumptions to be carried over between social contexts, as when Swedish students have to be told that the utility of interpreting society in terms of "whiteness" and "blackness" might be different when you write about small-town Sweden and when you write about small-town California. A recent example was an anthropological conference presentation analysing the relation between the racially indistinct Norwegian Sami and mainstream Norwegians in terms of "whiteness." Such terms are of course not only analytical categories but also terms for culturally specific ideas. By essentializing them in irrelevant contexts, researchers may not only obscure the meaningful analysis of the cultural underpinnings of racism but actually act to racialize a situation in new ways. Perhaps it creates a pedagogical problem to teach the eager, young power critic that inequality, too, is culturally varied and set in different clusters of meaning, but if we are to understand structures of discrimination and injustice, this insight is absolutely necessary. Reflexivity in social science also requires a critical look at the critic, and to what extent the role of critic itself is conventionalized. Modes of resistance, and of critical science, are no more immune to cultural domination than are other expressions of culture. It may be particularly difficult to reflexively look at the assumptions, roles, conventions, and practices of critical research, as they tend to be even more underpinned by normative and morally loaded stances. The risk of appearing cynical should nevertheless not detain us from such scrutiny, if we want to improve its quality by the organized skepticism that is the hallmark of all good science.

Much reflexive practice in anthropology, and the discourse about it, appears in contrast to depart from an assumption that our professional epistemic community is culturally homogenous. Fieldwork methods and writing conventions are assumed to be widely shared. Even when the notion of situated knowledge puts focus on the researcher's personal background, it is done in a typecasting way that does not recognize cultural variation and the path-dependence of meaning and frames of interpretation. We should localize both ourselves and those whom we study socially, culturally, and historically in a comparable terminology. I would like to argue that such cultural reflexivity in anthropology does not necessitate reference to stereotyped identities: it can as well depart from recognizing that culturally, social units have fuzzy boundaries. Ideas and sets of meaning travel and are transmitted in spatial flows; they are selected, elaborated, and reformulated. Notions of flux and flow do not change the fact of cultural and historical contingency; they only question the permanence or immutability of a certain cultural repertoire, and the idea of closed cultural borders. The global spread of higher education and more efficient communication has led to a more varied composition of our profession, even though it is still an empirical question to what extent non-Western anthropologists enter the profession with radically different perspectives or tend to have been similarly formed in a homogenizing educational system. Even heterodox standpoints may have a distribution with a definite center–periphery structure.

Too little attention has also been afforded to the effects of cultural differences between social contexts in parts of an assumedly homogenous West. Between class-related or regional subcultures even within Europe, there are strong differences in the emphasis on equality or hierarchy; in the rules of reciprocity; in the interpretation of the causation, conditions, and constraints for human agency; in patterns of responsibility, blame, and risk ascription; or in the prevalent reading of relations between the individual and the state. Between U.S. and Scandinavian researchers there are obvious differences in how you look at self-assertion and equality. Such notions are both unevenly distributed and in flux; they make up repertoires tied to particular social contexts, available resources for bricolage. Yet they are also examples of culturally based stances prone to be of some permanency at the individual level within a person's lifespan, even when their cultural setting is undergoing quick transformation. They are starting points very likely to be reflected in a person's theoretical effort. The question of how the anthropologist's descriptions and analyses of "reality" are affected by her own cultural presuppositions should therefore never be allowed to stop at a mention of some socially constructed label. It needs to depart from the understandings that the researcher so far has gained in her own life as a social and cultural being, situated in a dynamic flow of information and frames of interpretation, rather than in a static position.

Perhaps the main task of anthropology is to undermine common sense. Yet to be reflexive at the level of our own common sense is much more difficult than just labeling ourselves with stereotyped identity tags in order to demonstrate our positioning ("I am sorry, I am a rich, white woman"). It involves dealing with meaning, not just with interest or function. If radical rejection of taken-for-granted notions is what anthropologists have often spontaneously been forced to do in confrontation with other cultures, the question is if we do it systematically and rigidly enough when it comes to looking at our own backgrounds and how they influence our notions, concepts, and paradigms of interpretation.

Many anthropologists are not very preoccupied with careful definitions of terminology, partly because they know that concepts are culturally varied, perhaps also because of the uneasy relation that many anthropologists have to theory. As Henrietta Moore wrote, in the preface to *Anthropological Theory Today* (1999: 1), "anthropologists are often very unclear about the distinction between a generalization and a theory, and thus confusions arise about degrees of abstraction, or more precisely, about the relationship between observations, normative assumptions and theoretical propositions." Metaphors, paradigms, and concepts are the most significant tools of the anthropologist. Their function is to lead our attention in particular ways, to make us observe and systematize aspects of reality and allow us to formulate interesting questions. There are no ultimately correct, single definitions of scientific concepts. Still, no stringent analysis can do without a stringent use of terms: the author should make her own usage clear.

Analytical concepts are represented by terms often given a particular meaning in a particular epistemic community and with the purpose of solving some particular analytical task. Therefore, their meaning varies like that of other terms. Unlike the idealized scientific concept, the concepts we think with in everyday life are not joined with or set apart from each other by clear boundaries and conditions of necessity and sufficiency, but relate to each other in ways based on the presence or absence of family similarity (Lakoff 1987). The revolution of information technology, the opening of communication borders, and the internationalization of science have all resulted in many of the terms of social science referring to several different, sometimes contradictory notions. Nevertheless, the terms as words may themselves become fads. *Reflexivity*, as we have seen, is one such term. Each term and the concept it stands for is useful in relation to specific sets of concepts and particular analytical contexts. Yet, terms also tend to disentangle themselves from concepts and take on their own life. As words—that is, basically form rather than content—they acquire a particular symbolic value of their own in signaling timeliness (Dahl 2008). Overlapping abstract terms that are widely spread may create a sense of intersubjectivity but also a sense of confirmation that the researcher is dealing with relevant, real world problems. The conscious comparative juxtaposition of concepts that have developed in different scientific hothouses is a good source for identifying theoretical issues.

The theoretical terms we chose are not independent from the cultural baggage that we as individual researchers have carried over from our pre- or extrascientific lives, nor are they immune from the connotations they acquire in everyday life. Concepts lead political lives, and when they reach anthropology, their fashionability is not always derived only from their analytical fruitfulness. This situation is linked to "societal reflexivity," in the sense of social analysis contributing to shape society and also the institutions financing, ordering, or carrying out research. One case could be the concept of "civil society," allowed to structure one of the early meetings of the European Association of Social Anthropologists in the mid 1990s. This term, which has an ambiguous history (Foley and Edwards 1996), became popular mainly as an anti-state device, in the neoliberal wave after the fall of the Soviet bloc. Was this term, summarizing non-state forms of organization, really an analytic improvement to anthropology? I would suspect that by its inherent difficulties of delimitation, it on one hand clouded necessary distinctions and obscured the understanding of local meaning structures rather than clarified them—but on the other, made anthropology appear more relevant to contemporary policy debates. In retrospect, it is difficult to remember the extreme and unquestioning overevaluation of the democratic potential of NGOs that ruled in the mid 1990s. The category has over time become more circumscribed and the social institutions to which it corresponds have become more formalized in many countries. Today, as Juris (2008) has observed, *network* similarly not only is a descriptive term defining an organizational mode, but has increasingly become a societal ideal, even with the risk of being romanticized, presumably more because of the success of network technology than because of the utility of the concept as an analytical term in social science. A dream of authenticity and efficient direct democracy, which many of us presumably share, is likely to continue to produce labels like this. When used as categories for social science they appear as neutral descriptors, but when "loose on the street," they become normative, loaded panaceas for development.

Even within our own discipline, reflexivity in relation to concepts does not always come easily. As our students increasingly turn to an analysis of contemporary European culture, their studies become troubled by the fact that the terms used in the analysis are the same as those used in the social context they want to study. As in other disciplines, there is a constant risk of chronocentric blindness—critical reappraisal of conceptual tools is always easier through the comforting rear-view mirror.

The interaction between the idioms of social and cultural science and those of the surrounding society is more complicated that has ever been the case in natural sciences. The former language feeds into society as well as vice versa. Analytical terms such as *community* or *identity* acquire a value of desirability when reinscribed into political rhetoric. Fuzzy policy shibboleths such as *empowerment* or *sustainable development* structure the way research money is channeled, as if they represented clear-cut scientific concepts. What I wish to argue for here is the necessity to constantly scrutinize this interaction between social science and policy or political fads and the ramifications it has for our understanding not only of what is going on in our immediate present and presence, but also of what happens in other contexts and what happened long ago. Conversely, only by continuing to confront evidence from other times, places, and cultural settings can we find the tools for overcoming the trappings of our own time-bound consciousness and achieve farsightedness and afterthought.

Hannerz (1997) has emphasized the need to recognize the difference between "our" and "their" usage of words, and to add to the public scrutiny of the interconnected world, by publicly reflecting on the implications of words in our shared vocabulary. Looking at their meaning is, to me, one way to do this. Another is to cultivate a more conscious and systematic historical perspective on the political and economic embeddedness of our concepts. We should not just trace their history in terms of individual academic authorship as we do according to the rules of good manners when handling quotations. We need a more explicit recognition of the significance of where we pick up concepts, paradigms, and metaphors that we use. How do they relate to our own temporal and spatial situatedness in the flows of meaning and interpretational frameworks?

Scientific discourse is vulnerable to the changing trends of talking and writing about human conditions that arise outside the academic world, for better or worse. For us as anthropologists it is not difficult to accept that changes in temporally contingent mentalities affect our own tools for looking at social and cultural reality, taken as cultural constructions in themselves. Yet to be flexible and quick enough to maintain a reflexive critical stance also in relation to contemporary discursive fashions that are in the process of emerging is a formidable task. Since new concepts often come with the splendor of timeliness, the researcher questioning them always risks inviting accusations of conservatism. With hindsight of the breakthrough of neoliberal policy discourse, it is evident that new buzzwords do not necessarily appear on the local scene in the visible company of the ideological setup which later will appear as their inseparable context. In the mid 1990s there was an influx of new terms in both social policy and development work in Sweden, but the users of terms such as *empowerment, ownership,* and *partnership* were often unaware both that the words were widespread internationally, and that they occurred in parallel ways in the other policy sectors (Dahl 2008). Similarly, my impression is that in anthropology, self-reflexive awareness of time-contingent terminological change grows only slowly.

To make a clear distinction between moral discourse, political commitment, and neutral science is not possible other than as an ideal, and the ideal of neutrality itself has increasingly come to be questioned in favor of a committed science (for an early adherent of this view see Gouldner 1970, 1979). However, social science cannot withdraw from the duty to audit the overlaps between these discursive fields self-reflexively and to analyse, rather than to unquestioningly incorporate terms which have essentially contested character or significant moral connotations. As mentioned above, the term "reflexivity" is sometimes used to refer to propositions about reality, which are performative in the sense that they also impact on the very reality they describe. One needs to be particularly wary about the identification of long-term trends, especially when the projection comes close to important ideological currents and seems both politically and scientifically expedient. A good and often quoted example is Huntington's (1996) notion of the clash of civilizations, which has certainly added to the subsequent Muslim/Christian tensions. The notion of "reflexive modernization" may itself be another one.

The term "modernity" not only refers to a temporal dimension, but its meaning and connotations can also be shown to have changed substantially during the period the term has been in use. This is not only the case for the everyday usage of the term: the analytical concept has not escaped the influence of the researcher's own time-bound perceptions (Dahl 2012). Giddens' (1991; see also Beck et al. 1994) conceptualization of modernity as implying a situation where the individual decides how to fashion herself through a number of choices can hardly be understood unless in the context of the breakthrough of neoliberal ideology. After all, identity is both self-chosen and ascribed by others. Challenges to identity labeling, for example, are often not able to break the fetters of the stereotypes they question but imply a positive re-evaluation of negative terms rather than questioning their truth value. Whatever you act out and perform, you are constrained by how the performance will be read. Performance has to fall back on a socially shared system of signs. In a competitive situation, you are dependent on shared principles of rating. The range of choice is limited and neither the broadness and variety of options, nor the discontinuity and independence of new lifestyle models from traditions, should be exaggerated. The broad options of the freely self-fashioning individual in reflexive modernization may be spurious. If we look, for example, at the external (and somewhat superficial) signs that we can chose from in fashioning ourselves, fashion supply is more characterized by a rapid turnover than by a broad range of marketed styles at any particular time. The discourse of fashion companies in the last few years has emphasized that the options are limitless and no trend absolute, yet the range of colors of marketed clothes is often extremely limited. Is it that people nowadays chose who to be and whom to favor as customers, or is it that they are expected to do so by market suppliers? The neoliberal turn in the 1990s left many Western citizens desperately tired of the constant demands that one should chose energy supplier, telephone company, pension investment company, etc. In this case, the distinction between sociological analyst and megaphone for liberalism appears to be muddled: was Giddens depicting the reality or creating it? Free choice being a central value of liberal ideology, it is not particularly surprising that choice has been of more central interest than structure and constraints have been, during the period of neoliberal ideological rollout.

Similarly, anthropological texts from the 1970s and 1980s often manifest an urge to depict "the Other" as rational, in contrast to earlier forms of prejudiced denigration. In turn of the century anthropological literature, rationality had disappeared as the central criterion for how to write in a respectful way and been substituted by the trope "these people must be seen as agents, not victims." Both morally and theoretically, there was a new emphasis on agency, in sociological and anthropological discourse, the concept referring to either the agent's impact on history or the will and capacity to act. The new discursive trend has to be read in the context of an emphasis on action as a value, another part of the neoliberal political rhetoric specific to the time (Dahl 2009) and related to U.S. superindividualism, with roots in evangelical Christianity (Nilsson 2012: 130f.).

Since its inception, anthropology has had an awareness of the constraints that the concepts carried from our backgrounds to the field imply for our analysis and understanding. To stand back and treat our own concepts as exotic is no less important when we as anthropologists study our own society than it is when we do traditional anthropological fieldwork in an assumedly culturally different setting. It is time to consider the implications for anthropological reflexivity when we are working in and with cultural flux and drastic historical change, being particularly observant of key terms and popular discourse that have an overlap with our analytical terms. We need to be, even at the individual level, reflexive in relation to societal reflexivity.

References

Amory, Deborah. 1997. "African Studies as American Institution." In *Anthropological Locations: Boundaries and Grounds of a Field Science*, ed. Akhil Gupta and James Ferguson. Berkeley, Los Angeles, and London: University of California Press.
Anderson, Alison. 2000. "Environmental Pressure, Politics and the 'Risk Society.'" In *Environmental Risks and the Media*, ed., Barbara Adam, Stuart Allan, and Cynthia Carter. London: Routledge.
Aull Davies, Charlotte. 2007. *Reflexive Ethnography: A Guide to Researching Selves and Others*. The ASA Research Methods. London and New York: Routledge.
Bartholdson, Örjan. 2007. *From Slaves to Princes: The Role of NGOs in the Contemporary Construction of Race and Ethnicity in Salvador, Brazil*. Stockholm: Department of Social Anthropology, Stockholm University.
Beck, Ulrich, Anthony Giddens, and Scott Lash. 1994. *Reflexive Modernization: Politics, Tradition and Aesthetics in the Modern World Order*. Stanford: Stanford University Press.
Bourdieu, Pierre. 2003. "Participant Objectivation." *Journal of the Royal Anthropological Institute* 9(2): 281–294.
Bourdieu, Pierre and Loïc Wacquant. 1999. "On the Cunning of Imperialist Reason." *Theory, Culture and Society* 16(1): 41–58.
Bronäs, Agneta. 2003. "Aldrig mötas de två? Funderingar kring teori och praktik i lärarutbildning." In *Till frågan om teori och praktik i akademisk yrkesutbildning*, ed. Agneta Bronäs and Staffan Selander. Unpublished compendium, Stockholm Teacher Training College.
Clifford, James and George E. Marcus. 1986. *Writing Culture: The Poetics and Politics of Ethnography*. Berkeley: University of California Press.

Collier, Jane F. 1997. "The Waxing and Waning of 'Subfields' in North American Sociocultural Anthropology." In *Anthropological Locations: Boundaries and Grounds of a Field Science*, ed. Akhil Gupta and James Ferguson. Berkeley, Los Angeles, and London: University of California Press.

Dahl, Gudrun. 2008. "Words as Moral Badges: A Continuous Flow of Buzzwords in Development Aid." In *Sustainable Development in a Globalized World, Studies in Development, Security and Culture*, ed. Björn Hettne. Basingstoke and New York: Palgrave Macmillan.

———. 2009. "Agency, Victimization and the Ethics of Scientific Writing." *Asian Journal of Social Science* 37(3): 391–407.

———. 2012. "Modernities on the Move: Introduction." In *Modernities on the Move*, ed. Gudrun Dahl, Örjan Bartholdson, Paolo Favero, and Shahram Khosravi. Stockholm Studies in Social Anthropology 4. Stockholm: Acta Universitatis Stockholmiensis, pp. 9–32.

Foley, Michael W. and Bob Edwards. 1996. "The Paradox of Civil Society." *Journal of Democracy* 7(3): 38–52.

Garsten, Christina and Jan Turtinen. 2000. "'Angels' and 'Chameleons': The Cultural Construction of the Flexible Temporary Employee in Sweden and the UK." In *After Full Employment: European Discourses on Work and Flexibility*, ed. Bo Stråth. Brussels: European Interuniversity Press, pp. 161–196.

Gershon, Ilana. 2005. "Seeing like a System." *Anthropological Theory* 5(2): 99–116.

Giddens, Anthony. 1991. *Modernity and Self-Identity: Self and Society in the Late Modern Age*. Stanford: Stanford University Press.

Gouldner, Alvin W. 1970. *The Coming Crisis of Western Sociology*. New York: Basic Books.

———. 1979. *The Future of Intellectuals and the Rise of the New Class*. New York: Seabury Press.

Gupta, Akhil and James Ferguson. 1997. "Discipline and Practice: The Field as Site, Method and Location in Anthropology." In *Anthropological Locations: Boundaries and Grounds of a Field Science*, ed. Akhil Gupta and James Ferguson. Berkeley, Los Angeles, and London: University of California Press.

Hannerz, Ulf. 1992. *Cultural Complexity: Studies in the Social Organization of Meaning*. New York: Columbia University Press.

———. 1997. "Fluxos, fronteiras, híbridos: palavras chave da antropologia transnacional" [Flows, Boundaries, Hybrids: Keywords in Transnational Anthropology]. *Mana* 3(1): 7–39.

Haraway, Donna. 1988. "Situated Knowledges: The Science Question in Feminism and the Privilege of Partial Perspective." *Feminist Studies* 14(3): 575–599.

Howell, Signe and Aud Talle. 2011. *Returns to the Field*. Bloomington and Indianapolis: Indiana University Press.

Huntington, Samuel. 1996. *The Clash of Civilizations and the Remaking of World Order*. New York: Simon & Schuster.

Juris, Jeffrey S. 2008. *Networking Futures: The Movements against Corporate Globalization*. Durham, NC: Duke University Press.

Lakoff, George. 1987. *Women, Fire and Dangerous Things: What Categories Reveal about the Mind*. Chicago: Chicago University Press.

Lash, Scott. 1994. "Reflexivity and its Doubles: Structures, Aesthetics, Community." In *Reflexive Modernization. Politics, Tradition and Aesthetics in the Modern Social Order*, eds. Ulrich Beck, Anthony Giddens, and Scott Lash. Stanford: Stanford University Press, pp. 110–173.

Lindhart, Lars and Birthe Lund. 2006. "Det problematiska med lärarutbildningen." In *Verklighet, Verklighet: Teori och Praktik i Lärarutbildning*, ed. Agneta Bronäs and Staffan Selander. Stockholm: Norstedts akademiska förlag, pp. 149–170.

Luhmann, Niklas. 1982. "The World Society as a Social System." *International Journal of General Systems* 8: 131–138.

———. 1995. *Social Systems*. Stanford: Stanford University Press.

Lynch, Michael. 2000. "Against Reflexivity as an Academic Virtue and Source of Privileged Knowledge." *Theory, Culture and Society* 17(3): 26–54. http://tcs.sagepub.com/content/17/3/26.

Moore, Henrietta L. 1999. "Anthropological Theory at the Turn of the Century." In *Anthropological Theory Today*, ed. Henrietta Moore. Cambridge: Polity Press, pp. 1–23.

Mouzelis, Nicos. 2007. "Habitus and Reflexivity: Restructuring Bourdieu's Theory of Practice." *Sociological Research Online* 12(6). http://www.socresonline.org.uk/12/6/9.html.

Nilsson, Erik. 2012. *Conserving the American Dream: Faith and Politics in the US Heartland*. Stockholm Studies in Social Anthropology New Series 7. Stockholm: Acta Universitatis Stockholmiensis.

Pollner, Melvin. 1991. "'Left' of Ethnomethodology." *American Sociological Review* 56: 370–380.

Rose, Nicholas. 1996. *Inventing Ourselves: Psychology, Power and Personhood*. Cambridge: Cambridge University Press.

Ruby, Jay. 1980. "Exposing Yourself: Reflexivity, Anthropology, and Film (1)." *Semiotica* 30: 153–179.

Sarajeva, Katja. 2011. *Lesbian Lives: Sexuality, Space and Subculture in Moscow*. Stockholm Studies in Social Anthropology 4. Stockholm: Acta Universitatis Stockholmiensis.

Sarnecki, Jerzy. 2001. *Delinquent Networks: Youth Cooffending in Stockholm*. Cambridge: Cambridge University Press.

Strathern, Marilyn. 2004. "Bullet Proofing: A Tale from the UK." In *Documents: Artefacts of Modern Knowledge*, ed. Annelise Riles. Ann Arbor: University of Michigan Press, pp. 191–205.

Thomas, Nicholas. 1999. "Anthropology and Cultural Studies." In *Anthropological Theory Today*, ed. Henrietta Moore. Cambridge: Polity Press, pp. 262–279.

Weston, Kath. 1997. "The Virtual Anthropologist." In *Anthropological Locations: Boundaries and Grounds of a Field Science*, ed. Akhil Gupta and James Ferguson. Berkeley, Los Angeles, and London: University of California Press, pp. 163–184.

Yamba, Bawa. 1985. "Other Cultures, Other Anthropologists: The Experiences of an African Fieldworker." *African Research and Documentation* 37.

Chapter 10

ON THE SHORES OF POWER
The Cultural Diversity Turn, Cultural Policies,
and the Location of Migrants

Ayse Caglar

Prologue

On February 15, 2004, at the fifty-fourth Berlin International Film Festival, the Golden Bear went to Fatih Akın and his film *Gegen die Wand* (literally, "Against the Wall"; released in English as *Head-On*). Akın was praised as one of the most promising young filmmakers. His success placed Germany back in the winners' camp at the Berlinale after eighteen years. The decision of the jury was unexpected. But Fatih Akın's triumph was the success of a German filmmaker's with a twist. The fact that he was the son of a Turkish *Gastarbeiter* (guest worker), born in Hamburg, and thus belonged to the so-called "second generation"[1] of German Turks, meant that his origin, his location within the New German Cinema, and the particularity of his films in relation to this position in German society all became part of the news about his success. This discursive field constrained the way he and his films were represented in both the German and Turkish media. As a filmmaker, Fatih Akın, a German citizen, born and raised in Germany, stood for the country, and his film *Gegen die Wand* won the first prize as a *German* film. Yet in every piece of news about the winner of the fifty-fourth Berlinale in German media, Akın's Turkish origins and his parents' Turkishness were mentioned, thereby identifying him as a "German Turkish" filmmaker. The autobiographical references in his films and his intimate knowledge of the underground world of foreigners in Germany found their place in the news. However, contrary to the hegemonic discourse in the 1970s and 1980s, his German "Turkishness" was not conceived of as a problem, or a pathology to be explained, but taken as one of the sources of his creativity.

Fatih Akın had to face questions about migrants' positioning vis-à-vis "tradition," heritage, and roots in his country of origin from media correspondents in a manner that a German filmmaker—without a migration background—would not have been exposed to. Some of these questions reduced his film to one about Turkish immigrants and their problematic location within German society.[2] Other critics designated *Gegen die Wand* as a back-to-roots film. Some wondered whether it could be considered a "German" film and answered in the affirmative. In fact, no one denied the "Germanness" of the film in terms of its production.

On the other hand, Fatih Akın, who understandably desired to be defined only as an artist[3] without any qualifying adjective referring to his origin, nationality, and ethnicity, reacted quite strongly at the mention of words, such as *Gastarbeiter* or *Auslaender* (foreigner), in relation to himself and his films.[4] The discourse around his dual citizenship[5] and his and his parents' origin succeeded in drawing Akın into an arena in which he felt obliged to position himself vis-à-vis these issues.[6]

Irrespective of how Akın's success was received in Germany, it was marked by the attempts of the critics and the media to situate the film with reference to Akın's Turkish origins. His ethnic and cultural origins were always made into an issue, though these were only sometimes seen as a positive resource that the film and the director drew on. At times he was relegated to the confines of his migrant background as a cultural mediator. In Turkey and in the Turkish press, Fatih Akın's prize was hailed as the success of a Turkish filmmaker living abroad. Other than a few exceptional reports referring to him as a German Turk (*Alman-türkü*), almost all reports in the Turkish media praised him as a Turk.[7] These divergent representations of Fatih Akın's success mark the tensions in the way he and his works are incorporated into public discourses about culture and diversity in Germany and Europe. Following Hannerz' (1998) suggestion of "studying sideways," this chapter will use the idioms, tropes, and repertoires the journalists mobilized to interpret Akın, his film, and cultural difference as a vantage point from which to explore the tensions and disjunctions surrounding cultural diversity as a discourse and instrument of governance within European cultural policies in the 2000s.[8]

Introduction

Cultural diversity as a global policy discourse has been around since the beginning of the 2000s. Especially after the UNESCO Convention on the Protection and Promotion of the Diversity of Cultural Expression (2005), cultural diversity has increasingly acquired popularity and presence in international policy, law-making, and the governance of difference in society. Cultural diversity, as a concept and as an instrument of governance, has been on the rise in a wide variety of knowledge-production institutions and in public policies for the regulation and management of difference in the U.S. and, later, in Europe.

The rise of cultural diversity as a corpus of normative discourses, practices, and policies about the regulation of difference in a wide range of areas from public sector to corporate business has followed different trajectories in the U.S. and Europe (Vertovec 2012). In the U.S., the origins of cultural diversity discourse and policies lie in the civil rights movements of the 1960s, which addressed the historical and structural discrimination of disadvantaged minorities. "Affirmative action" policies and institutional structures were the outcome of measures to overcome structural discrimination against the disadvantaged minorities, mostly defined on the basis of race and gender, so that they could be provided with opportunities to correct the past injustices (ibid.). As Vertovec shows in detail, the racial and gender emphases of these anti-discrimination policies and institutional measures, aimed to correct past injuries, were later expanded to other groups to accommodate a wide array of differences defined in terms of culture, ethnicity, religious beliefs, and sexual orientation (ibid.: 288–290) under the rubric of cultural diversity. Vertovec identifies these discourses and policy practices designed to regulate difference to be future-oriented, in that they are not designed to combat past injuries but to adjust to, and benefit from, the changing demographic composition of a society and most importantly its workforce. Incorporated into a semantic field of creativity, innovation, success, and competitiveness, cultural diversity—entailing all sorts of differences—came to be defined as an asset and a resource. It was celebrated, promoted, and developed by the corporate world through various schemes of diversity monitoring and measuring. The worldwide diffusion of "cultural diversity" as a nebulous body of discourses, measures, and practices of openness to difference was facilitated by institutions such as UNESCO which promoted it. The discourse of "cultural diversity" arrived thus in Europe.

With a different history, legacy, and politics of incorporating minorities and difference in Europe, several European Union (EU) institutions and policies played a crucial role in spreading and grounding ideas and practices of cultural diversity. By means of several measures and conventions, EU institutions facilitated the institutionalization of cultural diversity policies in the state sector to manage and govern different groups' intercultural relations, particularly in cities. Since the 2000s, cultural diversity policies have increasingly dominated the terrain of multicultural discourses and policies that are designed to provide minorities with access to resources on a collective basis.

This chapter situates the cultural diversity turn in European cultural policies and in urban governance by exploring its genealogy and semantic fields, as well as by mapping its tensions through the lens of migration and migrants in Europe. How does this turn locate the migrants within the social, economic, and cultural sphere of Europe and within what kind of semantic field? This chapter focuses particularly on third-country nationals (TCNs), i.e., on people residing in the EU whose countries of origin are not members of the EU. These migrants provide an important lens through which to analyse the cultural diversity turn in cultural and urban policies in Europe. First, these migrants constitute the main group of minorities referred to in European cultural-diversity policies and discourses. Although they are not the only group with a "migration background," they are the ones who are most often classified as culturally (and religiously) "diverse." Thus, not so-called member-country nationals, such as French, German, or Belgian citizens residing in other EU countries, but the TCN migrants, such as Turks, Moroccans, Algerians, etc., compose the crucial publics of the intercultural dialogue. Their changing representations over time reflect their transition from a group designated with a deficit (thus needing to be integrated) to a group defined with a potential (as a resource). Moreover, such groups are ambiguously positioned in terms of geographies of inclusion and exclusion and therefore provide a fruitful lens for reflexivity that casts light on the organizing principles of society (Boyer and Hannerz 2006; Caglar and Mehling 2013; and Boyer, in this volume). They provide an analytically fruitful location from which to analyse how society reflects on itself and also defines its problems, fault lines, and potentials.

These sites are important to explore the challenges facing the political community and imaginings of what "community," "membership," and "belonging" mean in Europe, especially in the context of the contemporary debates on the "limits" of Europe. All these debates have been centred on the regulation of "difference" within European social, cultural, and political spheres and the presence today of social groups that have been historically absent from formal representation in the public sphere. Using such a framework, the following sections concentrate on the location of migrants within European cultural policies that aim to accommodate and regulate difference, and to delineate the broader context and dynamics of these politics.

As Shore and Wright (2011) rightly emphasise, policies provide a window to explore larger social processes and new terms and forms of governance. They allow us to understand the new classificatory logics and regulatory powers along with the new semantics that accompany them (ibid.: 1–3). What kinds of subject positions are opened by these policies and for whom? A study of the cultural diversity turn in cultural policies in Europe enables us to analyse them as instruments of governance with new rationalities and regimes of knowledge and power especially in relation to migrants.

This chapter demonstrates the ways in which the cultural diversity turn is assembled with its multiple sources, agencies, and narratives. First it will explore the tensions, ambiguities, and contested narratives involved in cultural policies vis-à-vis migrants' participation in the European social, cultural, and political space. Then, it will address the consequences of this turn on migrants' positioning within the European public, cultural, and economic spheres. This will be followed by the contextualization of the cultural diversity turn in Europe within the global trade regimes, as well as within the frame of urban governance in times of neoliberal globalization.[9]

The Tense Landscape of European Cultural Policies

The terrain of European cultural policies that foster and regulate diversity and intercultural dialogue in relation to migrant minorities is a tension-ridden terrain, which entails discrepancies. In the early 2000s, there were two kinds of policy clusters, which operated with different notions of culture and envisioned the place of migrants within Europe in a disjointed, almost oppositional way. One type of European cultural policy regarding (TCN) migrants operates with a *territorialized* concept of culture and is anchored in the cosmology of the nation-state. It envisions the incorporation of the immigrants into the European cultural space — as secluded publics under the regime of multiculturalism. In these, migrants are incarcerated in the cultured territory of their homeland. The isomorphism between territory, culture, and people (Gupta and Ferguson 1992; Caglar 1998) is still very strong in these policies targeting migrants particularly from Turkey and the Mediterranean border of the EU. The Barcelona Declaration (1995) articulates, for instance, the spirit and the conceptual framework of these policies. Within the universe of these policies, Fatih Akın, for example, despite his incorporation into the social, economic, and political sphere of Europe, remains incarcerated in the cultured terrain of birth and/or descent so that at best he becomes a cultural mediator. Akın becomes a German filmmaker of Turkish descent through a past-fixated understanding of his present.

The second type of policy operates with a *deterritorialized* and dynamic concept of culture and conceives of migrants as part of the cultural complexity of the European landscape. Their aim is to secure migrants' participation and inclusion as a creative force in the European public sphere instead of as secluded publics defined as cultural communities. Within this universe of policies, Fatih Akın finds a place through the appraisal of his film and his cultural diversity as one of the sources of his creativity. Although these two kinds of policies are embedded into different conceptual frameworks they operate simultaneously in Europe. While concepts such as *mutual understanding*, or *intercultural* and *interreligious dialogue*, mark the terrain of the first group of policies, the second group employs concepts such as *cultural diversity, cultural citizenship, participation* and *democracy*. In the early 2000s, these almost contradictory policies that coexisted within the European cultural policy landscape have provided very different institutional opportunity structures – especially for migrants from the Mediterranean.

Although the origin of the first group of policies could be traced back to the European Cultural Convention in 1954, they were translated into programs elaborated in the Barcelona Declaration (1995). To explore the first group of cultural policies, here the focus will be on EUROMED (the European–Mediterranean Partnership), as this directly targeted migrant communities from the Mediterranean through EU institutions and schemes. The Barcelona Declaration launched EUROMED in three separate chapters. The third one on culture aimed at promoting cooperation between the Euro-Mediterranean countries in radio, television, and film production to increase mutual understanding between the two shores of the Mediterranean (EUR-Lex 1998). Mutual understanding and cultural (cross-border) cooperation were the key terms of the EUROMED policies.[10]

EUROMED policies have publicly and institutionally sanctioned the migrants in Europe from the Mediterranean as cultural intermediaries. They are designated "the cultural communicators for cooperation, contributing to a better flow of communication and exchange between Europe and its neighbors of North Africa and the Middle East" (Council of Europe 2003). Cast as agents of cooperation (Civil Forum Marseilles 2000), migrants have been incorporated as active partners in the codevelopment between receiver and sender countries and in the development of the partnership (Civil Forum Marseille 2000). They are conceived as "genuine intermediaries between the cultures of the home and the host countries" (European Commission High Level Advisory

Group 2003). The aim is to foster and sustain a dialogue between "cultures" and particularly between "religions" in the Euro-Mediterranean space in order to secure mutual understanding, peace, and security.

Within these cultural policies the topos of neighbor and concomitantly a bridging metaphor is used to refer to migrants.[11] Migrants are supposed to bridge the (cross-border) cultured spaces with their "neighbors" and initiate cross-border cooperation, intercultural, and interreligious dialogue inside the Euro-Mediterranean space.[12] At this level, the EUROMED policies first incarcerate those immigrants in the cultured territories of their homeland, which in this case is the territory of the neighbor in the Mediterranean, and then attribute to them agency for creating a dialogue bridging the two cultural shores as reflected in the depiction of Akin and his film at the beginning of the chapter.

The EU schemes of the 1990s in the realm of the media illustrate this territorial topos of migrants' incorporation into the EU public and media spaces quite clearly. Cultural difference and diversity are conceptualized in close relation to territoriality. The Mercator project (comprising Mercator-Education, Mercator-Legislation, and Mercator-Media) is one such scheme, which seeks to accommodate diversity following the logic of the first group of cultural policies. It is financed by the European Commission and was established to protect and foster the territorially based non-state languages of the European Union (such as Catalan, Basque, Frisian, Welsh, and Breton).[13] Interestingly, the schemes of the Mercator Project do not cover the (im)migrant minorities in the EU.[14] It is noteworthy that the EUROMED programs are all conceptualized as the EU's *external* relations. So even if the immigrants are incorporated into the schemes of EUROMED, they are not incorporated into EU programs from within but via the countries included in the regional cooperation. In all these policies, (TCN) migrant residents of Europe are still conceived as the "other" within, who has to be incorporated usually through their countries of origin.[15] Hence, such schemes result in strengthening the "homeland" ties of the immigrants, which also become part of their cultural expression. This constitutes the "excess" (the qualifying adjective in front of their names) in their encounters, relations, and subject positions that sets them apart from their fellow citizens in the European social and cultural sphere.

The Cultural Diversity Turn in European Cultural Policies

The second group of policies was explicitly formulated in the Declaration on Cultural Diversity by the Council of Europe Committee of Ministers in 2000 but their trajectories could also be traced back to the early 1990s. However, they were adopted as clear cultural policies of most European countries only in 2000. Since then cultural diversity has become one of the main policy aims of those institutions which set the agenda of European cultural policy in most European countries. The earliest explicit formulation of the principles of cultural diversity policy is to be found in the "Declaration of Cultural Diversity" of the Committee of Ministers of Council of Europe in December 7, 2000."[16] Based on the recognition that "respect for cultural diversity is an essential condition of human society" (Civil Forum Marseille 2000: 1) and "cultural diversity has always been a dominant European characteristic and fundamental political objective in the process of European construction" (ibid.: 1), the declaration calls upon the member states "to examine ways of sustaining and promoting cultural and linguistic diversity in the new global environment at all levels" (ibid.: 4).

The declaration requests the competent organs of the Council of Europe "to identify those aspects of cultural policy which are in need of special consideration in the context of the new global economy, and to elaborate a catalogue of measures, which may be useful to member states in their quest to sustain and enable cultural diversity" (ibid.). This declaration laid the ground for policy formulations on other related topics.[17] What is referred to as cultural diversity in this crucial document is "the co-existence and exchange of culturally different practices and ... the provision and consumption of culturally different services and products" (ibid.: 3).

Since 2000, cultural diversity has been adopted by different organs and committees of the European Council and turned into the guideline for cultural policies. As part of the program of transversal studies of cultural policies developed by the Council of Europe's Directorate of Culture and Cultural and National Heritage, sociologist Tony Bennett was commissioned to do a study on cultural diversity, which resulted in the report "Differing Diversities, a Mapping of Policy Issues" in 2000.[18] The same year, the commissioned report approached the question of cultural diversity from within the changed social and cultural landscape of Europe and within the frame of current debates on globalization and European dynamics. The report lays the theoretical ground for dealing with the challenges that migration and migrants pose to the existing cultural policies in Europe.

The Europeanized notion of cultural diversity is based on a broad concept of culture and Europe. The main objectives of all these cultural policy formulations are twofold: to create a better understanding of a more inclusive and wider Europe in cultural terms; and to foster the cultural development of Europe by policies that could meet the challenge of the complexity of the European cultural ecosystem (European Commission Working Group 2003: 6). According to these position papers and declarations, diversity is a part of European heritage, which construes European specificity and Europe's identity (Lebon 2002: 1–2). Moreover, although this aspect of European heritage has not been properly acknowledged, and has even been neglected during the age of nationalism and nation-state in Europe, it needs to be fostered and utilized now.

However, these documents do not identify European heritage as the sole source of cultural diversity in Europe. In addition to the existing minorities, they explicitly indicate that waves of migrants and refugees have changed the cultural landscape of Europe in such a way that the new cultural-policy formulations need to encompass the expectations of these newcomers to Europe, ensure their participation in the public sphere, and foster their potential to contribute to the social and cultural vitality of Europe (UNESCO 2005). Accordingly, they have to be incorporated into the cultural diversity complex of Europe.

It is important to note that the culture concept informing the cultural diversity perspective is dynamic, non-essentialized, and non-territorial. Thus, the task is not to map out different cultural groups and formulate policies to ensure that the existing landscape of cultural diversity will be preserved, as has been the case with the multiculturalism policies that foster communal segregation.[19] The aim is to enhance sustainable diversity where diversity is a continuing resource (UNESCO 2005). The cultural diversity perspective is envisaged to offer a theoretical space that accommodates formations of new cultural practices and values particularly those of "third cultures" or "hybrid cultures" (Lebon 2002: 8).[20] Crossbreeding of cultural formations is identified as an important source of diversity. On this ground, the cultural-diversity perspective envisions Europe as inclusive and changing. Since it aims for the protection and promotion of cultural diversity, the objective of cultural diversity policies is sustainable cultural diversity, thereby assuming a culturally changing Europe.

It is important to distinguish that in this case, cultural diversity policies are projects not of identity but of democratic public policy, which need to be reconciled with the changing conditions of cultural diversity in Europe in the age of globalization (Civil Forum Marseille 2000; Bennett 2001; Lebon 2002; European Commission Working Group 2003; UNESCO 2005). Accordingly, cultural policies for sustainable cultural diversity need to "be recognized as a force for democratic development" (Lebon 2002: 2). Their main objective is to ensure the fairness of collective and cultural participation including the participation of the marginal groups and those who are excluded from formal citizenship schemes.[21] The aim of fostering cultural diversity is to create a public space for cultural communication and to enable the marginal, the excluded, and the socially and economically worse off to access this public space. Thus equity, growth, and sustainability, as well as democratic participation and cultural citizenship, compose the case of its semantics.

In the position papers, the premises of new cultural policies are coupled with cultural citizenship. The recognition of difference is related to social justice and recognition of cultural rights and entitlements. Thus, the cultural diversity project is closely related to cultural development, to democracy, and consequently to human rights agendas (Civil Forum Marseille 2000; Bennett 2001; Lebon 2002). It is a project of expanding the circle of democratic inclusion in Europe. If public policy is going to come to terms with the changing context of the relations between peoples and policies in the global world, cultural policies that foster cultural diversity need to forge and ensure new channels and forms of engagement to pave the road for cultural democracy beyond the limitations of citizenship reduced to its canonized understanding of political participation (Bennett 2001). The cultural diversity turn in European cultural policies opens new subject positions for migrants as compared to those anchored in the Barcelona Declaration (1995). Rather than being the cultural intermediaries bridging between the cultured territories of their homeland and Europe, now migrants are seen as embedded in a conceptual grid of growth, democratic governance, equity, and sustainable cultural vitality. Migrants are now hailed as a resource, as a group with potential rather than a group with deficits to overcome.

Intercultural dialogue is assembled anew in relation to cultural diversity and it becomes the new tool of managing cultural diversity (Council of Europe 2008). Old approaches to the management of cultural diversity, namely multiculturalism and assimilation approaches are declared inadequate to cope with the current realities of diversity. These older approaches are not suitable for the management of diversity as both of them operate with a social division of majority/minority, which is inadequate to capture and address the complexity of the increasing diversification of diversity (which becomes "superdiversity" in Vertovec's (2007) terminology) in European societies. Furthermore, by fostering segregated communities and publics, as well as disregarding social equity, these models are seen to fall short from coping with the demands of democratic governance (Council of Europe 2008: 4). In the White Paper on "Intercultural Dialogue: In Living Together as

Equals in Dignity" (2008), migrants, identified as "the vectors of development stimulating innovation and the cross-fertilization of ideas" are situated as "the pioneers of intercultural dialogue" (ibid.: 6). However, by emphasizing the freedom to choose one's culture and adopt different cultural affiliations—that is, by not being incarcerated into the cultured homelands—the intercultural dialogue, which is reshaped in conjunction with the cultural diversity turn, opens subject positions to migrants beyond the idiom of cultural intermediaries between the cultures of their homeland and the place of settlement in Europe. If managed properly, culturally diverse societies, through migrants, can be a resource anchored in Europe rather than a threat. The European Council has been designated as the main agency for the management of diverse populations and the fostering of intercultural dialogue.

Situating the Cultural Diversity

> At a recent international meeting of cultural policy specialists, a UNESCO official lamented that culture is invoked to solve problems that previously were the province of economics and politics; Yet she continued, the only way to convince government and business leaders that it is worth supporting cultural activity is to argue that it will reduce social conflicts and lead to economic development. (Yudice 2003: 10)

There is no doubt that the cultural diversity turn of European cultural policies breaks with the cultural policies that incarcerate migrants to cultured spaces.[22] As a project of democratic inclusion, these policy formulations theoretically envision the insertion of migrants, the marginal, and the minorities in the European public sphere beyond the multicultural and culturalist policies of the 1980s and 1990s. However, it is important to attend to the "historical contingency" of this turn in Europe; that is, to situate the dynamics and processes through which such a social and cultural order as that envisioned by cultural diversity came to be conceived and constituted (Boyer and Hannerz 2006; Boyer, in this volume). This requires reflexivity. In embedding the cultural diversity turn in Europe within broader forces, two dynamics come to the forefront: the multilateral trade relations, especially in cultural goods between U.S. and Europe; and the cultural industries and their prominence in urban development in the context of neoliberalism.

Cultural Goods and Multilateral Trade Relations

It is clear that questions of minority rights and reconciliation of equality and difference within the context of intensified globalization pose challenges to the cultural policies grounded in the cosmology of the nation-state. However, situating this turn in broader dynamics, within the context of U.S. and Europe multilateral trade relations, agreements, and negotiations, enables us to see the dynamics of the Europeanization of cultural diversity. Cultural diversity is not only about the management of diverse populations, but is also located within discourses and policies of trade and culture.

The cultural diversity turn is very much embedded in the question of protecting cultural industries. In fact cultural protectionism has evolved from "cultural exception" to "cultural diversity" (Burri 2011: 4). Thus it is closely connected with agendas of cultural exemption against uncontrolled global trade in culture — particularly with regards to the ever-expanding cultural and creative industries, including the audiovisual sector. It is no coincidence that the Declaration on Cultural Diversity (Committee of Ministers of the Council of Europe 2000), which set the agenda for cultural diversity policies, came in 2000 after the World Trade Organization (WTO) meeting in Seattle in 1999. In today's world, culture functions as an engine of capital development. The agreements of trade and intellectual property such as GATT (the General Agreement on Tariffs and Trade, 1948–1994) and the WTO have been crucial to facilitate as well as coordinate the culturalization of economy. It has been repeatedly underlined that the audio-visual industry in U.S. is second only to the aerospace industry (Yudice 2003: 17).

Cultural exemption aims at "exempting any product or service that is culture-related from the rules of the negotiated WTO agreements" (Burri 2011: 2). The shift in cultural policies is also entangled with the French draft of general exception for cultural industries.[23] The cultural diversity agenda is developed as a strategy in close relation to the notion of cultural sovereignty, pitted against the "consumer sovereignty" motto of the U.S., in order to secure an advantage for domestic cultural industries, including television and the audiovisual sector, in Europe.

Once "completely free trade" in culture was identified as a threat to cultural diversity, then the cultural diversity perspective became an important terrain and strategy for European countries to secure trade protectionism for cultural industries in global trade talks. Especially after the Convention on Cultural Diversity (UNESCO 2005), the first legally binding instrument on cultural matters, the global discourse on cultural diversity increasingly acquired popularity in international policy (Burri 2011). In short, the cultural diversity turn in European cultural policies is embedded into some European countries' efforts to pursue protectionism in cultural industries.[24] All the milestone documents arguing for cultural diversity in cultural policy underline the special needs of the cultural sector as different from other sectors that are subject to the logics of free trade, and consequently they all plead for regulation in this sector.[25] Trade protectionism in cultural industries is depicted as a necessary measure to secure cultural diversity.

In the report "Towards a New Cultural Framework Program of the European Union" (European Commission Working Group 2003), the necessity of a new cultural policy is argued for with respect to the challenges the European Union is confronted with (the need for a European public sphere, enlargement of the EU, and intercultural dialogue with neighboring countries). This new policy, according to the report, "must also include regulatory aspects of the cultural sector, which have to be applied with considerable sensitivity to the special needs of the sector and in recognition of its difference to other economic sectors" (ibid.: 20). In a similar vein, the Culture Declaration recognizes that "globalization and evolving multilateral trade policies have an impact on cultural diversity" (Committee of Ministers of the Council of Europe 2000: 1) and argues that "cultural and audiovisual policies which promote and respect cultural diversity ... [are] necessary compliment[s] to trade policies" (ibid.: 3). In this document, there is a clear call for measures to sustain and protect cultural diversity within European cultural and media policies, because media pluralism (which will be otherwise destroyed through free trade policies) is identified as essential for European democracy and cultural diversity (ibid.: 2).

In order to secure media pluralism, minority cultural production in general and minority media production in particular need to be protected from what are deemed to be pure market forces. If special protection, incentives, and subsidies are not introduced, the cultural production and entertainment of minority groups (especially of migrants) will arguably be ill-served by national policies and will be a completely deregulated cultural sector, with grave consequences for the institutions of democracy in Europe. Thus, the cultural diversity arguments of European cultural-policy papers not only tie in and defend non-tariff barriers to cultural industries, cultural rights, and subsequently, human rights agendas, but they also situate the minorities in Europe on a footing very different from the national modernism that characterized national(izing) policies for a long time (Beale 2002: 81). The cultural diversity turn in Europe, which is embedded in a matrix of global trade, culture, sustainable media pluralism, intellectual property, and human rights, opens up new ground for not only the cultural, but also the economic positioning of migrants in the culturalized economies of Europe.

Cultural Diversity, Urban Regeneration, and Urban Governance

It is important to note that cultural diversity is not only about cultural vitality, but also about economic and social performance. The economic aspect of culture and cultural industries is not limited to global trade in cultural goods. Diversity is believed to foster economic innovation and creativity. Being one of the essential drivers of cultural and creative industries, which are among the fastest-growing economic sectors in Europe, cultural diversity is closely related to economic growth. The Council of Europe advocates that diversity, if managed properly, becomes a resource for gaining a competitive advantage in the economic and social performance of societies (Wood 2010). The advocates of a similar perspective argue that diversity stimulates creativity and that creativity promotes growth (Jacobs 1985; Florida 2002). Moreover, in the context of postindustrialism, the economic fortunes of cities and cultural diversity are increasingly linked, whereby the latter becomes the new motto for urban growth. Despite the caution expressed by some urban scholars against the necessary connection between diversity and equity in producing just societies (Sandercock 2002; Fainstein 2005; Rath 2005), cultural diversity became the banner of pro-growth coalitions in urban policy.

The impact of cultural diversity in fostering urban development is particularly evident in culture-led regeneration narratives, strategies, and policies of cities. In fact, the relationship between cultural diversity and urban development policies could be better understood with reference to scholarship that examines the neoliberal restructuring of cities within the context of the uneven spatialization of globalization. This scholarship on the contemporary neoliberal restructuring of cities, urban regeneration, and competitive urban rebranding and remarketing provides a suitable context in which to situate the cultural diversity policies' emphasis on diversity, urban growth, and governance in a more comprehensive way (Smith 1995; Brenner 1999; Brenner and Theodore 2002; Harvey 2006). This scholarship argues that all cities are forced to compete for the investments necessary to transform their postindustrial structures into bases for "new economy" so that they gain competitive advantage in positioning themselves in relation to each other and to states, within power hierarchies. According to these scholars, all cities are being rescaled in relation to new forms of capital accumulation.

The changing public discourse about the representation of particular cities, concentrating on the city's image and the resources available to its residents, like cultural diversity, is shaped by this context of scalar politics. All the resources, including human resources, are evaluated anew in the context of rescaling processes (Caglar 2007). Within this context, migrants acquire a crucial role in culture-led urban regeneration and growth. That is, migrants' insertion into urban economies and politics is entangled with the new role that culture and cultural industries acquire in neoliberal urbanism. Migrants come to be situated as both agents and subjects of the urban development processes that reposition the cities within and across state boundaries. Cities draw attention to their capacities to mobilize human resources with intercultural competencies and to their diverse populations, including migrants. Thus, migrants are one of the crucial actors of this process (Caglar and Glick Schiller 2011: 7–10).

The Intercultural Cities joint program of the Council of Europe and the European Commission—developed in 2010 in relation to the Intercultural Dialogue program of 2008—illustrates quite clearly how the relations between cultural diversity, urban regeneration, urban governance, and the role of migrants within these dynamics are envisaged. This is a model developed as part of "the capacity-building and policy development field programme" (Council of Europe 2008: 41). It gives priority to cultural diversity in urban areas and aims to initiate, through its Intercultural Cities network, a group of cities "to work towards intercultural strategies for the management of diversity as a resource" (Council of Europe 2008: 42). Based on an analysis of innovative practices of cities across Europe, it experiments with a model of the integration of migrants and minorities (ibid.).

Migrants occupy multiple roles in the Intercultural Cities program and network. Migrants' transnational reach and networks and their entrepreneurial aspirations and solidarity networks, as well as their reproductive behavior, all find their place in the "intercultural cities" model (Wood 2010). Most importantly, all these qualities are linked to the repositioning struggle of cities regionally as well as globally. It is not only migrants' future-orientedness and related entrepreneurial aspirations, which give impetus to urban economies that come to the fore in this model-program. As stated in the Intercultural Cities program documentation, migrants "may add a welcome to a flat or low-aspirational local economy, particularly if they resettle in cities experiencing stagnation or decline" (Wood 2010: 27).

Clearly, in this program, diversity and openness to diversity are important in terms of their impact on the stimulation of creativity and inventiveness, which in turn are crucial for the acquisition of a competitive advantage among cities (Wood 2010: 28). Culture and creative industries are hailed as being at the top of Europe's most dynamic economic sectors. Moreover, they themselves are seen to be essential drivers of cultural diversity in Europe. Within this context, migrants' cultural production acquires a central place in fostering and sustaining the desired cultural diversity as part of cultural industries.

Once culture becomes an essential component of the knowledge economy and is hailed as a sector with crucial economic potential, migrants and their cultural production attain a different position vis-à-vis urban economies than they used to have as skilled or unskilled labor force in the former models of integration. However, in order to be able to make use of diversity as an advantage, it needs to be managed properly. Thus not only does the management of cultural diversity become an important tool of urban governance, but also migrants have acquired a new salience in urban governance.

Conclusion

To come back to Fatih Akın's success and celebration as the prize-winning filmmaker of the 2004 Berlinale: no matter whether he was designated as German-Turkish or a German filmmaker of Turkish origin, he represented Germany and his film received the prize as a German film. However, the depiction of Akın's success in the media was still marked by the tensions and contested narratives of the cultural policies vis-à-vis migrants in Europe. On one hand, there was insistence on his "distinct" ethnic and cultural origins that set him apart but also provide one source of his creativity. At the same time, the narratives about him and his success often situated him as a cultural intermediary between his "Turkish roots and heritage" and the German society. All these representations and the subject positions opened by them were marked by excess, an excess against which he strongly expressed himself in interviews to the media. No matter how much the "cultural diversity turn" reassembled the territorial understanding of culture of the 1990s intercultural dialogue, tensions have remained. Traces of those narratives, which inscribed Akın first into the cultured territories of his own—or rather, his parents'—"homeland" before relating him to the European social and cultural space, were strikingly present in the discourses and events surrounding his celebrations. Although there is no way to precisely link Akın's success and his films to European cultural policies, his prize-winning film might be considered a product of collaboration schemes that are facilitated by the cultural policies that enable cultural but also economic spaces for such productions. As Yudice underlines in his critical analysis "The Expediency of Culture" (2003: 18): "[t]oday, a film or an art festival or biennale are as much international composites as the clothes we wear or the cars we drive with parts made from steel produced in one country, electronics in another, leather and plastic in still others, and finally assembled in yet other countries."

Although one of the dynamics behind the cultural diversity policies in Europe has been the effort to secure protectionism for (European) cultural industries within global trade regimes, this turn has had crucial consequences in the way migrant/minority cultures and cultural productions are situated, are supported, and have found voice(s) within the European public space. These policies have provided opportunities and opened new avenues for migrant/minority cultural productions within the growing cultural and creative industries. The empowerment that has come with their presence in these growing sectors is an unintended consequence of the cultural-protectionist desires of Europe. Despite their limitations, the cultural policies based on cultural diversity include these migrants in the European cultural space beyond the schemes of secluded communities and carry the potential to pose a challenge to the self-definition of "the public" in Europe. No matter what the agendas and dynamics behind the prominence of migrants within cultural diversity policies may be, these policies succeed in questioning the assumed boundaries of "the public" in Europe by including migrants in social, cultural, and political spheres. The policies, which enable (TCN) migrants to occupy such an interstitial position, carry with them a subversive potential to open up the boundaries of the realm of "the public" in Europe.

Similarly, the increasing importance of culture and cultural diversity for the economic and social performance of cities gives a different but related prominence to populations marked as "diverse," as seen for example in the role of migrants in urban growth and governance. Flagging "cultural diversity" is a common trend in culture-led urban development. However, the "success" of cities in converting their "diversity" into economic assets that would provide opportunities and open up new avenues of participation and presence for migrants lies in the dynamics of the competitive positioning of a particular city within global power hierarchies (Caglar and Glick Schiller 2011). For this reason, without the political economy of cultural diversity, the narratives on cultural diversity remain confined to shallow representations of migrants' presence and cohabitation. Approaching cultural diversity from this perspective might function as a reminder that discursive constructs in the cultural diversity debate need to be grounded in a broader field of global forces.

Notes

1. For a critique of this concept and the problems involved in the assumptions informing the notion of "second-generation" see Caglar (1997); Soysal (1999); and Karakayali (2005).
2. Several questions in the interview ("Your film is about Turkish immigrants in Germany. Immigrants need to drop their tradition and heritage in a new society or whether the immigrants can find peace only in the place where they come from" [*Deutsche Welle*, February 14, 2004]), left out any enquiries about the cinematography or the filmmaker's positioning in the cinema world.
3. Fatih Akın defines himself simply by saying "I am a filmmaker" (*Rheinische Post Online*, September 25, 2007). At this point, his position is very similar to the filmmakers from Africa who refuse to be designated as African filmmakers, regardless of whether or not their Africanness enabled them to reach certain markets.
4. When some journalists mentioned the concepts of *Gastarbeiter* and *Auslaender*, during the press conference after he received the prize at the Berlinale, he reacted angrily and underlined that the former word does not have any reality for him (Nicodemus 2004).
5. Germany, contrary to Turkey, does not recognize dual citizenship, except for exceptional cases.
6. Akın, who was born to Turkish parents, had to take position vis-à-vis his parents' and his origins, and his real 'home'—Germany or Turkey. Confronted with this, he stated that he considers his film an international movie, since it is produced by someone with a dual cultural background (Bax 2004; Tosun 2004b).
7. Like some of the journalists in Germany, Turkish columnists preferred to discuss issues about his position towards tradition in reference to "generational differences" among German Turks. They somehow disregarded the fact that, in this comparison, the views of a worker who came from Turkey to Germany and the views of an artist were at stake (Tosun 2004a; Frankfurter Allgemeine Online 2004).
8. Here, my aim is neither to situate Fatih Akın's cinematography within the New German Cinema, nor to explore his films' differences from other German Turkish films. These tasks lie beyond my interest and competencies. For comprehensive reviews of the New German Cinema and particularly Akın's place within it, see Göktürk (2002) and Jones (2003).
9. Though policies acquire new meanings in every different setting (Shore and Wright 2011), here, rather than following the transformation of cultural diversity policies, with their implications and effects, in different

places around Europe, the focus is on the subject positions that the policies open up for the migrants—their potentials as well as their limits.
10. Here it has to be noted that mutual understanding was one of the central goals of cooperation in the cultural area in the European Cultural Convention (1954). Though its original focus was to create and mediate understanding between nations, migrants, national minorities, linguistic and cultural communities, and religious groups were increasingly included into it.
11. It is important, however, to note that the concept of "neighbor" is defined by the interplay between proximity and distance, and as such, characterized by ambiguity. Neighborhood entails dangerous proximity with a great deal of potential for conflict. Neighbors are not only intimately connected, but also mutually estranged. "The neighbour is both too close to be entirely reified or abstracted, and too distant to count among the subject's group of intimates" (Reinhard 1997: 1).
12. It has to be noted that the discourse on Europe's eastern and southern neighbors shows differences. While the aim of cultural dialogue in the south always comes together with an *interreligious dialogue*, the relation with the eastern neighbors is taken care of by the milder concept of *mutual understanding*.
13. The Kuijpers Resolution (1987) instructed the European Commission to bear in mind the interests of the smaller languages in the areas of education, the media, and local and regional administration. The Mercator project was the consequence of this instruction. This emphasis put on territoriality is apparent in the journal Mercator Media Forum, published within the *Mercator Media Project* framework. "The journal is being launched to promote discussion and the flow of information between those who work in the territorially-based non-state languages of the European Union in the field of media, very broadly defined to include book publishing, radio and television, newspapers and magazines, archives and libraries, electronic networks and databases" (Thomas 1995: 3). This is how the objectives of the journal are formulated in the first issue. In fact, in all the four issues published until 2000, the questions of multilingualism and multiculturalism and the minority media are only approached from the point of territorial minority-language groups of the European Union.
14. Strikingly, within the frame of the Mercator project, the questions of media, multiculturalism, or multilingualism in Europe are not discussed in relation to the immigrant communities (TCNs) in Europe. The only article, for example, in *Mercator Media Forum* dealing with a group outside of Europe is interestingly an article on the Kurds and Kurdish television. However, this topic was included not to expand the scope of the journal to immigrant communities, but because Kurdish is a non-state language and refers to a trans-border territorial minority.
15. The ambiguity between the inclusion and exclusion of immigrants in the EU runs throughout the recommendations. On one hand, they are accepted to be an integral part of European identity (see the first clause of the Recommendations); on the other hand, different schemes are adopted to encourage their contact with their country of origin, "to assist the pro-

duction of broadcasting of programs on intercommunity relations and immigration" (recommendation h) and to promote the coproduction of films with producers from immigrant communities' countries of origin, including films dealing with migrants and ethnic minorities (recommendation j). For an excellent study of the challenge immigrants in the EU pose to the European polity, see Aziz (2001). She assesses the role of law in perpetuating the divide between a political community defined in national terms and a transnational economic and social community in the EU.
16. This refers to Europe-specific, direct initiatives of the Council of Europe. In fact, the report "Our Creative Diversity," resulting from the UNESCO initiative the "World Decade on Cultural Development," dates back to 1996. This report was followed by three meetings of the International Network on Cultural Policy in 1998 and 1999. See Beale (2002: 850) for a detailed discussion of this development.
17. For example, in the project "Intercultural Dialogue: A Project of the Council of Europe. The Unifying Aspects of Culture," the aim of cultural diversity is coupled with the aim of fostering coexistence of religious diversity.
18. This report was later published as a book titled "Differing Diversities: Cultural Policy and Cultural Diversity" by Tony Bennett in 2001.
19. From this point of view, the cultural diversity perspective is different from the multiculturalist perspective, which is dedicated to the preservation of a pre-given cultural mosaic that is based on an isomorphism between territory, culture, and ethnicity.
20. For the complex relationship between hybridity and essentialism see Friedman (1997) and Caglar (1997). However, as the cultural diversity perspective, at least in Bennett's report, succeeds in avoiding any kind of isomorphism between ethnic and cultural diversity, it does not share the problems of hybridity criticized in these works.
21. "The Working Group wishes to stress the importance of recognizing the value of and supporting cultural groups that operate 'at the margins' or outside traditional cultural structures" (Civil Forum Marseille 2000: 7). The new cultural framework clearly operates with a broader concept of cultural and artistic activities, including popular music and youth culture. It has to be noted that the cultural policies target the participation of all peoples of Europe, beyond the criterion of citizenship (see Lebon 2002 and Civil Forum Marseille 2000). This aspect of the inclusive formulation of Europe in cultural policies is informed by cultural diversity. The other important aspect of these policies is the notion of culturally inclusive Europe as opposed to "Fortress Europe" (European Commission Working Group 2003: 20). Policies aim to involve those from the neighboring countries who are not included in "formal Europe" (ibid.).
22. It has to be recognized that the concepts of culture, participation, and citizenship with which these policy formulations operate are tuned to the most up-to-date critical positions in the social sciences.
23. It is important to note that France and Canada "tried to pursue a concentrated strategy for a cultural exemption in trade talks" (Beale 2002: 85). In fact, it was first Canada with whom the U.S. failed to have cultural industries incorporated into the Free Trade Agreement in 1988. After this failure,

U.S. trade officials put extra effort into preventing the European Community (as it was then) to impose import quotas on audio-visual texts (Miller 1996: 75). Canada's relationship with the U.S. regarding the exemption of cultural industries from free-trade agreements made Canada an important ally for Europe, in positioning Europe against the U.S. Canada's presence in the Council of Europe's transversal Study on Cultural Policy and Cultural Diversity (Council of Europe 2001) becomes meaningful within this context.
24. The U.K.'s take on this matter was different from the French position. The U.K. remained skeptical about French notions of culture. See Miller (1996: 81).
25. However, one has to be cautious in building two oppositional fronts in this debate, such as that the EU was for protectionism and the U.S. for the complete removal of trade barriers. The U.S. exercises protectionism in its domestic market and protects its domestic production in several areas, including the audio-visual sector. For an elaboration of this argument see Miller (1996).

References

Aziz, Miriam. 2001. "What Makes the European? EU Citizenship and an (O)ther." Paper presented to the Conference *Stranger*, November 8. RSCAS, EUI, Florence.

Bax, Daniel. 2004, March 11. "Ey, das ist nur eine Geschichte." Available at http://www.taz.de/1/archiv/?id=archivseite&dig=2004/03/11/a0212. Accessed 15 March 2004.

Beale, Alison. 2002. "Identifying a Policy Hierarchy: Communication Policy, Media Industries, and Globalization." In *Global Culture: Media, Arts, Policy and Globalization*, ed. Diana Crane, Nobuko Kawashima, and Kenichi Kawasaki. London and New York: Routledge, pp. 78–89.

Bennett, Tony. 2001. *Differing Diversities: Cultural Policy and Cultural Diversity*. Strasbourg: Council of Europe Publishing. Available at http://www.coe.int/t/dg4/cultureheritage/culture/completed/diversity/EN_Diversity_Bennett.pdf. Accessed 10 December 2007.

Boyer, Domenic and Ulf Hannerz. 2006. "Introduction: World of Journalism." *Ethnography* 7(1): 5–17.

Brenner, Neil. 1999. "Globalisation as Reterritorialisation: The Re-scaling of Urban Governance in the European Union." *Urban Studies* 36(3): 431–451.

Brenner, Neil and Nik Theodore. 2002. "Cities and Geographies of Actually Existing Neoliberalism." *Antipode* 34(3): 348–379.

Burri, Mira. 2012. "Cultural Protectionism 2.0: Updating Cultural Policy Tools for the Digital Age." In *Transnational Culture in the Internet Age*, ed. Adam Candeub and Sean Pager. Cheltenham: Edward Elgar Publishing, pp. 182–202. Available at http://www.wti.org/fileadmin/user_upload/nccr-trade.ch/wp3/3.1/Burri_reviewed.pdf/. Accessed 12 November 2013.

Caglar, Ayse. 1997. "Hyphenated Identities and the Limits of 'Culture': Some Methodological Queries." In *The Politics of Multiculturalism in the New Europe: Racism, Identity, Community*, ed. Pnina Werbner and Tariq Modood. London: Zed Books, pp. 169–185.

———. 1998. "Popular Culture, Marginality and Institutional Incorporation: German-Turkish Rap and Turkish Pop in Berlin." *Cultural Dynamics* 10(3): 243–261.

———. 2007. "Rescaling Cities, Cultural Diversity and Transnationalism: Migrants of Mardin and Essen." *Ethnic and Racial Studies* 30(6): 1070–1095.

Caglar, Ayse and Nina Glick Schiller. 2011. "Introduction: Migrants and Cities." In *Locating Migration: Rescaling Cities and Migrants*, ed. Nina Glick Schiller and Ayse Caglar. Ithaca, NY: Cornell University Press, pp. 1–19.

Caglar, Ayse and Sebastian Mehling. 2013. "Sites and the Scales of the Law: Third-Country Nationals and EU Roma Citizens." In *Enacting European Citizenship*, ed. Engin Isin and Michael Saward. Cambridge: Cambridge University Press, pp. 155–177.

Civil Forum Marseille. 2000. *Culture Declaration*. Available at http://90plan.ovh.net/~euromedp/spip/spip.php?rubrique142. Accessed 23 April 2008.

Committee of Ministers of the Council of Europe. 7 December 2000. *Draft Declaration on Cultural Diversity*. 733rd Meeting of the Ministers' Deputies. Available at https://wcd.coe.int/ViewDoc.jsp?Ref=C-M(2000)180&Ver=rev&Language=lanEnglish&Site=COE&BackColorInternet=DBDCF2&BackColorIntranet=FDC864&BackColorLogged=FDC864. Accessed 12 June 2011.

Council of Europe. 2003. "Cultural co-operation between Europe and the South Mediterranean Countries." Resolution 1313. Available at http://assembly.coe.int/Mainf.asp?link=/Documents/AdoptedText/ta03/ERES1313.htm#_ftn1. Accessed 13 February 2003.

———. 2008. "Living Together as Equals in Dignity." White Paper on Intercultural Dialogue. CM. 2008. 30. Available at http://www.coe.int/t/dg4/intercultural/whitepaper_interculturaldialogue_2_EN.asp. Accessed 17 March 2012.

Deutsche Welle. 2004, February 14. "Interview with Fatih Akın." Available at http://www.dw.de/interview-with-fatih-akin/a-1114779. Accessed 16 February 2004.

EUR-Lex. 1998, August 7. "EuroMed Audiovisual—EuroMed Audiovisual Cooperation Programme." Official Journal of the European Communities 41 C247/15. Available at http://eur-lex.europa.eu/LexUriServ/LexUriServ.do?uri=OJ:C:1998:247:0015:0015:EN:PDF. Accessed 9 December 2009.

European Commission High Level Advisory Group. 2003. *Dialogue between Peoples and Cultures in the Euro-Mediterranean Area*. Brussels. Available at http://institut-medea.be/wp-content/uploads/2004/01/Rep_HL_Adv_Group_11_2003.pdf. Accessed 14 April 2004.

European Commission Working Group. 2003. *Towards a New Cultural Framework Program of the European Union*. Brussels. Available at http://www.ccp-deutschland.de/fileadmin/user_upload/3_Infos_und_Service/5_Pub-

likationen/towards_framewor_programme_juni2003.pdf/. Accessed 14 June 2006.
Fainstein, Susan. 2005. "Cities and Diversity. Should We Want it? Can We Plan for it?" *Urban Affairs Review* 41(1): 3–19.
Florida, Richard. 2002. *The Rise of the Creative Class*. New York: Basic Books.
Frankfurter Allgemeine Online. 2004, February 14. "Goldener Bär für Gegen die Wand." Available at http://www.faz.net/aktuell/feuilleton/berlinale-2009/berlinale-2004-goldener-baer-fuer-gegen-die-wand-1147554.html. Accessed 10 March 2004.
Friedman, Jonathan. 1997. "Global Crises, the Struggle for Cultural Identity and Intellectual Pork-Barrelling: Cosmopolitans, Nationals and Locals in an Era of De-hegemonization." In *Debating Cultural Hybridity: Multi-cultural Identities and the Politics of Anti-racism*, ed. Pnina Werbner and Tariq Modood. London: Zed Books, pp. 70–89.
Göktürk, Deniz. 2002. "Beyond Paternalismus: Turkish German Traffic in Cinema." In *The German Cinema Book*, ed. Tim Bergfelder, Erica Carter, and Deniz Göktürk. London: British Film Institute, pp. 248–256.
Gupta, Akhil and James Ferguson. 1992. "Beyond "Culture": Space, Identity, and the Politics of Difference." *Cultural Anthropology* 7(1): 6–23.
Hannerz, Ulf. 1998. "Other Transnationals: Perspectives Gained from Studying Sideways." *Paideuma* 44: 109–123.
———. 2010. *Anthropology's World: Life in a Twenty-first Century Discipline*. London and New York: Pluto Press.
Harvey, David. 2006. *Spaces of Global Capitalism: Towards a Theory of Uneven Geographical Development*. London: Verso.
Jacobs, Jane. 1985. *Cities and the Wealth of Nations*. New York: Vintage.
Jones, Stan. 2003. "Turkish-German Cinema Today: A Case Study of Fatih Akın's Kurz und Schmerzlos (1998) and Im Juli (2000)." In *European Cinema: Inside Out: Images of the Self and the Other in Postcolonial European Film*, ed. Guido Rings and Rikki Morgan-Tamosunas. Heidelberg: Winter, pp. 75–91.
Karakayali, Nedim. 2005. "Duality and Diversity in the Lives of Immigrant Children: Rethinking the 'Problem of Second Generation' in Light of Immigrant Autobiographies." *Canadian Review of Sociology and Anthropology* 42(3): 325–344.
Lebon, France. 2002. "Colloque d'experts: Dialogue au service de la communication interculturelle and inter-religieuse, Strasbourg, 7–9 October 2002—Séance de travail 3, 'Le défi de la diversité culturelle,' Contribution de France Lebon." Strasbourg: Conseil de l'Europe.
Miller, Toby. 1996. "The Crime of Monsieur Lang: GATT, the Screen, and the New International Division of Cultural Labour." In *Film Policy: International, National and Regional Perspectives*, ed. Albert Moran. New York and London: Routledge, pp. 72–84.
Nicodemus, Katja. 2004. "Ankunft in der Wirklichkeit." Available at http://www.zeit.de/2004/09/Berlinale-Abschluss. Accessed 28 October 2007.
Rath, Jan. 2005. *Tourism, Ethnic Diversity and the City*. London: Routledge.
Reinhard, Kenneth. 1997. "Freud, My Neighbor." *American Imago* 54(2): 165–195.

Rheinische Post Online. 2007, September 25. "In Deutschland keine Integration." Interview with director Fatih Akın. Available at http://www.rp-online.de/kultur/in-deutschland-keine-integration-aid-1.2030607. Accessed 27 September 2007.

Sandercock, Leonie. 2002. "Toward Cosmopolis: Utopia as Construction Site." In *Readings in Planning Theory*, ed. Scott Campbell and Susan Fainstein. Oxford: Blackwell, pp. 401–410.

Shore, Cris and Susan Wright. 2011. "Conceptualizing Policy: Technologies of Governance and the Politics of Visibility." In *Policy Worlds: Anthropology and the Analysis of Contemporary Power*, ed. Cris Shore, Susan Wright, and Davide Però. Oxford: Berghahn, pp. 1–26.

Smith, Neil. 1995. "Remaking Scale: Competition and Cooperation in Pre-national and Post-national Europe." In *Competitive European Peripheries*, ed. Heikki Eskelinen and Snickars Folke. Berlin: Springer Verlag, pp. 59–74.

Soysal, Levent. 1999. *Projects of Culture: An Ethnographic Episode in the Life of Migrant Youth in Berlin*. Ph.D. dissertation. Harvard University, Department of Anthropology.

Thomas, Ned. 1995. "The Mercator Media Forum." *Mercator Media Forum* 1: 2–11.

Tosun, Murat. 2004a, February 15. "Altın Ayı Fatih Akın'a." Available at http://hurarsiv.hurriyet.com.tr/goster/haber.aspx?id=202802. Accessed 10 March 2004.

Tosun, Murat. 2004b, February 16. "İki kültürlü olmak yaratıcılığımı artırdı." Available at http://hurarsiv.hurriyet.com.tr/goster/haber.aspx?id=202889. Accessed 10 March 2004.

UNESCO. 2005, October 20. "Convention on the Protection and Promotion of the Diversity of Cultural Expressions." Available at http://portal.unesco.org/en/ev.php-URL_ID=31038&URL_DO=DO_TOPIC&URL_SECTION=201.html. Accessed 13 November 2008.

Vertovec, Steven. 2007. "Super-diversity and its Implications." *Ethnic and Racial Studies* 30(6): 1024–1054.

———. 2012. "'Diversity' and the Social Imaginary." *European Journal of Sociology* 53(3): 287–312.

Wood, Phil, ed. 2010. *Intercultural Cities: Towards a Model for Intercultural Integration. A Practical Handbook, with Good Practice Examples and Guidance*. Strasbourg: Council of Europe Publishing.

Wright, Susan. 2011. "Studying Policy: Methods, Paradigms, Perspectives." In *Policy Worlds: Anthropology and the Analysis of Contemporary Power*, ed. Cris Shore, Susan Wright, and Davide Pero. Oxford: Berghahn, pp. 27–32.

Yudice, George. 2003. *The Expediency of Culture: Uses of Culture in the Global Era*. Durham, NC and London: Duke University Press.

Chapter 11

EMERGENT CONCEPT CHAINS AND SCENARIOS OF DEPOLITICIZATION
The Case of Global Governance as a Future Past

Ronald Stade

As the Cold War came to an end, American pundits tried to guess where the world was headed. They thought up a number of future scenarios in which the United States either epitomized the final stage of human history or was faced with new threats and evils. Because many pundits invoked cultural differences as the cause of impending geopolitical conflicts, Ulf Hannerz (2009) calls these scenarios "geocultural." Such geocultural scenarios include everything from a clash of civilizations to a world in need of U.S. soft power. An interesting, although not entirely new, aspect of the scenario industry was its creation of a common academic-public-political sphere. In a case study, with the utilization of a new analytical model, the workings and logic of this type of common sphere will be investigated. The case study is that of a specific post–Cold War scenario: global governance. The analytical model is one of an emergent concept chain.

Geocultural Scenarios

In and around the end of the Cold War, a number of U.S. pundits tried to guess what would happen next, now that the East–West conflict was over. They conceived future scenarios and marketed them to the public and to an academic and expert audience in the United States and beyond. Not many of their scenarios came with a happy face; most exhibited a worried (or snarling) face.[1] Several scenarios contended that cultural differences would be the cause of impending geopolitical conflicts, which is why Ulf Hannerz (2009) refers to them as "geocultural scenarios." Most notorious among these was Samuel Huntington's (1993) prophecy that the Cold War would be replaced by a clash of civilizations on a global scale, in which Islam would reveal itself as the latest menace to U.S. hegemony. Other pundits identified alternative, culturally defined, conflict scenarios: the coming anarchy wrought by the uncivilized urban poor (Kaplan 1994); the unwillingness of effete Europeans to defend the North Atlantic security zone (Kagan 2002); the need for the U.S. to project the soft power of American pop culture (Nye 1990); the threat from cultures that resist development and modernization (Harrison 1993); etc.[2] The basic constellation in all these scenarios is as simple as it is trite. The West—or, more precisely, the United States—is pitted against the rest. The genre of geocultural scenarios relies on the image of a United States that is in a perpetual state of siege and forever must be poised to attack. The underlying assumption is that, to the U.S.A., the world is enemy country.

Huntington's geocultural augury was a refutation of another post-Cold War scenario: Francis Fukuyama's (1989) prediction that history had come to an end. Fukuyama thought that, with the collapse of the Soviet empire, "liberal democracy" and capitalism had run out of competitors. Humanity had arrived at the end point of ideological evolution; the ideal of capitalist society could not be improved upon. While Huntington and other geocultural pundits would go on to warn against the United States lowering its guard, Fukuyama assumed that the world soon would become one big U.S.A.: a global capitalist society with just a few, marginalized dissidents. Fukuyama believed that the U.S. had won; Huntington worried that new wars were headed its way. Despite this apparent difference between their scenarios, Fukuyama, Huntington, and the rest of the geocultural ideologues agreed on one crucial issue: they were all convinced that the era of politics was over. From now on, human affairs would be a matter of administration and consumption (Fukuyama) or of distinct religious affiliations and intercultural relationships (Huntington), or of some other non-political development. Just a few years later, it seems that the xenophobic—and, in the case of Fukuyama, triumphant—scenarios have been debunked by the course of events. Actual scenarios turned out to be so much more complex and unpredictable than one-liner divinations like "the clash of civilizations" and "the end of history." Huntington did not predict the liberation movements, as well as the divisions, within "Muslim civilization," and, most importantly, trivialized the fact that cynicism (called "realism" by its practitioners and by political scientists)—rather than cultural identity—continues to play a decisive role in domestic and international politics. Fukuyama's imagination was equally limited. Even (or, perhaps, especially) if one adopts his metaphor of ideological evolution, it should be clear that history knows no end.

An excellent example of this is the Muslim reformation. Jihadists who sympathize with, support, or are members of movements like al-Qaeda already have achieved changes in what Huntington naïvely thought of as a single, immutable "Muslim civilization." For millions of young people, the jihadists may have created a contemporary, generic Muslim identity that bears little resemblance to what Huntington took to be a centuries-old civilization. On closer inspection, the new, electronically diffused identity is a creolized and creolizing version of Sufi, Shia, Sunni, Arabic, and non-Arabic versions of Islam. To quote Faisal Devji (2005: 162): "In the long run, violence is probably Al-Qaeda's most superficial and short-lived effect, though it is certainly one of great importance for the moment. Far greater and almost incalculable in its effects is the jihad's democratization of Islam, accomplished by its fragmentation of traditional forms of religious authority and dispersal of their elements into a potentially endless series of re-combinations." If we add to this analysis the uprisings in the Arab countries, conducted by a motley crew of protesters with radically different agendas and loyalties, we are able discern ideological leaps and bounds, not an end to history or a civilization that fossilized millennia ago and has not changed since. If anything is to be learned from history—itself a questionable proposition—it is that major upheavals and ruptures always come as a surprise. The most consequential historical changes have been of the unforeseen and unintended kind.

Depoliticization

The geocultural scenario business—and it is a business—carried on a consequential legacy: the ideology of depoliticization. What is meant by depoliticization? The answer to this question depends on how we define politics or the political. A common definition centers on two aspects: politics as a normative order (rules, principles, meanings, etc.) and politics as the enforcement of this order (coercion, power, violence, etc.). Different political theories have stressed one of these aspects and reduced the relative importance of the other. Theorists like Hannah Arendt and Jürgen Habermas emphasize the normative aspect of the political, considering consensus and communication the essence of politics. In this view, the public realm of politics is concerned with the common good (not private interests), the principles of which one agrees upon through unimpeded deliberation on equal terms.[3] Other scholars, like Carl Schmitt and Chantal Mouffe, take conflict to be the essence of the political. Schmitt concluded that enforcement therefore is the ultimate truth of the political: in any political order one must ask who is entitled to abrogate the normative order; for instance, by declaring a state of emergency (see, e.g., Schmitt 1922 and 1927). Mouffe has other reasons for endorsing the view that the political must consist of conflict. She believes that unless politics is contestation, the ties between political representatives and those who vote them into office are weakened and finally severed. When in liberal democracies[4] there is political consensus on vital issues, potential voters turn their back on mainstream politics (see, for example, Mouffe 2005).

In accordance with the first definition of the political, depoliticization is brought on by a breakdown of communication and an end to consensus. The political dissolves into incompatible private interests and irreconcilable conflict. If we keep to the second definition, depoliticization is a consequence of conflict avoidance. Instead of admitting that conflict, power, and violence are the essence of the political—and inversely, that issues of conflict, power, and violence are political—agents and advocates of depoliticization turn political contention into technical, procedural, managerial problems. A classical anthropological treatment of this type of depoliticization is James Ferguson's (1990) study of how the international development apparatus treats political conflicts as matters of bureaucratic reform. International aid agencies redefine reality so that it fits their own mission and organizational logic. The same occurred in an even more dramatic context, when the United Nations (UN), due to its inner technocratic workings, refused to intervene in Rwanda to put an end to the genocide (for a participant observation account from inside the UN, see Barnett 2002).

In our era of public management ideology and audit cultures (Strathern 2000)—only that which can be audited may exist—depoliticization in both senses, i.e., both as the suppression of issues of power and conflict and as an obstruction of communication on equal terms and the public negotiation of political consensus, has become a near-universal problem. This ideology was formulated by people like Friedrich von Hayek, Milton Friedman, and James Buchanan (all of whom won the Nobel Memorial Prize in Economic Sciences). The essential message is that political conflict and deliberation really is a problem of rational choice and management—that is, of "scientific" procedure.[5] Metaphysically, ideologues like von Hayek, Friedman, and Buchanan are "enemies of the state": they reject the idea that there is such a thing as a separate public sphere, a polis, where consensus and equity supersede private interest and selfishness. Historically speaking, this metaphysics of depoliticization, in the U.S. and the U.K., soon mutated into a moral crusade against "government." The mutation was an unintended consequence of deeper cultural processes. The "enemies of the state" had rallied round the flag of liberty. They opposed liberty to equity. For decades, the promise of increased equity had served as a guiding political principle, at the rhetorical as well as at the institutional level. Profound moral convictions had been associated with this principle, which was now dismantled in a concerted effort by American right-wing think tanks (the Heritage Foundation, the Manhattan Institute, the American Enterprise Institute, etc.), U.S. media (Fox News, most talk radio stations in the U.S., the Wall Street Journal, etc.), and U.S. political movements (e.g., elitist ones like the Bohemian Club, and white middle-class ones like the Tea Party Movement). The Thatcher–Reagan axis of neoliberal ideology provided another institutional outlet for this movement. The strategic dismantling of egalitarian ideals created a moral void, which was filled not just by faith in the infallibility of the market, but also by a moral crusade for "cultural values" like heterosexual marriage, religion, and patriotism and against intellectual doubt. Moral values were put before self-interest; *homo probus* was to replace *homo economicus*. A considerable portion of the U.S. electorate that has been touched by the spirit of the crusade nowadays votes individuals and parties into office, who divest it of its prosperity and welfare but promise to take uncompromising action against abortion, homosexual marriage, and secularism.[6]

The latter type of depoliticization in the name of "cultural values," which moves not just beyond norms of equity but also beyond liberty as a guiding principle, merits a study of its own. At this point, it may suffice to note that depoliticization in whatever shape it appears—be it as geo-cultural scenarios, neoliberalism, or right-wing populism—displaces political conflicts and inhibits political communication. This brings us to the question of how to study phenomena like depoliticization.

Emergent Concept Chains

Over the most recent decades, calls for the reinvigoration of ethnographic methodology have been frequent.[7] Hugh Gusterson (1997: 116), for instance, suggests that our ethnographic engagements necessarily must be polymorphous. Talking to people, observing them, reading books and newspapers, surfing the Internet, exchanging emails: these are all part of fieldwork nowadays. Then again, one may ask what sets apart the polymorphous engagements of the ethnographer from the polymorphous engagements of everyone else. In terms of method, nothing; which is why Talal Asad's comment on ethnographic methodology strikes me as crucial: "In my view anthropology is more than a method, and it should not be equated—as it has popularly become—with the direction given to inquiry by the pseudoscientific notion of 'fieldwork' .... What is distinctive about modern anthropology is the comparison of embedded concepts (representations) between societies differently located in time or space" (Asad 2003: 17). As will become apparent, this study is very much a comparison of embedded concepts—or, rather, of a particular embedded concept. Asad's definition calls for a comparison of embedded concepts. The concepts, writes Asad, are embedded in societies "differently located in time or space." This prompts the question of what we mean by a "society." A more or less integrated system? A metaphysical entity that is both cause and effect of individual actions? Or just another concept that is embedded in a particular context (and that refers to other concepts and contexts)? To avoid—or, rather, to acknowledge—the fallacy of self-referentiality ("society is a concept that is embedded in society"), we may want to do away with the notion of society as a temporally and spatially delimited context for concepts. The social, just like the political, is about consensus and conflict, about association and dissociation, and about shifting forms and degrees of accord and alienation. Therefore, it is better to think of concepts as being embedded in a wide range of ever-changing fields of association and dissociation, of understanding and misunderstanding, of cohesion and division. Concepts tend not to be embedded in societies (whatever is meant by that), but in shifting contexts of meaning.

Naturally, my ethnographic engagements were polymorphous—ethnographic engagements always are. I traveled to think tanks in Washington, D.C. and Germany; I conducted interviews over the telephone; I visited archives and libraries; I talked to colleagues; I followed the news, etc. I did all this to follow a concept across time and space and contexts, which is why, for the purpose of this study, one call for methodological reform deserves special attention. George Marcus (1995), in proposing a multisited ethnography of connections, urges us to follow the thing, metaphor, plot, story, allegory, life, biography, or conflict. Ethnography ought to be a kind of tracking—which it, strictly speaking, has been at least since the days of Seligman's and Malinowski's description of the inter-island exchange network, the *kula* ring. Going even further back in time, the entire diffusionist school in anthropology could be considered an example of tracking methodology (see Stade 2001 for a discussion of diffusionism and its legacy). A more recent example of such a research strategy can be found in *The Social Life of Things: Commodities in Cultural Perspective* (1986), edited by Arjun Appadurai. In this volume, Brian Spooner (1986), for example, tracks the changes in symbolic value of oriental carpets across international borders and social contexts, from production to consumption (and back again). George Marcus, in his discussion of tracking strategies, refers not just to Appadurai's book but also to Immanuel Wallerstein's concept of commodity chains. Wallerstein's concept was picked up and systematized by Gary Gereffi and Miguel Korzeniewicz (1994), who analyzed global capitalism as cascading chains of exchange that link together producers and consumers. They differentiate between up- and downstream sections of commodity chains. To give an example, one can follow a specific commodity item along the exchange chain. An athletic shoe decorated with the logo of the U.S. company Nike on display in an American or European shopping mall is likely to have been assembled in a shop in Indonesia or Vietnam or China or some other low-income country (in 2005, Nike had 705 independent contract factories in its network).[8] The largest portion of the price the consumer is expected to pay for the athletic shoe, i.e., most of its economic value, is not added in the upstream process of production in an Asian factory, but downstream at the designing and marketing stages. (How much does the Chinese woman earn who works for ten to twelve hours a day in one of Wenzhou's assembly lines compared to a copywriter or creative director at the American advertising agency Wieden and Kennedy, which, among other things, came up with Nike's slogan, "Just do it"?)

The concept of commodity chains is a useful tool for analyzing global capitalism. It lends itself to breaking down the analytical barriers between system and lifeworld, between macro- and micro-levels of analysis. The life of a factory worker in Asia can be connected to the life of an American advertising professional, both in terms of macro-economic and geopolitical structures and effects and as different forms of everyday life and subjectivity. At the theoretical level, making such connections involves both simultaneity (the juxtaposition in space of up- and downstream positions in the global system) and process (the movement of a commodity along a time axis; from upstream production to downstream consumption). In what is to follow, the model of commodity chains will be appropriated and applied to the investigation of concepts. For the purpose of this study, the model needs some adjustment. As far as concepts are concerned, a marked difference in structural position or subjectivities may not be found between up- and downstream sections of the chain. The upstream producer of a concept, for instance, may be in a similar structural position as the downstream user of the same concept. This is particularly true of contemporary social and political key concepts. It may be illustrated as follows. The social and political key concept of "zero tolerance" was invented by

Charles Murray and launched by the Manhattan Institute in the mid-1980s to signify a harsh policy that no longer would tolerate any form of social deviance (Wacquant 1999). The idea was that there would be no tolerance whatsoever for even the most insignificant offense, because today's petty theft and graffiti will be tomorrow's armed robbery and murder. The policy of zero tolerance led to the systematic punishment and incarceration of the U.S.A.'s urban poor (ibid.). The European relay station for the concept was the British Institute of Economic Affairs, from which it diffused across the continent. Nowadays, well-meaning individuals and organizations wish to impose zero tolerance for sexual harassment and bullying in the workplace, or zero tolerance for child abuse and human trafficking. The concept of zero tolerance may lose some or most of its ideological charge when it is being used in these circumstances, which, as will be shown, is a common feature in the downstream section of concept chains. The Manhattan Institute has as its slogan, "Turning intellect into influence." The problem is that it may be difficult for those at the upstream section of the concept chain to predict of what kind the influence will be further downstream.

The point in adopting the metaphor of chain for the study of concepts, then, is not to argue that, as in the case of commodity chains, specific sections of the chain are associated with specific positions in the system of global capitalism, but to allegorize the international traffic in political concepts as a chain that consists of identifiable, sequentially linked sections, in which the upstream section of production is connected with the downstream section of consumption or usage. This sort of tracking strategy in the research of social and political keywords is not new. The most notable, in terms of archival thoroughness and theoretical sophistication, among established research strategies of tracing concepts, is Reinhart Koselleck's *Begriffsgeschichte* (conceptual history), which, inter alia, has resulted in large-scale projects like the multivolume encyclopedias *Geschichtliche Grundbegriffe: Historisches Lexikon zur politisch-sozialen Sprache in Deutschland* (Brunner et al. 1972–1997) and *Handbuch politisch-sozialer Grundbegriffe in Frankreich 1680–1820* (Reichardt et al. 1985–2000).[9] Those of Koselleck's major theoretical contributions that are relevant for the current discussion can be condensed in three of his analytical terms: *Sattelzeit* (saddle period, ca 1750–1850); *Bewegungsbegriff* (concept of movement); and *Vergangene Zukunft* (future past). The first term, "saddle period," according to Koselleck, denotes a period in European history when key political and social concepts became future-oriented and utopian. In pragmatic terms, these new concepts—these concepts of movement—did the work of creating expectations of something new, something yet to come. This is Koselleck's

(2002: 129) own short formula for the new concepts of movement: "The lower their content in terms of experience, the greater were the expectations they created." As an example, one can think of all the "isms" that were conceived in the saddle period. Studying the history of concepts of movement amounts to studying futures past. That is, concepts of movement—say, "emancipation" or "enlightenment"—which, by being used, created expectations and imaginations of a possible future, can be studied in retrospect, as a future past; i.e., as unfulfilled expectations. This is also the case here.

The differences between Koselleck's conceptual history and the model of concept chains are many and various. Most consequential is the difference in timescale and intentionality. Whereas conceptual history traces semantic changes in social and political key concepts over several centuries, the model of concept chains, as elaborated here, follows a particular political key concept for just a couple of decades. Also, whereas the origins of the key concepts, with which *Begriffsgeschichte* concerns itself, may be shrouded by the mist of centuries (at least at times), the kind of concepts that make up the chains in the present model have a sender, an identifiable author, who formulates a concept with certain discernible intentions. Contemporary political key concepts are produced in a process that can be understood as cultural engineering.[10] The expression *cultural engineering*, as it is used here, is derived from that of social engineering, which is the application of sociological principles to social problems.[11] One could argue that cultural engineering is the application of hermeneutic principles to political problems. Cultural engineers come up with concepts for the sake of political change. The intentional authoring of political concepts by academics, spin-doctors, think tanks, speechwriters, etc. has become a veritable industry in our time. It is not least for this sake that the analytical model of concept chains may be of use.

As they travel down the chain, away from the context of cultural engineering, concepts are subjected to interpretation and exegesis. The semantic charge of a concept is likely to change in a process of emergence through contestation: the meaning of social and political key concepts will be contested as they travel downstream. Every act of exegesis—of critical interpretation—repositions a concept. In this sense, concepts are like Paul Ricœur's (1974: 317) myths: "There is no myth without exegesis, no exegesis without contestation." Exegetic conflict is inevitable, which is why concept chains are emergent. The direction of the concept chain, as well as the concept chain itself, emerges through exegetic contestation.

Global Governance

As the Berlin Wall came down and the Soviet empire burst asunder in flames, a professor of political science applied, to the new world order, the idea of complex adaptive systems; that is, self-organizing systems, which, firstly, consist of separate elements; secondly, readily adapt to their environment; and, thirdly, produce new features at the macro-level due to the interaction between their constitutive elements. He eventually gave this idea the name "global governance." The professor was James Nathan Rosenau, born in 1924 in Philadelphia, U.S.A., and with a doctoral degree in political science from Princeton University. Early in his career, while still working on his doctoral thesis, Rosenau began teaching at the History and Political Science Department of the New Jersey College for Women (later Douglass College of Rutgers University). There had been a sudden opening in May of 1949 and Rosenau seized the opportunity. Then, he had to wait eleven years for tenure. From early on, he took an interest in systems theories of complexity. The concept of global governance, in some sense, was the end product of this research interest (about which more later). Global governance also fit Koselleck's definition of a concept of movement: it was low in content in terms of experience and therefore great in terms of the expectations it created. To here and now study this concept is to outline a future past.

When I first met him in 2002, Rosenau was professor emeritus of international affairs at the Elliott School of International Affairs at George Washington University, in Washington, D.C. He was still teaching and commuted from upstate New York, where he lived with his young wife and recently born daughter (Rosenau was seventy-eight at the time). We went out for lunch and I asked him about some of his comments in an interview with the *Review of International Studies*.[12] To the question of what books he had read recently that had made him think deeply about world politics, Rosenau, in the published interview, had replied: "Two come immediately to mind, both by anthropologists. One is Appadurai's *Modernity at Large* and the other is Hannerz' *Transnational Connections*. They are both exciting and creative probes into the underpinnings of globalization" (Review of International Studies 2000: 474). He told me that nowadays he would sooner read sociological and anthropological literature than political science.[13] The reason was that most political scientists, when discussing globalization, seemed unwilling or unable to abandon their focus on international politics; i.e., on relations and interactions between governments.

This comment allowed me to ask Rosenau about the concept of global governance. He began explaining the concept in terms of a disaggregation of authority. Instead of concentrating on government, political scientists ought to study governance; that is, the way in which an almost infinite array of globally diffused decision-making constitutes a complex self-organizing system, whose underlying structure no single actor can undo. Having read his writings on the concept (to which this study will return), I was familiar with his account and steered the talk to a more specific issue: whether he had come up with the concept of global governance himself or borrowed it from somewhere or someone else. Rosenau assured me that he had not borrowed the concept and that he assumed that it originated with him. Thus, I seemed to have found the point furthest upstream in the concept chain of *global governance*.

Of course, Rosenau had not invented the two words that make up the concept of global governance. The word *global* was widely popular in the post-Cold War era. In part, this may have reflected a growing awareness of the world as a single place—what Roland Robertson (1992: 8) calls "globality"—i.e., "the intensification of consciousness of the world as a whole." Robertson, however, also observes that globality is not a modern phenomenon. In fact, globality not only precedes modernity, according to Robertson: it is the very precondition of modernity (see, e.g., Robertson 2004). The popularity of the adjective *global* may have been associated with globality in a more cynical sense: as the Cold War drew to a close, some, feeling victorious, may have believed that the world now was a single place—*for them*.

The second word in the expression global governance is an old one. It derives from the Greek word *kybernan*, "to steer or pilot a ship, to direct," which in Latin became *gubernare*, "to direct, rule, guide." Already the Greeks had used *kybernan* in the metaphorical sense of "leading men." Both *governance* and *government* hail from this metaphor. In the English language, *governance* seems to be the older word of the two. In Geoffrey Chaucer's poem *The Legend of Good Women* (ca 1385), in the legend of Thisbe, is the line, "Fortune that hath the world in governaunce." *Governance* here refers to the act of governing. It is the nominalization of the verb *to govern*. When the word form *government* starts to be used in the English language in the sixteenth century, it serves as a synonym of *governance*. Only later, toward the eighteenth century, is *government* also used to denote a political body that governs (as in, "the prime minister forms the government"). The word *governance*, on the other hand, has retained its original reference to the act of governing to this day, which is why Rosenau used it and opposed it to the word *government* (see Rosenau and Czempiel 1992). More specifically, Rosenau's approach was to disaggregate the concept of "government" into its opposite, "governance." Disaggregation had already previously been Rosenau's preferred methodology. He had disaggregated the domestic–foreign policy distinction (Rosenau 1964, 1967, and 1969), the concept of power (Rosenau 1971 and 1976), and the bifurcation of macro- and micro-levels of analysis (Rosenau 1990). Disaggregating the concept of government in terms of governance, therefore, was a logical step in Rosenau's ongoing theoretical work.

Governance, according to Rosenau, exhibits certain traits: it bridges the domestic–foreign and macro–micro levels of analysis, and it replaces the notion of international regimes (which are always defined in terms of issue areas, like "the environmental regime," "the disease-control regime," "the global trade regime," etc.) with a concept of global governance; i.e., globally diffused processes of decision-making and governing that are not limited to what is usually considered the political sphere. The governance concept thus may be taken to either extend the concept of the political or represent another form of depoliticization. The question of politicization/depoliticization will be revisited in the conclusion. Now, the time has come to follow Rosenau's concept of global governance further downstream; but before this, a parallel concept chain will be identified.

A Parallel Flow

An emergent chain of the governance concept, which runs parallel to the one initiated by Rosenau, can be traced back to a 1989 report, entitled, *Sub-Saharan Africa: From Crisis to Sustainable Growth, a Long-Term Perspective Study* (World Bank 1989). The report was the last in a series of five encompassing reports on Africa that the World Bank published in the 1980s. The 1989 report differed from the previous ones in that many more experts were consulted and that two-thirds of them were Africans. As the principal author of the 1989 report and of the other pan-African reports in the series, Indian economist Ramgopal Agarwala, put it: the explicit wish was to put "Africans in the driver's seat in designing and implementing their development program." The final report goes where previous World Bank reports had not dared to venture. In the report, the World Bank (1989: 60) addresses political issues: "By governance is meant the exercise of political power to manage a nation's affairs." The report criticizes the governance of African countries and demands political reforms.

> Ultimately, better governance requires political renewal. This means a concerted attack on corruption from the highest to the lowest levels. This can be done by setting a good example, by strengthening accountability, by encouraging public debate, and by nurturing a free press. It also means empowering women and the poor by fostering grassroots and nongovernmental organizations (NGOs), such as farmers' associations, cooperatives, and women's groups. (ibid.: 6)

Why is it reasonable to claim that this report ventures into forbidden terrain? Because formulations like the ones just quoted constitute a violation of the Bank's statutes. The Bank is prohibited from engaging in political activities by its articles of agreement.[14] The introduction of the concept of governance therefore marked the birth of a new, more openly political agenda in the sphere of Bretton Woods institutions like the Bank and the International Monetary Fund (IMF) (which is not to say that the Bretton Woods system, ideologically and in its workings ever was apolitical). The concept of governance made it possible for the Bank to openly interfere in the political affairs of member states. The concept spread throughout the entire network of international aid and development assistance at the apex of which the Bank and the IMF are located. This spread was accompanied by meaning-adding activities; that is, by cultural engineering. *Governance* became another word for public management and the privatization of the polis. Whereas the 1989 report pleaded for governance as democratization and political regulation, subsequent Bank reports charged the governance concept with neoliberal content. This created a bifurcation in the concept chain of governance: on one hand, the Bretton Woods institutions used *governance* as a synonym for *public management*; on the other, international institutions like the United Nations Development Programme and its sister organizations, in particular the United Nations Economic and Social Council (ECOSOC), the United Nations Children's Fund (UNICEF), the Office of the United Nations High Commissioner for Human Rights (OHCHR), and the International Labour Organization (ILO), continued to use the "governance" concept in the spirit of the 1989 report.

The two rival concepts of governance reflect the kind of division in the world of international aid and development assistance that Jean-Philippe Thérien (1999) discusses in his article on two alternative and paradigmatic definitions of poverty. On one hand, there is the Bretton Woods paradigm, which posits that poverty is not caused by asymmetrical structures biased against the global South, but by temporary misadaptations of national markets. The Bretton Woods paradigm's long-term analysis is that poverty is a residual phenomenon that is waning geographically (that is, disappearing from more and more places). The UN paradigm, in contrast, identifies the causes of poverty as consisting in the inequitable distribution of resources at all levels of social organization—at the global, national, regional, and household levels. Rather than regarding poverty as a waning problem, the UN paradigm defines poverty as a deepening problem. According to this paradigm, there is a widening gap between rich and poor all over the world. Poverty is not so much a matter of dysfunctional markets but of exclusion from tangible and intangible resources. The solution is to subordinate the global economy, as well as its constituent parts, to objectives of intergenerational and gender equity and development sustainability. The difference between the two paradigms is equal to the distinction between politicization and depoliticization. The UN paradigm politicizes the question of poverty; the Bretton Woods paradigm does the opposite: it depoliticizes the problem. In retrospect, it may be noted that the depoliticizing paradigm of public management defeated the UN paradigm. In everything from structural adjustment programs to the promotion of free economic zones, the Bretton Woods paradigm defined international policies and made itself felt in the southern hemisphere of this planet.[15]

Tracking the concept of governance in the spheres of international aid and development assistance yields two realizations: one, political key concepts like "governance" can move rapidly along emergent concept chains, whose direction and bifurcation may be predetermined by already carved out ideological riverbeds (in the above case, the conflict between the Bretton Woods and UN paradigms); two, the end of the Cold War was a boom period for scenarios of depoliticization, and it is in this ideological climate that the "governance" concept rose to popularity.

Commissions

Rosenau's concept of global governance, meant to substitute analytical metaphors like *government* and *regime,* became an item of debate in political science.[16] A former professor of political science at Odense University in Denmark, Peter Hansen, took part in this debate. Hansen had begun working for the United Nations in 1978, serving first as UN assistant secretary-general for program planning and coordination and then, for seven years, as assistant secretary-general and executive director of the United Nations Centre on Transnational Corporations (UNCTC). The history of UNCTC went back to November 1972. Chile's President Allende had delivered a speech at the General Assembly in which he (rightly) accused the U.S. corporation ITT of intervening in Chile's domestic affairs.[17] The Chilean situation was important in triggering the establishment of UNCTC with the purpose of bringing about a new international economic order, which, among other things, would set limits to the intervention of multinational corporations in the domestic affairs of individual countries. Hansen brought with him his experience as executive director of UNCTC when he was appointed as executive director of a new, independent, international commission. The commission would be the latest in a series of similar commissions dealing with global issues, in particular with the global division between the northern and southern hemispheres. These commissions linked the UN system with the Socialist International, and with "progressive forces" more generally.[18] The commissions served as vehicles for the circulation and popularization of key political concepts, many of which have become common property—for example, global commons, sustainable development, and human security (on the commissions, see Table 1).

First among these commissions was one created by Robert McNamara and led by Willy Brandt. In the eventful year of 1968, former U.S. secretary of defense Robert McNamara took office as president of the World Bank. Under his leadership, the Bank changed its policy from a paradigm of development by means of industrial and agricultural production to one of poverty alleviation at the level of individual human beings (rather than at the level of "poor countries").[19] This implied a fundamental shift of focus. Instead of measuring development simply on the level of GNP (or GNP per capita), the Bank was now required to reckon with the social and political problem of wealth distribution. This reorientation may have been prompted by Lyndon Johnson's domestic "unconditional war on poverty" (that is at least what Gunnar Myrdal believed; see Myrdal 1968: xii–xiii). Johnson's war on poverty was part of his Great Society program, which he himself thought of as the completion of Franklin D. Roosevelt's New Deal program. Both in the new World Bank policy of poverty alleviation and in Johnson's Great Society program, poverty and its abatement were no longer defined in terms of individual failure and trickle-down benefits, or of savings and investments, but in terms of social causes and political solutions. At the international level, this meant that plans for a global welfare system of sorts would have to be fashioned. Global capitalism would have to be regulated politically.

The task of developing a global vision for the war on poverty was handed to Willy Brandt, who could pick up where a prior commission had left off. Already, McNamara's predecessor at the World Bank, George Woods, had initiated a commission, headed by former Canadian prime minister Lester B. Pearson, that was to review the previous twenty years of development assistance and to make recommendations for the future. The Pearson Commission, however, did not have the new Bank policy of poverty reduction as its starting point. Therefore, its proposals were of a more conventional, macroeconomic nature. At the same time, the Pearson Commission has already introduced the theme of an interdependent world community, whose existence subsequent commissions would take for granted. In 1977, McNamara created the Independent Commission on International Development Issues. He asked Brandt, who headed the Socialist International at the time, to chair the commission, which subsequently became known as the Brandt or North–South Commission. Brandt adopted Pearson's vantage point of world community. He also identified the core problem as economic and social disparities dividing this community. A massive attack on poverty was necessary. The Brandt Commission, among other things, proposed a twenty-year Marshall Plan for developing countries.

The first report of the Brandt Commission was published in 1980; that is, in the midst of a neoliberal counter-revolution against equity as fundamental political principle and cultural guiding light. The counter-revolution was slowly gaining ground. Margaret Thatcher had come into office the preceding year. Ronald Reagan was ahead in the polls in the U.S. presidential election of 1980 at the time the Commission presented its report to UN Secretary-General Kurt Waldheim. The report politicized that which previously had been expressed in a language that was ostensibly technical and procedural ("capital mobilization," "sector-led growth," "economic diversification," etc.). The 1970s had been a time of politicization. Everything from intimate relationships to global affairs had been subjected to politicization, which meant that every aspect of social life was measured against perceived standards of equity (and justice, the common good, and authenticity). At the level of international relations, independent international commissions worked in the same spirit, trying to politicize the global agenda.

The internal negotiations and subsequent recommendations of the Brandt Commission revealed a crucial paradox: commission members endorsed views and proposals, which they then, as government officials of their respective countries, turned down (Seers 1980). If a commissioner suddenly were to be recalled to government service, he or she would have to denounce the views he or she had just formulated as a commissioner. Most national governments were, in other words, not prepared to follow the recommendations of the Brandt Commission. Brandt was nevertheless determined to press ahead with the agenda of development and peace. To this end, he initiated the establishment of

Table 1: Independent international commissions, 1977–2002

Name of commission	Duration	Initiated by	Chaired by	Report
Independent Commission on International Development Issues	1977–1979	Robert McNamara, president of the World Bank	Willy Brandt	1980, North–South: A Programme for Survival; 1983, Common Crisis, North–South: Cooperation for World Recovery
Independent Commission on Disarmament and Security Issues	1980–1982	Olof Palme, possibly together with David Owen	Olof Palme	1982, Common Security: A Blueprint for Survival
World Commission on Environment and Development	1984–1987	1983 UN General Assembly Resolution, A/RES/38/161	Gro Harlem Brundtland	1987, Our Common Future
South Commission	1987–1990	Mahathir Mohamad, prime minister of Malaysia, at the 8th Meeting of the Non-Aligned Countries, held in Harare, Zimbabwe, in September 1986	Julius K. Nyerere	1990, Challenge to the South
Commission on Global Governance	1992–1995	Willy Brandt, who brought together the members of the Brandt, Brundtland, South, and Palme commissions to a 1990 meeting in Stockholm	Ingvar Carlsson and Shridath Ramphal	1995, Our Global Neighbourhood

Source: Lapeyre (2004: 9), with author's revisions

a more permanent think tank, the *Stiftung für Entwicklung und Frieden* (Development and Peace Foundation) in Bonn, which ever since has held in trust Brandt's vision of global justice.[20] As the Cold War drew to a close, Brandt, grasping the new geopolitical situation, thought that the time had come to formulate a new political agenda. In January 1990, he invited the chairs and select members of previous commissions, as well as some other politicians and experts, to a meeting in Königswinter, Germany. Ingvar Carlsson, Shridath Ramphal, and Jan Pronk were asked to author a report that would, on one hand, summarize and continue the work of the previous commissions, and, on the other, identify new global problems and prospects in light of post-Cold War developments.

The report, later referred to among commissioners as the Stockholm document, formed the basis of the next meeting of the group in Stockholm, in April 1991. The meeting, officially entitled Stockholm Initiative on Global Security and Governance, called for the creation of an international commission to address not specific areas of concern, as previous commissions had done, but international cooperation across all major policy areas. A small secretariat was set up in Geneva. The focus of the new commission was to be the institutional settings within which policy is made, rather than lofty ideals or the policies themselves.

Our Global Neighborhood

The new commission needed an original and pellucid name. It was Hansen who came up with the designation, Commission on Global Governance. Hansen had arranged a series of seminars in Denmark, Norway, and the U.S., for the benefit of the twenty-eight commission members, among whom one could note the co-chairmen, Ingvar Carlsson, former Social Democrat prime minister of Sweden, and Shridath Ramphal, former foreign minister of Guyana and Commonwealth secretary-general, as well as Dutch politician Jan Pronk and UN veteran Brian Urquhart. To the seminars, Hansen had invited political scientists like Ernst and Peter Haas, Robert Keohane, Johan Galtung (who probably would reject the designation "political scientist"), and James Rosenau. The purpose was to make the commission members understand that decision-making was not solely, or even mainly, a clearly centralized, patently top-down process. Decisions were made at all levels of social and political organization, creating intricate webs of institutional connections. According to Hansen, the concept of global governance referred to "civil society," rather than to governmental and legal structures. Hansen envisioned a report that would advocate the development of civil society on a global scale.[21]

The scholarly presentations and background papers presented to the commission were later published as *Issues in Global Governance: Papers Written for the Commission on Global Governance* (Commission on Global

Governance 1995a). Rosenau is given the space of several chapters to elaborate his theory. Ernst and Peter Haas (father and son), as well as Johan Galtung, are the ones who, on the whole, and besides Rosenau, are responsible for conceptualizing "global governance." The papers of the other experts for the most part deal with specific policy areas. Rosenau and Haas, senior and junior, associate the theme of civil society to that of decision-making. Haas emphasizes the expert knowledge on which decision-making is based; Rosenau couples the notion of decision-making to that of global consciousness and the exercise of authority beyond national borders. Global governance, then, comprises behavior, activities, and systems of rule at the international, transnational, and regional levels. These levels, in turn, consist of inter- and transnational organizations, networks, forums, and relationships (for instance, in the shape of epistemic communities and transnational action networks). Rosenau's conceptualization of global governance is one in which spheres of authority multiply and globalization simultaneously creates integration and fragmentation. In this model, political decision-making is disaggregated and grafted on a model of global civil society.

Several commission members, especially Carlsson and Urquhart, objected to using *global governance*. They thought that *global governance* sounded too much like *global government*, and that the general public surely would perceive the name in the latter sense. Hansen thinks that Carlsson, Urquhart, and others in fact wanted to arrive at something that looked much more like a global government, but that they hesitated to signal such intentions. The commissioners, for instance, were more concerned with the legal authority of the Security Council than with abstract ideas about governance, according to Hansen. To quote Hansen: "The key players in the commission probably would have preferred an organigram."

Carlsson has a somewhat different recollection of the discussions that took place. He claims that his and other commission members' major objection was that *global governance* was difficult to translate into other languages.[22] At the same time, Carlsson admits to not being able to recall the exact details of the discussion. Hansen's recollections are more detailed. They are also more in line with the general tenor of the commission report. A key sentence in the report starts with the words, "The ultimate process has to be intergovernmental and at a high level"; that is, the authors of the report consider international decision-making at the highest level to be the most important part of "global governance." This is hardly what Rosenau had had in mind when he coined the expression and this was not why Hansen chose the concept as the name for the commission. To quote Hansen once more: "In a sense, one can say that the commission members preferred a type of soft power that is not as soft as the concept of governance suggests an international organization like the United Nations is able to wield." The commission members, used as they were to thinking in conventional terms about governmental, intergovernmental, and legal structures and processes, were preoccupied with the reform of existing procedures and institutions, rather than with reconceptualizing the institutional conditions of governance.

In the end, the Commission on Global Governance produced a report, entitled *Our Global Neighborhood* (1995), which (thus far) marks the end of the socialist-led international commissions. The report states that global governance rests on shared global values (Commission on Global Governance 1995b: 47). Such values include respect for life, liberty, justice and equality, mutual respect, caring, and integrity (ibid.: 48–49). The report goes on to detail the conditions and requirements of global governance: growing globalization; increasing global risks; the realities of global interdependence; the need for vision in these uncertain times; the ethics of being a neighbor; the reconceptualization of security in terms of "security of people" and "security of the planet"; the necessity of reforming the Security Council and of strengthening the General Assembly; and the need for an Economic Security Council, an International Criminal Court, and a World Conference on Governance. The report, then, homes in on institutional reforms. Global governance is implemented through international organizations and institutions, of which the United Nations is considered the most central one. The recommendation to "implement" global governance through the governing organs of an international organization—that is, through two UN councils (for Security and Economic Security)—contradicts the definitions of *governance* and *global governance* contained in the same report:

> Governance is the sum of the many ways individuals and institutions, public and private, manage their common affairs. It is a continuing process through which conflicting or diverse interests may be accommodated and co-operative action may be taken. It includes formal institutions and regimes empowered to enforce compliance, as well as informal arrangements that people and institutions either have agreed to or perceive to be in their interest. Examples of governance at the local level include a neighbourhood co-operative formed to install and maintain a standing water pipe, a town council operating a waste recycling scheme, a multi-urban body developing an integrated transport plan together with user groups, a stock exchange regulating itself with national government oversight, and a regional initiative of state agencies, industrial groups, and residents to control deforestation. At the global level, governance has

been viewed primarily as intergovernmental relationships, but it must now be understood as also involving non-governmental organizations (NGOs), citizens' movements, multinational corporations, and the global capital market. Interacting with these are global mass media of dramatically enlarged influence. (Commission on Global Governance 1995b: 4)

On one hand, then, the report disseminates the agenda of the commission members (reforming the UN Security Council); on the other, Hansen manages to include Rosenau's definition of global governance (as disaggregation of government). Downstream the concept channel, in the Commission report, Rosenau's concept of "global governance" bifurcates: one flow continues in the same direction as the upstream section; the other meanders in the opposite direction. The first stream is represented by Hansen's retaining Rosenau's concept in its original sense; the other by the commissioners' undoing Rosenau's disaggregation, aggregating *governance* back to *government*. The bifurcation of the *global* concept chain prompts the question: Which of the flows proceeds toward depoliticization and which runs toward politicization? Does Ingvar Carlsson's reaggregation of the governance concept imply a move toward depoliticization or politicization? Is Rosenau's concept of global governance, which Hansen imported from an academic sphere to the realm of international politics, a more sophisticated version of those scenarios of depoliticization, which U.S. pundits promulgated as the Cold War ended in violent convulsions? An answer to these questions may come to light in following the emergent concept chain of "global governance" along its last leg.

The Last Leg

Peter Hansen is responsible for extracting Rosenau's concept of global governance from its upstream scholarly source and injecting it into the downstream context of institutionalized international politics. Hansen tried to do two things at once: he tried to preserve the academic intricacy of the concept and to instrumentalize it by highlighting its association with the concept of civil society. The latter concept served as another keyword in the post-Cold War push for depoliticization. The other commission members took a more conventional political stance and engineered an odd version of the "global governance" concept, which in effect was closer to the concept of global government, in contradistinction to which the concept of global governance originally had been created.

Hansen went on to become the commissioner-general of the United Nations Relief and Works Agency for Palestine Refugees in the Near

East, UNRWA (a post from which he eventually was fired due to pressures from the U.S. and Israel). The "global governance" concept continued its journey downstream, along the riverbed of international politics. The work of the Commission on Global Governance did not yield the results Ingvar Carlsson had hoped for. The Security Council has not been reformed and an Economic Security Council has not been set up. Carlsson sounds frustrated these days when he tells me that the commission has done its job and that it is now up to the politicians to do theirs.[23] Carlsson's, and the commission's, efforts, however, did transport the concept of global governance further downstream in a couple of directions. One flow ended up in Davos, the other in metropolitan meetings of third-way political leaders. Let us begin by turning our attention to the first of these two flows.

A particular outcome, which can be related to the report Our Global Neighbourhood, is the adoption of the United Nations Millennium Declaration by the UN General Assembly on September 18, 2000.[24] The declaration opens with the heads of state and government (in their own terminology) recognizing that they "have a collective responsibility to uphold the principles of human dignity, equality and equality at the global level." The heads of state and government then go on to "reaffirm" what in fact is the central contradiction of the UN Charter: that the UN must uphold both individual human rights and the territorial integrity of all states. In the absence of a mandate to secure social and economic rights for individual human beings—i.e., a minimum of welfare and social inclusion—by violating the territorial sovereignty of states, the UN must rely on the goodwill of its member countries to abide by joint declarations of intent. This has also been true of the Millennium Declaration. The most significant and widely publicized feature of that declaration is that it specifies a number of Millennium Goals. The goals are to accomplish a number of tasks by the year 2015: to halve the proportion of the world's population whose income is less than one U.S. dollar a day, who suffer from hunger, and who are unable to reach or to afford safe drinking water. By the same date, children (boys and girls alike) shall be able to complete a full course of primary schooling, and girls and boys shall have equal access to all levels of education. In addition, maternal mortality shall be reduced by three-quarters and mortality of children under five years old by two-thirds. By 2015, the spread of HIV/AIDS, as well as malaria and other major diseases, shall have been halted and begun to be reversed. By 2020, a significant improvement in the lives of at least one hundred million slum dwellers shall have been achieved.

A hallmark of the Millennium Goals was their auditability: whether or not the goals had been attained by the set dates could be measured. The Millennium project was another attempt at depoliticizing development issues that are political in nature—as when powerful governments lend financial, military, and, often enough, moral support to regimes that clearly violate the human rights of their citizenries or turn a blind eye to policies and international economic relations that produce negative development for large sections of the world population. The depoliticization of global economic issues has been a preferred method of the World Economic Forum (WEF), also known as the Davos Club, ever since it was founded as the European Management Forum in the early 1970s with the mission to dissolve the boundary that separates the public realm of the polis from the private sphere of for-profit market activities. Just like similar associations—the Bilderberg Club, the Trilateral Commission, the Bohemian Club, etc.—the WEF or Davos Club is a by-invitation-only organization, which brings together members of the political, financial, and cultural elites. A common attribute of these clubs is their pro-U.S.A., neoliberal, public-management agenda of depoliticization: (a) the common-good realm of the polis ought to be run like a business and (b) private business should be exempt from political regulation as much as possible. In the language these clubs tend to use this would be called, "envisioning public–private and multistakeholder projects."

It is from this perspective and position that the WEF tried to seize the Millennium project. The WEF took it upon itself to keep track of the progress made toward achieving the Millennium Goals. For this purpose, a Global Governance Initiative was set up, which, according to the mid-2000s version of the WEF homepage, "monitors the efforts of governments, the private sector, international organizations and civil society towards achieving the United Nations Millennium Development Goals." The Global Governance Initiative was managed by Richard Samans, a former corporate lending officer with Crédit Lyonnais and erstwhile economic advisor to Bill Clinton, and by Ann Florini, who holds a Ph.D. in political science and at the time was a senior fellow with the Brookings Institution, a think tank situated close to Dupont Circle in Washington, D.C. In a couple of interviews I conducted with her at Brookings, Florini explained to me that the WEF wanted her and Samans to produce annual report cards on the progress toward the different Millennium Goals. Her ambition was that the Global Governance Initiative's annual report would become as widely cited as Transparency International's annual report on corruption. This goal was never achieved. Aided by various expert groups, Florini authored a number of scarcely noticed annual reports before taking up a new position in Asia and the Global Governance Initiative silently being put to rest. Florini did not want to discuss the exact circumstances of how and why the Global Governance Initiative failed, claiming that it had not. In all likelihood, it soon became apparent that, given the deregulation of financial markets, the dismantling of the public sector, and the realities of geopolitical conflict, there was no way of achieving the Millennium Goals. For the UN and organizations like the WEF, which also make much of the enlightenment and goodwill of "global leaders," the Millennium Declaration had become an embarrassment.

It is important to remember that the years in which all this took place—that is, from the early 1990s to the mid 2000s—were the triumphant years of the Third Way.[25] Parts of the political Left in western Europe and the U.S. decided to abandon key political principles to conquer what they saw as the ideological middle ground. The most important principle to be relinquished was that of equity. No longer should every policy have to conform to an ethics of equity. No longer should equity serve as a key concept of movement (*Bewegungsbegriff*)—that is, as a utopia to be realized in the future, toward which all developments must be directed. The perseverance of social inequality in the face of decades of political reforms made it difficult to proclaim, year in, year out, that equality was within reach or was at all attainable. In the U.K., Tony Blair launched New Labour; in the U.S., Bill Clinton left the post of chair of the Democratic Leadership Council, an organization of and for the so-called New Democrats, when he decided to run for president. The political program of New Labour and the New Democrats is said to combine neoliberal economic policies with liberal social ones. In hindsight, one can note that neoliberal economics tended to leave little scope for social programs and that New Labour, as well as most New Democrats, like U.S. senators Joe Lieberman, Sam Nunn, and Evan Bayh, actually took up right-wing positions not just on economic issues, but in social matters as well.

Third-way leaders soon created their own global network. U.S. president Bill Clinton initiated the so-called Progressive Governance Network (PGN), which would serve as an alternative to the Socialist International. The PGN functioned as a policy forum for new (social) democrat leaders around the world. In 1998, at the New York University School of Law, the conference, "Strengthening Democracy in the Global Economy: An Opening Dialogue," featured one panel that included, among others, Hillary Rodham Clinton, Ronald Dworkin, and Anthony Giddens, and another with Tony Blair, Bill Clinton, Swedish prime minister Göran Persson, European Commission president Romano Prodi, and Petar Stefanov Stoyanov, then president of Bulgaria. The following year, at the European University Institute in Florence, the conference, "Progressive Governance in the 21st Century," gathered President Clinton, premiers Massimo d'Alema of Italy, Tony Blair of the U.K., and Lionel Jospin of France, and German chancellor Gerhard Schröder, as well as Romano Prodi, secretary-general of the EU Council Javier Solana, and Brazilian president Fernando Henrique Cardoso. At the conference, D'Alema called for a permanent "cultural forum for world progressive leaders," to which Jospin responded that Europe's social democrats already had a forum, the Socialist International, and that this particular meeting was a "political event," not the inauguration of a new "Atlantic International" (Gill 2000). In 2000, yet another conference, entitled "Modern Governance in the 21st Century," was held in Berlin. It was hosted by Chancellor Schröder, and attended by presidents Clinton, Cardoso, Ricardo Lagos of Chile, Fernando de la Rúa of Argentina, and Thabo Mvuyelva Mbeki of South Africa, as well as by prime ministers Blair, Jospin, D'Alema, Persson, Helen Clark of New Zealand, Wim Kok of the Netherlands, António Guterres of Portugal, and Ehud Barak of Israel.

In a brief comment on a Swedish newscast, then Swedish prime minister Persson summarized the PGN conferences as follows: "This thing is huge. It is one big political seminar." The purpose of this long seminar was to globalize the third-way agenda—out with equity and politics, in with the public-management doctrine and strategic depoliticization—as preformulated by the New Democrats and New Labour. One of the *éminences grises* in the process of formulating and spreading the third-way ideology is Will Marshall, a journalist turned think-tank director. The think tank he established in 1989 and has directed ever since is called the Progressive Policy Institute. It is located in Washington, D.C., and competes (unsuccessfully) with the Democratic Leadership Council for the title of the foremost Democrat think tank.[26] Cultural engineering, it should not be forgotten, is as competitive a business as any. The Progressive Policy Institute brands itself as promoting "progressive, market-friendly ideas."[27] Will Marshall, an avowed supporter of the Clintons, likes to drop names when he talks about his involvement in the PGN.[28] "Tony," he would say without further explanation, when referring to British prime minister Tony Blair, and "Gordon" when mentioning Blair's successor, Gordon Brown. According to Marshall, it was Bill Clinton who inspired Tony Blair. New Labour was an outgrowth of the New Democrats, in other words. Behind the scenes, people like Peter Mandelson, a British politician who went from being a member of the Young Communist League to being appointed a life peer by Queen

Elizabeth II, worked hard to hijack the Labour Party with the ideological and practical support of American colleagues like Will Marshall. The hijackers had to struggle with opponents like Robert Kuttner, a liberal (in the American sense of the word) pundit, who fought the New Democrats and New Labour and whom Marshall pointed out specifically as a representative of the old-fashioned Left.

The terms Clinton and Blair spent in office did not result in sweeping political change at the level of international politics. Internationally, Clinton seems to have accomplished less than his predecessor, George Bush, Sr., who, according to Ingvar Carlsson, did more to strengthen the UN than Clinton, who (according to Carlsson) first and foremost was a tactician.[29] Despite his rhetoric, Clinton always put U.S. domestic interests before anything else. If anything, what Carlsson calls the "negative coalition"—the motley group of countries that block any attempt to reform the UN—grew stronger during Clinton's presidency. Carlsson's vision of global governance as a reformed UN system with a more potent government—an improved Security Council and an Economic Security Council—contrasts with Clinton's and the PGN's third-way politics. Whereas the former is guided by the political principle of (global) equity, the latter has parted with this principle. In the subsequent periods of social neoconservatism and continued economic neoliberalism, President Bush, Jr. turned the tacit discarding of equity as a guiding political principle into an often-publicized moral virtue.

On the other side of the Atlantic, in Bonn, Germany, a small think tank, the *Stiftung Entwicklung und Frieden* (Development and Peace Foundation), founded in 1986 on the initiative of Willy Brandt (mentioned briefly above), continues to fly the flag of global equity. The foundation still uses the concept of global governance to signal its commitment to Brandt's legacy and the Carlsson Commission's call for the political regulation of global capitalism. With the Development and Peace Foundation we have reached the end of the concept chain. The PGN has faded away, as has the Global Governance Initiative of the Davos Club. The concept of global governance moved between different spheres: the academy, international politics, elitist clubs, and think tanks. It was exposed to, and moved on by, exegetic conflict; in particular when it was used as the designation of the Carlsson Commission. Finally, the stream of global governance dried up. In the academy, a considerable number of articles and books were devoted to the concept; but soon, this wave also seeped away. Global governance had gone from an analytical concept to a future-oriented concept of movement. The concluding section returns to the question of the political and that of depoliticization. More specifically, it will consider what the concept chain of global governance can reveal about the post-Cold War trend toward depoliticization.

Conclusion: The Return of the Political?

In the beginning of this chapter, it was mentioned that the political could be defined as a normative order (rules, principles, meanings, etc.) and as the enforcement of this order (coercion, power, violence, etc.). Further on, it was claimed that the principle of equity had been part of an earlier normative order, but that this principle had been abandoned due to a long-term, right-wing strategy of replacing equity with conservative social values and economic laissez-faire. Even the previous champions of equity (at least at the rhetorical level)—the Democrats in the U.S. and Social Democrats across the world—dispensed with this principle and focused their energies on public management; that is, on public-sector managerialism. Some of the key ingredients in public-management ideology are: (a) the idea that politicians are motivated by self-interest; (b) the notion that self-interest, while leading to positive results in the market sphere, creates pathologies in the political sphere (pathologies like "free-riding," "rent-seeking," and "special interests"); (c) the belief that inefficient resource allocation and poor governance are caused by government bureaucrats ("public managers") maximizing their budgets; and (d) the ideological conclusion that the state therefore needs to be reduced to a minimum, and that the individual member of society should be given as many choices as possible. Citizens are turned into consumers of goods and services.

As can be gleaned from his writings, James Rosenau was aware of the spread of public-management ideology when he formulated the concept of global governance. In contrast to the downstream users of his concept, Rosenau had descriptive, not prescriptive, intentions. Nevertheless, the timing of Rosenau's conceptualization is hardly coincidental. Global governance was conceived at a time when Fukuyama, Huntington, and other American pundits declared the end of ideology.[30] The time of political conflicts and debates was over, they argued. And, indeed, the 1990s and 2000s were a period of depoliticization, if by depoliticization we mean either the ideological dissolution of the common good into incompatible private interests and irreconcilable conflict or the transformation of political issues into technical, procedural problems to be resolved not by debate but by standardized management principles. In either definition of depoliticization, the allocation of resources is decoupled from equity as a political principle. "The market," that supernatural fantasy, was to guarantee a most effective resource allocation. It was time for the social sciences and humanities to abdicate and leave everything to economic theory.[31] In extreme cases, depoliticization could produce absurdities like Richard Posner's recommendation to permit mothers to auction off their newborn babies.[32]

Depoliticization diffuses political accountability, as does the normative use of *global governance* as an organizing concept. As Hannah Arendt (1970: 39) once remarked, "if, in accord with traditional political thought, we identify tyranny as government that is not held to give account of itself, rule by Nobody is clearly the most tyrannical of all since there is no one left who could even be asked to answer for what is being done." The anti-politics machine, which is what James Ferguson (1990) calls the international development and aid industry, but which, as has been shown here, is at work in a much wider global context, has permeated ever more political domains and is now all around us. From the social life and cultural biography of the "global governance" concept, the ideological—and political—nature of the anti-politics machine may be gathered. Tracking political and social key concepts through emergent concept chains allows us to realize the political dimensions of exegetic conflict. What may appear to be squabbles about inconsequential semantics, like that between Ingvar Carlsson and Peter Hansen at the Commission on Global Governance, turn out to be indicative of larger ideological shifts of tide. Ideology can be said to be the fuel that drives the anti-politics machine, which chews up political notions like accountability and equity. Then again, Rosenau's conceptualization could be taken to mean that the ideology of depoliticization is a sign or side effect of systemic change: as the process of globalization accelerates, decision-making is disaggregated and diffused. Choosing between an analysis that focuses either on the production of ideology or on the systemic characteristics of decision-making is not just a matter of intellectual preferences; it is political as well.

Acknowledgments

My research on global governance was part of a larger project, entitled, "Kosmopolit: Culture and Politics in Global Society," which was led by Ulf Hannerz. The project was funded by the Bank of Sweden Tercentenary Foundation. I wish to thank all my colleagues in Project Kosmopolit for their stimulating comments, collaborative efforts, and good company. This is a fitting place to express my gratitude to Ulf

Hannerz, friend, mentor, and trailblazer, for two decades of support, encouragement, and dialogue.

Notes

1. See Hannerz (2004) on two versions of cosmopolitanism, one with a happy, the other with a worried, face.
2. The last-mentioned scenario is not discussed by Hannerz. It came to my attention when I conducted interviews at the World Bank Institute (WBI) with the intention of finding out more about the use of the governance concept in the Bretton Woods sphere. In one of the interviews, David Dollar, who at the time headed the macroeconomics and growth group at the WBI, told me in so many words that he had resigned himself to the fact that international aid simply does not work. Dollar thought that instead of trying to force systemic change on "developing" societies, it may be better to direct investments toward free economic zones that operate independently from corrupt governments and national legislations. He advised me to read Jared Diamond's book, *Guns, Germs, and Steel: The Fates of Human Societies*, in order to understand why human development has been uneven and continues to be unjust. Diamond, a physiologist turned geographer, offers causal explanations that focus on environmental factors: its natural environment determined the fate of each human society. Another simplistic explanation was provided in the book, *Culture Matters: How Values Shape Human Progress* (2001), edited by Lawrence Harrison and Samuel Huntington: cultural values determine human development. Harrison (2000: xxii), referring to right-wing Argentinian pundit Mariano Grondona's typology of cultural values, goes so far as to suggest that there is such a thing as "development-resistant cultures."
3. Other normative approaches to the political than Arendt's and Habermas' are both possible and widespread.
4. The term, "liberal democracy" is vague and contested. It is used here as shorthand for a constitutional political order with extensive citizenship rights, political representation, and the rule of law. Providing such a definition of course only defers the problem of explanation to the next set of concepts: what is meant by "constitution," "citizenship," "rights," "representation," etc.?
5. Just as there can be no such thing as a political *science*, there can be no economic science—at least not in the sense political scientists and economists like to make believe.
6. See Frank (2004) for an entertaining, disturbing, and more or less ethnographic account of local and national strategies by America's right wing, which succeeded in convincing poor U.S. citizens to vote against their own economic interests.
7. See, for example, Rabinow (1977), Crapanzano (1980), Sahlins (1993), Marcus (1995), Gusterson (1997), and Faubion and Marcus (2009).

8. The source for the number of Nike's contract factories is the website Corporate Watch: http://www.corpwatch.org/article.php?id=12463 (accessed July 18, 2011).
9. In Anglophone academia, Raymond Williams' (1976) *Keywords* and, possibly, the Cambridge School of Quentin Skinner and J. G. A. Pocock may be better known than Koselleck's approach of *Begriffsgeschichte*. All of these versions of semantic history share the common roots of Ludwig Wittgenstein's and John Austin's pragmatics and the French Annales School's combining of social and intellectual historiography. For a discussion of the various approaches to semantic history, one can go to Melvin Richter's many treatments of the issue. Particularly helpful is Richter 1995.
10. To my knowledge, the concept of cultural engineering was first introduced by Ali Mazrui in his *Cultural Engineering and Nation-Building in East Africa* (1972).
11. The concept of social engineering seems to have been coined by William Tolman (1909), given symbolic value by Karl Popper (1961), and been instrumentalized by Gunnar and Alva Myrdal (see, e.g., Myrdal and Myrdal 1934).
12. My first interview with James Rosenau was conducted on Friday, November 15, 2002, in Washington, D.C.
13. A couple of years later, I brought Rosenau and Hannerz together at a conference I organized in Falsterbo, Sweden. Also, see Rosenau (2003) for his use of Appadurai's and Hannerz' theses.
14. Article IV, Section 10 of the articles of agreement reads: "The Bank and its officers shall not interfere in the political affairs of any member; nor shall they be influenced in their decisions by the political character of the member or members concerned. Only economic considerations shall be relevant to their decisions."
15. In the intellectual environment of the Bretton Woods institutions, culturalist arguments circulate that explain poor governance with the prevalence of certain cultural traits (see Harrison and Huntington 2000). Societies could be divided into two categories: development-prone and development-resistant (Grondona 2000). Anthropologists are likely to smile at the simple-mindedness and naïveté of such a classification. They should remind themselves, however, that the almost exact same cultural distinctions once were made in their own discipline (of which Mariano Grondona and Lawrence Harrison, as well as the anthropologists who have contributed to the volume edited by Harrison and Huntington, seem wholly ignorant). In 1939, for example, Felix Keesing wrote about hard-shelled vs. soft-shelled cultures and how they differed in being able to develop (in those days referred to as "acculturate"). In 1949, John Adair and Evon Vogt presented a study of "contrasting modes of culture change," in which they analyzed why the neighboring Indian tribes of Zuni and Navaho reacted differently to veterans returning from World War II. The distinction between development-prone and development-resistant cultures is thus neither original nor an advance over the distinctions made by anthropologists in the 1930s and 1940s. If anything, the current use of the distinction represents an analytical and intellectual step backward, even if compared to methods and

theories of anthropology that are fifty to sixty years old. Yet, coupled to issues of governance, the division of the world's cultures into resistant and receptive types grows in popularity.

16. See for example, Rayner (1994), Desai and Redfern (1995), Finkelstein (1995), Held (1995), Young (1997), Hewson and Sinclair (1999), Risse (1999), or Held and McGrew (2002).
17. In those days, ITT not only owned 70 percent of Chitelco, the Chilean Telephone Company, it also funded *El Mercurio*, a Chilean right-wing newspaper. More importantly, ITT, in collaboration with the Nixon administration and the CIA, financially helped opponents of Allende's government prepare a military coup.
18. A *Washington Post* journalist once described one of the commissions (the Palme Commission) as being made up of "out-of-power Western liberals," "neutralists," "leftists," "communists," and "Third Worlders" (Rosenfeld 1982: 19; quoted in Wiseman 2005: 48). The denunciatory tone of these comments aside, it has to be admitted that members of the Socialist International chaired most independent international commissions. A few commissions, however, do not necessarily belong to this category. Examples of the latter type of commissions include the Independent Commission on International Humanitarian Issues, chaired by Sadruddin Aga Khan and Hassan bin Talal, and the Commission on Population and Quality of Life, chaired by Maria de Lourdes Pintasilgo.
19. See Finnemore (1996: 89–127) for a discussion of changing World Bank policies and McNamara's role in this normative reorientation.
20. In addition, a university department, the *Institut für Entwicklung und Frieden* (Institute for Development and Peace), was set up at the University of Duisburg-Essen.
21. Interview with Peter Hansen conducted by the author on August 3, 2005.
22. Interview with Ingvar Carlsson conducted by the author on May 10, 2005.
23. Interview with Ingvar Carlsson conducted by the author on May 10, 2005.
24. See United Nations Resolution 55/2 adopted by the General Assembly (retrievable at http://www.un.org/millennium/declaration/ares552e.pdf).
25. The literature on Anthony Giddens' role in formulating and banging the drum for third-way politics is too vast to be quoted or reviewed here. Suffice it to say that Giddens is neither the inventor of what commonly is considered the third-way position, nor the one who set this particular ideological train in motion. It may nonetheless be interesting to consult his statements of a Third Way (Giddens 1994, 1998, 2000, and 2002).
26. The think-tank business continues to thrive in places like Washington, D.C. Another contender for the title of foremost New Democrat think tank is the New Democrat Network, which, at the time of writing, is launching the think tank New Politics Institute.
27. See http://www.progressivepolicy.org/about/ (retrieved on April 6, 2014).
28. Interview with Will Marshall conducted by the author at the Progressive Policy Institute, Washington, D.C. on November 13, 2003.
29. Interview with Ingvar Carlsson conducted by the author on May 10, 2005.
30. This, of course, was not the first time that ideology had been pronounced dead. Daniel Bell had done so already in 1960 (see Bell 1960).

31. Cf. e.g., Gary Becker's research on sociological topics like race discrimination (Becker 1957), family and sexual life (Becker and Posner 1993), and addiction (Becker, Grossman, and Murphy 1994); Richard Posner's speculations on law (see, e.g., Posner 1972); Robert Fogel on historical issues like American slavery (see, e.g., Fogel and Engerman 1968); and, most important in this context, James Buchanan, Gordon Tullock, and Anthony Downs on political science topics like democracy and public administration (see, e.g., Downs 1957 and Buchanan and Tullock 1962).
32. See Landes and Posner (1978). Abraham Maslow's quip comes to mind: "When the only tool you own is a hammer, every problem begins to resemble a nail."

References

Adair, John, and Evon Vogt. 1949. "Navaho and Zuni Veterans: A Study of Contrasting Modes of Culture Change." *American Anthropologist* 51: 547–561.

Appadurai, Arjun, ed. 1986. *The Social Life of Things: Commodities in Cultural Perspective*. Cambridge: Cambridge University Press.

Appadurai, Arjun. 1996. *Modernity at Large: Cultural Dimensions of Globalization*. Minneapolis: University of Minnesota Press.

Arendt, Hannah. 1970. *On Violence*. New York: Harcourt, Brace, and World.

Asad, Talal. 2003. *Formations of the Secular: Christianity, Islam, Modernity*. Stanford, CA: Stanford University Press.

Barnett, Michael. 2002. *Eyewitness to a Genocide: The United Nations and Rwanda*. Ithaca, NY: Cornell University Press.

Becker, Gary. 1957. *The Economics of Discrimination*. Chicago: University of Chicago Press.

Becker, Gary and Richard Posner. 1993. "Cross-Cultural Differences in Family and Sexual Life: An Economic Analysis." *Rationality and Society* 5(4): 421–431.

Becker, Gary, Michael Grossman, and Kevin Murphy. 1994. "An Empirical Analysis of Cigarette Addiction." *American Economic Review* 84(3): 396–418.

Bell, Daniel. 1960. *The End of Ideology: On the Exhaustion of Political Ideas in the Fifties*. Glencoe, IL: Free Press.

Brunner, Otto, Werner Conze, and Reinhart Koselleck, eds. 1972–1997. *Geschichtliche Grundbegriffe: Historisches Lexikon zur politisch-sozialen Sprache in Deutschland*. Stuttgart: Klett-Cotta.

Buchanan, James and Gordon Tullock. 1962. *The Calculus of Consent: Logical Foundations of Constitutional Democracy*. Ann Arbor: University of Michigan Press.

Commission on Global Governance. 1995a. *Issues in Global Governance: Papers Written for the Commission on Global Governance*. London, The Hague, and Boston: Kluwer Law International in association with the Commission on Global Governance.

———. 1995b. *Our Global Neighbourhood: The Report of the Commission on Global Governance*. Oxford: Oxford University Press.

Crapanzano, Vincent. 1980. *Tuhami: Portrait of a Moroccan*. Chicago: University of Chicago Press.
Desai, Meghnad and Paul Redfern, eds. 1995. *Global Governance: Ethics and Economics of the World Order*. London: Pinter Publishers.
Devji, Faisal. 2005. *Landscapes of the Jihad: Militancy, Morality, Modernity*. Ithaca, NY: Cornell University Press.
Downs, Anthony. 1957. *An Economic Theory of Democracy*. New York: Harper.
Faubion, James and George Marcus, eds. 2009. *Fieldwork Is Not What it Used to Be: Learning Anthropology's Method in a Time of Transition*. Ithaca, NY: Cornell University Press.
Ferguson, James. 1990. *The Anti-Politics Machine: "Development," Depoliticization, and Bureaucratic Power in Lesotho*. Cambridge and New York: Cambridge University Press.
Finkelstein, Lawrence S. 1995. "What Is Global Governance?" *Global Governance* 1: 367–372.
Finnemore, Martha. 1996. *National Interests in International Society*. Ithaca, NY, and London: Cornell University Press.
Fogel, Robert and Stanley Engerman. 1968. "The Economics of Slavery." Report 6803, Center for Mathematical Studies in Business and Economics. Chicago: Department of Economics and Graduate School of Business University of Chicago.
Frank, Thomas. 2004. *What's the Matter with Kansas? How Conservatives Won the Heart of America*. New York: Metropolitan Books.
Fukuyama, Francis. 1989. "The End of History?" *National Interest* (Summer): 3–18.
Gereffi, Gary and Miguel Korzeniewicz, eds. 1994. *Commodity Chains and Global Capitalism*. Westport, Connecticut, and London: Praeger.
Giddens, Anthony. 1994. *Beyond Left and Right: The Future of Radical Politics*. Cambridge: Polity.
———. 1998. *The Third Way: The Renewal of Social Democracy*. Cambridge: Polity.
———. 2000. *The Third Way and its Critics*. Cambridge: Polity.
———. 2002. *Where now for New Labour?* Cambridge: Polity.
Gill, Tom. 2000. "Blair Fails to Replace Socialist International." *Socialist Campaign Group News*, January 1, p. 150.
Grondona, Mariano. 2000. "A Cultural Typology of Economic Development." In *Culture Matters: How Values Shape Human Progress*, ed. Lawrence E. Harrison and Samuel P. Huntington. New York: Basic Books, pp. 44–55.
Gusterson, Hugh. 1997. "Studying Up Revisited." *Political and Legal Anthropology Review* 20(1): 114–119.
Hannerz, Ulf. 1996. *Transnational Connections: Culture, People, Places*. London: Routledge.
———. 2004. "Cosmopolitanism." In *A Companion to the Anthropology of Politics*, ed. David Nugent and Joan Vincent. Oxford: Blackwell, pp. 69–85.
———. 2009. "Geocultural Scenarios." In *Frontiers of Sociology*, ed. Peter Hedström and Björn Wittrock. Leiden: Brill, pp. 267–290.
Harrison, Lawrence. 1993. *Who Prospers? How Cultural Values Shape Economic and Political Success*. New York: Basic Books.

———. 2000. Introduction. In *Culture Matters: How Values Shape Human Progress*, ed. L. Harrison and S. Huntington. New York: Basic Books.
Harrison, Lawrence E. and Samuel P. Huntington, eds. 2000. *Culture Matters: How Values Shape Human Progress*. New York: Basic Books.
Held, David. 1995. *Democracy and the Global Order: From the Modern State to Cosmopolitan Governance*. Cambridge: Polity Press.
Held, David and Anthony McGrew, eds. 2002. *Governing Globalization: Power, Authority and Global Governance*. Cambridge: Polity Press.
Hewson, Martin and Timothy J. Sinclair. 1999. *Approaches to Global Governance Theory*. New York: State University of New York Press.
Huntington, Samuel. 1993. "The Clash of Civilizations?" *Foreign Affairs* 72(3): 22–49.
Kagan, Robert. 2002. "Power and Weakness." *Policy Review* 113: 1, 3–5, 7.
Kaplan, Robert. 1994. "The Coming Anarchy." *Atlantic Monthly* 273(4): 44–76.
Keesing, Felix. 1939. "Some Notes on Acculturation Study." *Proceedings of the Sixth Pacific Science Congress* 4: 62.
Koselleck, Reinhart. 2002. *The Practice of Conceptual History: Timing History, Spacing Concepts*. Stanford, CA: Stanford University Press.
Landes, Elisabeth and Richard Posner. 1978. "The Economics of the Baby Shortage." *Journal of Legal Studies* 7(2): 323–348.
Lapeyre, Frédéric. 2004. *The Outcome and Impact of the Main International Commissions on Development Issues*. Working Paper 30. Geneva: International Labour Organization.
Marcus, George. 1995. "Ethnography in/of the World System: The Emergence of Multi-sited Ethnography." *Annual Review of Anthropology* 24: 95–117.
Mazrui, Ali Al'Amin. 1972. *Cultural Engineering and Nation-Building in East Africa*. Evanston, Ill.: Northwestern University Press.
Mouffe, Chantal. 2005. *On the Political*. Abingdon: Routledge.
Myrdal, Gunnar. 1968. *Asian Drama: An Inquiry into the Poverty of Nations*. 3 volumes. London: Allen Lane, Penguin Press.
Myrdal, Gunnar and Alva Myrdal. 1934. *Kris i befolkningsfrågan*. Stockholm: Bonniers.
Nye, Joseph S., Jr. 1990. "Soft Power." *Foreign Policy* 80: 153–171.
Popper, Karl. 1961. *The Poverty of Historicism*. London: Routledge and Kegan Paul.
Posner, Richard. 1972. *Economic Analysis of Law*. Boston: Little, Brown, and Co.
Rabinow, Paul. 1977. *Reflections on Fieldwork in Morocco*. Berkeley, CA: University of California Press.
Rayner, Steve. 1994. *Governance and the Global Commons*. Discussion Paper 8. London: Centre for the Study of Global Governance.
Reichardt, Rolf, Eberhard Schmitt, and Hans Jürgen Lüsebrink, eds. 1985–2000. *Handbuch politisch-sozialer Grundbegriffe in Frankreich 1680–1820*. Munich: Oldenbourg.
Review of International Studies. 2000. "Interview with Jim Rosenau: Washington DC, March 1999." *Review of International Studies* 26(3): 465–475.
Richter, Melvin. 1995. *The History of Political and Social Concepts: A Critical Introduction*. Oxford: Oxford University Press.

Ricœur, Paul. 1974. *The Conflict of Interpretations: Essays in Hermeneutics.* Evanston, IL: Northwestern University Press.

Risse, Thomas. 1999. "Democratic Global Governance in the 21st Century." Paper presented at the international conference *Progressive Governance in the 21st Century*, Florence, Italy, 20–21 November. Available at http://www.iue.it/General/Risse.PDF/.

Robertson, Roland. 1992. *Globalization: Social Theory and Global Culture.* London: Sage.

———. 2004. "Globality." *International Encyclopedia of the Social and Behavioral Sciences.* Amsterdam: Elsevier, pp. 6254–6258.

Rosenau, James N. 1971. *The Scientific Study of Foreign Policy.* New York: Free Press.

———. 1976. "Capabilities and Control in an Interdependent World." *International Security* 1(2): 32–49.

———. 1990. *Turbulence in World Politics: A Theory of Change and Continuity.* Princeton, NJ: Princeton University Press.

———. 2003. *Distant Proximities: Dynamics beyond Globalization.* Princeton and Oxford: Princeton University Press.

Rosenau, James N., ed. 1964. *International Aspects of Civil Strife.* Princeton, NJ: Princeton University Press.

———. 1967. *Domestic Sources of Foreign Policy.* New York: Free Press.

———. 1969. *Linkage Politics: Essays on the Convergence of National and International Systems.* New York: Free Press.

Rosenau, James N. and Ernst-Otto Czempiel, eds. 1992. *Governance without Government: Order and Change in World Politics.* Cambridge: Cambridge University Press.

Rosenfeld, Stephen. 1982. "Just Propaganda, or Is it?" *Washington Post*, 4 June, p. A19.

Sahlins, Marshall. 1993. "Goodbye to Tristes Tropes: Ethnography in the Context of Modern World History." *Journal of Modern History* 65: 1–25.

Schmitt, Carl. 1922. *Politische Theologie. Vier Kapitel zur Lehre von der Souveränität.* Munich and Leipzig: Duncker & Humblot.

———. 1927. "Der Begriff des Politischen." *Archiv für Sozialwissenschaften und Sozialpolitik* 58: 1–33.

Seers, Dudley. 1980. "North–South: Muddling Morality and Mutuality." *Third World Quarterly* 2(4): 601–693.

Spooner, Brian. 1986. "Weavers and Dealers: The Authenticity of an Oriental Carpet." In *The Social Life of Things: Commodities in Cultural Perspective*, ed. Arjun Appadurai. Cambridge: Cambridge University Press, pp. 195–235.

Stade, Ronald. 2001. "Diffusion: Anthropological Aspects." *International Encyclopedia of the Social and Behavioral Sciences*, volume 6. Amsterdam: Elsevier.

Strathern, Marilyn, ed. 2000. *Audit Cultures: Anthropological Studies in Accountability, Ethics and the Academy.* London: Routledge.

Thérien, Jean-Philippe. 1999. "Beyond the North–South Divide: The Two Tales of World Poverty." *Third World Quarterly* 20(4): 723–742.

Tolman, William. 1909. *Social Engineering: A Record of Things Done by American Industrialists Employing Upward of One and One-Half Million People.* New York: McGraw.

Wacquant, Loïc. 1999. "US Exports Zero Tolerance: Penal 'Common Sense' Comes to Europe." *Guardian Weekly*, April 1999: 1, 10–11.

Williams, Raymond. 1976. *Keywords: A Vocabulary of Culture and Society*. London: Fontana.

Wiseman, Geoffrey. 2005. "The Palme Commission: New Thinking about Security." In *International Commission and the Power of Ideas*, ed. Ramesh Thakur, Andrew F. Cooper, and John English. Tokyo: United Nations University Press, pp. 46–75.

World Bank. 1989. *Sub-Saharan Africa: From Crisis to Sustainable Growth. A Long-Term Perspective Study*. Washington, D.C.: The International Bank for Reconstruction and Development/The World Bank.

Young, Oran R., ed. 1997. *Global Governance: Drawing Insights from the Environmental Experience*. Cambridge, MA: MIT Press.

Chapter 12

Lusotopy as Ecumene

João de Pina-Cabral

In a now famous essay, Ulf Hannerz suggested that we should look at our contemporary world as an ecumene; that is, as an undivided space of human intercommunication, a network of networks (1991). A few years later, Sidney Mintz argued that, within this larger space, one could identify areas where intercommunication is more intense due to historical reasons—he famously suggested that the Caribbean, too, must be seen as an ecumene (1996). A similar notion of areas of density of intercommunication that define humanity as historically constructed can be found in Tolkien's fiction writing, where the notion of ecumene plays a centrally creative role—he calls it "the middle-earth." An ecumene, thus, is constituted by the sharing of a historical past which functions as a catalyst for "amity" (*amicitia*)—the principle that, according to Meyer Fortes' famous suggestion, is at the root of all kinship phenomena (1970).

In this chapter, it is argued that such a formulation can open up new vistas concerning a type of human proximity (historically rooted but not necessarily spatially contiguous) for which the social sciences during the twentieth century provided no ready description. In this way, it is hoped that the disturbing propensity of recent postcolonial critique to read imperial and postimperial socialities in nationalist terms might be avoided. Thus, I propose that, within our globalized world, the space/time originating in the historical expansion of the Portuguese (Lusotopy) shares the features of a "middle-earth," an ecumene. This is due not only to the sharing of a language, cultural codes, or political and civic institutions; rather, the very choice of the concept of "amity" to characterize what makes Lusotopy emerge is meant to highlight the fact that, over and above these more perceptible features, less immediately visible features can be found, such as kinship networks, family histories, friendships, relations of homonymy, etc.—all of those things that mark primordially our social personhood.[1]

I propose, therefore, that Hannerz' and Mintz' concept of "ecumene" can provide a valid alternative, to bypass some of the limitations that have recently plagued more traditional concepts, such as "group," "culture," or "society" (cf. James et al. 2010).

A Catalyst for Amity

When I meet someone new, I invariably carry out a process of comparison of his or her condition to mine. The first thing that happens is that I access what I share with this new person. This involves an exercise in memory—do we speak the same languages, do we hold similar types of knowledge, do we have similar tastes, have we lived in the same cities, do we know people in common? Although the process usually takes place subconsciously, I have found out that it makes for a peculiar intensity in the situation. The proof is that, if on a certain occasion one meets new people, one is prone to getting tired more quickly. Greater effort is involved in encountering new people than people we already know.

The context of the meeting, however, matters immensely. As a young man, I discovered that, in Johannesburg, South Africa, a person who had heard about my parents counted as a friend in the ethnically hostile environment of the Transvaal, where being Portuguese was, on the whole, a stigmatized condition. Then, I went on to discover that, if I came across that very same person in a street in Lourenço Marques (present-day Maputo, Mozambique, then a Portuguese colony), where my parents lived, she would not greet me in the same effusive way. Similarly, in England, a few years later, simply speaking Portuguese was a sufficient passport for being received as a friend in someone's home.

The point I want to establish here is that we approach people on the basis of who we are by relation to who they are—but context matters. Thus, sharing a past somehow brings people closer and, depending on context, might even have the effect of allaying solitude in the way that Epictetus famously described when he said that finding oneself in the middle of a group of thieves while traveling abroad hardly reduces one's solitude: "it is not the sight of a man as such that relieves us from being forlorn, but the sight of one who is faithful and self-respecting and serviceable" (2004 [1916], II: 24). Thus, I chose to speak of amity—a notion that Meyer Fortes placed at the root of kinship relations and Julian Pitt-Rivers extended to apply to close relations of neighborhood and friendship (Fortes 1970; Pitt-Rivers 1973). By using it, I mean to stress that what is at stake in these encounters is a process of interaction that is also a process of constant human co-construction, which is akin to and associated with the processes of emotional constitution that characterize kinship and friendship. It is, of course, an "intermediate category" (Pina-Cabral 2010a) that serves our purposes as anthropologists to the extent that it condenses and coheres a set of observations that, seen in the reductionist light of psychoanalysis, cognitive psychology, or neurophysiology, would be addressed in far denser detail and with other contextual implications (cf. Bråten 1998).

In his classical essay on the issue, Pitt-Rivers defines *amity* in the following terms: "All these 'amiable' relations imply a moral obligation to feel—or at least to feign—sentiments which commit the individual to actions of altruism, to generosity. The moral obligation is to forego self-interest in favour of another, to sacrifice oneself *for the sake* of someone else" (1973: 90, italics in original). However, this definition of the concept is problematic, as it bears the marks of the modernist conceptions that characterized the period of writing, in that it assumes a polarized relation between individual and group. Today, we find ourselves obliged to rework the concept of amity in order to avoid the implication that the person's interests are in any way monadic and that, therefore, all "generosity" sits on some sort of reciprocity between individuals.[2] In short, we must work with a relational notion of personhood: person as "dividual," not individual—not only in Melanesia (see Strathern 1988), but everywhere (see Pina-Cabral 2010b).

Amity, thus, must be taken to remit to an extended notion of "fraternity," of co-responsibility, such as that which Emmanuel Lévinas has proposed. The philosopher warned against the dangers of polarizing alterity. He called attention to the fact that the categories of social belonging on which anthropologists have traditionally focused (individual x, group y, culture z) coexist with another, far more constitutive, form of alterity: an interpersonal, face-to-face interaction that implies a deep and unavoidable sense of ethic co-responsibility and which is at the root of the recognition of our common humanity. The asymmetry of that anterior alterity is what launches the relational dynamics that constitute the person as a never-completed process, always in the throes of constitution (see Pina-Cabral 2013a, 2013b).

Lévinas warns that "alterity [cannot] be justified uniquely as the logical distinction of *parts belonging to a divided whole*, which rigorous reciprocal relations unite into a whole" (1996: 165, italics in the original). Modernist anthropologists focused on the latter type of alterity, thus forgetting about the former: the face-to-face confrontation, the basic fraternity that is constitutive of our own selves as humans and that cannot possibly be understood in contractualist terms (cf. Pina-Cabral 2010a). Lévinas' notion of the essential asymmetry of the relation between identity and alterity is especially useful to the social sciences today, as it is highly compatible with recent developments in the cognitive sciences (e.g., the stress on "alterocentric participation" or "self-with-other mirroring"; see Stern 2004), in the evolutionary study of human communication (e.g., Tomasello's notion of "shared intentionality," 2008), and in the psychological study of early ontogenesis.

This basic fraternity is a precondition of all human sociality because it is constitutive of human beings, but it is constantly subject to the strains of political belonging: that is, to culturally elaborated forms of alterity. Therefore, in my view, the intermediate category of "amity" must be taken to refer to the way in which human persons construct themselves out of a drive for recognizing the humanity of other humans. This process involves the channeling of one's initial collaborative dispositions and the fields of attention that they define. This is amity as constituted in kinship relations, friendship relations, ethnic belonging, etc.—that is, the identifications/differentiations that mark the person primordially in ontogenetic terms and whose implications, whilst susceptible to being altered at a latter moment, leave deep marks in the person's position before the world throughout their lifetime.

The Proprietorial Distortion

Let us now return to the analysis of the unspoken claims hidden in the examples of encounter with which this chapter began, to examine two contrasting cases. W.V. Quine, the prominent Anglo-American philosopher, was a fluent speaker of Portuguese—indeed, one of his very first books was published in Portuguese, in Brazil (1944). Does this make his work an instance of the Portuguese-speaking cultural contribution to contemporary philosophy? Most people would think not. Yet it might well have opened up the door of someone's home for him in some distant context. In fact, the eminent sociologist Hermínio Martins reports that, when the two met at a party in Oxford, they spoke amicably together at length in Portuguese.

Now, the philosopher Spinoza was the son of Portuguese-speaking Jews residing in Amsterdam. In his correspondence with Blyenbergh (2006 [1664]) he complains about not being able to debate philosophy in the language that he most feels as his own—which was, of course, a variety of Portuguese. In fact, he was forced as an adult to learn Latin in order to be able to write his philosophical œuvre. Spinoza decidedly is part of the Portuguese-speaking world and of the Portuguese cultural heritage in a way that Quine will never be. But why? Do the Dutch have a better claim to him? Do the Jews have a better one still, as he was Jewish—even although he had been ostracized? Or, since he made his living as a grinder of lenses, do the opticians have a greater right to claim his intellectual heritage?

How did this argument pass so easily from the recognition of the sharing of a language to the ownership of a claim over a heritage? Surely that was an unsound passage! In fact, the examples given above were meant to suggest just that. Unfortunately, the issue is not so easily settled. It is beyond doubt that, in a globalized world where "cultural politics" has come to the forefront, the sharing of all that goes with a common language brings people together; makes them feel they share one another's fate; fosters mutual interest. António Damásio, the famous neurophysiologist, has written a book about Spinoza where it becomes abundantly clear that the fact that the two of them share some association with Portugal is not irrelevant (2003). And yet, I would not want to impute to Damásio's mind some sort of pathetic claim to national ownership of Spinoza's œuvre. As a matter of fact, the sense that one gets from reading his book is that what really mattered was not only that they shared a language or a culture (as the "national" and the "religious" issues are clearly beside the point in their case); rather, it was the combination of language with a diasporic condition.

These perplexities can hardly be resolved by reference to linguistic norm. What counts or does not count as Portuguese, strictly speaking, from some sort of normative linguistic standpoint is clearly not what is at stake here. In other words, Spinoza's relevance for this discussion is not affected by any debate concerning the precise nature of the dialectical variety of Portuguese that Amsterdam Portuguese Jews spoke in the late seventeenth century. The proprietorial distortion that leads to the silly debate concerning who "owns" Spinoza's heritage is produced by a tendency to identify automatically language with culture, culture with nation, nation with groupness—and we are lucky if our interlocutor does not go on to identify *a* people with *a* religion, succumbing to incurable confusion. Part of the problem is the proclivity inherited from our modernist ancestors of the early twentieth century to discuss human interaction in terms that reify politically self-defined groupness—in anthropology, this kind of proclivity is called by the name that Émile Durkheim and Marcel Mauss gave to it when they advocated it: sociocentrism (1963).

These kinds of doubts are especially poignant when diasporic situations are the order of the day. And this is why I started this chapter by giving examples of my own African experience. These were situations where the fact that I was perceived as sharing something with these people made it more likely for us to create social trust in the midst of an essentially hostile environment, increasing the intensity of the intersubjectivity that arose during our encounters. This thing we shared was a catalyst for amity. But it was also the putty that brought Damásio to Spinoza in the throes of their mutual diasporas, or that produces in me such a feeling of intimacy when I read the book of Duarte Barbosa—the Malayalam-speaking clerk of the Cannanore factory (now called Kannur in Kerala, India, where the famous Nayars resided), one of the greatest proto-anthropologists of the sixteenth century (Barbosa 1984 [ca 1516]; Reis 1948; Pina-Cabral 2007).

Error and Irritation

What is it that brings us closer together, then? Is it to do with sharing a common language? I reckon it is not, since I have met people who do not speak Portuguese and yet whose relations to me give evidence of the presence of that catalyst for amity. My experience with the Eurasians of Macao and Hong Kong and my contacts with the Timorese have left me with no doubt that one can feel distinctly the presence of this catalyst even among people who do not speak more than a few shreds of Portuguese (see Pina-Cabral 2002a).

Is it, then, a "culture"? Well, frankly, if Spinoza and Damásio are said to share the same culture only because they both share this catalyst for amity, then really the concept of culture has to be stretched to such a point that it means very little. Damásio clearly shares much more concerning his definitions of the world with any contemporary Dutch person than with Spinoza. "Culture," then, also will not suffice.

This line of enquiry will be taken no further, as it surely has become obvious by now that "nation," "group belonging," "genetics," "knowledge of historical facts," etc. are all categories that will fare no better as exclusive terms for defining this catalyst—even if they all belong to the chain of identifications that are usually associated to the constitution of an ecumene. There is, of course, the possibility of simply denying that it exists at all; claiming that I made a mistaken assessment concerning the sense of amity that I shared with those people or that Damásio shares with Spinoza; in short, that it is a confabulation. But I am hardly the first one to have noticed it (see e.g., Sousa Santos 2001; Fry 2005). So, for the moment, it will just be taken for a fact that there is indeed "something," the nature of which has not yet quite been determined.

It has often been noted that one of the best ways of starting an analysis is to test the notion through error. Ever since Malinowski, we have known that ethnographic misunderstanding is a valuable tool for interpreting other people's actions and their assumptions concerning the world more generally (cf. Fabian 2001). Through it, we can start working at identifying the boundaries of operation of what we want to analyze.

Now, in my own experience as a bearer of this Lusotopic catalyst, I have learnt to recognize a potential for misunderstanding in our exchanges leading to intense mutual discomfort: a source of error in communication that is not always easy to pinpoint. For example, in Mozambique, I have learnt that my accent, conjoined with my skin color, functions as an irritant. Somehow this conjunction has the potential to bring down my local interlocutors on first approach even though, in time, the old process of constitution of amity eventually prevails. Then again, in Brazil, I have often been the butt of ethnicist jokes concerning the supposed stupidity of "the Portuguese." My interlocutors' irrepressible compulsion to perform these jokes in front of me is a clear expression of their discomfort before me. But there again, when faced with third parties, who somehow do not share this catalyst with us, the same Brazilians always give clear signs of its presence. Again, in Portugal, when speaking about such matters, it is I who often feel irritated as I notice that my interlocutors are prone to presuming proprietorial claims to "language" and "culture" that imply the subalternization of all the people around the world who share this catalyst of amity with us but who do not categorize themselves as "Portuguese."

Over the years, I have learnt that these misunderstandings have to do with that sense of "claim" identified above concerning Spinoza's heritage. It is a claim to privileged representation, to ownership rights—in it, cultural phenomena (custom, language, food, etc.) and political domination somehow conjoin. One does not actually need to openly stake the claim before one's interlocutors feel its effects; the isomorphism between language, culture, and nation is so deeply ingrained into our presuppositions concerning the world that it is automatically presumed. Its political corollary is that those who rule in the place where the language historically originated have greater claim to represent that language and, by implication, the groups which that language brings together. Yet, in our postcolonial era, no one in their right mind would be willing to condone such a position, due to its imperialist and racialist implications. In his theorization on these issues, Boaventura de Sousa Santos rightly identifies these problems (2001).[3]

It is, therefore, a surprise to me that there is at the moment no way of referring conjointly to the space/time that is demarcated by the sharing of this catalyst for amity. *Lusophony*, as a term to describe those who hail from countries where Portuguese is the state language, leaves out many people and places around the world where the catalyst's presence is nevertheless very strongly felt: both (a) people who do not speak Portuguese in Goa, Africa, Macao, or Timor, and (b) people who, though they might speak Portuguese at home, live in countries where other languages are dominant, such as Canada, the United States, Venezuela, South Africa, Australia, France, Luxembourg, Switzerland, or Germany. In fact, in Macao, Mozambique, and Timor, I have personally found that affinity to a Portuguese football club is probably a far better marker of this shared sense of destiny than the actual capacity to use the Portuguese language (Pina-Cabral 2002/3). As was stated above, strictly speaking, sharing a language, a culture, or a national identity will not suffice. A case in point might be the sense of amity that a student of mine encountered when he went to Manchester to study Hindus whose ancestors originated in Diu, once a Portuguese colony, but resided for various generations in Mozambique and then came to Europe, first settling in Portugal and then moving on to England?[4]

While it might be observed that the putty that brings together these experiences is not strictly speaking a linguistic one, there is a yet stronger reason why I prefer not to start with *Lusophone* as an adjective. And that is, once we start to define a social space by a language, it becomes almost impossible to avoid the sociocentric convergence of language, culture, and nation. Lusophony surely is an important (I would say even central) aspect of the space that is delineated by the sharing of this catalyst for amity. But referring to the space by the language inevitably leads to the type of proprietorial distortion that was warned of above.

Therefore, I propose to characterize our object as a space/time and not as a language. I propose to adopt the word *Lusotopy*, which the political historians from *Sciences Po* in Bordeaux invented and which they use as the name for their interesting journal (*Lusotopie*). In short, to be part of Lusotopy is to possess the modes of identification/differentiation that are the key for entering into the network of relations that it constitutes. Each one of us that possesses these modes of identification (that carries them in his or her past and signals them in a reified manner by his or her presence) creates a space/time by being part of it. So Lusotopy as a space/time affirms itself in its enactment. This enactment occurs in the moment of recognition—that is, simply put, when two people who possess those modes of identification realize it by experiencing and assuming reflexively the operation of the catalyst for amity.

Note, experiencing the identification does not necessarily mean to acknowledge the identification. For example, I have encountered people who, for one reason or another, refuse to acknowledge openly the experience of identification. It might be the case that they actually do not feel it—in which case Lusotopy has simply not occurred. But it has happened to me to have come out of such an encounter with the conviction that the people in question were in denial, to use the Freudian expression. It has even occurred that, retrospectively, the person in question has later on acknowledged the equivocation. The situations of misunderstanding exemplified above are typical instances where one's presumed proximity functions initially in an almost perverse way as a factor for irritation. One's interlocutor's irritation or his or her need to perform some sort of ritual of exclusion (of the kind exemplified by Portuguese jokes in Brazil) is already a sign that the catalyst is in operation.

Ecumene

Lusotopy, therefore, is not a contiguous space, nor can it be defined in any regional manner. In short, so as to avoid the risk of any further confusion, I propose that, in attempting to define Lusotopy, instead of relying on culture, language, and nation and their presumed isomorphism, Ulf Hannerz' lead should be followed in having recourse to an earlier use of the concept of culture as expressed in the work of the American diffusionist anthropologist Alfred Kroeber. The latter suggested that these phenomena of cultural diffusion and the way in which they create a human world of intercommunication should be viewed using the Greek concept of *oikoumenê* (1963 [1923, 1948]: 231). The word *oikoumenê* derives from a verb meaning "to inhabit." It was used literally to describe the part of the earth inhabited by humans. The radical *oikos* refers to household (and specially the large room in ancient Greek homes where the women lived) and points to the element of human fostering. The usage of *ecumene* to mean the part of the world known to a civilization, which Kroeber espoused, further captures the Christian sense that the word has acquired since then, when used to describe the whole and most widely defined community of the Christians (as in the adjective *ecumenical*).

My favorite, however, is the use that Tolkien gives to the concept of ecumene by defining it as "the abiding place of men": 'the physical world in which man lives out his life and destiny, as opposed to the unseen worlds, like Heaven or Hell."[5] The synonym he ultimately adopts in his fiction writing is "middle-earth," a translation of the Old English expression *middangeard*, of which he declares that it "is not my own invention. It is a modernization or alteration ... of an old word for the inhabited world of Men, the *oikoumenê*."[6]

The concept is useful here, because it points to the existence of levels of convergence that exist within a much more broadly conceived sociocultural universe. Thus, we can speak of areas of global integration and areas of local specificity. The middle-earth or ecumene is that area where struggle, construction, and destruction occur, which allows for human co-construction. It is the area of human action. In that sense, it is an area of relative freedom; it allows both for a certain freedom from local constraints and a certain freedom from global hegemonic imperatives.

It should be noted that I specifically want to avoid any similarity with the opposition in canon law, which Mary Douglas made famous as a principle of social organization (2001), between modality (the local organization of the Church in terms of parishes and dioceses) and sodality (task-oriented, non-local, religious organizations)—that is, the difference between local allegiances and transversal, non-local allegiances. This will not serve our purposes. Whilst Lusotopy functions as a sodality in as much as it links people across nations and continents; at a local level, it is often the very historicity of the reified Lusotopy that gives rise to a localized sense of community. I believe Timor-Leste—the nation-state that has recently emerged through the help of the United Nations out of an attempt by Indonesia to annex by extreme force an ancient Portuguese colony—is probably the best example of how a distant, historical Lusotopic ferment can function as the basis for a future-oriented project of national community (see Feijó 2008). Many other examples can be found throughout Asia, from the Catholic communities of Larantuka in the Solor Islands, to Catholic communities in India, to the burghers of Sri Lanka, to the Kristang of Malacca, to the Eurasian middle class of Macao and Hong Kong that I studied in the 1990s (Pina-Cabral 2002a).

The tendency enshrined most recently in so-called "postcolonial" literature to focus on colonial history from the Eurocentric perspective of nation, power, and rule means that we have not developed sufficiently our analytical language for dealing with the way in which, in the long term, colonial encounters write themselves into people's worldviews, paving the way for new negotiations of self-respect and self-determination. Elizabeth Traube, in her superb ethnography of the Mambai of Timor-Leste, has carried out a study of the way in which colonial rule wrote itself into Timorese myth, giving rise to complex processes of identification/differentiation (Traube 1986: 55).

[S]trictly speaking, Mambai have no tradition of foreign invaders from the outside, nor do they have any real conception of a larger outside world which might encompass their own society. By Mambai theories of origin, the Malaia [a category which includes all non-Timorese] are autochthonous, their relationship to the Timorese is based on kinship, and their arrival on Timor signifies the return of the legitimate defenders of order. (Traube 1986: 53)

Decolonization was formulated to the ethnographer as "this matter of our younger brothers going away" (Traube 1986: 54).

Now, a process such as this one is local and unique and cannot be observed in any other Lusotopic space/time. Still, each of these local charters of identification/differentiation, when looked at from a distance, comes to constitute a foundation (local, diversified, and unrepeatable) for an ecumene that, in contrast, is a function of globalization. Paradoxically, this is the case even when, as it happens with the Mambai, there is no local category to formulate the larger, outside world.

In fact, the question is even more complex than that. As historian David Jackson has reminded us, something like this loop effect could be found also in the obsessive search for Christian roots in exotic places that characterized the Portuguese expansion in the sixteenth century (the search for Prester John, for the tomb of St. Thomas, for the Nestorians in Mendes Pinto, etc.). "In abstract terms, to identify oneself with the lost origins means to assimilate being with its own absence. One might say that the Portuguese navigated in order to reach their own 'lost' bodies, thus completing themselves" (Jackson 1997: 17).

In light of these considerations, I was impressed by the way in which Sidney Mintz mobilizes the concept of ecumene proposed by Ulf Hannerz. It is especially useful because it focuses on the historical way in which "ecumene" emerges as a compound factor, rather than on each of the reified aspects of its manifestations (e.g., language, custom, law, etc.). What unites the Caribbean, Mintz argues, cannot really be pinned down to language, custom, or nation (including, of course, ethnicity)— for these are all very varied in the region. And yet, in spite of all that, the Caribbean has a distinct "coherence not so much cultural as sociological" (1996: 289). Thus, he sustains,

the basis for constructing a Caribbean *oikoumenê*, then, lies with the social frameworks created for culturally diverse migrant people who were subjected to century-long processes of mostly forced cultural change by European rulers; and with the long-term effects of those processes upon Caribbean life. It has nothing to do with language or food or dress or like cultural indices as *such*, but with a transmuted vision of the world itself, engrafted upon countless strangers, who came or were brought to the region over the centuries, replacing those who had died or who had been killed off by disease, war and European imperial enterprise. (Mintz 1996: 297, italics in original)

Now, obviously, I am not claiming that Lusotopy as ecumene has the same history, the same process of construction, or the same regional type of reach as Sidney Mintz' Caribbean. It shares a similar condition, however, in that it operates as a kind of "middle-earth." Lusotopy is something that most of us that belong to it can identify when it arises. Being spread out throughout the world, it is not a region but a space/time; but it is, as Benítez-Rojo says of the Caribbean, "a union of the diverse" (1997: 2). I favor the spatial metaphor for the sole reason that it marks better Lusotopy's proneness to call onto itself by encompassment those who come close to it.

The point being made here is simple: as an ecumene, Lusotopy is a network of contacts; but, when it fires up, it has effects upon the world; thus, it leaves reified marks (cities, statues, modes of cuisine, musical styles, manners and etiquettes, narratives and texts, language games, etc.); so, the world feeds back the ecumene onto those who produce it. Thus, the ecumene is triggered, as it were, by the reified products of its former occurrences, even when one is alone. When this happens, the dispositions of identification within the single person involved are deepened and reinforced, predisposing this person to greater ulterior recognition.

For example, I go to a foreign land, Sarajevo, at a time in which a violent civil war is brewing up and everyone around me is, as it were, fevered up by a sense of foreboding (Pina-Cabral 1988). In a museum, I start reading a liturgical text written in Serbo-Croatian alphabetical style in a beautiful silver mounting. As I pronounce it aloud, I discover that it is a Serbo-Croatian rendering of Portuguese Jewish prayers—although it looks like Serbo-Croat, it bears Hebrew words, and it reads out as an archaic-sounding Portuguese. The experience grabs my breath with a poignant identification that brings me close to tears. I will never forget it for it disposed me to look at Sephardic history in a new, Lusotopic manner. Thus, unwittingly, at that moment, I became an agent of the Lusotopification of Sephardic history, in much the same sort of movement that results from Damásio's approximation of Spinoza's hideouts in Rijnsburg near The Hague.

The reader will pardon that this is a personal example but it is useful precisely because of that—as I can report on the internal emotional dynamics that it produced which, in other people, would have remained relatively obscure to me. The process is not unlike that of Freud's reliance on the analysis of his own dreams or of his own reaction to Austrian jokes concerning Jews (1960).

Lusotopy's strange inescapability is largely produced by the way in which one's subject condition is dependent on one's insertion into chains of historical events, making one prone to recognize the people whose past went past those same events. In this sense, Lusotopy is a *continued identity*—it is a proneness to recognize in others a certain kind of mutuality caused by a common past (cf. Pina-Cabral 2003, 2013b). Note: the strangeness of the feeling is created by the imposition of a number of veils. Descendants of former enemies find one another mutually comforting against their own expectations; national foes find themselves sharing an unstated common ground when faced with third persons; people whose trajectories are ethnically divergent find ground for silent common recognition. As Oswald de Andrade said for Brazil, "only anthropophagy unites us"—the struggles of the past bring people together in the present (see Pina-Cabral 1999).

Particularly strange is the feeling of pride that people experience in the face of past events that, officially, are often held to be disreputable: empire, slavery, war, migration, hunger, religious fanaticism, dictatorship, etc.[7] Ever since the eighteenth century, the Lusotopic subject has lived a strangely dual condition: whilst being part of imperial nations, he or she is also subaltern in geopolitical and economic terms. Brazil inherited from Portugal this same sense of being both modern, Western, and imperial and, at the same time, backward, impoverished, and dominated (Schwartz 2000 [1977]). Faced with the Anglo-American hegemonic alliance that has ruled the world since then, the subjects of Portugal, Brazil, and their ex-colonies were ever placed before a dilemmatic identity, which made up for a type of hurt pride. Lusotopy, thus, when faced with Anglo-American might (cultural, economic, political, or military) is often experienced as a stigma.

In these past postcolonial decades, the children of the Portuguese and the children of the former subjects of the Portuguese empire have found themselves in a global atmosphere where their continued identity is seen as a source not of prestige but mostly of a lack of prestige. This gives rise to both anger and shame; both rejection and repression; both fascination and enforced oblivion. Many are those who learnt to hide the ghosts in their closets by means of de-Lusotopifying narratives of their personal histories—as when they opt for passing to their children their mothers' non-Portuguese surnames or to anglicize the patronym, as frequently happens in the United States (Almeida 2010).

Now, if we learn Erving Goffman's (1974) lesson, we can detect the logic of stigma in operation—the process that often makes the stigmatized their own worst enemies, fraternity breeding love as well as hatred. As a young man in South Africa, I witnessed the arrival of the refugees from the African colonies. These were becoming independent in 1976 as a result of the revolution that had taken place in Portugal in 1974, bringing to an end four decades of fascist-colonialist rule. In both Angola and Mozambique, these violent and undemocratic processes eventually led to prolonged and bitter civil wars. The Portuguese refugees hurriedly leaving the ex-colonies were arriving in South Africa in hoards. They were disoriented people who had been unprepared for such a sudden eviction from their homes by the backward and irresponsible regime that had governed Portugal and its colonies. The prosperity of the late colonial period had turned them, nearly all of whom had left Portugal in relative penury, into a rising middle class. Overnight, however, they were disowned and exiled. To witness the scenes of abuse, pillage, and maltreatment that were enacted against them by many of the already settled Portuguese migrants that lived in South Africa was an experience that I found deeply troubling and that probably goes into explaining why, over thirty years later, I am concerned with this topic to the point of writing this essay.

Lusotopy and Diaspora

At this point, it might well be pointed out that whilst the argument has managed to identify the vague historical links that go into making Lusotopy, the bearers of those links themselves are often ignorant of their presence and nature. Immersed as they are in universes of everyday life that feel locally integrated, they cannot tell which aspects demonstrate a Lusotopic ascent and which do not. What, then, makes Lusotopy a middle-earth, a world of human cohabitation?

The question is legitimate in as much as each of these bearers of Lusotopy are also the bearers of many other types of links; some of a local nature, but others of a global nature. For example, members of my generation born in China, Africa, Brazil, America, or Portugal, independent of whether or not they are bearers of Lusotopy, are capable of singing aloud the starting words of the song "Yesterday," by The Beatles. So, what is special about Lusotopy by contrast to Beatlemania? Well, the answer is that the difference is not one of essence but one of relevance. As opposed to Beatlemania, Lusotopy is far more constitutive of people's everyday universes. In short, when two bearers meet, they find echoes in each other that make them mutually recognizable which, in that way, allows for greater and easier contact. This does not necessarily mean that these people will immediately, due to it, become "friends." The notion of amity discussed here does carry that ultimate meaning of mutual docility, but it hardly implies constant and absolute agreement. Fraternal fights, as we have known since Cain, are the most homicidal (cf. Pina Cabral 2005a and Finkielkraut 1997). That ultimate sense of docility is hardly an emotional disposition of each bearer individually. It has to do with the fact that we are all socially constructed — all humans were created by humans in a process of gradual evolution that is lost in the infinitesimal nature of the intervening steps (an autopoetic ontogenesis, to quote Christina Toren 1999). For that reason, when we speak of amity, it is not a localized or determinable emotion that is at stake. Rather, it is the architecture of a person's world that mobilizes "e-motional" dispositions (cf. Bråten 1998).

In order for us to become people, we had to link up into a series of meanings that were created long before each one of us came into existence. That process of linkage is a process of acceptance, of docility in the face of the meanings of others. That original docility, however, need not be interpreted to mean that we are all easygoing, nice sort of fellows (cf. Thompson 1998: 156–157). To the contrary, all it means is that the very process of becoming human has involved us in negotiated meanings. Pastness, therefore, is written into our condition as humans in such a way that we are all historical. Thus, when a little baby in Brazil babbles her first words, those words produce echoes that reverberate throughout the world and that give rise to harmonies wherever there is Lusotopy. These harmonies, we have seen, might not even be conscious to those who experience them and, in turn, reproduce them. Never mind, because the whole process, whilst being human, is one that goes on in the world outside (or, better still, beside) humans. It is in this sense that Lusotopy is an ecumene — a world of human cohabitation with characteristics of its own when compared with others: not always the same characteristics everywhere; not always with the same intensity; not always as tightly bound to each other. But then, as this essay has never claimed that Lusotopy is a sharply delineated territory, but rather that it is a loosely defined space/time that comes into existence whenever it occurs, we need not be troubled by the impossibility of drawing it out precisely on a world map; though, of course, there is no problem in attempting to draw out on a map the areas of its strongest occurrence. In short, it is a statistical, not a mechanic, occurrence.

As an ecumene, therefore, Lusotopy is the network constituted by a continued identity that originated in the Portuguese expansion of the sixteenth century but that acquired immediately a complexity and dynamic of its own. One can follow the process along the sea routes. It is possible, for example, to trace the musical style that accompanied the Portuguese expansion all the way along the south Atlantic and into the Indian Ocean and, beyond that, to Malacca and into what is today Indonesia and, still beyond, to Macao (see Jackson 1990). The mutual and multilayered process that created these musical affinities and prolonged them over the next five centuries no longer has a single direction. The local musicians that carry this musical line of descent are generally unaware of the web of links that their interiorized musical practice transports. When the Sinhalese modernizing youth of the 1970s rocked and danced away to the sound of what they thought to be the latest thing in modern chic (*baila*), they hardly could know that they were building on musical resources that this web of Lusotopic music had provided for them (see Shihan de Silva Jayasuriya 2008).

In short, their music is written onto the world with implications that far outreach them; but once inscribed in the world, their music produces echoes and triggers recognitions (nostalgias, memories, traumas) that the musicians had not planned for. In this way, a musical gesture produced with one set of localized personal aims gets to echo somewhere else. In some places, it gives rise to sheer disharmony—many have been the people who have turned their noses up at Sinhalese Lusotopic rock, at the Macanese tuna's music, or at the folk dancing of the Malacca Kristang. For such people, Lusotopy did not occur. But, unbeknownst to those who produce those musical gestures, there will be many other people around the world for whom the very same echoes produce Lusotopic chords, so to speak.

The reader will excuse me for using musical metaphors to speak about music, but I hope the point has been taken that the way Lusotopy is inscribed in the world operates largely independently of the actors. Through human action, Lusotopy is reified; and, once that occurs, it becomes a mould for human action. It does not constrain, it entices—and that is why I do not speak of conversion, of cultural domination, of acculturation, or anything of the kind, but of echoes that give rise to harmonies.

As with musical styles, much the same applies to the present-day descendents of the naval creole that installed itself round the world in the sixteenth century or, for that matter, of the basic cooking methods that, adapting themselves to different foodstuffs and condiments, can still be seen in operation from Portugal to Brazil, from there to Africa and on to Asia, all the way to Macanese food and Japanese *tempura* or *castilla* cake.

There are too many examples like this for it to be worthwhile to list them. The ones to do with music and dance or with language and literature are probably the most visible and striking, but I would not like to leave the reader with the sense that it is all to do with "culture," "language," and "literature." There are many ecumenical phenomena in other areas: food and drink; legal practice; business dispositions; etc. Where such things go deeper, however, is precisely where they are less easy to formulate. Peter Fry has shown the way that the dynamics of racial differentiation are structured by long-term Lusotopic trends (2005). I myself have argued that the Lusotopic traditions of anthroponomy transport dispositions concerning the construction of the person (Pina-Cabral 2008).

Lusotopy in Portugal

Considering the drift the argument has taken, it might well be asked whether Lusotopy is something strictly to do with exile and diaspora. In short, is it something that necessarily occurs outside of Portugal?

There are two seemingly contradictory replies to this question. The first is that exile and diaspora are in Portugal, too: today, Portuguese cities are terrains of Lusotopic colonization. The second is that the Portuguese in Portugal have always been the bearers of two interconnected but distinct kinds of sociocultural strains: one, linking them to Iberia, southern Europe, and the Catholic world as heirs to the Roman Empire; the other, linking them to the Atlantic world they were forced onto through economic need and Castilian political pressure (see Pina-Cabral 2002/3). Portugal, therefore, is as much part of Lusotopy as anywhere else.

This issue links up with the question of misplaced proprietorial claims. This is, in fact, a problem inherent in the initial use of the notion of ecumene. At the beginning of the last century, Kroeber writes, for example, that the concept has "a modern utility as a convenient designation of the total area reached by traceable diffusion influences from the main higher centres of Eurasia at which most new culture had up to then been produced" (1963 [1923]: 231). This directionality of ecumene deserves attention. A noteworthy aspect of Mintz' treatment of the concept is that he actually avoids this colonizing implication.

To put the issue plainly, is it not true, after all, that it was the Portuguese "discoveries," as it were, that opened up Lusotopy? Can we, thus, speak of Lusotopy without presuming the directionality (the one-way movement) that this historical process implies? Linear time produces directionality in sociocultural influence. The thing with linear time, however, is that it is never the only temporal mode; other modes of temporality always interplay with it. In short, Lusotopy was not instituted in Brazil the moment that Pedro Álvares Cabral arrived there, but rather the moment that the famous letter written by his pilot, Pedro Vaz de Caminha, reached the king back in Lisbon. Empire is created in an expansion outwards, but the historical implications of what it sets up are always dependent on a dialectics of return, as is apparent from the work of all the major sixteenth-century Portuguese traveler-scholars.

The only problem today is that Portugal gives the feeling of being unchanged. This is a mirage caused by cultural hegemonies that far outreach the influence of the Portuguese elite itself. Portugal's role as the point of origin does not imply by any means that it stands outside of its creation, as an unchanged, elementary core. No such thing happens in history and that has never actually been the case. For example, the registers of the Inquisition studied by Laura de Mello e Souza (2005 [1986]) bear patent evidence to the fact that, ever since the sixteenth century, the religious and moral life of the Portuguese was being marked by the cargo of the return trip, the counter waves of empire (cf. Sansi-Roca 2007). One of the ways in which this mirage of a pristine, unchanged condition is fostered is by associating Portugal and things Portuguese with the other axis of sociocultural foundation of Portugal—the European axis, which we are prone to call "Western" these days.

For instance, we are ready to see how people like Matteo Ricci or Tomás Ribeiro went from Portugal and Italy to China, there to implant notions of neo-Aristotelian philosophy and European music making. At the same time, we fail to see what came in the Jesuits' baggage on the return trip. Leibniz, for example, invented binary mathematics after having read a description of the Chinese notion of Dao by a Portuguese Jesuit (1994). Binary mathematics, which made the computer revolution possible, is strongly considered a Western thing. Here is the hegemonic mirage at work, hiding the return trip. Directionality cannot be written out of the ecumene, but the counterdirectionality can be written back into it.

When that happens, suddenly, things that were invisible earlier start to become visible. For example, over the past ten years or so the best fiction writing in Portuguese has not come out of Brazil or Portugal but out of Africa. We might, thus, be tempted to claim that the two seats of Lusophony have lost their nerve, have exhausted their genius, and that the newer communities are showing their vigor. This, however, would be to miss the point that, in the present postcolonial world, Lusotopic literature is written in a kind of delocalized space that reflects the globalization of the lives of the inhabitants of modern metropolises. The point is not one of directionality, but one of increasing transnationality.

Conclusion

Racism, ethnocentrism, and class prejudice can all be found in Portugal, as well as Brazil, Angola, Mozambique, or the Asian ex-colonies: Lusotopy is as much a terrain of encounter as one of mutual fear and distrust (see Pina-Cabral 2012). The characteristic proclivity of the twentieth century to formulate observations concerning sociocultural proximity in utopian terms may suggest an incorrect reading of the above argument. As an ecumene, one thing Lusotopy is not is a utopia.

Utopian thought, by attempting to escape history, encourages a kind of blindness to the unfathomable richness of history. When history inevitably touches the plans of action drawn along utopian modes, it does so in ways no one could have predicted. People who bear utopian dispositions are not prepared for the complexity and depth of the encounter with history and react in fear, producing monstrosities. In this sense, much as we have to allow ourselves to be inspired by the great visionaries of Lusotopy—António Vieira, Fernando Pessoa, Agostinho da Silva—we have to avoid their utopianism if we are to produce in the twenty-first century a more humane world than that which we produced in the last century, with its poisonous dreams of perfection.

Before closing the argument, however, I would like to refer back to another characteristic of Tolkien's notion of middle-earth which is implicit in Ulf Hannerz' proposal of the notion of ecumene. Tolkien says that, in his fiction, the *oikoumenê* is in the middle "because [it is] thought of vaguely as set amidst the encircling Seas and ... between the ice of the North and the fire of the South." I want to argue that Lusotopy shares much the same fate. In our globalized world, it is neither Western nor non-Western—it places its subjects in a middle-earth between today's rich North and today's highly diversified South. Some authors, such as Viveiros de Castro, adopt the Western perspective *par courtoisie*, as he puts it (2009: 9); others, take a distance *par précaution* (Pina-Cabral 2005b). In coming years, when the unifocal world we have lived in since the fall of the Berlin Wall again polarizes politically and culturally, the condition of those who are intermediate will again be queried. In the past, this condition has often proved to be a disadvantage for Lusotopic subjects. Today, however, Agostinho da Silva's suggestion that we should own that condition as a middle-earth might well turn out to be useful.

Ulf Hannerz' own, decentralized condition, as a Swede in an Anglo-American world, has given him greater sensibility to these questions of human historical complexity than many of his contemporaries that have written about our present postcolonial condition. Following his lead, this chapter was an effort at inserting old concepts into new frameworks. The sociocentric framework which presumes the unitariness of identity and sees all alterity as essentially dyadic is no longer satisfactory to most of us; but anthropological theory has not taken sufficient steps to salvage some of its central concepts (concepts of immense theoretical might, such as *amity* or *ecumene*) from the sociocentric interpretations that were written into them by the modernists. It is Kroeber's and Tolkien's humanist preoccupations—as well as the cosmopolitanism in Hannerz and Mintz—that allow their concept of ecumene to rise above diffusionism, medievalist nostalgia, or localized ethnography, making it decidedly useful to understand our contemporary world, where the unitariness of cultures, societies, or individuals is no longer desirable or, in any case, self-evident.

Acknowledgments

An earlier, Portuguese version of this chapter has been published in *Revista Brasileira de Ciências Sociais* 25 (74), 2010: 5–20.

I am indebted to comments and suggestions from Mónica Chan, Omar Ribeiro Thomaz, Michel Cahen, Hermínio Martins, Wilson Trajano Filho, Rui Graça Feijó, and Luiz Eduardo Dias Duarte. I am grateful to Cristiana Bastos for having called my attention to Ulf Hannerz, many years ago.

Notes

1. For this particular use of the concept of "primordiality" as associated to the person's ontogenesis, see Pina Cabral (2002b).
2. This is the case even if reciprocity is conceived in terms of Marshall Sahlins' "generalized reciprocity" (1972). One can now see that this useful concept performed an interesting role of logical mediation in that it allowed non-contractual relations to fit into a contractualist theoretical mode.
3. Unfortunately, I feel that the "Calibanization of Lusophony" that he proposes dehistoricizes the process, leading to the constitution of a kind of Lusophonic destiny that is inevitably utopian, even if, in having recourse to the image of Shakespeare's ugly character Caliban, it presents itself initially as dystopian (cf. Pina-Cabral 2004).
4. I thank Nuno Dias for our long and interesting talks concerning his fieldwork experience.
5. http://en.wikipedia.org/wiki/Oikoumene.
6. Tolkien (1995 [1981]): Letter 211.

7. One of the best exemplars of this process is the recent novel *Barroco Tropical* (2009) by the Angolan writer José Eduardo Agualusa.

References

Agualusa, José Eduardo. 2009. *Barroco Tropical*. Lisbon: Dom Quixote.
Almeida, Onésimo Teotónio de. 2010. *O Peso do Hífen—ensaios sobre a experiência luso-americana*. Lisbon: Imprensa de Ciências Sociais.
Barbosa, Duarte. 1984/c. 1516. *Livro do Oriente. Além-Mar, Códice Casanatense. Os Portugueses na Índia: Viagens, aventuras, conquista*. Introd. Fernand Braudel et al. Lisbon: Bertrand & Franco Maria Ricci.
Benítez-Rojo, Antonio. 1997. *The Repeating Island: The Caribbean and the Postmodern Perspective*. Durham: Duke University Press.
Bråten, Stein. 1998. "Introduction." In *Intersubjective Communication and Emotion in Early Ontogenesis*, ed. Stein Bråten. Cambridge: Cambridge University Press, pp. 1–14.
Damásio, António. 2003. *Looking for Spinoza: Joy, Sorrow, and the Feeling Brain*. New York: Harcourt.
Douglas, Mary. 2001. *In the Wilderness: The Doctrine of Defilement in the Book of Numbers*. Oxford: Oxford University Press.
Durkheim, Émile and Marcel Mauss. 1963. *Primitive Classification*, transl. Rodney Needham. Chicago, Ill.: Chicago University Press.
Epictetus. 2004/1916. *Discourses*, transl. P.E. Matheson. Mineola, NY: Dover Publications.
Fabian, Johannes. 2001. "Ethnographic Misunderstanding and the Perils of Context." In *Anthropology with an Attitude: Critical Essays*. Stanford, Calif.: Stanford University Press, pp. 85–104.
Feijó, Rui Graça. 2008. "Língua, nome e identidade numa situação de plurilinguismo concorrencial: o caso de Timor-Leste." *Etnográfica* 12(1): 143–172.
Finkielkraut, Alain. 1997. *The Wisdom of Love*, transl. Kevan O'Neill and David Suchoff. Lincoln: University of Nebraska Press.
Fortes, Meyer. 1970. *Kinship and the Social Order: The Legacy of Lewis Henry Morgan*. London: Routledge & Kegan Paul.
Freud, Sigmund. 1960. *Jokes and their Relation to the Unconscious*, transl. James Strachey. New York: Norton.
Fry, Peter. 2005. *A persistência da raça: ensaios antropológicos sobre o Brasil e a África Austral*. Rio de Janeiro: Civilização Brasileira.
Goffman, Erving. 1974. *Stigma: Notes on the Management of Spoiled Identity*. New York: J. Aronson.
Hannerz, Ulf. 1991. "The Global Ecumene as a Network of Networks." In *Conceptualizing Societies*, ed. Adam Kuper. London: Routledge, pp. 34–56.
Jackson, K. David. 1990. *Sing without Shame: Oral Traditions in Indo-Portuguese Creole Verse*. Macao: Instituto Cultural de Macau.
———. 1997. *Os construtores dos oceanos*. Lisbon: Assírio & Alvim.
James, Deborah, Evie Plaice, and Christina Toren, eds. 2010. *Culture Wars: Context, Models and Anthropologists*. Oxford: Berghahn Books.

Jayasuriya, Shihan de Silva. 2008. *The Portuguese in the East: A Cultural History of a Maritime Trading Empire*. London: I.B. Tauris.
Kroeber, Alfred and Clyde Kluckhohn. 1963. *Culture: A Critical Review of Concepts and Definitions*. New York: Vintage Books.
Leibniz, Gottfried Wilhelm. 1994. *Writings on China*, ed. Joseph Campbell. Chicago, Ill.: Open Court.
Lévinas, Emmanuel. 1996. *Basic Philosophical Writings*, ed. Adriaan Peperzak, Simon Critchley, and Robert Bernasconi. Bloomington: Indiana University Press.
Mello e Souza, Laura de. 2005/1986. *O Diabo e a Terra de Santa Cruz: feitiçaria e religiosidade popular no Brasil colonial*. São Paulo: Companhia das Letras.
Mintz, Sidney W. 1996. "Enduring Substances, Trying Theories: The Caribbean Region as Oikoumenê." *Journal of the Royal Anthropological Institute* N.S. 2: 289–293.
Pina-Cabral, João de. 1999. "O retorno da Laurentina: A simbolização das relações étnicas no Moçambique colonial e pós-colonial." *Novos Estudos — CEBRAP* 53: 85–96.
———. 2002a. *Between China and Europe: Person, Culture and Emotion in Macao*. LSE Anthropology Series 74. New York: Continuum Books/Berg.
———. 2002b. "Dona Berta's Garden: Reaching across the Colonial Boundary." *Etnográfica* 6(1): 77–91.
———. 2002/3. "'Agora podes saber o que é ser pobre': identificações e diferenciações no mundo da lusotopia." *Lusotopie* 10: 215–224.
———. 2003. *O homem na família*. Lisboa: Imprensa de Ciências Sociais.
———. 2004. "Cisma e continuidade em Moçambique." In *A persistência da história*, ed. Clara Carvalho and João de Pina Cabral. Lisbon: Imprensa de Ciências Sociais, pp. 375–392.
———. 2005a. "Crises de fraternidade: Literatura e etnicidade no Moçambique pós-colonial." *Horizontes Antropológicos* 24: 229–253.
———. 2005b. "The Future of Social Anthropology." *Social Anthropology* 13(2): 119–128.
———. 2007. "Aromas de Urze e de Lama: Reflexões sobre o gesto etnográfico." *Etnográfica* 11(1): 191–212.
———. 2008. "Recorrências Antroponímicas Lusófonas." *Etnográfica* 12(1): 5–16.
———. 2010a. "Xará: Namesakes in Southern Mozambique and Bahia (Brazil)." *Ethnos* 73 (3): 323–345.
———. 2010b. "The Truth of Personal Names." *Journal of the Royal Anthropological Society* 16(2): 297–312.
———. 2012. "Charles Boxer and the Race Equivoque." In *Racism and Ethnic Relations in the Portuguese-Speaking World*, ed. Francisco Bethencourt and Adrian Pearce. London: Oxford University Press for British Academy, pp. 99–112.
———. 2013a. 'The Core of Affects: Namer and Named in Bahia (NE Brazil)." *Journal of the Royal Anthropological Institute* 19(1): 75–101.
———. 2013b. "The Two Faces of Mutuality: Contemporary Themes in Anthropology", *Anthropological Quarterly* 86(1): 257–274.
Pitt-Rivers, Julian. 1973. "The Kith and the Kin." In *The Character of Kinship*, ed. Jack Goody. Cambridge: Cambridge University Press, pp. 89–105.

Quine, W.V. 1944/1996. *O sentido da nova lógica*. Rio de Janeiro: Livraria Martins.
Reis, Eduardo. 1948. *Duarte Barbosa: pioneiro revelador dos costumes das Índias: relação biográfica*. Macao: Imprensa Nacional.
Sahlins, Marshall. 1972. *Stone-Age Economics*. London: Tavistock.
Sansi-Roca, Roger. 2007. "The Fetish in the Lusophone Atlantic." In *Cultures of the Lusophone Black Atlantic*, ed. Nancy Naro, Roger Sansi-Roca, and David H. Treece. New York: Palgrave-Macmillan, pp. 19–39.
Schwartz, Roberto. 2000/1977. *Ao vencedor as batatas*. São Paulo: Duas Cidades/Editora 34.
Sousa Santos, Boaventura de. 2001. "Entre Prospero e Caliban: Colonialismo, pós colonialismo e interidentidade." In *Entre ser e estar: Raízes, percursos e discursos de identidade*, ed. Maria Irene Ramalho and António Sousa Ribeiro. Porto: Edições Afrontamento.
Spinoza, Baruch. 2006/1664. *Lettres sur le Mal: Correspondance avec Blyenbergh*. Paris: Gallimard.
Stern, Daniel .N. 2004. *The Present Moment in Psychotherapy and Everyday Life*. New York: Norton.
Strathern, Marilyn. 1988. *The Gender of the Gift: Problems with Women and Problems with Society in Melanesia*. Berkeley: University of California Press.
Thompson, Ross A. 1998. "Empathy and its Origins in Early Development." In *Intersubjective Communication and Emotion in Early Ontogenesis*, ed. Stein Bråten. Cambridge: Cambridge University Press, pp. 144–157.
Tolkien, John Ronald Reuel. 1995/1981. *The Letters of J. R. R. Tolkien*, ed. Humphrey Carpenter. New York: Harper Collins Publishers.
Tomasello, Michael. 2008. *Origins of Human Communication*. Cambridge, Mass.: MIT Press.
Toren, Christina. 1999. *Mind, Materiality and History: Explorations in Fijian Ethnography*. London: Routledge.
Traube, Elizabeth. 1986. *Cosmology and Social Life: Ritual Exchange among the Mambai of East Timor*. Chicago, Ill.: University of Chicago Press.
Viveiros de Castro, Eduardo. 2009. *Métaphysiques canibales*. Paris: PUF.

Chapter 13

An Anthropologist of the World
Interview with Ulf Hannerz, September 2012

Dominic Boyer

Q: More so than most of us, Ulf, you are truly an "anthropologist of the world." And, it so happens that these are very challenging times, but also in some ways very inspiring times, for the world. The Washington Consensus, for example, seems more fragile than ever before and an anthropologist is set to lead the World Bank for the first time. Yet austerity reigns and the eurozone is in turmoil. Latin America is blossoming with new social and political experiments. Yet the United States seems in the grip of slow and possibly very ugly decline. I wanted to ask you to reflect on anthropology's role in today's world. Or, not to be so parochial, what the ethnographic and conceptual work of transnationally oriented human scientists (forgive the German conceit!) could contribute to the navigation of times like these. Is this a good time to resurrect the 1980s image of anthropology as cultural critique, for example?

A: I will certainly follow the activities of the World Bank with renewed interest (although the alternative, which would have been a Nigerian woman economist heading it, would have been appealing as well).

I think "cultural critique" remains one of the uses of anthropology—and of course, although it was revived in the 1980s, it goes way back, to Margaret Mead and Bronislaw Malinowski. But overall, I would want to see more experimentation with diverse styles and genres in anthropological writing—particularly in reaching out to audiences outside the discipline, in or outside academia. At present, anthropologists, not least in the United States, seem to be writing almost entirely for each other. It is striking that a number of historians seem to do so much better in writing for wider readerships—I am thinking of people like Timothy Garton Ash, Simon Schama, the late Tony Judt, or Niall Ferguson (whatever one may think of some of the latter's political stances). But then it is also notable that these are all British immigrants, or commuters, to the American academic scene.

Thank you for describing me as an "anthropologist of the world." I really do think that anthropology as a truly worldwide discipline in its research interests has a particular public role. I just read Amin Maalouf's *Disordered World*, an essay on various troubles now facing humanity—Maalouf is a Lebanese writer, long in the Paris diaspora, so the book has an emphasis on the changing Arab world. Anyway, he sees coping with cultural differences as perhaps *the* major challenge, globally and locally, and suggests that if everyone were to become enduringly passionate about one culture other than his or her own, the result would be "a closely woven cultural web covering the whole planet." Now that is obviously a utopian idea, but it struck me that anthropologists, with their commitments to widespread fields, could be seen as a kind of avant-garde here. But then they have to find ways of disseminating their understandings effectively, in an information landscape which is now very different from that of the classic anthropology of "other cultures." On the one hand, knowledge (or misunderstandings) can now flow through so many parallel or competing channels; on the other hand, I am afraid the result of current media saturation is often more narcissism rather than more cosmopolitanism. Will such efforts at informing the public about the world elsewhere take the form of cultural critique? Sometimes, no doubt. But I am reminded of Marshall Sahlins' comment somewhere that we should not make it seem as if other people have constructed their lives for our purposes, in answer to the evils of Western society. This could turn into only a higher form of narcissism.

Q: Ulf, let's talk a bit more about reaching out to wider audiences through our writing. Two questions come immediately to mind given your career: the first is whether you feel there are particular experimental lessons to be learned from Scandinavian anthropology, where, perhaps especially in Norway and Sweden, anthropology has shown a remarkable capacity to participate in public debate. The second question is what, if anything, you think we can learn from news journalists today about communicating our forms of expertise to wider publics. One tends to hear lamentation that news media are not more interested in what we have to say or in how we say it. But of course this way of thinking amounts at some point to its own alibi.

A: I think our Norwegian colleagues have been particularly successful here, but to what extent there are "experimental lessons" I am not quite sure. In part I think they have simply tried harder. One of them had a regular newspaper column for quite some time, in the 1970s and 1980s or so, and then in the next generation there were several who took an interest in reaching a wider public, and who may also have stimulated each other. This has been true not only of anthropologists; I think a number of other Norwegian social scientists have been noticeable as public commentators as well.

Now for one thing one should note that even these anthropologists have in large part offered views on Norwegian affairs, not so much on matters relating to other countries or cultures (although immigration and minority issues have been an important theme). But I think one should also keep in mind that in terms of population size, the Scandinavian countries are all rather small. So I believe there is a kind of familiarity, accessibility, transparency that helps. Journalists have some sense of who is who in academia and vice versa. It is far from perfect, but scholars who want to cultivate media contacts have a better chance to do so.

There is another factor which I think I should emphasize. These are countries with strong national languages, which are weak internationally. My friend Abram de Swaan, a Dutch sociologist, has described the "world language system" as one of three tiers: English now far above anything else, then languages like French, Spanish, German, Arabic, Chinese, and a few others; then the third tier of languages which have few people using them as a second language. That obviously is where Scandinavian languages (as well as Dutch, and a great many others) belong. This means that Scandinavian academics who want to participate in international academic life must write in a foreign language, most likely English, and some get very good at this. The other side of the coin may be that they can then become fairly invisible at home, among audiences who do not habitually read English, and do not see those publications, in foreign journals or from foreign publishing houses, anyway. That may not worry these scholars—but if they care to reach home audiences, writing in the national language may become more of a conscious choice where one knows that one is very likely writing for another audience, outside the discipline, perhaps outside academic life altogether. I think there is a kind of informal division of labor here. Some people are more focused on their more or less global community of colleagues; others are more intent on contributing to public knowledge at home.

But then I see a current complication. Academic institutions, and politicians of higher education, in Europe and various other regions, now seem much more obsessed with streamlined research assessment exercises, publication rankings—what is sometimes referred to as the academic "audit culture"—than I believe is yet the case in the more pluralistic American academic world. I think it is in large part a matter of these institutions being state institutions, so you can impose rules on them very effectively from the top. And the way these measurements work, you climb in the rankings with articles in what are considered the leading international journals, which will be mostly in English (and published or at least distributed by a handful of commercial publishing houses, but that is to a degree another matter). The ranking procedure obviously in large part has its origins in the natural sciences and medicine, so not much thought is given to the built-in logics of different disciplines, especially those in the humanities and social sciences. This means that books are undervalued, and so are writings in other languages, for other audiences. There is, for one thing, a contradiction here. At least our Scandinavian national academic systems tend officially to celebrate the "three tasks" of universities: research, teaching, but also reaching out with its knowledge to the public. Now the first of these may at least seem rather easily measurable—that is at least the assumption behind those auditing procedures. There is some preoccupation, too, with ways of evaluating teaching quality. In contrast, there seems to be very little systematic attention to that third task: contributing to public knowledge. Unless the agents of audit culture get serious about this, the reasonable response, from university presidents all the way down to young faculty struggling to get tenure, will be not to bother much with that scholarly public service. So that could actually decline, and public culture would be further impoverished. I know universities in countries with severe societal problems—no names mentioned—where some more input into public debate from the human sciences would seem desirable, but when you point this out to a university leadership with its eyes on global ranking lists, you may not find good listeners.

Forgive me for dwelling on this, but I think it is a tendency we must really be concerned with. Your second question: what if anything can we learn from journalists? Now there is certainly a lot of variety in journalism. Some of it is dreadful, some very good. Academics and journalists may have a kind of habitual aversion to one another; for anthropologists that aversion easily comes to focus on foreign correspondents. Forgive me again, but when I engaged in a research project on the work of foreign correspondents some years ago (mostly those writing for print media of higher quality), I quite often found that they were doing very good work, considering the practical circumstances. And they could know much more than they had a chance to show. Especially in their feature stories, I think they were sometimes quite impressive in getting mini-ethnographies into one thousand words or so, in ways that could attract readers. So if we want to reach wider audiences ourselves with some of our work, I think we may do well to read at least some foreign correspondents, and some other investigative reporters, with some care. Not least would I think we should try to develop a sense of the "big picture," if we can credibly find one. Ethnographers still tend to handle miniatures well, but techniques of zooming may be a bit neglected.

Q: *I'd like to come back to the issue of audit culture in a moment. But while we're on the subject of publics and publicity (again in the German sense of* Öffentlichkeit), *do you see conditions changing, or new opportunities opening, with new media and social media? For example, there are now probably hundreds of anthropologists engaged in blogging of some form and this format could be one way of offering the thousand-word mini-ethnographies that you just mentioned. On the other hand, blogs, like other new and social media, tend to operate through networks rather than to address broad (anonymous) publics in the traditional sense. Another example: I enjoy Keith Hart's Facebook posts and he seems to take this work very seriously. But again, he may be posting only to an immediate audience of a few hundred people many of whom already belong to his professional networks. But that's rather symptomatic of our media environment today, no? The broadcast publicity that you and I grew up with is being hollowed out by these new meshes of lateral connectivity. Do we need to rethink our modes of public outreach accordingly? Or should the objective still be to write more op/ed pieces for newspapers or to find ways to get ourselves on TV?*

A: Perhaps we should be doing all these things—perhaps the one format I am really doubtful about is the kind of TV talk show where the entire idea seems to be to get people to shout at each other. But I do not think I am really technologically up to date on all new possibilities. Keith is an old friend of mine—we first ran into each other in the Cayman Islands over forty years ago, and have been in touch ever since. I think he has continued to be one of the original minds, the gadflies, of our field. But I believe it is true that his ongoing electronic networking effort is another instance of anthropologists talking mostly to each other. And I am afraid much blogging, in and out of anthropology, is more a matter of self-expression than of communication.

Now I am not sure why the *Mumbai Theatre Guide* and the *Circassian World Newsletter* appear regularly in my e-mail inbox. I never asked for them, and I certainly do not always, or even often, open these messages, but at least they are there, without my having to make the effort to seek them out. I think if we are really interested in contributing to public knowledge, we cannot sit and wait for audiences to come to us.

I would see more potential in collaborative enterprises, regularly feeding knowledge and opinion about particular themes, rather than some undifferentiated "public anthropology," to audiences who really define their interests in other ways than a curiosity about our discipline as such.

I see a need for a greater organizing effort here. In my most recent English-language book, *Anthropology's World* (2010), I devote a chapter to pointing to some "usable past" that we could still do well to think about again—contemporary anthropology seems to me too much inclined to amnesia. And there I devote some passages to the efforts of the "modernologist" Kon Wajiro in Japan and the "Mass Observation" movement in Great Britain in the 1920s and 1930s. Both of these basically recruited teams of amateur observers to do ethnographic observations in varied contexts, on current issues. I would not suggest we would want to return precisely to this, but the fact that there are now professional anthropologists everywhere might make possible a kind of collaborative "world watch" drawing on local knowledge, continued access and informed interpretation which hardly any news organization could match. In early 2011, during the Arab Spring, I found in my e-mail a flow of messages organized by the lively media anthropology section of EASA, the European Association of Social Anthropologists. Some of them were from people who had been right there, on Tahrir Square and other sites. Especially if we could develop a genre of "rapid ethnography," drawing probably on local anthropologists rather than parachutists, we might find new, interested audiences.

Q: I like this "collaborative world watch" idea very much and agree with you that there is an important opportunity for anthropology here parallel to the work of parachutists but also to networks of stringers. I'm deeply committed to the importance of long-form, "slow ethnography" as well, but just because we do that doesn't mean that we cannot also do rapid ethnography. These are different modes of writing for different venues. But to accomplish something on the scale of a collaborative world watch would require significant coordination and sponsorship I think. Could this be a project for our professional associations like AAA and EASA? In general, I'd be interested to know how you, as a former chair of EASA and long-time participant in AAA, feel that professional associations can best contribute to the intellectual vitality of the field. Could they be doing more than they are?

A: Certainly, as with so many things, this is not an "either-or," but a "both-and" matter: trying, if we can, to do both slow and rapid ethnography. I am sure both AAA and EASA, as major regional organizations, can play a part in supporting this sort of world-watch endeavor. But I think it is very important to get African, Asian and Latin American colleagues involved as well. My friend Virginia Dominguez, a former AAA president, tells me of a new outfit that she has played a part in initiating, an *Anthropologists Without Borders*, at present with a base in Brazil. Perhaps that could play a part in stimulating and coordinating rapid public ethnographic reporting as well.

Q: You wisely caution in Anthropology's World *that "the ideal of building intelligibility in the world … does not seem to be fully realizable as long as opportunities for observation, reflection and reporting remain very unevenly distributed, and unevenly controlled." Perhaps this gets us back to the less than optimal institutional conditions under which academic and non-academic anthropology is practiced in many parts of the world. How can one strive for the kind of global "world-building anthropology" you have in mind in a world still defined by uneven opportunities?*

A: That is a difficult question. Again, perhaps that new head of the World Bank can do something to support capacity-building in more places, in those social sciences which are most relevant to the purposes of his institution. I do hear of scholars in the more prosperous parts of the world seeking research grants which would also cover the collaboration with local colleagues in their fields in countries where there is little or no funding available. Yet there is the risk in such arrangements that the research agenda is set by the more affluent partner, and so it could become, to put it bluntly, another variety of "academic colonialism." And in the current situation, I doubt that much funding of this kind is readily available anyway.

One might also hope that in some of those countries that are now rising in the world, some of the new resources can go to a broad support for research institutions, and institutions cultivating public knowledge. That could at least diversify scholarly interests and perspectives. It is true, for one thing, that several of the BRICS countries already have strong anthropological traditions; it would be good if these could also expand to be a little less preoccupied with "anthropology at home," to contribute more to the "closely woven cultural web" about which I quoted Amin Maalouf before—that global cross-cutting of points of view.

Then certainly there is also a question of what we can do perhaps on a slightly more everyday basis, on this side of more utopian schemes. This involves things like scrutinizing our reading habits—Which journals do we read? Where do our books come from?—and using invitations for example to visiting scholars and to conferences in such a way that they do not always routinely strengthen existing center–periphery structures.

Q: Do you also share the worry that the cosmopolitan aspirations of anthropology are being undermined by the rise of what Strathern and others have termed "audit culture" in universities across the world? In your experience, how have "new public management"-style regimes impacted the way anthropology is practiced?

A: I would not claim to have a good overview of how all that actually works out. Audit culture has indeed spread widely, but the forms may vary. I remember that in the early 2000s, when my own department was undergoing the first Swedish assessment exercise, and I was involved in that at the ground-floor level, it all ended with a brief meeting of representatives of departments with the director-general of the national universities board, and I told her that I thought it had all turned out rather better than I had feared, after listening to the lamentations of British academic friends about their earlier experiences. And she smiled and said, "The first thing we decided was not to do it the British way." So there have been differences between places, and over time. Moreover, I would not be sure about how policies actually work their way through structures in different national and other contexts. I suspect that in some places the auditing is performed, measures are taken and reported—and then nothing happens, except that the administrative workload has increased. "New public management" shades into old public mismanagement.

But that said, to get to the specific impact on anthropology, I do not believe it is a good influence. To consider first its implications for graduate training, the imposition of standard time schedules for the completion of a doctorate, regardless of discipline, which is often part of the audit culture package, does not go well with a kind of professional cosmopolitanism which involves going to live in another country, even among those proverbial exotic Bongo-Bongo, learning a new language, and what have you. I think this is one factor—there are certainly others—which now pushes in the direction of more "anthropology at home." Some years ago, when I was invited to examine a Ph.D. candidate at a British university, I found that she looked strikingly young (and found that she was indeed younger than I had been when I got my doctorate—I have not been so used to that). It was a very good thesis, and she had completed it well before the deadline, but she had done her field work pretty much across the street.

As I said before, I still think audit culture has struck more uniformly across Europe, and in some other places, than it has in the United States. But then curiously, some of the decision-makers in higher education seem not necessarily to be very well informed about the facts of American academic life, although they find that American universities tend to rank highly on those ranking lists which they take very seriously, and must therefore be taken as models. So for one thing, they apparently often believe that those standard times for graduate degrees come from there. When, on the other hand, I ask my American friends in major departments if their students actually do their graduate training and finish their theses in four years, they seem all to shake their heads.

I also remember one prominent American (but British-trained) colleague, when we were at the same conference in Australia, warning local colleagues there that if their universities dutifully started turning out Ph.D.s with only a few years' training, these young scholars would be unable to compete for academic jobs in their own country; these jobs would go to Americans coming in with better qualifications.

Well, what about later career stages? It is sometimes said that at least after you have tenure, or whatever is its nearest equivalent, you can afford to do the research you want, change your research interests— perhaps go to other places for research than where you have been before. But things like research assessment exercises may impose peculiar rhythms on academic work at such levels as well. I hear of pressures to get things published, by whatever journal or press, even when they might have benefited from being allowed a little more time. I doubt that extensive retooling, such as reading up on a new area, taking on another language and other such activities, would be warmly welcomed by the captains of auditing either.

I certainly have no trouble with the principle that we must be accountable for the work we do, whether in teaching, research, or contributions to public knowledge. It is OK, too, if people at academic management levels get better informed about who does what, how much and how well, on the shop floor. Neither am I in favor of Ph.D. theses taking forever. But assessment procedures need to be better attuned to the pluralism of scholarship and its disciplines. Clearly there is now a fairly widespread understanding of that, at least in the human sciences, although it is not so certain how receptive policy-makers will be to this understanding.

Q: Cosmopolitanism has been a conceptual or theoretical interest of yours for some time as well as a problem of ethics and practice. At the risk of framing this too dualistically, is there a broader lesson to be drawn here as to how Ulf Han-

nerz navigates the relationship between anthropological theory and practice? What are the theoretical and practical issues of greatest concern to you today?

A: My engagement with cosmopolitanism really began rather accidentally. In the mid-1980s, when I gave a talk at Berkeley on my growing interest in globalization, Paul Rabinow, who was in the audience, asked if I had thought about cosmopolitanism. I had to reply that I had not (it later turned out that he had). But that irritated me, and I realized that I should. So a little later, for a rather unusual academic get-together called the "First International Conference on the Olympics and East/West and South/North Cultural Exchanges in the World System" in Seoul in 1987, I pulled together my thoughts in a paper which was really a sort of stream-of-consciousness piece. Then that paper made its way into one high-visibility publication, and hitting the first wave of revived interest in cosmopolitanism in several disciplines, it became one of my most-cited publications. I want to mention that history of the paper partly to show that it was done for a gathering engaged with cultural issues, but especially because it was done in what was still the Cold War era. (There was a Soviet sport sociologist among the participants in the Seoul conference, and he was followed around by South Korean plainclothes detectives with walkie-talkies.) Then in the 1990s that rapid growth of interest in cosmopolitan theory and practice occurred, with more of an emphasis on the ethics and politics of it all, in a period of optimism about what the world could do together. I am afraid in the early 2000s Vladimir Putin, George W. Bush, and Osama bin Laden together dampened that optimism. Anyway, so when I came back to cosmopolitanism, a main question seemed to be how the more cultural-experiential-esthetic dimension of the concept that I had been dealing with related to the more ethical-civic-political dimension. When I gave a talk on this to a cultural studies group in Tokyo, my colleagues there said there was no native term in Japanese that really covered both dimensions. So is this just a sort of disease of western languages, to conflate the two? I think they can at times exist quite separately, and potentially there can even be a certain tension between them, but I would also think they are often mutually supportive.

OK, that got to be quite long. What am I trying to do now? I have a long-term interest in another post-Cold War development, the genre of global future scenarios that began with people like Francis Fukuyama and Samuel Huntington on the academic side, and Thomas Friedman and Robert Kaplan on the journalist side, and which has continued to grow ever since. This is not just an interest in these as texts, to be critiqued as such, but also in their significance in forming a global public consciousness; mostly American in origin but translated into many languages, ubiquitously available in airport book stalls, remembered through those seductive one-liners and sound bites: "the end of history," "the clash of civilizations," "the world is flat." A blurb for the German edition of Huntington's book describes its thesis rather pithily as *"Kulturknalltheorie"* — I think that suggests something about why an anthropologist might be provoked by the kind of "culturespeak" you find in many of these scenarios.

Then as another current interest, which I have been developing particularly in a collaboration with Andre Gingrich in Vienna, I am exploring the anthropology of "small countries" (like the Scandinavian ones, and Austria). We had a small conference recently in Landskrona, a southern Swedish town which is close to my summer home but also conveniently close to the Copenhagen airport, so colleagues could fly in from places like New Zealand, Singapore and the United Arab Emirates to participate — we do not want this exercise to become too Eurocentric. We are certainly not aiming to identify some essence of smallness, but there are interesting family resemblances. At best, I think one may find a certain ease of access in networks internally (see what I said about Norway before), and some cosmopolitan inclinations in external relations. But certainly there may be some recurrent less attractive qualities as well.

Well, that may be mostly over on a theoretical side. But I think you can see that those, too, fit into my general concern with the way the world comes together, in academia and elsewhere — and the part anthropology can have in that. It would be nice if the world was flat, a more level playing field, but we are not there now. Even the order of production and circulation of those global future scenarios, and the debate over them, shows that.

Q: It seems to me as though there is an attractive symmetry between these two projects. On the one hand, you are looking at the epistemic work of envisioning "the global," and on the other hand, you are recognizing the enduring plurality of smallness in the world today. Does this balancing of large and small scales perhaps say something about the state of anthropology's own scenario building and "culturespeak" today? As one of anthropology's first analysts of the dynamics of globalization, I'd like to ask you to comment on the status of "the global as an analytic category for anthropology today. Where is it still useful, where less so?

A: I remember that in an afterword I wrote for a book on "globalization and identity" in the late 1990s, I suggested that the time was quickly coming when globalization as such might not be a focal research interest any longer. Whatever it may stand for would be normalized as a part of the significant context of a variety of kinds of studies. But it was never really a favorite term of mine. I have used "the global ecumene" some number of times, to indicate a more wide-reaching sociocultural openness, drawing on a notion that has deep historical roots. But apart from that, I have often preferred the term "transnational" to refer to phenomena that cross national boundaries—which certainly still does not mean that they are truly "global." That, then, has been a way of breaking out of the straitjacket of methodological nationalism which I think is still quite strong in many disciplines, although perhaps less so in anthropology. I think once anthropology broke out of its own commitment to "the local," its ethnographic discovery procedures helped it follow linkages wherever they took it.

It is true that I have had a certain interest in small-scale things, and in scale generally. I took an early interest in symbolic interactionism in more or less classic sociology, for insights into cultural process, and I tend to follow writings on micro/macro issues in social theory. But our "small countries" are not really small-scale in that sense. A country with ten million inhabitants is still *relatively* small, compared to China, or the United States, or Germany. We are concerned with scale in a comparative sense, but then we also want to explore what "country" stands for now, socially and culturally. If many other disciplines may have been overly committed to a national framework, anthropology has done remarkably little at this level, and with that attractive contrast of "the global and the local," too many intermediate levels have tended to be disregarded. Perhaps the main organized effort to do an anthropology of "the national" is still that of the national character studies of the 1940s? But that was in large part a war effort, during World War II, with Americans using unconventional ethnographic methods (and questionable theories) to understand adversaries, or more or less problematic allies. So then "countries" become obvious units, and in large part, fairly naturally, this was about "large countries": Japan, Russia, and to an extent Britain.

What should we do about "the global" now? I am not sure it was ever that much of an analytical term in any strict sense. It may cover too many things—and at the same time it is unfortunate that in some minds it is so strongly tied only to expanding markets. But I think we should understand the value of having some number of words which sensitize us in a general and preliminary way to types of phenomena, qualities, problems, issues. "The global" will probably remain among those. And so will "culture," and "civilization," and no doubt a great many others.

Many of them will remain in wide public use, and if we want to be in contact with wider publics and their concerns, as commentators or for that matter as whistleblowers (in relation to some culturespeak, for one thing), avoiding their keywords may not be a wise strategy. Dominic, I think that takes us back to where we started this conversation?

Acknowledgments

This interview was originally published as Dominic Boyer, "An Interview with Ulf Hannerz," in *Public Culture*, Volume 26, no. 1, pp 187–199. Copyright, 2014, Duke University Press. All rights reserved. Republished by permission of the copyright holder, Duke University Press.

Publications by Ulf Hannerz
(reprinted and translated articles, newspaper articles, unpublished conference papers, etc. not included)

Books

1969
Soulside: Inquiries into Ghetto Culture and Community. New York: Columbia University Press.

1973
ed., *Lokalsamhället och omvärlden*. Stockholm: Rabén & Sjögren.

1974
Caymanian Politics: Structure and Style in a Changing Island Society. Stockholm Studies in Social Anthropology, no. 1.

1980
Exploring the City: Inquiries toward an Urban Anthropology. New York: Columbia University Press.

1982
ed., with Rita Liljeström and Orvar Löfgren, *Kultur och medvetande*. Stockholm: Akademilitteratur.

1983
Explorer la ville. Paris: Éditions de Minuit. (French edition of Exploring the City.)
Över gränser: studier i dagens socialantropologi. Lund: Liber.

1986
Exploración de la Ciudad. Mexico City: Fondo de Cultura Económica. (Spanish-language edition of Exploring the City.)

1990
ed., *Medier och kulturer*. Stockholm: Carlssons.

1992
Cultural Complexity: Studies in the Social Organization of Meaning. New York: Columbia University Press.
Culture, Cities and the World. Amsterdam: Centrum voor Grootstedelijk Onderzoek (pamphlet).
Esplorare la città. Bologna: Il Mulino. (Italian edition of Exploring the City.)

1996
Transnational Connections: Culture, People, Places. London: Routledge.

1998
Conexiones transnacionales. Madrid: Ediciones Cátedra. (Spanish edition of Transnational Connections.)
La complessità culturale. Bologna: Il Mulino. (Italian edition of Cultural Complexity.)

2000
ed., with Kjell Goldmann and Charles Westin, *Nationalism and Internationalism in the Post-Cold War Era*. London: Routledge.

2001
ed., *Flera fält i ett: socialantropologer om translokala fältstudier*. Stockholm: Carlssons.
La diversità culturale. Bologna: Il Mulino. (Italian selection from Transnational Connections.)

2004
Foreign News: Exploring the World of Foreign Correspondents. Chicago: University of Chicago Press.
ed., *Antropologi/Journalistik: Om sätt att beskriva världen*. Lund: Studentlitteratur.
Soulside: Inquiries into Ghetto Culture and Community. Chicago: University of Chicago Press. (Second edition, with new afterword.)

2006
Odkrywanie miasta. Krakow: Wydawnictwo Uniwersytetu Jagiellonskiego. (Polish translation of Exploring the City.)
Powiazania transnarodowe. Krakow: Wydawnictwo Uniwersytetu Jagiellonskiego. (Polish translation of *Transnational Connections*.)

2010
Anthropology's World: Life in a Twenty-first Century Discipline. London: Pluto Press.
La complexité culturelle: Études de l'organisation sociale de la signification. Bernin: À la Croisée. (French translation of Cultural Complexity, new foreword.)

2011
Café du Monde: platser, vägar och människor i världsvimlet. Stockholm: Carlssons.

2012
Il mondo dell'antropologia. Bologna: Il Mulino. (Italian translation of *Anthropology's World*.)

Articles and Book Chapters

1966
The Anthropologist and Technical Aid Programs. *Ethnos*, 31 (supplement): 105–110.

1967
Gossip, Networks and Culture in a Black American Ghetto. *Ethnos*, 32: 35–60.

1968
Comment on Marcus S. Goldstein, *Anthropological Research, Action, and Education in Modern Nations: With Special Reference to the USA. Current Anthropology*, 9: 259–260.
The Rhetoric of Soul: Identification in Negro Society. *Race*, 9: 453–465.

1969
Den mångtydiga fattigkulturen. *Häften för Kritiska Studier*, 1(2–3): 19–25.

1970
What Ghetto Males Are Like: Another Look. In Norman E. Whitten, Jr., and John F. Szwed, eds., *Afro-American Anthropology*. New York: Basic Books.
The Notion of Ghetto Culture. In John F. Szwed, ed., *Black Americans*. New York: Basic Books.
Language Variation and Social Relationships. *Studia Linguistica*, 24: 128–151.

1971
The Study of Afro-American Cultural Dynamics. *Southwestern Journal of Anthropology*, 27: 181–200.

1972
Reflections on the Anthropology of the Metropolis. In *Yearbook of the Ethnographic Museum of the University of Oslo, 1970*. Oslo: Universitetsforlaget.
Comment on Charles A. Valentine, Racism and Recent Anthropological Studies of U.S. Blacks. *Human Organization*, 31: 99–100.
Socialantropologin och språket. In Bengt Loman, ed., *Språk och samhälle*. Lund: Gleerups.

1973
The Second Language: An Anthropological View. *TESOL Quarterly*, 7: 235–248.
The Great Chernichewski. *Current Anthropology*, 14: 172.
Marginal Entrepreneurship and Economic Change in the Cayman Islands. *Ethnos*, 38: 101–112.

1974
Ethnicity and Opportunity in Urban America. In Abner Cohen, ed., *Urban Ethnicity* (ASA 12). London: Tavistock.

1975
Research in the Black Ghetto: A Review of the Sixties. *Journal of Asian and African Studies*, 9: 139–159.
Comment on Jennie-Keith Ross, Social Borders. *Current Anthropology*, 16: 65–66.

1976
Some Comments on the Anthropology of Ethnicity in the United States. In Frances Henry, ed., *Ethnicity in the Americas*. The Hague: Mouton.
Methods in an African Urban Study. *Ethnos*, 41: 68–98.

1977
"Ibo sover aldrig": etnicitet och ekonomi i en nigeriansk småstad. *Rapport från SIDA*, 8(4): 2–4.

1978
Problems in the Analysis of Urban Cultural Organization. In Joyce Aschenbrenner and Lloyd R. Collins, eds., *Processes of Urbanism*. The Hague: Mouton.
Comment on Gerald D. Berreman, Scale and Social Relations. *Current Anthropology*, 19: 238–239.

1979
Två språk, två grupper, två kulturer. In Astrid Stedje and Peter af Trampe, eds., *Tvåspråkighet*. Stockholm: Akademilitteratur.
Town and Country in Southern Zaria: A View from Kafanchan. In Aidan Southall, ed., *Small Urban Centers in Rural Development in Africa*. Madison: African Studies Program, University of Wisconsin.
Complex Societies and Anthropology: A Perspective from 1979. *Ethnos*, 44: 217–241.

1981
Leva med mångfalden. In Kjell Öberg, ed. *Att leva med mångfalden: en antologi från Diskrimineringsutredningen*. Stockholm: Liber.
Sverige som invandrarsamhälle: några antropologiska frågeställningar. In Eva M. Hamberg and Tomas Hammar, eds., *Invandringen och framtiden*. Stockholm: Liber.
The Management of Danger. *Ethnos*, 46: 19–46.
Erich H. Jacoby, 1903–1979. *Ethnos*, 46: 147–151.

1982
Etnografie en het karakter van de stad. In Carolien Bouw, Frank Bovenkerk, Kees Bruin and Lodewijk Brunt, eds., *Hoe weet je dat?* Amsterdam: Uitgeverij De Arbeiderspers.
Washington and Kafanchan: A View of Urban Anthropology. *L'Homme*, 22(4): 25–36.

with Tomas Gerholm, Introduction: The Shaping of National Anthropologies. *Ethnos*, 47: 5–35.
Twenty Years of Swedish Social Anthropology: 1960–1980. *Ethnos*, 47: 150–171.
Delkulturerna och helheten. In Ulf Hannerz, Rita Liljeström and Orvar Löfgren, eds., *Kultur och medvetande*. Stockholm: Akademilitteratur.
Tjugo år med svensk socialantropologi: 1960–1980. In *Ymer '82: Antropologisk Forskning*. Stockholm: Svenska Sällskapet för Antropologi och Geografi/Esselte.

1984
Tools of Identity and Imagination. In Anita Jacobson-Widding, ed., *Identity: Personal and Socio-Cultural*. Stockholm: Almqvist & Wiksell International.

1985
History and Anthropology in Scandinavia: An Introduction. *Ethnos*, 50: 165–167.
City. In Adam Kuper and Jessica Kuper, eds., *Encyclopedia of the Social Sciences*. London: Routledge and Kegan Paul.
Structures for Strangers: Ethnicity and Institutions in a Colonial Nigerian Town. In Aidan Southall, Peter J.M. Nas and Ghaus Ansari, eds., *City and Society*. Leiden: Institute of Cultural and Social Studies.
The Informal Sector: Some Remarks. In Harald O. Skar, ed., *Anthropological Contributions to Planned Change and Development*. Gothenburg Studies in Social Anthropology, no. 8.

1986
Theory in Anthropology: Small Is Beautiful? The Problem of Complex Cultures. *Comparative Studies in Society and History*, 28: 362–367.
Immigrants in Sweden: An Introduction. *Ethnos*, 51: 145–147.

1987
Anthropology's Other Press: Training Ground, Playground, Underground. *Current Anthropology*, 28: 214–219.
The World in Creolisation. *Africa*, 57: 546–559.

1988
Kriterier för att identifiera ett kulturarv. In Per Sörbom, ed., *Kulturen vi ärvde*. Stockholm: Forskningsrådsnämnden, report 88:8.
The World as a Multicultural Society. In *Research on International Issues*. Stockholm: Faculty of Social Sciences, Stockholm University.
American Culture: Creolized, Creolizing. In Erik Åsard, ed., *American Culture: Creolized, Creolizing and other lectures from the NAAS Biennial Conference in Uppsala*, May 28–31, 1987. Uppsala: Swedish Institute for North American Studies.

1989
Notes on the Global Ecumene. *Public Culture*, 1(2): 66–75.
Culture between Center and Periphery: Toward a Macroanthropology. *Ethnos*, 54: 200–216.

1990
Cosmopolitans and Locals in World Culture. *Theory, Culture and Society*, 7: 237–251.
Genomsyrade av medier: kulturer, samhällen och medvetanden av i dag. In Ulf Hannerz, ed., *Medier och kulturer*. Stockholm: Carlssons.

1991
Scenarios for Peripheral Cultures. In Anthony D. King, ed., *Culture, Globalization and the World-System*. London: Macmillan.
Den "egna" kulturen? *Norsk Antropologisk Tidsskrift*, 2(1): 15–16.

1992
Center–Periphery Relations and Creolization in Contemporary Culture. In Annick Sjögren and Lena Janson, eds., *Culture and Management*. Botkyrka: Swedish Immigration Institute and Museum.
with Orvar Löfgren, Nationen i den globala byn. *Kulturella perspektiv*, 1: 21–29.
Stockholm: Doubly Creolizing. In Åke Daun, Billy Ehn and Barbro Klein, eds., *To Make the World Safe for Diversity*. Botkyrka: Swedish Immigration Institute and Museum.
The Global Ecumene as a Network of Networks. In Adam Kuper, ed., *Conceptualizing Society*. London: Routledge.
Networks of Americanization. In Rolf Lundén and Erik Åsard, eds., *Networks of Americanization*. Uppsala: Department of English, Uppsala University.

1993
The Cultural Role of World Cities. In Anthony Cohen and Katsuyoshi Fukui, eds., *Humanising the City?* Edinburgh: Edinburgh University Press.
Mediations in the Global Ecumene. In Gísli Pálsson, ed., *Beyond Boundaries: Understanding, Translation and Anthropological Discourse*. London: Berg.
Hvilken globale kultur? Seks teser om globalisering, kultur og mennesker. *Samtiden*, 4: 2–9.
When Culture is Everywhere: Reflections on a Favorite Concept. *Ethnos*, 58: 95–111.
with Orvar Löfgren, Introduction: Defining the National. *Ethnos*, 58: 15–16.
The Withering Away of the Nation? An Afterword. *Ethnos*, 58: 377–391.

1994
with Orvar Löfgren, The Nation in the Global Village. *Cultural Studies*, 8: 198–207.
Sophiatown: The View from Afar. *Journal of Southern African Studies*, 20: 181–193.
Mångfalden och världsvimlet. In Kaj Århem, ed., *Den antropologiska erfarenheten*. Stockholm: Carlssons.

1995
Continuity and Change in the Global Ecumene. In James W. Fernandez and Milton B. Singer, eds., *The Conditions of Reciprocal Understanding*. Chicago: Center for International Studies, University of Chicago.

"Kultur" in einer vernetzten Welt. Zur Revision eines ethnologischen Begriffes. In Wolfgang Kaschuba, ed., *Kulturen - Identitäten - Diskurse*. Berlin: Akademie Verlag.

1996
En väskas liv. In Stig Nordqvist, ed., *Farande och fraktande*. Stockholm: Kommunikationsforskningsberedningen.
Complex Society. In Alan Barnard and Jonathan Spencer, eds., *Encyclopedia of Social and Cultural Anthropology*. London: Routledge.
The Reorganization of Culture in Space. *Environment and Planning A*, 28: 1937–1939.
The Network of Perspectives: Between the Division of Labor and Occupational Subcultures. *Nordisk Arkitekturforskning (Nordic Journal of Architectural Research)*, 9(3): 7–13.

1997
Fluxos, fronteiras, híbridos: palavras-chave da antropologia transnacional. *Mana* (Rio de Janeiro), 3(1): 7–39.
Cultural Diversity in the Global Ecumene. In Partha Dasgupta, Karl-Göran Mäler and Alessandro Vercelli, eds., *The Economics of Transnational Commons*. Oxford: Oxford University Press, 1997.
Borders. *International Social Science Journal*, 154: 537–548.

1998
Other Transnationals: Perspectives Gained from Studying Sideways. *Paideuma*, 44: 109–123.
Of Correspondents and Collages. *Anthropological Journal on European Cultures*, 7: 91–109.
Transnational Research. In H. Russell Bernard, ed., *Handbook of Methods in Anthropology*. Walnut Creek, CA: Altamira Press.
Reporting from Jerusalem. *Cultural Anthropology*, 13: 548–574.

1999
Epilogue: On Some Reports from a Free Space. In Birgit Meyer and Peter Geschiere, eds., *Globalization and Identity*. Oxford: Blackwell.
Views of Culture in Globalization Studies. In Paul Gilroy, Lawrence Grossberg and Chantal Mouffe, eds, *The Contemporary Study of Culture*. Vienna: Turia und Kant.
Touring Soweto: Culture and Memory in Urban South Africa. In Louise Nyström, ed., *City and Culture*. Stockholm: Swedish Urban Environment Council.
Reflections on Varieties of Culturespeak. *European Journal of Cultural Studies*, 2: 393–407.
Världsbild, kultursyn, medborgarskap. In Erik Amnå and Anna Brink, eds, *Globalisering*. Stockholm: Demokratiutredningen. (Government Commission of Inquiry into Democracy.)

Studying Townspeople, Studying Foreign Correspondents: Experiences of Two Approaches to Africa. In Hans Peter Hahn and Gerd Spittler, eds., *Afrika und die Globalisierung*. Hamburg: LIT Verlag.
La cultura popular y la ciudad. *Arxius de Sociologia* (Valencia), 3: 69–86.
Cultural Debates in the Global Ecumene. *The Stockholm Journal of East Asian Studies*, 10: 1–15.
Comment on Christoph Brumann, "Writing for Culture: Why a Successful Concept Should not be Discarded." *Current Anthropology*, 40: S18–S19.
Comment on Jonathan Friedman, Rhinoceros 2. *Current Anthropology*, 40: 689–691.

2000
with Kjell Goldmann and Charles Westin, Introduction: Nationalism and Internationalism in the Post-Cold War Era. In Kjell Goldmann, Ulf Hannerz and Charles Westin, eds., *Nationalism and Internationalism in the Post-Cold War Era*. London: Routledge.

2001
Thinking about Culture in a Global Ecumene. In James Lull, ed., *Culture in the Communication Age*. London: Routledge.
Introduktion: när fältet blir translokalt. In Ulf Hannerz, ed., *Flera fält i ett*. Stockholm: Carlssons.
Dateline Tokyo: Telling the World about Japan. In Brian Moeran, ed., *Asian Media Productions*. London: Curzon.
Anthropology. *International Encyclopedia of the Social and Behavioral Sciences*. Oxford: Elsevier.
Center–Periphery Relationships. *International Encyclopedia of the Social and Behavioral Sciences*. Oxford: Elsevier.

2002
Among the Foreign Correspondents: Reflections on Anthropological Styles and Audiences. *Ethnos*, 67: 57–74.
Where We Are, and Who We Want to Be. In Ulf Hedetoft and Mette Hjort, eds., *The Postnational Self: Belonging and Identity*. Minneapolis: University of Minnesota Press.
Epilogue: Changing Europe, Changing Ethnography. *Anthropological Journal on European Cultures*, 11: 207–214.

2003
Being There...and There...and There! Reflections on Multi-site Ethnography. *Ethnography*, 4: 229–244.
Gorillas, Geishas and Holy Places: Variations in the Embedding of Foreign News. In Jan Hallenberg, Bertil Nygren and Alexa Robertson, eds., *Transitions: In Honour of Kjell Goldmann*. Stockholm: Department of Political Science, Stockholm University.
Several Sites in One. In Thomas Hylland Eriksen, ed., *Globalisation*. London: Pluto Press.

Foreword. In Dorle Dracklé, Iain Edgar and Thomas K. Schippers, eds., *Educational Histories of European Social Anthropology*. Oxford: Berghahn.
Macro-scenarios: Anthropology and the Debate over Contemporary and Future Worlds. *Social Anthropology*, 11: 169–187.

2004
Cosmopolitanism. In David Nugent and Joan Vincent, eds., *Companion to the Anthropology of Politics*. Oxford: Blackwells.
Perspectives toward Cosmopolitanism as a Cultural Resource. *Interdisciplinary Cultural Studies* (University of Tokyo, Komaba), 8: 5–17.
Introduktion: mellan två skrivarkulturer. In Ulf Hannerz, ed., *Antropologi/Journalistik: Om sätt att beskriva världen*. Lund: Studentlitteratur.

2005
Speaking to Large Issues: The World, if it Is not in Pieces. In Richard A. Shweder and Byron Good, eds., *Clifford Geertz and His Colleagues: A Colloquy*. Chicago: University of Chicago Press.
Exploring the Current Cultural Order: Center–Periphery Relations, Creolization and Cosmopolitanism. In Eliezer Ben-Rafael and Yitzhak Sternberg, eds., *Comparing Modernities*. Leiden: Brill.
Two Faces of Cosmopolitanism: Culture and Politics. *Statsvetenskaplig Tidskrift*, 107: 199–213.

2006
Minnen och scenarier. Om vägar genom antropologins historia till framtiden. *Norsk Antropologisk Tidsskrift*, 17: 7–21.
Studying Down, Up, Sideways, Through, Backward, Forward, Away and at Home: Reflections on the Field Worries of an Expansive Discipline. In Simon M. Coleman and Peter J. Collins, eds., *Locating the Field*. Oxford: Berg.
with Dominic Boyer, Introduction: Worlds of Journalism. *Ethnography*, 7: 5–17.
Theorizing through the New World? Not Really. *American Ethnologist*, 33: 563–565.
Afterthoughts. In Andre Gingrich and Marcus Banks, eds., *Neo-nationalism in Europe and Beyond*. Oxford: Berghahn.
Foreign Correspondents as Flaneurs: Journalists' Views of Urban Life in the Global Ecumene. In Günter H. Lenz, Friedrich Ulfers and Antje Dallmann, eds., *Toward a New Metropolitanism*. Heidelberg: Universitätsverlag Winter.

2007
Foreign Correspondents and the Varieties of Cosmopolitanism. *Journal of Ethnic and Migration Studies*, 33: 299–311.
Geokulturella scenarier. In Bodil Axelsson and Johan Fornäs, eds., *Kulturstudier i Sverige*. Lund: Studentlitteratur.
Editorial: The Neo-liberal Culture Complex and Universities: A Case for Urgent Anthropology? *Anthropology Today*, 23(5): 1–2.

2008
Afterword: Anthropology's Global Ecumene. In Aleksandar Boskovic, ed., *Other People's Anthropologies*. Oxford: Berghahn.
Scenarios for the Twenty-first Century World. *Asian Anthropology* (Hong Kong), 7: 1–23.

2009
Geocultural Scenarios. In Peter Hedström and Björn Wittrock, eds., *Frontiers of Sociology*. Leiden: Brill.
Afterword: The Long March of Anthropology. In Mark-Anthony Falzon, ed., *Multi-sited Ethnography*. Farnham, Surrey: Ashgate.

2010
Afterthoughts: World Watching. *Social Anthropology*, 18: 448–453.
Diversity is Our Business. *American Anthropologist*, 112: 539–551.
"The First Draft of History": Notes on Events and Cultural Turbulence. In Hans Joas and Barbro Klein, eds., *The Benefit Of Broad Horizons*. Leiden: Brill.
La complexité culturale réactualisée: regards en arrière, regards en avant. In Ulf Hannerz, *La complexité culturelle: Études de l'organisation sociale de la signification*. Bernin: À la Croisée. (French translation of Cultural Complexity, new foreword.)
The World and the City since the Iron Curtain: Changing Habitats of Meaning. In Alexandra Bitusikova and Daniel Luther, eds., *Cultural and Social Diversity in Slovakia III. Global and Local in a Contemporary City*. Banska Bystrica: Matej Bel University, Institute of Social and Cultural Studies.

2011
"Frihet att", "Frihet från" och globalisering: En personlig erinring, och en till litet längre fram. *Informanten* (Aarhus), Forår: 12–13.
Operation Outreach: Anthropology and the Public in a World of Information Crowding. *Archivio Antropologico Mediterraneo*, 13(1): 11–17. http://www.archivioantropologicomediterraneo.it/
Comment on Stuart Alexander Rockefeller, Flow. *Current Anthropology*, 52: 570–571.
Kosmopolitismus. In Fernand Kreff, Eva-Maria Knoll and Andre Gingrich, eds., *Lexikon der Globalisierung*. Bielefeld: Transcript.

2012
Foreword: Creolisation on the Move. In Tommaso Sbriccoli and Stefano Jacoviello, eds., *Shifting Borders: European Perspectives on Creolisation*. Newcastle: Cambridge Scholars Publishing.
Anthropologists Everywhere: Getting to Know Your Colleagues. *Anthropology News*, 53(8): 20–21.
Opinions: What Business Anthropology Is, What it Might Become...and What, Perhaps, it Should not Be. (Contribution to a debate.) *Journal of Business Anthropology*, 1(2): 254–256. http://www.cbs.dk/jba/

2013
A Detective Story Writer: Exploring Stockholm as it once Was. *City & Society*, 25(2): 260–270.
Prologue: From this Southeast Asian Food Court, Food for Thought. In Joshua Barker, Erik Harms and Johan Lindquist, eds., *Figures of Southeast Asian Modernity*. Honolulu: University of Hawaii Press.

2014
Confessions of a Hoosier Anthropologist, *American Anthropologist*, 116(1): 169–172.

Reviews

1966
Harold W. Scheffler, Choiseul Island Social Structure. *Ethnos*, 31: 82.
John J. and Irma Honigmann, Eskimo Townsmen. *Ethnos*, 31: 182–183.
Margaret Mead and Martha Wolfenstein, eds., Childhood in Contemporary Cultures. *Ethnos*, 31: 183.
Feliks Gross, World Politics and Tension Areas. *Ethnos*, 31: 183–184.
Alfred G. Smith, ed., Communication and Culture. *Ethnos*, 31: 184.
J.S. Slotkin, ed., Readings in Early Anthropology. *Ethnos*, 31: 184–185.
E.E. Evans-Pritchard, Theories of Primitive Religion. *Ethnos*, 31: 187–188.
G.M. Mes, Now-men and Tomorrow-men and G.M. Mes, Mr. White Man, What Now? *Ethnos*, 31: 192.
Louis C. Faron, Hawks of the Sun. *Ethnos*, 31: 194.
Rupert East, ed., Akiga's Story. *Ethnos*, 31: 195–196.

1967
Leonard Plotnicov, Strangers to the City. *Ethnos*, 32: 173.

1969
Charles A. Valentine, Culture and Poverty. *Current Anthropology*, 10: 185–186.

1970
Fredrik Barth, ed., Ethnic Groups and Boundaries. *Acta Sociologica*, 13: 132–133.
R. Lincoln Keiser, The Vice Lords. *American Anthropologist*, 72: 1514–1516.

1971
August Meier and Elliott Rudwick, From Plantation to Ghetto. Man, 6: 713.

1972
Stuart T. Hauser, Black and White Identity Formation. Man, 7: 168–169.
Walter Dostal, ed., The Situation of the Indian in South America. *Ethnos*, 37: 195–196.

1973
Peter J. Wilson, Crab Antics. *Ethnos*, 38: 180–181.
Frank E. Manning, Black Clubs in Bermuda. *Ethnos*, 38: 185–187.

1974
Kenelm Burridge, Encountering Aborigines. *Ethnos*, 39: 179–181.
W.H. Clarke, Travels and Explorations in Yorubaland; Ebiegberi J. Alagoa and Adadonye Fombo, A Chronicle of Grand Bonny; and Obaro Ikime, The Isoko People. *Ethnos*, 39: 181–183.

1977
Fred W. Voget, A History of Ethnology. *Ethnos*, 42: 77–80.
Paul Riesman, Freedom in Fulani Social Life. *Ethnos*, 42: 223–226.

1979
John B. Haviland, Gossip, Reputation, and Knowledge in Zinacantan, and Ralph L. Rosnow and Gary Alan Fine, Rumor and Gossip. *Ethnos*, 44: 142–144.
David Popenoe, The Suburban Environment, and Börje Hanssen, Familj, Hushåll, Släkt. *Ethnos*, 44: 154–157.

1980
Adrian Peace, Choice, Class and Conflict. *Man*, 15: 212–213.
Murray J. Leaf, Man, Mind, and Science. *Ethnos*, 45: 270–271.
James Borchert, Alley Life in Washington, and George Reid Andrews, The Afro-Argentines of Buenos Aires 1800–1900. *Ethnos*, 47: 294–295.

1983
Jason Ditton, ed., The View from Goffman. *American Journal of Sociology*, 89: 223–225.
Charles Keyes, ed., Ethnic Change, and Anya Peterson Royce, Ethnic Identity. *Ethnos*, 48: 104–107.

1984
Ronald Frankenberg, ed., Custom and Conflict in British Society, and Jana Salat, Reasoning as Enterprise. *Ethnos*, 49: 312–313.

1985
Eric Hobsbawm and Terence Ranger, eds., The Invention of Tradition. *Ethnos*, 50: 326–328.

1986
Robin Ward and Richard Jenkins, eds., Ethnic Communities in Business. *International Journal of Urban and Regional Research*, 10: 149–150.

1987
Martin Bulmer, Neighbours: The Work of Philip Abrams. *Man*, 22: 191.

1988
Igor Kopytoff, ed., The African Frontier. *Ethnos*, 53: 134–136.
Sally Falk Moore, Social Facts and Fabrications. *Ethnos*, 53: 136–137.

1989
Leith Mullings, ed., Cities in the United States. *International Journal of Urban and Regional Research*, 13: 168–170.

1991
Allan Pred, Lost Words and Lost Worlds. *American Anthropologist*, 93: 1012–1013.

1992
Christopher Alan Waterman, Jùjú. *Ethnos*, 57: 245–246.

1993
Anthony D. King, Urbanism, Colonialism and the World Economy. *Social Anthropology*, 1: 155–156.
Arnold L. Epstein, Scenes from African Urban Life. *Man*, 28: 390–391.
James Fentress and Chris Wickham, Social Memory. *American Anthropologist*, 95: 470–471.

1994
Steel Bands, Rastas, and Mrs. Thatcher (review of Abner Cohen, Masquerade Politics). *Current Anthropology*, 35: 198–199.

1995
Alisdair Rogers and Steven Vertovec, eds., The Urban Context. *American Ethnologist*, 23: 154–155.

1996
George W. Stocking, Jr., After Tylor. *Ethnos*, 61: 276–278.

1999
Micaela di Leonardo, Exotics at Home. *Journal of the Royal Anthropological Institute*, 5: 678.

2002
C.W. Watson, Multiculturalism. *Journal of the Royal Anthropological Institute*, 8: 412–413.

2003
Jeremy MacClancy, ed., Exotic No More. *Ethnic and Racial Studies*, 26: 766–767.

2005
Theodore C. Bestor, Tsukiji: The Fish Market at the Center of the World. *Journal of Japanese Studies*, 31: 428–431.
Jerry Gershenhorn, Melville J. Herskovits and the Racial Politics of Knowledge. *Ethnic and Racial Studies*, 28: 952–953.

2006
Aihwa Ong and Stephen J. Collier, eds., Global Assemblages: Technology, Politics, and Ethics as Anthropological Problems. *American Anthropologist*, 108: 254–255.

Interviews

1978
Black and White in the American City. Interview by Al Simon, Voice of America. In Peter I. Rose, ed., *Views from Abroad*. Washington, DC: Voice of America Forum Series.

1995
Towards a Social Anthropology of Culture: An Interview with the EASA Chairman, Ulf Hannerz. By Susana Matos Viegas and Nuno Porto. *EASA Newsletter*, 15: 4–6.

1999
Os limites de nosso auto-retrato. Antropologia urbana e globalizacao. By Fernando Rabossi. *Mana*, 5(1): 149–155.

2001
Interview with Professor Ulf Hannerz. By Shahram Khosravi. *Ensanshenasi* (Anthropology, in Persian), 1(1): 110–115.

2003
On Transnational Awareness: An Interview with Ulf Hannerz. By Peter Probst. *NAB: Newsletter of African Studies at Bayreuth University*, 2(1): 6–11.

2004
"Existe la posibilidad de ver el mundo como una gran comunidad imaginada." By Sergio López Martínez. *Revista de Antropología Iberoamericana*, 3: 91–98.

2007
A Transnational Cosmopolitan: An Interview with Ulf Hannerz. By Terhi Rantanen. *Global Media and Communication*, 3(1): 11–27.

2008
Questioning the Cosmopolitan: Ulf Hannerz about the Internally Quite Diverse. By Norma Deseke and Birgit Pestal. *Die Maske: Zeitschrift für Kultur-und Sozialanthropologie* (Vienna), No. 2, January.

2014
Ulf Hannerz interviewed by Dominic Boyer. *Public Culture*, 26(1): 187–199.

Notes on Contributors

Ayse Caglar is Professor in the Department of Social and Cultural Anthropology, University of Vienna. Trained as a sociologist and an anthropologist, she was the Head of the Department of Sociology and Social Anthropology at the Central European University, Budapest. She has published extensively on migration, transnationalization processes, urban regeneration and displacements, citizenship, and neoliberal globalization. Her work is inspired by Ulf Hannerz in multiple ways.

Dominic Boyer is Professor of Anthropology at Rice University and Founding Director of the Center for Energy and Environmental Research in the Human Sciences (CENHS), the first research center in the world designed specifically to promote research on the energy/environment nexus in the humanities and social sciences. He is the incoming editor of the journal *Cultural Anthropology* and editor of the *Expertise: Cultures and Technologies of Knowledge* book series for Cornell University Press. His most recent book is *The Life Informatic: Newsmaking in the Digital Era* (Cornell University Press, 2013).

Gudrun Dahl has been a colleague of Ulf Hannerz since 1979, before which he was her tutor for a number of years. She is Professor of Social Anthropology with emphasis on Development Studies at Stockholm University, where she has also been the Dean for the Faculty of Social Science. Her early work was on pastoral communities in northeast Africa (the Borana and the Beja). Later she became interested in the interface between scientific language, policy discourse and moral arguments especially in the development field. This also involves how academic discourse becomes influenced by political and moral fashions and by the ambition to appear at once righteous and timely. Presently she is working on issues relating to how (and what) moralizing arguments are mobilized in environmental work.

Thomas Hylland Eriksen is Professor of Social Anthropology at the University of Oslo. His research in complex societies ranges from identity politics to the cultural implications of new information technology, and he now, using the metaphor of "overheating," studies local responses to global crises in ways inspired by Ulf Hannerz' pioneering vision of a truly global anthropology. His books include *Ethnicity and Nationalism* (1993/2010), *Engaging Anthropology* (2006), and *Globalization: The Key Concepts* (2007/2014).

Thomas Fillitz is Associate Professor in the Department of Social and Cultural Anthropology, University of Vienna, and was encouraged by Ulf Hannerz to apply for the post of Secretary of the European Association of Social Anthropologists (EASA), a function he carried out between 2007 and 2013. Within the frame of his major research interests—global art, the art world, art markets, globalization, and transnational processes—Thomas strongly relies on concepts developed by Ulf Hannerz, such as global culture, cultural diversity, and transnational connections.

Christina Garsten is Professor of Social Anthropology at Stockholm University and recently joined Copenhagen Business School as Professor of Globalization and Organization. She is also Chair of the Executive Board of the Stockholm Centre for Organizational Research. Her interests in transnational organizations as drivers of globalization processes and their role in the shaping of social identities and forms of sociality bear strong traces of Ulf Hannerz' influence as a long-term source of inspiration. Her most recent book is *Organisational Anthropology* (co-edited with Anette Nyqvist, Pluto Press, 2013).

Andre Gingrich is a member of the Royal Swedish and of the Austrian Academy of Sciences, and is Professor for Social and Cultural Anthropology at the University of Vienna. His main research interests are the Middle East in the past and present, qualitative methodologies such as comparison, and the history of anthropology. He has collaborated with Ulf Hannerz on neonationalism and is coediting with him a book on anthropology's take on "small countries" in transnational and globalized contexts.

Thomas Blom Hansen is Professor of Anthropology at Stanford University and Director of the Center for South Asia at Stanford. His research on religious and political identity politics, urban violence, state formation, and sovereignty has focused on India and postapartheid South Africa. He has an abiding interest in urban anthropology and in the dynamics of everyday urban phenomenology in large, culturally complex cities. Ulf Hannerz' pioneering work on urban experience is a major influence in this work. His most recent book is *Melancholia of Freedom: Social Life in an Indian Township in South Africa* (2012). He is currently editing a book of new urban anthropology provisionally called *Urban beyond Measure: City Life in South Asia*.

Brian Moeran is Professor of Business Anthropology at the Copenhagen Business School. He has, however, had a checkered career. A would-be helicopter pilot in Her Britannic Majesty's Royal Navy back in the early 1960s, he got out in time to avoid killing people and became a television comedian in Japan instead. When people started dying of laughter, he turned anthropologist, and now does his best to prevent people from dying of boredom. In this he cannot guarantee to have been always successful, but is glad to note that Ulf himself has survived.

João de Pina-Cabral is Professor and Head of the School of Anthropology and Conservation at the University of Kent. He has been Academic Director of the Institute of Social Sciences of the University of Lisbon, President of the Portuguese Association of Anthropology, and President of the European Association of Social Anthropologists. He has published extensively on matters related to house and family, personhood, ethnicity in postcolonial contexts, and anthropological theory. He has carried out fieldwork on the Alto Minho, Portugal; Macao, China; and Bahia, Brazil. (For publications see http://www.pina-cabral.org/.)

Shalini Randeria is Professor of Anthropology and Sociology at the Graduate Institute for International and Development Studies. Her research addresses issues of changing contours of law, policy, and governance; the interplay between international organizations, the state, and social movements in India; and judicial contestation around dispossession and displacement. Recent coedited volumes include: *Unraveling Ties: From Social Cohesion to New Practices of Connectedness* (2002); *Worlds on the Move: Globalisation, Migration and Cultural Security* (2004); *Vom Imperialismus zum Empire: Nicht-westliche Perspektiven auf Globalisierung* (2009); *Border Crossings: Grenz-verschiebungen und Grenzüberschreitungen in einer globalisierten Welt* (2014); and *Jenseits des Eurozentrisumus* (2002/2013).

Ronald Stade is Professor of Peace and Conflict Studies and Anthropology at Malmö University, Sweden. He has conducted fieldwork on the island of Guam and among scholars, experts, and politicians engaged in operationalizing the concept of global governance. The thematic priorities of his research have included cultural and, in particular, institutional diffusion, semantic history, cosmopolitanism, and philosophical anthropology. As Guest Professor at Hitotsubashi University in Tokyo he also worked on the topics of military metaphysics, the lessons of war, and the subjectivities of perpetrators, which, most recently, has led him to focus on the human capacity for absurdity.

Helena Wulff is Professor in the Department of Social Anthropology, Stockholm University. Her current research is in the anthropology of communication and aesthetics based on a wide range of studies of the social worlds of literary production, dance, emotions, and the visual arts in a transnational perspective, presently on contemporary Irish writers as cultural translators and public intellectuals. She was Editor-in-Chief of *Social Anthropology/Anthropologie Sociale*, the journal of the European Association of Social Anthropologists (EASA), and Chair of the Anthropological Association of Sweden (SANT). As a graduate student, she was trained by Ulf Hannerz.

Index

accountability 272
    cultural interpretation and 120–21
Actor Network Theory (ANT) 12, 49
Adams, Matthew 133
adjacencies 36–8, 41
advertising revenues 45–6
aesthetic frame of beauty and quality 41–4
African governance, Agarwala's take on 216–18
African National Congress (ANC) 120
Against the Wall (Fatih Akin film) 181–2
agency
    individual agency, Hannerz' concern with 2
    reflexivity and 177–8
    of things, cultural interpretation and 124
    transnational connections and 49, 61, 63–4, 66–7
Akin, Fatih 181, 182, 185, 186, 187, 196, 197
al-Houthi family 52, 56, 57, 60
Al-Qaeda 206
Alexander, Jeffrey C. 133
Allende, Salvador 218
Almeida, Onésimo Teotónio de 253
alterity 112, 124, 125, 126, 128n5, 243–4, 260
altruism 243
American Anthropological Association (AAA) 4, 122, 269–70
amity, Lusotopy as catalyst for 242–4, 248, 259–60

Amory, Deborah 168
analytical concepts 173–4
Anderson, Alison 165
Anderson, Benedict 100
anthropocene era 165
anthropological enquiry 149
anthropological knowledge 95, 96–7, 98–9
anthropological reflexivity 92, 93–6, 97, 101, 104–6, 106–7, 108, 178
    eventual (re)invention of 96–101
Anthropological Research on the Contemporary (ARC) 103
Anthropological Theory Today (Moore, H.L.) 173
anthropology
anthropological authority 114
    biological anthropology 124–5
    centrality of reflexivity to 92–3, 99–100, 143, 162, 166
    conceptual vocabulary of 112
    cosmopolitan aspirations of 271
    critical anthropology 125–6
    cultural critique in 264
    demise and death of? 111–12
    Durban, fieldwork in 119–21
    ethnography and 111–12
    future for, Hannerz' perspective on 8
    global cultural movement, role in 111–12, 124
    informant and anthropologist, similarities between 149–50
    of literature and writing 147–8
    Mumbai, fieldwork in 115–18
    non-linguistic turn in 122–3

prestige of 111
reflexivity as tool 173
reinvention of anthropological reflexivity 96–101
of small countries 274
sociology and, division of labour between 2
writing, reflexivity and 167–8
Anthropology and Literature (Benson, P., Ed.) 147
Anthropology's World (Hannerz, U.) 1, 8, 147, 159, 269, 270
Appadurai, Arjun 29, 30, 43, 48, 49, 112, 115, 133, 138, 210, 211, 214
Arab Spring 269
Archetti, Eduardo 147
Arendt, Hannah 207, 232
art biennials 133, 140–41, 142, 143
Asad, Talal 100, 209, 210
Ash, Timothy Garton 264
audit cultures 266–7, 271–2
public management ideology and 208–9
Aull Davies, Charlotte 166
authority, disaggregation of 215–16
autopoetic social systems, self-reproduction of 163–4

Bailey, F.G. 81
Banu Awfan 54, 57, 58, 61, 62–3, 63
Barak, Ehud 229
Barbaso, Duarte 246
Barcelona Declaration (1995) 185–6
Barley, S.R. 72
Barnett, Michael 208
Barry, Sebastian 151
Barth, Fredrik 2, 21, 22
Barthes, Roland 45, 46
Bartholdson, Örjan 171
Bashar al-Asad 57
Bath, Youssouf 135, 136
Bauman, Zygmunt 13, 49
Bayh, Evan 228
Beale, Alison 193
Beck, U. et al. 132, 133, 137–8, 143, 164, 177
Beck, Ulrich 49, 132, 143

Behar, Ruth 107
Belting, Hans 133, 138, 139
benchmarks for self-comparison 164, 166
Benítez-Rojo, Antonio 252
Benjamin, Walter 154, 157
Bennett, Jane 123, 124
Bennett, Tony 189, 190
Benson, Paul 147
Berghahn, Marion 67
Bergson, Henri 123
Bergsten, C.Fred 75, 76
Bhardwaj, Vishal 115
Bin Laden, Osama 71
bin Laden, Osama 273
Binchy, Chris 148, 151
Birdsall, Nancy 75, 76
Black Friday (Zaidi, H.) 116
The Blackwater Lightship (Tóibín, C.) 153–4, 156–7
Blair, Tony 228, 229, 230
Blom, Jan Petter 7
Boas, Franz 96
Boissevain, J. 81
boundaries, frontiers and 24–7
Bourdieu, P. and Wacquant, L. 92, 168, 171
Bourdieu, Pierre 95
Boyer, D. and Hannerz, U. 150, 184, 191
Boyer, Domenic 184, 191
Boyer, Dominic 91–108, 291
interview with Ulf Hannerz (September 2012) 264–76
Brandt, Marieke 57
Brandt, Willy 219, 220, 221, 230
Bråten, Stein 243, 255
Brenner, Neil 194
Brookings Institution 70
Brooklyn (Tóibín, C.) 157, 158
Brown, Gordon 229
Brundtland, Gro Harlem 221
Buchanan, James 208
Buddensieg, Andrea 138
Bunz, Matti 106
bureaucracy 23
Burri, Mira 192, 193

Bush, George ,Sr. 230
Bush, George W. 23, 230, 273
Business Week America 80–81
Bydler, Charlotte 133

Cabral, Pedro Álvares 257
Café du Monde (Hannerz, U.) 3
Caglar, A. and Glick Schiller, N. 195, 197
Caglar, A. and Mehling, S. 184
Caglar, Ayse 181–201, 185, 195, 291
Cahen, Michel 260
Calhoun, C. and Sennett, R. 74
Calhoun, Craig 14
Campbell, Craig 107
canon law, social organization and 250
capitalism 15, 16, 22–3, 44, 206
    global capitalism 12, 211–12, 219, 230
    networked capitalism 16
Cardoso, Fernando Henrique 229
Caribbean region, sociological coherence of 251–2
Carlsson, Ingvar 221, 222, 223, 225, 226, 230, 232
Carlyle, Thomas 43
Carnegie Endowment for International Peace 70
Casanova, Giacomo 158
Castells, Manuel 12, 14
Castles, S. and Davidson, A. 14
Caton, Steven C. 62
cellphone technology 51, 57–8, 61, 64, 66
Center for Global Development (CGD) 71, 74–5, 75–7, 79–81, 83–4, 85
Césaire, Aimé 123
Chan, Mónica 260
Chandavarkar, Raj 115
Chandra, Vikram 116
chaos theory 17
Chaucer, Geoffrey 215
civil society, concept of 174
Clark, Helen 229
Classen, Constance 122

Clastres, Pierre 125
Clifford, J. and Marcus, G.E. 91, 100, 113, 147, 167
Clifford, James 91
climate change 14, 16–17
Clinton, Bill 227, 228, 229, 230
Clinton, Hillary Rodham 228, 229
co-responsibility, ethic of 243
coda 45–6
Cohen, A.P. 19
Cold War, end of
    contemporary world, making sense of 15
    global governance and 205
collaborative world watch 269
collectivity, primitive philosophy and 95
Collier, Jane F. 170
Columbus, Christopher 21
commissions 218–22
Commitment to Development Index (CDI) 83–4
commodity chains, concept of 211, 212
common sense and reflexivity 173
communicative self-reflexivity 163–4
communitas 112
community and belonging in Europe 184
competitive reflexivity 164
complementarities 34–6
concept chains 209–13
concepts
    fashionability of 174
    reflexivity and 174–6
    timelessness of 176
connectedness, social and material 11–12, 29–46
    adjacencies 36–8, 41
    advertising revenues 45–6
    aesthetic frame of beauty and quality 41–4
    coda 45–6
    complementarities 34–6
    connections 29, 30–31
    contemporary world, making sense of 25

ethnoscapes 30
exchanges 31–3
fashion magazines 45–6
flows 34–6
frames 41–4
gender complimentarity 34–5
information technology 29–30
land, importance of 31–3
methodology 30
mingei movement 42–4
networks 29, 30
pottery, transformations in making of 38–41
social frame of working together 41–4
social norms, conjuncture with aesthetic ideals 35–6
social organization 33
Stockholm Anthropology Round Table (September 2007) 29
togetherness, community and 43–4
transactions 31–3
transformations 38–41
connections 29, 30–31
long-distance remote connections 65–6
military operations and 64–5
transnational connections in Upper Yemen 49–50, 66–7
Connolly, Cressida 152
Connolly, William 123
The Conquest of America (Todorov, T.) 21
Contemporary African Art Collection (CAAC) 139–40, 142
contemporary world, making sense of 15–27
accelerated world 16–18
boundaries, frontiers and 24–7
bureaucracy 23
capitalism 22–3
chaos theory 17
climate change 16–17
Cold War, end of 15
connectedness 25
contradictory claims, flurry of 17–18
cosmopolitanism/identity politics conflict 17
cultural autonomy/quest for recognition conflict 17
cultural variation, novel forms of 26
culture
 cultural differences and 25–6
 globalization of 26
democracy, consumerism and 24
economic globalization 16
entrepreneurialism 22
environmentalism/development conflict 17
fragmentation in identity politics 23
freedom and insecurity, search for 18–19, 20
Global South 16
global warming 16–17
globalization
 anti-globalization conflict 17
 processes of 25–6
Hindu nationalism, growth of 15
human nature, optimism on 23
identification 22
identity, uncertainty in 18–120
ideological conflict 24
inclusion/exclusion conflict 17
insecure sociality 21–2
Internet, beginnings of 15–16
Islamic identity politics, growth of 16
life opportunities, contrasts in 25
Mandela, freedom for 15
market deregulation 16
mobile telecommunications 16
modernity 15, 26
moral correctness 23
networked capitalism 16
new world order, conservative perspectives on 23–4
open-mindedness, need for 23
personal identity 19–20

personal identity, tortoise metaphor in West Africa for 20
postmodernism 17
purity and simplicity, search for 18–19
recognition 23–4
social belonging, identity and 19
social relations, instrumentalization of 23
sociality, security in 20
Swedish national identity 26–7
tensions and frictions, intensification of 16
uniformity/diversity conflict 17
Wesensville, concept of 20
Yugoslavia, dismantlement of 15
context
  cultural differences between social contexts 172–3
  relationships in 242–3
corporate social responsibility (CSR) 74
cosmopolitanism 1, 265, 272–3
cosmopolitanism/identity politics conflict 17
creolization 1, 5–6, 82–3
  cultural creolization 2, 26
critical interpretation, conceptual repositioning and 213
cultural artifacts 112
cultural authenticity 112–13
cultural autonomy/quest for recognition conflict 17
Cultural Complexity (Hannerz, U.) 1, 4–5
cultural connections, mapping of 139–40
cultural diversity, migrants and 181–98
  Barcelona Declaration (1995) 185–6
  community and belonging in Europe 184
  cultural deterritorialization 186
  cultural diversity as global policy discourse 182–3
  cultural diversity in European cultural policies 184, 188–91, 197
  cultural formations, crossbreeding of 189
  cultural goods, multilateral trade relations and 192–4
  cultural policies in Europe, tense landscape of 185–7
  Declaration of Cultural Diversity (Council of Europe, 2000) 188, 192, 193
  dual citizenship 182
  EUROMED (European-Mediterranean Partnership) 186–7
  European Cultural Convention (1954) 186
  'The Expediency of Culture' (Yudice, G.) 197
  German Turk, definition as 181, 182, 198n7, 198n8
  human rights, cultural diversity and 190
  Intercultural Cities joint program 195
  intercultural dialogue 190–91
  knowledge economy, culture and 196
  media pluralism, cultural diversity and 193–4
  Mercator project 187
  migrants, cultural diversity and positioning of 181–2
  minorities and difference in Europe, incorporation of 183–4
  multilateral trade relations, cultural goods and 192–4
  reflexivity on organizing principles of society 184–5
  representations of success, divergent nature of 182, 196–7
  situating cultural diversity 191
  social processes, exploration of 185
  studying sideways 182

third-country nationals (TCNs) 184, 197
UNESCO Convention on the Protection and Promotion of the Diversity of Cultural Expression 182–3, 189, 192–3
urban regeneration and governance, cultural diversity and 194–6, 197–8
Against the Wall (Fatih Akin film) 181–2
World Trade Organization (WTO) 192
cultural engineering 213
cultural flows, complexity of 4–5
cultural formations, crossbreeding of 189
cultural goods, multilateral trade relations and 192–4
cultural initiation 136–7
cultural interpretation 111–27
    accountability 120–21
    African National Congress (ANC) 120
    agency of things 124
    American Anthropological Association (AAA) 122
    anthropology
        anthropological authority 114
        biological anthropology 124–5
        conceptual vocabulary of 112
        critical anthropology 125–6
        demise and death of? 111–12
        Durban, fieldwork in 119–21
        ethnography and 111–12
        global cultural movement, role in 111–12, 124
        Mumbai, fieldwork in 115–18
        non-linguistic turn in 122–3
        prestige of 111
    communitas 112
    cultural artifacts 112
    cultural attachment 112
    cultural authenticity 112–13
    culture writing itself 113–18
    Durban, Indian township in 118–21
        alien minority, Indians as 119
        cultural practices, selectivity in writing about 119–21
        Group Areas Act 118
        inhabitants 118–19
        political and cultural struggles, need for imaginative understandings of 120–21
    ethnographic authority, resurrection of 125
    expert knowledge 113, 114
    language, attention to 122
    language and meaning, new materialism and hostility to 123–4
    Mumbai, megacity of 115–18
        capitalist modernity, undersides of 117–18
        conflict and pogroms in 115–16
        police corruption 116–17
        serial blasts (1993) in 116
    Négritude movement 123–4
    observation and observability 121–6
    ontology, deployment of 125–6
    participant observation 119–20
    self-making among Muslims in Cairo 123
    study and studied, epistemological distinction between 127
    thinking and consciousness, Descartes' distinction between 123
    writing about culture 118–21
cultural politics 245
cultural values, depoliticization and 209
cultural variation, novel forms of 26
culture
    cultural differences and 25–6
    culture flows, global scenarios of 78

deterritorialization of 186
globalization of 26
processual view of 5
and society, division of labour between study of 2
writing itself 113–18
culturespeak 274, 276

da Silva, Agostinho 259
Dahl, Gudrun 5, 162–78, 174, 176, 177, 178, 291
Dakpogan, Calixte 140
d'Alema, Massimo 229
Damásio, António 245, 246, 252
Dancer: A Novel (McCann, C.) 157
The Dancers Dancing (Dhuibhne, É. N.) 155–6
Darnell, Regna 96
Das, Veena 49
Davis, Mike 16
de Caminha, Pedro Vaz 258
de Castro, Viveiros 259
de la Rúa, Fernando 229
De Swaan, Abram 266
Declaration of Cultural Diversity (Council of Europe, 2000) 188, 192, 193
decolonization 251
Deeb, H. and Marcus, G.E. 104
Deleuze, Gilles 123
Demian, Melissa 132
democracy, consumerism and 24
depoliticization 207–9
derived (ideological) reflexivity 132–3
Descartes, René 123, 125, 131
Development and Peace Foundation 221–2
Devji, Faisal 207
Diario Financiero 81
diaspora
    Lusotopy and 243–6, 254–7
    sociocentrism and 245–6
Dib, Lina 107
Disordered World (Maalouf, A.) 265
Dominguez, Virginia 270
Dornfeld, Barry 45, 46
Douglas, Mary 21, 22, 250

Doyle, Roddy 148, 152
Dresch, Paul 53, 55
dual citizenship 182
Duarte, Luiz Eduardo Dias 260
Dumont, Jean-Paul 100
Duranti, Alessandro 49
Durban, Indian township in 118–21
    alien minority, Indians as 119
    cultural practices, selectivity in writing about 119–21
    Group Areas Act 118
    inhabitants 118–19
    political and cultural struggles, need for imaginative understandings of 120–21
Durkheim, Émile 94, 245
Dworkin, Ronald 228

economic globalization 16
ecumene
    concept of 241–2, 246, 249–54, 255–6, 259–60
    ecumenical phenomena 249, 257
    global ecumene 2, 275
Elhaik, Tarek 107
Elizabeth II 229–30
Elkins, John 133
embedded concepts, comparison of 210
Empire (Hardt, M. and Negri, A.) 12
Enright, Anne 148, 153
entrepreneurialism 22
environmentalism/development conflict 17
Epictetus, 242
epistemic contingency, reflexive attention to conditions of 99, 101
Epstein, Arnold L. 1
equity, guiding political principle of 209
Eriksen, Thomas Hylland 1–9, 11–27, 291–2
error, irritation and 246–9
ethnographic authority, resurrection of 125
ethnographic engagement 210–11

ethnographic methodology 209–10
ethnographic understanding 247
ethnographic writing 269
Ethnos 131–2
ethnoscapes 30
Eurasia Center 70
Eurocentrism
    knowledge practices 133
    Lusotopy and 250
EUROMED (European-Mediterranean Partnership) 186–7
European Association of Social Anthropologists (EASA) 4, 174, 269
European Cultural Convention (1954) 186
Evans-Pritchard, E.E. 94
exchanges 31–3
'The Expediency of Culture' (Yudice, G.) 197
expert knowledge 113, 114
Exploring the City (Hannerz, U.) 1

Fabian, Johannes 247
Fainstein, Susan 194
Falzon, Mark-Anthony 102
family structure, changes in 9
Farmer, Paul 107
fashion magazines 45–6
Faubion, James 100
Faubion, J.D. and Marcus, G.E. 104
feedback processes 164
Feierman, Steven 95
Feijó, Rui Graça 250, 260
Feld, Steven 122
Ferguson, James 208, 232
Ferguson, Niall 264
fieldwork
    Durban, fieldwork in 119–21
    Hannerz in Africa and US 2
    Mumbai, fieldwork in 115–18
    reflexivity and 162, 166, 168–9
    in Washington D.C. 74–5
Filho, Wilson Trajano 260
Fillitz, Thomas 131–44, 292
financial sector policy-making 80–81
Finkielkraut, Alain 255

Fitzpatrick, David 155
flexians 73–4
flexible accumulation 14
Florida, Richard 194
Florini, Ann 227, 228
flows
    connectedness, social and material 34–6
    transnational connections in Upper Yemen 49, 57, 66
fluidity and reflexivity 13
Foreign News (Hannerz, U.) 1
Fortes, Meyer 241, 242
Fox, Jonathan 24
Fox, Swallow, Scarecrow (Dhuibhne, É. N.) 151
frames 41–4
fraternity 243, 244
Frazer, Sir James G. 93–4, 96
freedom, insecurity and 18–19, 20
Friedman, Milton 208
Friedman, Thomas 273
Friedrich, Paul 107
Fry, Peter 246
Fukuyama, Francis 24, 206, 231, 273
future reflexivity 107–8

Galtung, Johan 222, 223
Garsten, Christina 1–9, 70–87, 292
The Gathering (Enright, A.) 153, 158
Geertz, Clifford 147
Gell, Alfred 126
Gellner, Ernest 7–8
gender complimentarity 34–5
general reflexivity 131–2
generosity 243
genetic engineering 14
geocultural imagination 78
geocultural scenarios, global governance and 205–7
Gereffi, Gary 211
Gerholm, Tomas 3
German Turk, definition as 181, 182, 198n7, 198n8
Gershon, Ilana 131, 132, 142, 163, 164
Ghosh, Amitav 107

Giddens, Anthony 13, 132, 138, 177, 228
Giesen, Bernhard 95
Gill, Tom 229
Gillis, John 155
Gingrich, Andre 48–67, 274, 292
Global Art and the Museum (GAM) project 138, 140
global art culture
  knowledge practices 133
  reflexivity and 133–4, 238–9
global capitalism 12, 211–12, 219, 230
global ecumene 2, 275
global financial markets 14
global future scenarios 273–4
global governance 205–33
  African governance, Agarwala's take on 216–18
  audit cultures, public management ideology and 208–9
  authority, disaggregation of 215–16
  Cold War, end of 205
  commissions 218–22
  commodity chains, concept of 211, 212
  concept chains 209–13
  critical interpretation, conceptual repositioning and 213
  cultural engineering 213
  cultural values, depoliticization and 209
  depoliticization 207–9
  Development and Peace Foundation 221–2
  embedded concepts, comparison of 210
  equity, guiding political principle of 209
  ethnographic engagement 210–11
  ethnographic methodology 209–10
  geocultural scenarios 205–7
  global capitalism, analysis of 211–12

global governance
  institutionalized international politics and 225–31
  Rosenau's concept of 214–16, 231–2
Issues in Global Governance (Commission on Global Governance) 222–3
global government and 225
global neighborhood 222–5
Our Global Neighbourhood (Commission on Global Governance) 224
globality 215
governance, government and 215–16, 217
independent international commissions (1977-2002) 221
Johnson's Great Society 219
Koselleck's Begriffsgeschichte (conceptual history) 212–13
Modernity at Large (Appadurai, A.) 214
Muslim reformation 207
neoliberal ideology 209
North-South Commission (Brandt Commission) 220
Office of UN High Commissioner for Human Rights (OHCHR) 217
Pearson Commission 220
political sphere, return to? 231–2
poverty, definitions of 217–18
public management ideology 208–9
Review of International Studies 214
Rosevelt's New Deal 219
self-referentiality, fallacy of 210
Stockholm Initiative on Global Security and Governance (1991) 222
Sub-Saharan Africa (World Bank) 216–17
Transnational Connections (Hannerz, U.) 1, 214

UN Centre on Transnational
    Corporations (UNCTC) 219–
    20
UN Children's Fund (UNICEF)
    217
UN Development Programme
    (UNDP) 217
UN Economic and Social
    Council (ECOSOC) 217
United Nations (UN) 217–18
World Bank 219–20
zero tolerance, concept of 211–12
global population 11
global processes, cultural complexity
    and 5
Global South 16
global warming 16–17
globality 215
globalization
    anthropology of 2, 3, 5–6
    anti-globalization conflict and 17
    art in era of 138
    globalization discourse 13–14
    identity and 274–5
    processes of 25–6
glocality, glocalization and 12–13, 275
Gluckman, Max 1
Godelier, Maurice 7
Goffman, Erving 64, 253
González, Roberto J. 107
Goody, Jack 122
Gouldner, Alvin W. 176
Graeber, David 105, 107
Graham, Mark 67
Gray, John 15
The Guardian 156
Gupta, A. and Ferguson, J. 168, 170,
    185
Gusterson, Hugh 72, 107, 209
Guterres, António 229

Haas, Ernst 222, 223
Haas, Peter 222, 223
Habermas, Jürgen 23, 207
Hage, Ghassan 125
Hand, Derek 151

Hannerz, Ulf
    Africa and US, fieldwork in 2
    'anthropologist of the world' 265
    bilingual in writings 3, 4
    Boyer's interview with
        (September 2012) 264–76
    citizen-anthropologist 4
    collectivities, different kinds of 6
    cosmopolitanism 1
    creolization 1, 5–6
    cultural creolization 2
    cultural flows, complexity of 4–5
    culture, processual view of 5
    culture and diversity 1
    culture and society, division of
        labour between study of 2
    future for anthropology,
        perspective on 8
    global ecumene 2
    global processes, cultural
        complexity and 5
    globalization, anthropology of 2,
        3, 5–6
    individual agency, concern with
        2
    intellectual tools 12
    network of networks 2
    networks, interest in 1, 2
    non-English publications,
        valorization of 4
    novelty in writings of 1–2
    ourselves, flexibilities in
        understandings of 5, 6
    participant observation 2
    political implications in works of
        5
    public works, span of 1, 5–6
    publications by 277–90
    reflexivity, central place of
        notion in writings of 8
    scholarship of 1–2, 3–4, 5–6, 9
    sociology and anthropology,
        division of labour between 2
    transnational connections 1, 5–6,
        7–8
    urban life, ethnographies of 1–2

Hansen, Peter 218, 219, 222, 223, 224, 225, 232
Hansen, Thomas Blom 111–28, 292–3
Haraway, Donna 101, 167
Harney, Elisabeth 135
Harrison, Lawrence 206
Hart, Keith 268
Harvey, David 14, 194
Heaney, Seamus 148
Hénelon, Serge 135, 136, 137
heritage, language and 245, 247
Hervik, Peter 132, 142
Herzfeld, Michael 95
Hindu nationalism, growth of 15
Hirschkind, Charles 123, 124
Højbjerg, Christian Kordt 131
Holbraad, Martin 125
Holmes, Doug 102
Holmquist, Kate 151
Houphouët-Boogny, Félix 135
al-Houthi revolt in Upper Yemen 56–60, 63
human nature, optimism on 23
human rights, cultural diversity and 190
human universals, Lévi-Strauss' theory of 11
Huntington, Samuel 24, 176, 205, 206, 207, 231, 273, 274
Hussein, Saddam 55
Hymes, Dell 100

Ibrahim, Dawood 115
Ibsen, Henrik 18, 19
ideas
    competition for 79
    diffusion of 78
identification
    acknowledgement of 249
    contemporary world, making sense of 22
    identification/differentiation, processes of 250–51
identity
    alterity and 244
    identity politics, fragmentation in 23
    mutuality in 253
    uncertainty in 18–120
ideological basis for reflexivity 99
ideological conflict 24
ideological reflexivity 132–3, 137
inclusion/exclusion conflict 17
independent international commissions (1977-2002) on global governance 221
individual agency, Hannerz' concern with 2
individual reflexivity, social context and 168
inequalities 15, 83, 85, 86–7, 99–100, 170, 171, 228
influence
    derivation of 86–7
    distinction between impact and 80
    educational activities and 79–80
informant and anthropologist, similarities between 149–50
The Information Society (Castells, M.) 14
information technology 9, 14, 265
    connectedness, social and material 29–30
    reflexivity and 164, 173–4
    transnational connections in Upper Yemen 64
initiatives 83–4
insecure sociality 21–2
institutional development and reflexivity 164
intellectual tools 12
intentionality 49–50
    interactive intentionality 66
intercommunication 241, 249
Intercultural Cities joint program 195
intercultural dialogue 190–91
interface position of think tanks 86
internal displacement in Upper Yemen 59
International Monetary Fund (IMF) 70
Internet, beginnings of 15–16

306 • Index

intersectionality 170–71
intersubjectivity 49–50, 174, 246
introspective representation 131
Ireland, literary world of 147–59
    anthropological enquiry 149
    Anthropology and Literature
        (Benson, P., Ed.) 147
    anthropology of literature and
        writing 147–8
    The Blackwater Lightship (Tóibín,
        C.) 153–4, 156–7
    Brooklyn (Tóibín, C.) 157, 158
    Dancer: A Novel (McCann, C.) 157
    The Dancers Dancing (Dhuibhne,
        É. N.) 155–6
    Fox, Swallow, Scarecrow
        (Dhuibhne, É. N.) 151
    The Gathering (Enright, A.) 153,
        158
    informant and anthropologist,
        similarities between 149–50
    Irish soil, significance of 154–6
    Irish writing, lengthy history of
        147
    Irish Writing in the Twentieth
        Century (Pierce, D.) 150–51
    land of Ireland, physical form
        and location in perceptions
        of 155–6
    literary tradition, contemporary
        writers in 148–9
    Literature and Anthropology
        (Dennis, P.A,. and Aycock,
        W.) 147
    London Review of Books 149
    The Master (Tóibín, C.) 154–5, 156,
        157, 158
    Molly Fox's Birthday (Madden, D.)
        152, 153, 158
    New York Review of Books 156
    Open-handed (Binchy, C.) 151–2
    reflexive informants 149
    reflexivity, studying sideways
        and 157–9
    The Secret Scripture (Barry, S.) 151
    stories from afar 156–7, 157–8
    studying sideways and 147, 148–9

    tropes of Irish storytelling 150–54,
        158
    Ulysses (Joyce, J.) 152
Islamic identity politics, growth
    of 16

Jackson, David 251
Jackson, John 107
Jackson, K. David 256
Jackson, Michael 98, 107
Jacobs, Jane 194
James, Deborah 81
James, Henry 154, 156, 157
John, Prester 251
Johnsen, Gregory D. 55, 57
Johnson, Lyndon B and Great Society
    219
Johnston, Barbara Rose 107
Jones, Donna 123
Jospin, Lionel 229
journalism 267–8
Joyce, James 148, 152, 157
Judt, Tony 264
Juris, Jeffrey S. 174

Kagan, Robert 206
Kahn, Rahman 74
Kanjirō, Kawaii 42
Kaplan, Robert 206, 273
Keane, Robbie 152
Kenkichi, Tomimoto 42
Keohane, Robert 222
Khomeini, Ayatollah Ruhollah 55
Kiberd, Declan 148
kinship phenomena 241
kinship relations 242–3
Kluckhohn, Clyde 2
knowledge brokerage 81–3
knowledge economy, culture and
    196
knowledge generation 77–8
knowledge packaging 86
knowledge practices 131–43
    art biennials 133, 140–41, 142, 143
    Contemporary African Art
        Collection (CAAC) 139–40,
        142

cultural connections, mapping of 139–40
cultural initiation 136–7
derived (ideological) reflexivity 132–3
Eurocentrism 133
general reflexivity 131–2
Global Art and the Museum (GAM) project 138, 140
global art culture 133
   reflexivity and 133–4, 238–9
globalization, art in era of 138
ideological reflexivity 132–3, 137
introspective representation 131
local cultures, reorientation towards 135–6
Négritude movement 134–5
post-traditional society, concept of 138
reflexive modernization, concept of 132, 133, 137–8, 143
reflexivity, anthropological enterprise and 131–2
reflexivity, *bricolages* and 138, 142
reflexivity, consequences of 132–3
reflexivity, cultural technique for self-reflection 132
reflexivity, 'other-awareness' and 142–3
relational reflexivity 141–3
spaces of reflexivity 137–41
Stockholm Anthropology Round Table (September 2007) 131
times of reflexivity 134–7
vohou-vohou movement in Ivory Coast 133, 135–6, 136–7, 140, 142, 144n3
West African art, reflexive turn in 134–5
Knox, Julene 67
Kok, Wim 229
Konrad, Monica 65
Korzeniewwicz, Miguel 211
Koselleck, Reinhart 214
   Begriffsgeschichte (conceptual history) 212–13

Koudougnon, Théodore 135, 136
Kra, N'Guessan 135
Kristang, Malacca 256
Kroeber, Alfred 249, 257, 260
Kuttner, Robert 230

labour market, changes in 9
Lagos, Ricardo 229
Lakoff, George 173
land, importance of 31–3
language
   attention to 122
   meaning and, new materialism and hostility to 123–4
   sociocentric convergence of 248
   uses of 266
   see also words
Lapeyre, Frédéric 221
Lash, Scott 132, 133, 137, 138, 143, 165
lateral connectivity 268
Latin America Adviser 81
Latour, Bruno 12, 49, 82, 101, 122, 123, 124
Lattier, Christian 135
Leach, Bernard 42, 43
Lebon, France 189, 190
Lee, Harmonie 156
The Legend of Good Women (Chaucer, G.) 215
Leibniz, Gottfried Wilhelm 258
Lévi-Strauss, Claude 11, 12
Lévinas, Emmanuel 243, 244
Lévy-Bruhl, Lucien 94
Lieberman, Joe 228
life opportunities, contrasts in 25
literary tradition, contemporary writers in 148–9
Literature and Anthropology (Dennis, P.A,. and Aycock, W.) 147
local cultures, reorientation towards 135–6
local relations, shifts in 55
Lomnitz, Claudio 95
London Review of Books 149
Luhmann, Niklas 163, 164
Lusotopy 241–60
   alterity 243–4

altruism 243
amity, catalyst for 242–4, 248, 259–60
canon law, social organization and 250
Caribbean region, sociological coherence of 251–2
co-responsibility, ethic of 243
cultural politics 245
decolonization 251
diaspora 243–6, 254–7
　sociocentrism and 245–6
ecumene, concept of 241–2, 246, 249–54, 255–6, 259–60
ecumenical phenomena 249, 257
error, irritation and 246–9
ethnographic understanding 247
Eurocentrism 250
fraternity 243, 244
generosity 243
heritage, language and 245, 247
identification, acknowledgement of 249
identification/differentiation, processes of 250–51
identity and alterity 244
identity and mutuality in 253
intercommunication 241, 249
invention of 248
irritants, misunderstandings and 247
kinship phenomena 241
kinship relations 242–3
language, sociocentric convergence of 248
middle-earth, Tolkien's notion of 241–2, 249–50, 252, 254, 259
musical style and 255–6
network of contacts 252
　in Portugal 257–8
postcolonial literature 250
pride in past events 253
proprietorial distortion 244–6
reciprocity between individuals 243
relationships in context 242–3
Sarajevo, civil war in 252

sociocentrism 245
as sodality 250
as space/time 248
stigma, logic of 253–4
Timor-Leste, emergence of 250
utopianism 259
Lynch, Michael 132, 166

Maalouf, Amin 265, 271
McCann, Colum 157
McLagan, Meg 107
McNamara, Robert 219, 220, 221
macro/micro issues in social theory 275
Madden, Deirdre 148, 152, 157
Maeckelbergh, Marianne 16
Magnin, André 139, 140
Malinowski, Bronislaw 2, 96, 210, 247, 264
Mandela, Nelson, freedom for 15
Mandelson, Peter 229
Mannheim, Karl 92
Marcus, George E. 74, 77, 91, 101, 102, 103, 104, 132, 137, 141, 210, 211
market deregulation 16
Marley, Bob 20
Marshall, Will 229, 230
Martins, Hermínio 244, 260
Marx, K. and Engels, F. 98
Mass Observation 269
Massumi, Brian 123
The Master (Tóibín, C.) 154–5, 156, 157, 158
Mauss, Marcel 19, 245
Maximum City (Mehta, S.) 115–16
Mbeki, Thabo Mvuyelva 229
Mead, Margaret 264
media pluralism, cultural diversity and 193–4
media saturation 265
Mehta, Suketu 115, 116
Mercator project 187
Merleau-Ponty, Maurice 126
Meyer, Birgit 122
middle-earth, Tolkien's notion of 241–2, 249–50, 252, 254, 259
migration, process of 8–9

Mille Plateaux (Deleuze, G. and
    Guattari, F.) 12
Miller, Daniel 126
mingei movement 42–4
Mintz, Sidney 241, 242, 251, 252
Mistry, Rohinton 115
Mitchell, Clyde 1
mobile telecommunications 14, 16
    see also cellphones
modernity 12
    contemporary world, making
        sense of 15, 26
    reflexivity and 176–7
Modernity at Large (Appadurai, A.) 214
modernology 269
Moeran, Brian 29–46, 293
Mohamad, Mahathir 221
Molly Fox's Birthday (Madden, D.) 152,
    153, 158
Moore, Henrietta 173
moral correctness 23
Morris, William 42, 43
Mouffe, Chantal 207, 208
Mouzelis, Nicos 163
multilateral trade relations, cultural
    goods and 192–4
Mumbai, megacity of 115–18
    capitalist modernity, undersides
        of 117–18
    conflict and pogroms in 115–16
    police corruption 116–17
    serial blasts (1993) in 116
al-Munabbihi, Shaykh Ali Hussayn 59
Munebbih 50–51, 53–4, 58–60, 61–3,
    65, 67n2
    civil war, stand in 53–4
Murray, Charles 212
musical style, Lusotopy and 255–6
Muslim Brotherhood 55–6
Muslim reformation 207
Myrdal, Gunnar 219

Nader, Laura 95, 107, 148
narcissism 265
national character studies 275
nations
    belonging, criteria of 7–8

cultural variation within 7, 9
French nation 8
identification and cohesion
    within 6–8
nationalist ideology 6, 7–8
similarity, principle of 8
transnational connections 7–8
Négritude movement
    cultural interpretation 123–4
    knowledge practices 134–5
neoliberal ideology
    breakthrough of 177
    global governance and 209
network society 14
network tracking 74–5
networked capitalism 16
networks
    concept of 12
    connectedness, social and
        material 29, 30
    of contacts 252
    Hannerz' interest in 1, 2
    of networks 2
    reflexivity 174–5
    Upper Yemen, transnational
        connections in 48
neutrality, ideal of 176
new world order, conservative
    perspectives on 23–4
New York Review of Books 156
The New Yorker 156
Ní Dhuibhne, Éilís 148, 151, 155
Nilsson, Erik 178
North-South Commission (Brandt
    Commission) 220
Nunn, Sam 228
Nureyev, Rudolph 157
Nyamnjoh, Francis 107
Nye, Joseph S. Jr. 86, 206
Nyerere, Julius K. 221

Ó Giolláin, Diarmuid 148, 155
Obama, Barack 84
O'Brien, Edna 148
observation and observability 121–6
O'Donoghue, Bernhard 151
Okely, Judith 142

Onabolu, Aina 134
online engagement 79
ontology, deployment of 125–6
Open-handed (Binchy, C.) 151–2
open-mindedness, need for 23
Ortner, Sherry 149
O'Toole, Fintan 156, 157
ourselves, flexibilities in understandings of 5, 6
Owen, David 221

Palme, Olof 221
para-ethnography 102–3
para-sites, Irving Center, modular research and 103–5
Parsons, Talcott 2
participant observation 2
    cultural interpretation 119–20
Patel, Sujata 115
Paul H. Nitze School of Advanced International Studies at Johns Hopkins University 70
Pearson, Lester B. and Pearson Commission 220
Pedersen, Morten A. 126
Pels, Dick 132
personal identity 19–20
    tortoise metaphor in West Africa for 20
Persson, Göran 228, 229
Persson, Magnus 3
Pessoa, Fernando 259
Peter G. Peterson Institute for International Economics 70
Pierce, David 150
Pigozzi, Jean 139
Pina-Cabral, João de 241–61, 293
Pink, Sarah 122
Pitt-Rivers, Julian 242
Pollner, Melvin 166
Portugal, Lusotopy in 257–8
Posner, Richard 232
post-traditional society, concept of 138
postcolonial literature 250
postcolonial situation in Upper Yemen
    Cold War scenario 52–4

'dethroned' minority and opponents 54–60
postmodernism 17
pottery, transformations in making of 38–41
poverty, definitions of 217–18
Powell, M.G. and Schwegler, T. 92
The Practice of Conceptual History (Koselleck, R.) 212–13
Primitive Man as Philosopher (Radin, P.) 93
Prodi, Romano 228–9
professional reflexivity 165
Progressive Era 72
Pronk, Jan 222
Prophet Muhammad 52
proprietorial distortion 244–6
Public Culture 276
public culture, impoverishment of 267
public management ideology 208–9
publication rankings 266–7
publications by Ulf Hannerz 277–90
publicity, ethics of 107
Puin, Gerd R. 52
purity and simplicity, search for 18–19
Putin, Vladimir 273
Puzo, Mario 116

Quine, W.V. 244, 245

Rabinow, Paul 92, 100, 101, 103, 273
Radin, Paul 93, 94, 95, 96
Randeria, Shalini 1–9, 143, 293
Rath, Jan. 194
Ratnam, Mani 115
Razsa, Maple 107
Reagan, Ronald 220
reflexivity 91–108, 162–78
    agency and 177–8
    analytical concepts 173–4
    anthropocene era and 165
    anthropological enterprise and 131–2
    anthropological knowledge 95, 96–7, 98–9

anthropological reflexivity 92,
    93–6, 97, 101, 104–6, 106–7,
    108, 178
  eventual (re)invention of 96–
    101
Anthropological Research on the
  Contemporary (ARC) 103
anthropological tools 173
anthropological writing and 167–
  8
autopoetic social systems, self-
  reproduction of 163–4
bases for 166–7
benchmarks for self-comparison
  164, 166
bricolages and 138, 142
as buzzword 165
central place of notion in writings
  of Hannerz 8
centrality to anthropology of 92–
  3, 99–100, 143, 162, 166
civil society, concept of 174
collectivity, primitive philosophy
  and 95
common sense and 173
communicative self-reflexivity
  163–4
competitive reflexivity 164
concept of 162–3
concepts, fashionability of 174
concepts, timelessness of 176
concepts and 174–6
consequences of, knowledge
  practices and 132–3
cultural differences between
  social contexts 172–3
cultural emphasis on 165
cultural technique for self-
  reflection 132
currency of term 91
discursive emphasis on 165, 172
encouragement of 164
epistemic contingency, reflexive
  attention to conditions of 99,
  101
European Association of Social
  Anthropologists 174

feedback processes 164
fieldwork and 162, 166, 168–9
fluidity and 13
forms in society of 163
future reflexivity 107–8
global growth and 165
ideological basis for 99
individual reflexivity and issue
  of social context 168
inequalities 170
information technology and 164,
  173–4
institutional development and
  164
intersectionality 170–71
as method of life rather than
  expert knowledge 107
modernity 176–7
moral discourse, political
  commitment and neutral
  science, distinction between
  176
neoliberal ideology,
  breakthrough of 177
networks 174–5
neutrality, ideal of 176
on organizing principles of
  society 184–5
'other-awareness' and 142–3
para-ethnography 102–3
para-sites, Irving Center,
  modular research and 103–5
professional reflexivity 165
publicity, ethics of 107
radical reflexivity 166
reality and 176
reflective observation 163–4
reflectivity and 163
reflexive anthropology 91–3, 96,
  100–101, 105–6, 107, 173–4
  anthropological reflexivity
    and 105–8
  third generation of 101–5
reflexive elaboration 167
reflexive modernity, idea of 164,
  165
reflexive modernization 176, 177

reflexive modernization,
    concept of 132, 133, 137–8,
    143, 176, 177
reflexive practice in
    anthropology 172
reflexive research 167–9
reflexive scrutiny 165
reflexive turn in anthropology
    95–6
reinvention of anthropological
    reflexivity 96–101
scientific discourse 176
scientific reflexivity 166, 167
self-awareness and 166
self-control, decentralized
    governance and rule by 164–5
self-monitoring 163–5, 166
situated knowledge and 169–70
social and cultural reality 176
social and cultural science,
    interaction between idioms of
    175
social constructions and 168, 169
social contexts, cultural
    differences between 172–3
in social science 91–2, 171–2
societal reflexivity 163–4, 174, 178
sociological reflexivities 166–7
studying sideways 102, 157–9
theoretical terms, choice of 174
typecasting 169–70, 172
words in shared vocabulary,
    implications of 175
Reis, Eduardo 246
relational reflexivity 141–3
research assessments 266–7
Review of International Studies 214
Ribeiro, Tomás 258
Ricci, Matteo 258
Ricoeur, Paul 213
rights issues 13
Riles, Annelise 79
Robertson, Roland 12, 215
Rojas-Suarez, Liliana 80
Roosevelt, Franklin D. and New Deal
    219
Rose, Nicholas 164

Rosenau, James Nathan 214, 215,
    216, 218, 222, 223, 225, 231, 232
Ruby, Jay 166
Rushdie, Salman 31, 115
Ruskin, John 43

Sacred Games (Chandra, V.) 116
Sahlins, Marshall 66, 92, 265
Salzmann, Philip O. 132
Samans, Richard 227
Sandercock, Leonie 194
Sandywell, Barry 131
Sansi-Roca, Roger 258
Santos, Sousa, Boaventura de 246,
    247
Sarajeva, Katja 171
Sarajevo, civil war in 252
Sarkozy, Nicolas 11
Sarnecki, Jerzy 171
Sassen, Saskia 77, 78
scale-making 85–6
Scandinavian anthropology 265–7
Schama, Simon 264
Scheper-Hughes, Nancy 107
Schmitt, Carl 207, 208
scholarship 115, 194
    pluralism of 272
    scholarly interests,
        diversification of 270
    of Ulf Hannerz 1–2, 3–4, 5–6, 9,
        134
Schröder, Gerhard 229
Schwartz, Roberto 253
scientific discourse, reflexivity in 176
scientific management movement 72
scientific reflexivity 166, 167
Scott, Edward W. Jr. 75–6, 84
The Secret Scripture (Barry, S.) 151
Seers, Dudley 220
self-awareness, reflexivity and 166
self-control, decentralized
    governance and rule by 164–5
self-making among Muslims in
    Cairo 123
self-monitoring 163–5, 166
self-referentiality, fallacy of 210
Seligman, Charles G. 210

Senghor, Léopold Sédar 123, 134
Serjeant, Robert B. 52
Shakespeare, William 19
Shōji, Hamada 42, 43
Shridath, Ramphal 221, 222
Silva Jayasuriya, Shihan 256
Simmel, Georg 1
situated knowledge 169–70
small-scale things 275
Smith, J.A. 72
Smith, Neil 194
social and cultural reality 176
social and cultural science, interaction between idioms of 175
Social Anthropology 131
social belonging, identity and 19
social constructions, reflexivity and 168, 169
social contexts, cultural differences between 172–3
social frame of working together 41–4
The Social Life of Things (Appadurai, A., Ed.) 210–11
social media 268–9
social norms, conjuncture with aesthetic ideals 35–6
social organization 33
social processes, exploration of 185
social relations
  instrumentalization of 23
  unintentional connections and 60–67
social science, reflexivity in 91–2, 171–2
social theories 12
sociality, security in 20
societal reflexivity 163–4, 174, 178
sociocentrism 245
sociological reflexivities 166–7
sodality 250
Solana, Javier 229
Soulillou, Jacques 139
Soulside (Hannerz, U.) 1, 71
Souza, Laura de Melloe 258
spaces of reflexivity 137–41

Spinoza, Baruch 244, 245, 246, 247, 252
Stade, Ronald 5, 205–36, 293–4
Standing, Guy 16
Stern, Daniel 244
Stewart, Charles 24
stigma, logic of 253–4
Stockholm Anthropology Round Table (September 2007)
  connectedness, social and material 29
  knowledge practices 131
Stockholm Initiative on Global Security and Governance (1991) 222
Stoyanov, Petar Stefanov 229
strategic networking 86
Strathern, Marilyn 84, 92, 125, 164, 208, 243
Stroller, Paul 122
studies on think tanks, methodological challenges for 73–4
study and studied, epistemological distinction between 127
studying sideways
  cultural diversity, migrants and 182
  Ireland, literary world of 147, 148–9
  reflexivity 102
Sub-Saharan Africa (World Bank) 216–17
subjectivity 49–50, 64, 66, 211
success, divergent nature of representations of 182, 196–7
Sulgrave Club 70
Summers, David 133
Sunni radicals in Upper Yemen 53, 55–6, 57, 63–4
Svenska Dagbladet 3
Swedish national identity 26–7

Taylor, Lucien 95, 107
The Telegraph 152
Thatcher, Margaret 220
Therborn, Göran 133
Thérien, Jean-Philippe 217

think tank activities *see* Washington D.C., Dupont Circle in
thinking and consciousness, Descartes' distinction between 123
third-country nationals (TCNs) 184, 197
Thomas, Nicholas 169
Thomaz, Omar Ribeiro 260
Thompson, Ross A. 255
times of reflexivity 134–7
Timor-Leste, emergence of 250
Tocqueville, Alexis de 72
Todorov, Tzvetan 21, 23
togetherness, community and 43–4
Tóibín, Colm 148, 153, 154, 156, 157
Tolkien, John Ronald Reuel 241, 249, 259, 260
Tomasello, Michael 244
Tönnies, Ferdinand 20
Toren, Christina 255
Touré, Yacouba 135, 136
tracking 72–5
transactions 31–3
transformations 38–41
transnational connections 1, 5–6, 7–8, 48
Transnational Connections (Hannerz, U.) 1, 214
transnational networks 14
transnational phenomena 275
transnational reconnection 50–52
Traube, Elizabeth 250, 251
Trouillot, Michel-Rolph 14
Tsing, Anna L. 78, 86
Turner, Terence 107
Turner, Victor 95, 147
Tylor, Edward B. 93, 96
typecasting 169–70, 172

Ulysses (Joyce, J.) 152
uniformity/diversity conflict 17
United Nations (UN) 217–18
    Centre on Transnational Corporations (UNCTC) 219–20
    Children's Fund (UNICEF) 217
    Development Programme (UNDP) 217
    Economic and Social Council (ECOSOC) 217
    Office of United Nations High Commissioner for Human Rights (OHCHR) 217
    UNESCO Convention on the Protection and Promotion of the Diversity of Cultural Expression 182–3, 189, 192–3
Upper Yemen, transnational connections in 48–67
    actor-network theory (ANT) 49
    agency 49, 61, 63–4, 66–7
        transnational connections and 63–4
    Banu Awfan 54, 57, 58, 61, 62–3
    cellphone technology 51, 57–8, 61, 64, 66
    civil war, Munebbih's stand in 53–4
    connections 49–50, 66–7
        long-distance remote connections 65–6
        military operations and 64–5
    flows 49, 57, 66
    global flows 48
    al-Houthi revolt 56–60, 63
    information technology 64
    intentionality 49–50
    interactive intentionality 66
    internal displacement 59
    intersubjectivity 49–50
    local relations, shifts in 55
    migrant workers, exclusion from Saudi Arabia 54–5
    Munebbih 50–51, 53–4, 58–60, 61–3, 65, 67n2
    Muslim Brotherhood 55–6
    networks 48
    postcolonial situation
        Cold War scenario 52–4
        'dethroned' minority and opponents 54–60
    social relations, unintentional connections and 60–67

subjectivity 49–50
Sunni radicals 53, 55–6, 57, 63–4
transnational connections 48
transnational reconnection 50–52
Zaydi version of Shiite Islam 52–3, 54, 56, 57
urban life, ethnographies of 1–2
urban regeneration and governance, cultural diversity and 194–6, 197–8
urbanization, process of 8–9
Urquhart, Brian 222, 223
Urry, John 14
utopianism 259, 265

Van de Port, Matthijs 122, 130
Van Maanen, John 31
Varma, Ram Gopal 115
Verdery, Katherine 95
Vertovec, Steven 183, 190
Vieira, António 259
Viveiros de Castro, Eduardo 125
vohou-vohou movement in Ivory Coast 133, 135–6, 136–7, 140, 142, 144n3
von Hayek, Friedrich 208

Wacquant, Loïc 212
Wajiro, Kon 269
Waldheim, Kurt 220
Wallace, Anthony 1
Wallace-Wells, B. 74
Wallerstein, Immanuel 211
Walshe, Eibhear 153, 156
warfare, deterritorialization of 14
Warren, Kay 95
Washington D.C., Dupont Circle in 70–87
　attention and impact, competition for 78–9
　audience groups 80
　Brookings Institution 70
　Business Week America 80–81
　Carnegie Endowment for International Peace 70
　Center for Global Development (CGD) 71, 74–5, 75–7, 79–81, 83–4, 85
　Commitment to Development Index (CDI) 83–4
　corporate social responsibility (CSR) 74
　creolization 82–3
　culture flows, global scenarios of 78
　Diario Financiero 81
　Eurasia Center 70
　fieldwork 74–5
　financial sector policy-making 80–81
　flexians 73–4
　geocultural imagination 78
　ideas, competition for 79
　ideas, diffusion of 78
　influence
　　derivation of 86–7
　　distinction between impact and 80
　　educational activities and 79–80
　initiatives 83–4
　interface position of think tanks 86
　International Monetary Fund (IMF) 70
　knowledge brokerage 81–3
　knowledge generation 77–8
　knowledge packaging 86
　Latin America Adviser 81
　network tracking 74–5
　online engagement 79
　Paul H. Nitze School of Advanced International Studies at Johns Hopkins University 70
　Peter G. Peterson Institute for International Economics 70
　policy impacts 79
　Progressive Era 72
　scale-making 85–6
　scientific management movement 72

strategic networking 86
studies on think tanks, methodological challenges for 73–4
subcultural inclinations 70
Sulgrave Club 70
tracking 72–5
Washington Post 81
World Bank 70
Weber, Max 23
Wedeen, Lisa 56
Wedel, Janine 73–74
Weibel, Peter 138
Weir, Shelagh 53
Wesenswille, concept of 20
West African art, reflexive turn in 134–5
Westbrook, David A. 75, 103
Weston, Kath. 170
whistleblowers 276
Wilde, Oscar 156
Wood, Phil 194, 195, 196
Woods, George 219
words
    buzzwords 48, 176
    connectedness of 30–31
    'our' and 'their' usage of 175
    sensitization through uses of 275–6
    in shared vocabulary, implications of 175
    symbolic values of 174
    see also language
World Bank 270
    global governance 219–20
    Washington D.C., Dupont Circle in 70
world-building anthropology 270
World Council of Anthropological Associations (WCAA) 3–4
World Trade Organization (WTO) 192
writing about culture 118–21
Writing Culture (Clifford, J. and Marcus, G.) 100, 113–14, 120
Wulff, Helena 147–59, 294

Yamba, Bawa 170
Yanagi, Sōetsu 41, 42, 43, 44
Yeats, W.B. 148
Yemen *see* Upper Yemen, transnational connections in
Yudice, George 191, 192, 197
Yugoslavia, dismantlement of 15

Zaidi, Hussain 116
Zaydi version of Shiite Islam 52–3, 54, 56, 57
zero tolerance, concept of 211–12